The Ethics of Epicurus and its Relation to Contemporary Doctrines

Re-inventing Philosophy as a Way of Life

Series editors: Keith Ansell-Pearson, Matthew Sharpe, and Michael Ure

For the most part, academic philosophy is considered a purely theoretical discipline that aims at systematic knowledge; contemporary philosophers do not, as a rule, think that they or their audience will lead better lives by doing philosophy. Recently, however, we have seen a powerful resurgence of interest in the countervailing ancient view that philosophy facilitates human flourishing. Philosophy, Seneca famously stated, teaches us doing, not saying. It aims to transform how we live. This ancient ideal has continually been reinvented from the Renaissance through to late modernity and is now central to contemporary debates about philosophy's role and future.

This series is the first synoptic study of the re-inventions of the idea of philosophy as an ethical pursuit or 'way of life'. Collectively and individually, the books in this series will answer the following questions:

1. How have philosophers re-animated the ancient model of philosophy? How have they revised ancient assumptions, concepts and practices in the light of wider cultural shifts in the modern world? What new ideas of the good life and new arts, exercises, disciplines and consolations have they formulated?
2. Do these re-inventions successfully re-establish the idea that philosophy can transform our lives? What are the standard criticisms of this philosophical ambition and how have they been addressed?
3. What are the implications for these new versions of philosophy as a way of life for contemporary issues that concern the nature of philosophy, its procedures, limits, ends, and its relationship to wider society?

Other titles in the series:

The Selected Writings of Pierre Hadot: Philosophy as Practice, Pierre Hadot, trans. Matthew Sharpe and Federico Testa
Effort and Grace: On the Spiritual Exercise of Philosophy, Simone Kotva
The Late Foucault: Ethical and Political Questions, ed. Marta Faustino and Gianfranco Ferraro

The Ethics of Epicurus and its Relation to Contemporary Doctrines

Jean-Marie Guyau

Edited by Federico Testa & Keith Ansell-Pearson
Translated by Federico Testa

BLOOMSBURY ACADEMIC
LONDON • NEW YORK • OXFORD • NEW DELHI • SYDNEY

BLOOMSBURY ACADEMIC
Bloomsbury Publishing Plc
50 Bedford Square, London, WC1B 3DP, UK
1385 Broadway, New York, NY 10018, USA
29 Earlsfort Terrace, Dublin 2, Ireland

BLOOMSBURY, BLOOMSBURY ACADEMIC and the Diana logo are trademarks of
Bloomsbury Publishing Plc

First published in 1878 in France as *La morale d'Épicure et ses rapports avec les doctrines contemporaines*, by Jean-Marie Guyau

First published in Great Britain 2022
This paperback edition published 2023

Copyright © Federico Testa and Keith Ansell-Pearson, 2022

Federico Testa and Keith Ansell-Pearson have asserted their right under the Copyright, Designs and Patents Act, 1988, to be identified as Editors of this work.

Federico Testa has asserted his right under the Copyright, Designs and Patents Act, 1988, to be identified as Translator of this work.

Series design by Charlotte Daniels
Cover image: Epicurus, marble bust (© colaimages / Alamy Stock Photo)

All rights reserved. No part of this publication may be reproduced or transmitted in any form or by any means, electronic or mechanical, including photocopying, recording, or any information storage or retrieval system, without prior permission in writing from the publishers.

Bloomsbury Publishing Plc does not have any control over, or responsibility for, any third-party websites referred to or in this book. All internet addresses given in this book were correct at the time of going to press. The author and publisher regret any inconvenience caused if addresses have changed or sites have ceased to exist, but can accept no responsibility for any such changes.

A catalogue record for this book is available from the British Library.

Library of Congress Cataloging-in-Publication Data
Names: Guyau, Jean-Marie, 1854-1888, author. | Ansell-Pearson, Keith, 1960-editor. | Testa, Federico, editor.
Title: The ethics of Epicurus and its relation to contemporary doctrines / Jean-Marie; edited by Federico Testa & Keith Ansell-Pearson; translated by Federico Testa.
Other titles: Morale d'Épicure et ses rapports avec les doctrines contemporaines. English
Description: London, UK; New York, NY, USA: Bloomsbury Academic, 2022. | Includes bibliographical references and index. |
Identifiers: LCCN 2021013500 (print) | LCCN 2021013501 (ebook) | ISBN 9781350013919 (hb) | ISBN 9781350013902 (epdf) | ISBN 9781350013926 (ebook)
Subjects: LCSH: Hedonism. | Epicurus.
Classification: LCC B573.G813 2022 (print) | LCC B573 (ebook) | DDC 187–dc23
LC record available at https://lccn.loc.gov/2021013500
LC ebook record available at https://lccn.loc.gov/2021013501

ISBN: HB: 978-1-3500-1391-9
PB: 978-1-3502-6102-0
ePDF: 978-1-3500-1390-2
eBook: 978-1-3500-1392-6

Series: Re-inventing Philosophy as a Way of Life

Typeset by RefineCatch Limited, Bungay, Suffolk

To find out more about our authors and books visit www.bloomsbury.com and sign up for our newsletters.

Contents

Note on the Translation	vii
Editors' Introduction: Jean-Marie Guyau on Epicurus and the Art of Living: A Novel Approach to the History of Philosophy	xi
Foreword: On the Method Used for the Exposition of Systems	xxvi
Introduction: Epicureanism in Antiquity and Modernity	1

Book One: The Pleasures of the Flesh

1	Pleasure: The End of Life and the Principle of All Ethics	11
2	Fundamental Pleasure: The Stomach	21
3	The Rule of Pleasure: Utility. – Happiness, The Sovereign Good	27
4	Desire – The Ultimate End of Desire: Rest, Enjoyment of Self	35

Book Two: The Pleasures of the Soul

1	Intellectual and Moral Serenity – Science, Opposed by Epicurus to the Idea of Miracle	49
2	Freedom – Contingency in Nature, the Condition of Human Freedom	61
3	Tranquillity in the Face of Death. – Epicurean Theory of Death, and its Relation to Contemporary Theories	89

Book Three: Private and Public Virtues

1	Courage and Temperance. Love and Friendship. The Genesis of Friendship. The Conduct of the Sage in Human Society	111
2	Justice and Social Contract	125
3	Progress in Humanity	133
4	Epicurean Piety. The Struggle against Divinity understood as Efficient Cause	147
	Conclusion: Epicureanism and its Analogies with Modern Positivism. The Success of Epicureanism in Antiquity	155

Book Four: The Modern Successors of Epicurus

1 The Epoch of Transition Between Ancient Epicureanism and
   Modern Epicureanism – Gassendi and Hobbes   163
2 La Rochefoucauld – The Psychology of Epicureanism   177
3 Spinoza – Synthesis of Epicureanism and Stoicism   195
4 Helvétius   205
5 The Spirit of Epicureanism in Eighteenth-Century France   229
   Conclusion: Contemporary Epicureanism   239

Bibliography   247
Index of Names   259
Index of Subjects   263

Note on the Translation

The Ethics of Epicurus was originally written as the first part of the dissertation (or *mémoire*) that Jean-Marie Guyau submitted to a competition of the Académie des Sciences Morales et Politiques on the history and critique of utilitarianism. In 1874, two authors received the Académie's prize (*prix de budget*): Ludovic Carrau, a professor at the Faculty of Letters of Besançon, and the young Guyau. From his awarded *mémoire*, Guyau extracted two books, *La morale d'Épicure et ses rapports avec les doctrines contemporaines* and *La morale anglaise contemporaine. Morale de l'utilité et de l'évolution*.

In his report to the Académie, Elme-Marie Caro praises Guyau, stressing the author's striking originality and independence with regards to 'every tradition or authority in the history of philosophy' (xxx). However, he points out that if the renewed picture of Epicurus presented in the dissertation is the product of a bold and daring effort of interpretation, 'I would not state that it is the true [*véritable*] one' (xxix). And he adds: 'the Epicurus presented in this *mémoire* is an Epicurus seen through [the lens of] John Stuart Mill' (xxx).

Although the utilitarian perspective is of key importance in Guyau's understanding of Epicureanism, the book we now read as *The Ethics of Epicurus* is partly Guyau's attempt to engage with Caro's criticism. When publishing his dissertation in 1879, Guyau revised and provided further textual evidence for his interpretations of Epicurus, including, for example, a series of references to ancient texts and to Cicero in particular. Guyau also wrote a few additional chapters, namely those on the Epicurean theory of death (book 2, chapter 3), piety (book 3, chapter 4) and friendship (book 3, chapter 1). Moreover, he also revised and developed the chapter on freedom and contingency (book 2, chapter 2), seeking to provide further philosophical and textual support for his explanation of the Epicurean theory of the swerve of atoms or *clinamen* – criticized by Caro in the report as a 'mere dialectical device'. For Guyau, this theory is an entirely rational and constitutive part of Epicureanism and essential for its understanding of moral freedom.

In my translation I have mainly used the seventh edition of *La morale d'Épicure et ses rapports avec les doctrines contemporaines*, from 1927 (Félix Alcan). During the long process of editing and revising my translation, together with Keith Ansell-Pearson, I have also consulted the 2002 edition by Jean-Baptiste Gourinat (Encre Marine), which reproduces the third edition from 1886 (Baillière & Félix Alcan).

I have decided to render the French word *morale* in the title as 'ethics' – a term that sounds familiar to the contemporary reader. I have also considered options such as 'morality', 'morals' and 'moral philosophy'. However, in my view, these terms could occasionally create ambiguity or present a distorted version of the original meaning. Guyau's understanding of the term *morale*, as the title indicates, is connected both to the idea of a domain of knowledge occupied with human moral action and conduct (he will characterize Epicureanism as an 'art of conduct'), and to the idea of a way of life, an *ethos* proposed by Epicureanism. The word 'ethics' is closer to the Greek root, designating the part of philosophy concerned with human action and echoing the traditional division of the different parts of philosophy in the Hellenistic period (logic, physics and ethics). In addition, the term 'ethics' is also more descriptive and does not have some of the potentially evaluative shades of meaning conveyed by the words 'morals' or 'morality', being therefore less prone to moralistic understandings, which is consistent with Guyau's construal of Epicurean philosophy. Throughout the text, and especially when discussing Epicurus' successors, it becomes clear that the use of the term *morale* also refers to the realm of knowledge – or science – that examines moral conduct, rather than moral prescriptions and specific behaviours. In this sense, I have used the English 'morality' to indicate patterns or systems of behaviour and moral action, and 'ethics' to indicate the domain of philosophical analysis that examines them. Furthermore, I found another reason for choosing the English word 'ethics' (preferring it to 'morals' or 'morality'), namely Alfred Fouillée's choice of title for this 1902 text on *The Ethics of Nietzsche and Guyau*.[1] Nevertheless, given the wide semantic field covered by the French term, as well as its sometimes ambiguous use by Guyau, I have opted for a more nuanced, contextual approach when translating other occurrences in the text. In any case, for the sake of consistency, I have, whenever possible, translated the French *morale* according to the distinction sketched above.

Guyau's style is singular and informed by his vitalist insights. This peculiar style, as well as the nineteenth-century use of the French language, and Guyau's elaborate and poetic formulations, constitute a particularly challenging situation for the translator. I have thus tried my best to be faithful to the original text, attempting to preserve Guyau's voice and style, rather than simply trying to make him sound 'English', which will no doubt explain some of the unusual sentences and formulations that the reader will find in this translation (such as the intransitive use of the transitive verb 'to enjoy') and which I ask them to forgive. Translating philosophy sometimes means learning a different and peculiar language, which is neither the original language in which the text was written nor the language into which one wishes to transpose it. Rather, it is the philosophical language of the author, his unique use of words and conceptual distinctions that the translator seeks to capture, which often reveal, to speak with Pierre Hadot, 'a vision of the universe which is extremely different from our own'.[2] In this sense, the reader should bear in mind that these at times awkward formulations are not accidental but have a philosophical import and contribute in their own ways to the general economy of the text. For this reason, my priority was to *not* correct Guyau, even when his sentences are difficult to understand. I believe that a philosophical text must exhibit its complexity, difficulties, limitations and blind spots also in translation. However, to render Guyau's text more readable in English (while preserving its philosophical tone and structure), I have often added terms in square brackets to the text for the sake of clarity. The reader will also find critical material and explanations of potentially obscure passages in the translator's notes (T.N.).

Another important choice was to translate Guyau's own translations of ancient texts, even when they differ quite significantly from existing English translations. The task of translation plays a central role in Guyau's interpretive enterprise. He had a solid philological background and started his work on the ancients as a translator. In this sense, his relation to the ancient sources is not naive, but marked by critical work; additionally, he sometimes makes unusual choices that are consistent with his arguments and interpretation. My decision to preserve the meaning and structure of Guyau's translations complements my effort to preserve his own voice. Additionally, in his often unorthodox readings of Epicurus and the Epicureans, the operation of translation is linked to a specific thought process and to decisive interpretive choices. My idea here was to assure the reader's access to every detail of Guyau's complex picture of Epicurus. I have done that by always seeking to compare Guyau's translations with original texts and several English translations, highlighting the singularities of his choices. When his renditions strikingly depart from the original or differ drastically from existing English translations, I have added an endnote signalling it.

Where Guyau quotes Greek and Latin texts, I have provided translations in endnotes after consulting the original texts and existing standard English editions (such as R. D. Hicks' edition for Diogenes Laertius), sometimes comparing different translations (as with Lucretius: I have consulted the original Latin text, along with English translations by W. H. D. Rouse and A. E. Stallings), as well as considering Gourinat's French translations. I have reproduced Latin passages as Guyau quotes them, and I have transliterated Greek passages. When transliterating the Greek, I have adopted a simplified method, always using the Latin *u* for the Greek *upsilon* [υ], making no distinction for cases of diphthong; I have largely neglected accents, and only differentiated between short and long vowels.[3]

Guyau's references – both to ancient and modern authors – are often abbreviated or incomplete. My attempt was always to provide the full references in the translator's notes, which I complement with two bibliographical lists at the end of this translation: ancient and modern references. In order to help the reader navigate scholarly work on Guyau, I have also provided a list of important texts by commentators.

Some of the key concepts of *The Ethics of Epicurus* are difficult in translation. An example is the notion of *jouissance*, which I have translated as 'enjoyment'. An easy solution could have been to simplify Guyau's text by referring this notion of *jouissance* back to the Epicurean notion of pleasure. Such a procedure would not be incorrect. However, Guyau also had the French word *plaisir* available, which, like its English counterpart, conveys that precise idea. It is for philosophical reasons that Guyau chose to use the word *jouissance*. The term undoubtedly signifies the feeling of pleasure, but it also has a scope broader than pleasure: it designates the process of enjoyment, as well as the fact of having obtained, of being in possession of, a desired object, property or right. One can enjoy one's freedom – but also one's food. One can enjoy a wide range of different pleasures. The notion points therefore to a sense of well-being and satisfaction, which is also present in the word 'delight'. Nevertheless, the term 'enjoyment' seems to better convey the processual aspect of the experience of pleasure as Guyau understands it. Moreover, the French verb *jouir* ('to enjoy') also designates sexual pleasure and the orgasm. The complexity of this notion is difficult to capture in English, and I have adopted the path of consistency (using the word 'enjoyment'), without neglecting possible contextual variations. For similar reasons, I have preserved Guyau's use of the French *volupté*, by using the English 'voluptuousness'. However, since in this case the notions of both pleasure and voluptuousness refer back to the Latin *voluptas*, I have occasionally chosen the English 'pleasure'.

A similar situation occurs with the French *peine*, which is usually translated in the Epicurean context as 'pain', since it refers to the Greek *ponos*. However, *peine* is more encompassing than the English 'pain', which in French is *douleur*. *Peine* has a series of meanings involving effort, hardship, toil, trouble, difficulty, distress – but also anguish, grief and sorrow. Additionally, *peine* is the word used to designate juridical punishment, the sentence or sanction. Therefore, *pain*, despite its phonetic proximity, is not a literal equivalent. Facing this difficulty, I have adopted a fully contextual approach. For example, I have chosen the phrase 'absence of trouble and suffering' to convey the wide semantic field of the Greek word *aponia*, which Guyau renders as *absence de peine*. We could think of this state as one of freedom from pain and exemption from toil, and as a condition of relaxation and non-exertion. Like the French *peine*, the Greek *ponos* expresses both the idea of toil, effort and work, and the notion of suffering, distress, preoccupation, trouble and pain.

I am grateful to all those who were friends to this project. I would like to thank Ann Thomson, who has read the chapter on the eighteenth-century Epicureans and greatly aided me with La Mettrie's references. Michael Ure, Andre Okawara, Thomas Ryan, Aurelia Armstrong, Thomas Nail, Dimitri Vardoulakis and Daniela Voss have read different parts of the book, providing important feedback. I am grateful to Mitchell Abidor, Miguel de Beistegui, Charles T. Wolfe, Guy Longsworth, Daniele Lorenzini, Jenny Messenger, Emmanuelle de Champs and Annamaria Contini, who helped me at different stages of this work.

Finally, this translation would not have been possible without Keith Ansell-Pearson's philosophical insight, attentive reading and constant support and encouragement. Concerned with a recovery of Guyau's work, and his reading of Epicurus in particular, Keith first set this project in motion. His input throughout the whole process was of inestimable value and deeply increased the clarity, flow and readability of this translation. He has read all my translation drafts multiple times, providing extensive and detailed feedback, and making a series of important suggestions and improvements. Together we discussed and edited each chapter, and I hope that in this translation the reader will find a trace of the cheerfulness of our discussions.

Notes

1   Alfred Fouillée, 'The Ethics of Nietzsche and Guyau', *International Journal of Ethics*, Vol. 13, No. 1, 1902, 13–27.
2   Pierre Hadot, *Wittgenstein et les limites du langage*. Paris: Vrin, 2014, 97.
3   I have marked the rough breathing and neglected the *iota* subscript; I have used the Latin *ō* and *o*, for *omega* [ω] and *omicron* [o], respectively; and *ē* and *e* for *eta* [η] and *epsilon* [ε], respectively.

Editors' Introduction

Jean-Marie Guyau on Epicurus and the Art of Living: A Novel Approach to the History of Philosophy

Keith Ansell-Pearson & Federico Testa

Once called the 'Spinoza of France' and considered one of the 'greatest eudaemonist philosophers' of his century,[1] Jean-Marie Guyau remains an unjustifiably forgotten and marginal figure in the history of philosophy. During the time when Guyau produced most of his philosophical work he remained an outsider with regards to the academic institution. His state of poor health did not allow him to occupy the teaching position he obtained at the Lycée Condorcet,[2] and he was forced to seek refuge in the milder weather of southern France; he settled first in Nice, then in Menton, where he worked until the end of his short life. Despite Guyau's extra-institutional position his work met an enthusiastic reception during his lifetime and was later championed by his stepfather and life-long interlocutor Alfred Fouillée, which assured its reception in the first decade of the twentieth century.[3] Guyau's contemporaries praised his precocious philosophical maturity and intellectual boldness.

The stature and importance of the figures that intellectually engaged with Guyau's work is striking. Friedrich Nietzsche read the books of the philosopher he called 'the brave Guyau', filling the margins with enthusiastic, and also critical, comments.[4] The anarchist thinker Peter Kropotkin expressed his admiration for Guyau's attempt to establish ethics on a scientific foundation and judged his contribution to be 'remarkable'.[5] Henri Bergson read and reviewed Guyau's work on the philosophy of time. In his book on art Tolstoy praises Guyau's conception of beauty.[6] A young Émile Durkheim wrote a review of Guyau's 1887 book, *L'irréligion de l'avenir,* extracting from it the notion of *anomie.*[7] The philosopher and magistrate Gabriel Tarde engaged with Guyau's work on sanction, and lamented the fact that he was 'prematurely taken from us in the full bloom of a train of thought'.[8] Guyau's impact was not less remarkable in the Anglophone context. In the United States he was read by important and inspiring thinkers and ethicists, such as Josiah Royce and William James.[9] In England, Henry Sidgwick wrote a review of Guyau's *La morale d'Épicure* for *Mind.*[10] G. E. Moore also read and reviewed Guyau's work in 1899,[11] and discussed it again in his *Principia Ethica.*[12] As one can see, in the late nineteenth century Guyau was far from being an obscure figure; rather, he was a necessary reference for thinkers from different traditions and schools of thought.

Guyau was born in Laval on 28 October 1854. He began his classical and philosophical education at a very early age under the mentorship of his relative, Alfred Fouillée. At the age of 17 Guyau obtained the title of *licencié ès lettres,* translating and writing commentaries on a series of ancient texts.[13] Alongside the *Ethics of Epicurus*, Guyau published at least five other philosophy books and regularly contributed to the *Revue philosophique de la France et de l'étranger*, the *Revue bleue* and the *Revue des deux Mondes*. Additionally, he wrote poems and literary texts, as well as a series of schoolbooks.[14] This prolific output was interrupted by a serious lung disease, aggravated by an earthquake that occurred in southern France. Guyau died in Menton on 31 March 1888 at the tender age of 33. After a short-lived reception in French academia, and the deaths of Fouillée, and Guyau's son Augustin, his work gradually fell into oblivion, and the majority of his personal papers and manuscripts were lost.[15]

During his lifetime, Guyau was best known for two main works, the *Irréligion de l'avenir*, and the *Esquisse d'une morale sans obligation ni sanction*. In the *Esquisse* in particular, Guyau proposes a notion of life that stresses its expansive, social and cooperative character. He thinks life can best be defined by two fundamental movements. The first is that of 'gravitation upon itself', which consists in 'nutrition, appropriation, [and] transformation for itself of the forces of nature'.[16] This dimension explains the egoistic drives of the living being, such as self-preservation and hedonistic behaviours. The second movement is one of 'expenditure' of accumulated force, which gives rise to an expansive, generous and sociable drive. This aspect is the key to understanding one of the central notions of Guyau's philosophy of life: *fecundity*. Fecundity appears in its physical dimension in the reproduction of life: the expansion of life's force and energy through (and with) others. It also appears in what Guyau calls the superior or elevated pleasures, which presuppose the existence of others. For him, the most intense life is also the one that is more extensive and sociable, the one that communicates and associates itself with others. With this philosophy and ethics of life Guyau attempts to harmonize egoism and altruism, while also maintaining that the expansion of life also presupposes a bursting of the 'narrow shell of the self'.[17] The main philosophical issues occupying Guyau's attention and that will lead Guyau to formulate his philosophy of life are to be found in his book on Epicurus. In this work, he favours a notion of pleasure over conceptions of duty, and inquires into the different solutions found in the history of ethics – and in the Epicurean tradition in particular – concerning the relationship between individual enjoyment and collective well-being.

The *Ethics of Epicurus* constitutes one of the most significant receptions of Epicurean teaching in the nineteenth century. Although today it is a neglected source, a situation that this translation and edition aims to correct, Guyau's reception of Epicurus makes a major contribution to our understanding of Epicurean teaching as an ethics based on a refined and enlightened form of enjoyment, and for him this is an ethics that shapes the entire existence of those who adhere to it. Guyau sets out to reveal the emancipatory potential of the Epicurean way of life, while at the same time challenging its traditional depiction or, one should say, caricature, as a coarse form of hedonistic egoism, marked by lassitude and debauchery. Guyau is keen to demonstrate that Epicurean teaching does not amount to a simple-minded hedonism, but rather supposes an ethical way of living in the world, which is what he calls an 'art of conduct'. Through this mastery of conduct the Epicurean is able to govern himself, overcoming the bondage of vain opinions and fears, and shaping his life as a work of art.[18] For Guyau, no other doctrine has been the object of more attacks and criticism than ancient and modern Epicureanism, and this is largely because it goes so strongly against received opinion on those things that are most dear to the human heart, notably received moral ideas and religion: 'the moment seems to have arrived,' he writes, 'when we can more fairly appreciate the Epicurean doctrine and seek the portion of truth it contains' (381).

The Ethics of Epicurus

In 1871 a competition was announced by the 'Section de Morale' of the Académie de Sciences Morales et Politiques. The panel presided over by philosopher Elme-Marie Caro solicited contributions on the history and critique of utilitarianism. Three years later, in 1874, a lengthy dissertation won the competition. The author of this 1,300-page-long monograph was the 19-year-old philosopher Jean-Marie Guyau. In 1879 he published the first part of his dissertation as a separate book: *La morale d'Épicure et ses rapports avec le doctrines contemporaines*, while the second part would become *La morale anglaise contemporaine*.

The way in which Guyau chose to engage with the proposition of the Académie was rather peculiar and surprising: he historically displaces the main theme, resituating it in ancient Greece, and begins his dissertation with a reconstruction of Epicureanism. Guyau notes that Epicureanism was the most popular philosophy of ancient Greece and Rome. Indeed, he writes, 'the first Greek doctrine to enter Rome and to be expressed in Latin was the irreligious doctrine of Epicurus' (39). While their main adversaries, the Stoics, struggled against this teaching for the whole duration of the Roman Empire, the struggle was, he holds, largely in vain since they found it impossible to defeat its popularity or to escape its influence. As Guyau observes, Seneca, a strong critic of the Epicureans, was attracted to the very doctrines he fought against. The same is true of Marcus Aurelius, who although meditating under the influence of Epictetus, and himself a severe critic of Epicureanism, kept returning to Epicurus, the 'pagan master', as a model to be inspired by.

Guyau appreciates the significance of Epicurean teaching in a specific manner, which he develops in the context of a consideration of Epicureanism's defeat by Christianity. The Epicureans found themselves weak, he notes, when they confronted this religion simply because of their emphasis on the reality of our death and ultimate annihilation, when the vast majority of human beings crave immortality. 'At this time,' Guyau remarks, 'human beings were weary of life, overwhelmed by servitude and decadence. Saint Augustine rejects, as did his era, a doctrine that promised him only a happy life' (41). Over time the gardens of Epicurus, which for centuries had been graced by sages of every nation and surrounded by an enchanted crowd, became deserted and depopulated. Epicurus' words, which had been incorporated as sacred truths, were forgotten and effaced by what seemed to be a more powerful word.

However, although defeated, Epicurean teaching was not destroyed. After several centuries, Guyau notes, the teaching was rediscovered and 'the earth was found to have value and to be worth taking seriously' (42). Human beings eventually grew tired of having their eyes restlessly oriented to heaven, and the earth came to have importance for humanity once again. Guyau locates this development taking place in the thinking of Montaigne, whom he notes was not an Epicurean but a Pyrrhonian sceptic. Although Montaigne may have been keen to refute his despised nickname of being an Epicurean, Guyau contends that numerous Epicurean thoughts find a rebirth in his *Essays*: 'In this "handbook of the honest" ... it is not the scepticism of Pyrrho that will come out of this meditation, but rather the *ethics* of Epicurus' (2). Guyau's narrative then reaches the modern epoch, and he closely examines how in France the system of Epicureanism was reawakened by the erudition of Gassendi, and in England by the genius of Hobbes. Furthermore, this reawakening continues in the work of Helvétius and almost all eighteenth-century French philosophers, while from the time of Bentham onwards almost all English thinkers are Epicurean. Finally, notes Guyau, the influence of Epicureanism continues to grow in spite of the new Stoicism of Kant and the Kantian school.

As this narrative outline indicates, Guyau prudently brings the topic closer to his own intellectual background and the philological training in Classics, ancient philosophy and the Early Church fathers, which he had pursued under Fouillée's mentorship. It is, therefore, from the perspective of antiquity – and of Epicureanism in particular – that Guyau will propose to write an alternative critical history of utilitarianism. This fertile, and at first sight anachronistic, approach allows Guyau to interpret modern utilitarianism as an accomplished expression of Epicureanism. It also allows him to read Epicurus through the lens of John Stuart Mill, to quote Caro's expression in his report to the Académie, providing an original and stimulating reading of the philosopher of the garden.[19] In this sense, modern ideas such as utilitarianism, positivism and evolutionism will constitute the privileged perspective from which Guyau views the philosophy of Epicurus and his followers.

Indeed, for Guyau, 'Epicurus and Lucretius already embody the scientific spirit of modern utilitarians' (2). If, on the one hand, Epicureanism is chosen by Guyau as a privileged perspective for writing a history of ethics, which sheds light upon modern ideas, helping us understand their foundations and implications, then, on the other hand, Epicureanism itself is seen as a modern idea – the 'most modern' of ancient ideas (xxix). Evidently not in a chronological sense, but in what we could call a logical and normative one: for Guyau, the Epicurean system has generated ideas such as evolution and progress (which Guyau observes emerging for the first time in the work of Lucretius),[20] and has sought to put forward a secular, probabilistic and scientific account of natural and physical phenomena, challenging religious notions of miracles, as well as supernatural explanations. Guyau observes that despite preserving an ethical admiration for the gods – seen as models of tranquillity and ataraxia for the sage – and a political respect for the religious rites of the city, the system of Epicurus is essentially irreligious. For Epicurus, the natural seed of religion is held to reside in superstition, which refers back to fear, ignorance and man's innate penchant for hasty conclusions. Moreover, as Guyau argues, 'no master can be more tyrannical than the master that one gives to oneself'.[21] However, Guyau shows that Epicurus and Lucretius equally resist replacing the arbitrary tyranny of the pagan gods by the much deeper and inescapable tyranny of fate and necessity – both in their scientific and philosophical versions.[22] Finally, Guyau notes the successes of Epicureanism in his own time: the cosmological systems of Democritus and Epicurus are triumphing again in the natural sciences with the renewal of materialism and the atomistic system, and in the moral and social sciences the doctrines that derive from Epicureanism are receiving a vital renewal in the English school and its emphasis on utility. 'How many old ideas and rooted customs Epicureanism has contributed to ridding the moral domain of!' (245). These Epicurean ideas can be seen as constituting the core of a modern philosophical attitude and that reappears throughout Guyau's appreciation of the history of ethics, referring to thinkers such as Hobbes, La Mettrie and Helvétius, and the *philosophes* of the Enlightenment.

Guyau's apparently naive position cannot be reduced to a mere anachronism. It finds its philosophical foundations both in his underlying appreciation of the history of Western ethical thought and in his method in the history of philosophy. Let us seek to illuminate the latter.

Guyau's method rests upon a certain 'vitalist' premise according to which philosophical ideas form systems that are organized in such a way that each of their parts is organically connected, forming what Pierre Hadot called, following Schopenhauer, an 'organic type of system'.[23] Guyau sees philosophical systems as living beings and, ultimately, as organisms. This is why a merely structural or architectonic reconstruction of the system – which Guyau calls a 'geometric projection' or the 'anatomy of a philosophical system' (xxvii) – although it might provide an informative synchronic picture of the organization and structure of the system – is still insufficient for an understanding of its development, movement, and the transformations it undergoes through history. For Guyau, this understanding can only be achieved once the system is considered in motion and subject to development throughout time.

Guyau proposes, then, to study the genesis of philosophical systems in the same way one studies the formation of biological organisms, for 'the laws of life and the laws of thought are the same' (28). And how does an organism develop? The genesis of an organism can always be traced back to a cell or a small number of associated cells, which gradually develops into an increasingly complex entity. The same process, Guyau argues, characterizes the genesis and formation of a philosophical system; and the task of the historian of philosophy amounts to identifying this first seminal and fertile idea – or set of associated ideas – that Guyau calls the 'key idea' (*idée maîtresse*), and then to analyse its development and growing complexity in the course of time. In a word, to the 'architecture' or the 'anatomy of thought' that analyses the structure and the relations of a certain system of ideas, and that studies its different parts independently of time, one must add an 'embryogenesis of thought' (xxviii). This approach focuses on the genesis and gradual development of a living philosophical system, starting from a fertile principle, which encounters other ideas, and then undergoes differentiation in the course of time.

In this sense, Guyau's approach to the history of thought is defined by an *evolutionary* perspective: one cannot understand the dynamics and evolution of a living system, be it an organism or a system of thought, simply by analysing its internal constitution. The structure of a certain philosophical system is but a snapshot of a state of its living development and is, therefore, to be explained by this development. This is why, he maintains, we can only fully understand modern utilitarianism by looking at ancient Epicureanism, for they are different states of an evolving living system. Moreover, a sole focus on internal development only gives us a part of the story: it is only when we focus on the interaction of an organism with an environment – or what Guyau calls 'a resistant *milieu*' – and the obstacles and challenges it poses to it as a form of life – that we can begin to properly understand its evolution. Here, again, it is the consideration of the living system in time, and in relation to specific spatial coordinates, that will provide us with the key to understanding the living structures it presupposes as solutions to this dynamic, and sometimes conflictive, interaction with the environment.[24] In the case of a system of thought, this interaction is characterized by the different appropriations and subsequent transformations that the system undergoes in different linguistic, national and cultural contexts, and more importantly the particular challenges it confronts, including the objections and contradictions it is likely to encounter in its development.

What, then, initially appeared as an anachronistic approach is, in truth, Guyau's attempt to write a history of ethics from the perspective of the development and evolution of a philosophical system. In order to understand modern utilitarianism we must go beyond its present anatomy and current state of development so as to comprehend its formation, its embryogenesis, by looking at the 'key ideas' of pleasure and utility, which first emerge with Epicureanism. In a way, one could say that utilitarianism is but a chapter (although an important one) in a broader history of Epicureanism. However, there is another reason why Guyau thinks we should read utilitarian ethics as an instance of Epicureanism. This leads us to the philosophical presuppositions of the kind of history that Guyau is putting forward in the *Ethics of Epicurus*.

By highlighting a fundamental form of Epicureanism Guyau enables the reader to instructively conceive the history of ethics in terms of an antagonistic relationship it has with a fundamental Stoicism that embodies an ethics of duty and virtue. These two forces reappear, Guyau argues, every time religious enthusiasm and moral fanaticism dwindle, and human beings seek to freely investigate their ethical experience in the world. Consequently, we will also find exemplars of this fundamental Epicureanism and Stoicism in modernity:

> Epicurus' influence (…) is increasing despite the new Stoicism of Kant and his school. Everywhere, in theory and practice, we find two moralities (…) split philosophical thought and divide human beings. We can say that today the fierce half-a-millennium struggle between Epicureans and Stoics has rekindled and is burning anew.
>
> 43

If utilitarianism represents a modern version of the ethics of pleasure, Kant's moral philosophy represents the renewal of the ethics of duty.[25] This suggests that Epicureanism and Stoicism embody two fundamental organizing poles of human ethical experience, two irreducible principles both in thought and in action: pleasure and duty. The latter is centred upon the notion of *obligation*, which it seeks to found upon rational, formal and non-empirical principles and rules of action; the former, by contrast, focuses on action based on interest and characterized by an empirical principle of enjoyment.

A key aim of Guyau's text is to restore the dignity of the earthly pleasures advocated by Epicureanism against its detractors and against abstract and transcendent rules of action. This focus on the importance of pleasure allows him to uncover a forgotten, or at least overlooked, Epicurean tradition in the history of thought, one mainly concerned with human emancipation and happiness, and in which he situates the work of thinkers such as Gassendi, Hobbes, La Rochefoucauld, Spinoza, La Mettrie, Helvétius, Feuerbach and others. This tradition finds in pleasure and enjoyment a path to the achievement of personal independence to be attained through the victory over fear and superstition – the principal sources of trouble and anguish for human beings – and it inspires the creation of collective forms of emancipation. Indeed, as Guyau shows, Epicureanism and its modern successors were not concerned only with individual happiness and well-being: it is within the Epicurean tradition, and beginning with Epicurus himself and his analysis of friendship, that a series of reflections result in key political ideas, such as conventional justice and the social contract. Against the traditional reconstruction of Epicureanism as an egoistic and apolitical morality, characterized by a lack of attention to social concerns and a withdrawal from politics, Guyau shows that it was within the Epicurean tradition that important notions of modern political thought were first developed, such as a society founded on mutual agreements and the idea of social progress. To the Stoic tradition of natural law Guyau opposes the Epicurean 'pact of utility', which embodies the natural right of not harming and not being harmed by others. The pact, as Guyau sees it, is a way to come to terms with the tension existing between individual and society, between egoism and altruism. He writes: 'Epicurus in antiquity, and Hobbes in modernity, were the first thinkers to solve the issue in a utilitarian way. They invoked the interest of each one of its members as the end of society and, as a means for its organization [they posited] mutual consent, that is the mutual acceptance of burdens with a view to the common enjoyment of benefits; in a word, the social pact' (126). However, the social pact is not seen as a merely formal device since it also entails a community of ends founded on harmony and sympathy, and such a community of interests can only exist through mutual aid (120).

Guyau shows how the Epicurean approach to society is marked by a profound realism regarding the human condition: it does not deny the self-interested nature of human beings and the tendency of individuals towards pleasure and utility. The developments of this Epicurean view in psychology, which we witness in La Rochefoucauld's *Maxims*, for example, show the extent to which self-love and its transformations inform almost all human interactions, never fully disappearing in our encounters with others.[26] However, this realistic insight into the human heart, and the apparently pessimistic observation of human nature, do not amount to a form of moralistic contempt. Like Spinoza, the Epicurean tradition seeks not to 'bewail, or laugh at, or disdain, or (as usually happens) curse' the affects and actions of human beings.[27] In this sense modern Epicureanism, while deepening the social and political aspects of an ancient philosophy of pleasure, does not deny the affective and passionate nature of human beings. On the contrary, it is through the prism of the powerful naturalistic insights provided by Epicurus that his modern followers come to reflect upon the 'social problem'. Their great concern will be, then, how to create collective arrangements in which individual and common enjoyment and happiness can be most effectively and rationally brought together.

If Epicurean reflections on society seem to be merely founded upon utilitarian concerns, Guyau also stresses other aspects that, while based on utility, seem to exceed it, such as the importance accorded to friendship, which is seen as necessary for the attainment of virtue and happiness (115), as well as the importance of life lived in common, the *conspiratio amoris* that emerges from the habit of acting in common (116; 118). In the conclusion to the book Guyau claims that we have reached a time when our individual pleasure presupposes the pleasure of others: 'egoism will turn back and retreat further and further into ourselves, becoming less and less recognizable' and human beings 'will no longer be able to *enjoy* [pleasure] in solitude: their pleasure will be as if part of a *concert* in which the pleasure of others will take part as a necessary element' (241). Or, as he will later write in his *Esquisse*, the 'truly human pleasures are all (...) social. Pure selfishness (...) instead of being a real affirmation of self, is a mutilation of self'.[28]

Guyau guides us through the different attempts of the Epicurean tradition to come to terms with the problem of the pleasure of others, or that which he called 'the social ideal'. In the *Ethics of Epicurus*, Guyau thinks of the social contract, for example, as a collective and consensual organization of enjoyment and pleasure. He writes: 'According to Epicurus, the social idea consists of a strong union of all the contractors in mutual trust, in a form of happiness where everyone would have their share, and which everyone would enjoy at once' (128). However, if the Epicurean tradition has sought to harmonize self and others, Guyau writes, 'this is not a primitive and fundamental harmony. The egoisms of individuals function together like pendulums, without merging into one another, and without becoming deeply united. Ethics does not have as its goal to produce this union, since that would be ultimately impossible' (241).

Epicurean pleasure and self-cultivation

We now wish to illuminate how in his text Guyau conceives of an Epicurean ethics centred on the nature and tasks of self-cultivation.

Guyau's positioning of Epicureanism remains significant for one important reason: as we already mentioned it seeks to champion a pagan teaching against the menace of religious enthusiasm and moral fanaticism and, in so doing, it seeks to renew humanity's commitment to the earth as the place of its existential flourishing. For Guyau, modern human beings find themselves in a sceptical search for the truth about things – 'We are now less willing to believe, more willing to search' (4) – and Epicureanism can be enlisted as a mode of living and thinking that can greatly aid us in our search. For Guyau, Epicurean teaching is to play a fundamental role in developing a new research programme about ethics, in which, sceptically and honestly, we pose a series of daring questions, including: Does duty exist? Does morality exist? Should we replace duty by the common interest? Should we replace merit in action by the enjoyment of acting? For Guyau, it is the thought of Epicurus that echoes in the greatest minds of our own modern times and that may provide some answers to our searching questions. In short, for him Epicurean teaching is once again alive, and its enduring vitality shows that both history and its critical systems are never finished. For him, as for Nietzsche, 'Epicurus has been alive in all ages and he lives now.'[29]

In the opening chapter of his book Guyau highlights the distinctive character of Epicurus' teaching by making a helpful contrast with Aristotle. Where Aristotle holds that science in its highest forms is the thing that is least useful, Epicurus focuses on the positive and practical aspects of his doctrines, asking the question: What is the use or purpose of philosophy? Epicurus can thus be seen to be rejecting, Guyau says, 'every abstract speculation and every vain subtlety' (12). Most significantly perhaps, Epicurus 'breaks the Aristotelian distinction between contemplative and active virtue, between the goal of thought and that of action' (12).

The practical problem par excellence is to determine the end of our actions and the end or goal of our lives. As is well known, for Epicurus this end is pleasure; we delight in enjoyment (*jouissance*) and we revolt against pain. The challenge, Guyau notes, is to contend with the intelligence and reason that would judge pleasure as the end of life: when we live in accordance with the pleasure principle we are simply being faithful to nature and to our natural drives, so that when an animal inclines itself towards pleasure it is nature that judges in it and in its purity and integrity. For Guyau, this makes Epicurus the founder of naturalism: pleasure is the natural end of every being that lives. Let us be clear: for Guyau, nature and intelligence are not opposed; rather, the decisive point for Epicurus is that we cannot conceive of an abstract good divorced from a sensible element. It is only through an error that human intelligence conceives of an end that differs from the one pursued by the whole of nature since it is from sensation that thought first comes to life. The task is to do away with the abstractions of metaphysical thinking and to identify a good that is truly living (*vivant*), that is accessible to all, and that we cannot doubt. Even the self-denying Stoic, Guyau astutely notes, is, in effect, searching for a refined kind of satisfaction, namely, that of overcoming their suffering and pain, and in the process the desire for pain is transformed into some actual enjoyment. This curious kind of enjoyment in oneself, and in one's overcomings, plays a crucial role in the psychology of a refined egoism: it consists in taking a refined, even heroic, pleasure in oneself. This was also understood well by Nietzsche: 'There is a serenity the Stoic possesses whenever he feels constricted by the duties he has prescribed for his way of life: he takes pleasure in himself as the ruler.'[30]

In Guyau's reading, Epicurus' teaching results in a reconfigured doctrine of virtue: virtue is always a means to the end of pleasure and without pleasure the virtues would be neither commendable nor desirable. This is where Epicurus appeals to reason: if they are to serve the end of pleasure the virtues need to be rationally organized and subordinated to the end in a way that is skilful, and this is the task of science as well as the domain of wisdom. Here we can praise philosophy as this science and as this wisdom; we do not praise it on account it being the highest speculation of the intellect. We might think this is to subordinate physics, or the study of nature, to ethics, and to be worried by this. However, as Gilles Deleuze points out, there is a need of both: 'Everything happens as if physics were a means subordinated to practice, but practice would not have found this means all on its own and is incapable of achieving its end without it.'[31]

To be found in Epicurus' teaching is a temperate reason, and this forms an important component in Epicurus' conception of an art of living conceived as what Guyau calls 'the art of conduct', and to be conceived more fully as 'the art of spiritual and material direction' (15). This means that, for Epicurus, philosophy is not a pure, theoretical science but constitutes a practical rule of action. Indeed, for him, philosophy is in itself a *praxis*, 'an *energy* that seeks to produce, by discourses and reasoning, the blissful life' (15). As Guyau notes, thought without flesh (*chair*) is, for the Epicureans, nothing but a 'distant and uncoloured image, an effaced picture in which one can only glimpse the vaguest and most irresolute lines' (16). We thus need to pay attention to the pleasures of taste, of hearing, of sight, and those of Venus; but the principal pleasure, Guyau concludes, is the pleasure of living. James Porter has recently echoed this when he observes, with respect to Epicurean teaching: 'To love life is to be in an unqualified state of affirmation about what lies most immediately to hand: it is the pleasure, the unalloyed passion, and even thrill, of living itself.'[32] For Epicurus, then, a correct understanding of our mortality is one that should lead to the enjoyment of this mortal life. Moreover, this Epicurean love of life is not a longing for life, but 'rather an immediate expression of what is dear about life,'[33] what is most life worthy in life', and which makes it something fragile and easily ruptured.[34] Moreover, 'what an Epicurean enjoys is not some pleasure that is distinct from life, but life *qua* pleasure'.[35] Similarly, arguing against the idea that Epicurean pleasure is a merely negative or empty concept, Pierre Hadot conceives of it as a positive sentiment, namely, the pure pleasure of existing.[36]

Guyau, we think, is especially incisive in seeing that Epicurean ethical teaching is focused on seeing the cultivation of happiness (*bonheur*) as a task to be carried out over the course of a whole lifetime. The task is one of genuine, far-sighted wisdom in which happiness is the new element in the doctrine of pleasure and that can lead to the attainment of blessedness. This is where Epicurus differs from Aristippus. Guyau depicts Aristippus' position as a form of radical hedonism, an absolute fidelity to the present moment, and consequently to the pleasure that is possible to achieve in each singular ephemeral fragment of the present. For Aristippus, the present alone is ours (28); for who could tell what the future reserves to us? We must avoid every thought involving duration and succession in pleasure, making ourselves fully present to the sole actuality of enjoyment, and thus dispersing ourselves in the multitude of ephemeral instant pleasures we experience.

For Epicurus, by contrast, we must consider pleasures and pains from the perspective of the whole of our lives (*ho holos bios*). Passions and desires appear to us as completely dominant when considered in the present moment. However, when we consider them in time and, specifically from the perspective of the duration of our whole life, we can reassess their ethical significance and ultimately master them. Guyau explains this idea through a physical analogy: *time* is for our *passions* what *space* is for *atoms* (30). Take, for example, the shocks and collisions of atoms; they are less violent and frequent in a vast space than they would be when atoms find themselves compressed in a small space and have less room to move freely without the hindrance of other atoms. The same applies to our passions in the short and long term. When considered in the short span of the present they appear absolute and unconquerable. However, when we view them from the perspective of the duration of our whole life, what can their impact upon us be?

One of the unique aspects of Guyau's interpretation of Epicurus resides in the way he conceives the temporality of pleasure. While other interpreters from Nietzsche to Hadot have highlighted the value of the *present instant* in Epicureanism,[37] Guyau shows that the experience of the present moment, and the emphasis on the pleasure that can be found in it, is *not* distinctive of Epicureanism – since we also find it in other hedonist thinkers.[38] For Guyau, Epicureanism's distinctive character resides in also considering the *future* when acting in the present. For the Epicurean, the present must be linked to the future, and both present and future converge in the composition of a 'whole of life'.[39] It is this encounter between present and future in enjoyment that Guyau calls 'utility': utility is pleasure fecundated by the idea of time.

When Guyau proposes to shift our attention from this complete and total belonging to the pleasure in the instant, focusing instead on the duration of our whole life, he also shifts focus from the object and moment of enjoyment to the *subject* of enjoyment. It is this subject, which persists in pleasure and pain, that must craft his or her own existence as a coherent unity. Guyau's interpretation of Epicurus stresses the necessary cultivation of this subject who is capable of surrendering to present enjoyment when convenient, but also able to resist pain and even mobilize it as a means for achieving a superior and lasting pleasure in the future. This is why the introduction of the notion of temporality in the consideration of pleasure is concomitant with the appearance of the figure of the sage – who embodies the subject of this renewed experience of pleasure, conceived form the viewpoint of *ho holos bios*.[40] The sage is the moral agent and the philosophical persona that Epicureanism seeks to craft; one which perhaps only Epicurus himself had fully embodied.

The fundamental existential choice of the Epicurean sage is that of a coherent and consistent life over time, and that is why the Epicurean is not someone who pursues unstable and fleeting pleasures. He is neither the Cyrenaic hedonist who disperses himself in a multitude of fleeting instants nor the *stultus* depicted by Seneca, and who is never able to unify his desires. In order to accede to the underlying pleasure of existence the Epicurean sage must cultivate a rational organization of means that will allow him to achieve happiness, conquering the chaos and contradiction of desires and passions, directing his or her 'thought [and actions] towards the future'. The Epicurean subject cultivates the whole of his or her life as a work to which they endeavour to give a rational and beautiful form. This is why when the sage chooses a present pleasure, he does so considering it as a part in the process of the constitution of an ordered totality – that of a beautiful life. The assurance and confidence that the sage obtains in this process of self-cultivation allows him to cope with pain when it presents itself. If at times Guyau's picture of an austere and lofty Epicurus may recall the Stoic, it is important to bear in mind that the main force driving and sustaining this austerity – when it is necessary – is the achievement of a superior form of pleasure that one takes in life itself, and in the cultivation of one's own life as a masterpiece.

Guyau also casts valuable light on the aesthetic sensibility that informs Epicurean ethics. The cultivation of a consistent way of life can be understood as an ethical and aesthetical continuity in *style*. The style that the Epicurean applies to his whole life is characterized by a form of beauty to be found in harmony, that is, in a certain orderly relation of parts and whole, and that connects current instants with one's entire lifespan.

The modest pleasures one chooses to affirm in the correct doses, and the pains that one chooses to endure as a means for a greater, more stable and lasting delight with one's own existence, result in what Michel Foucault in our own time characterizes as an aesthetics of existence, an understanding of 'the *bios* as a material for an aesthetic piece of art'.[41] Similarly, Guyau uses the metaphor of the painter to depict the sage, this 'artist of happiness' painting emotions, pleasures and pains on the canvas of life, so making use of an aesthetic and ethical work of selection. As Guyau writes: 'Life then becomes this *cadre* of undetermined contours, in which the sage, this "artist of happiness" groups his emotions to come, placing some of them in the second plane, some others in the first, bringing these to light, and casting the shadows of oblivion over the others.' The aesthetic value and beauty of the work comes from its rational order, which emerges from the intelligent organization of a lifestyle, and in which certain pleasures are cultivated, aiming at a superior happiness.

Epicurus' teaching is significant since it brings heaven to earth and the happiness of the gods to human beings. It is on account of his appreciation of the whole of life that Epicurus' teaching amounts to an ethical one: it sets us the work of cultivation. As we have shown, it is even possible to appreciate this ethical teaching on aesthetic grounds, finding beauty in the rational disposition of life that subordinates the parts of life to the whole of it (31). Moreover, in Guyau's portrait of Epicurus we find a hedonistic morality that does not neglect the cultivation of virtue, but presupposes it: Guyau reveals the interdependence that exists between the enjoyment of pleasure and the care of self and others. Unlike typical conceptions and appreciations of utilitarianism as a straightforward hedonism, Guyau provides us with a rich ethics of self-cultivation that focuses on the subject and agent of pleasure rather than simply on the objects of pleasure. There is, then, a great deal to learn from an encounter with Guyau's appreciation of Epicurus and Epicureanism, including the continued inspiration we can draw from the art of cultivating earthly happiness.

Notes

1 See, respectively, Gertrude Kapteyn's 'Translator's Preface', in Jean-Marie Guyau, *Sketch of a Morality Independent of Obligation or Sanction*, translated by G. Kapteyn, London: Watts & Co., 1989, xii; Ilse Walther-Dulk, *De Guyau à Proust: Essai sur l'actualité d'un philosophe oublié*, translated by Marianne Dautrey, Weimar: VDG, 2008, 7.
2 Walther-Dulk, *De Guyau à Proust*, 15.
3 For example, in 1906, Gabriel Aslan defended his philosophy thesis at the Sorbonne, entitled *La morale de Jean-Marie Guyau* (see *Revue de métaphysique et morale*, 'Supplément', July 1906, 12–14). In 1905, the *Société française de philosophie* discusses Guyau's notion of life (see *Bulletin de la Société Française de Philosophie*, 6:43, 1906. 'De l'idée de vie chez Guyau'. Séance du 28 décembre 1905. Thèse: Georges Dwelshauwers, Discussion: R. Berthelot, Dauriac. Edité par A. Colin). See also Contini, *Jean-Marie Guyau. Una filosofia della vita e l'estetica*, Bologna: CLUEB, 1995, 66 ; Riba, *La morale anomique de Jean-Marie Guyau*, translated by Mariló Fdez Estrada, Paris: L'Harmattan, 1999, 52.
4 Friedrich Nietzsche, *Nachgelassene Fragmente 1884-5*, *Kritische Studienausgabe*, edited by Giorgio Colli & Mazzino Montinari, Berlin: Walter de Gruyter, 1988, 525. As

Mazzino Montinari has shown, Guyau was part of a constellation of authors that Nietzsche read during his stay in southern France (see Montinari, 'Nietzsche e la décadence', *Studia Nieztscheana*, 7 June 2014, 18).

4   Peter Kropotkin, *Ethics: Origin and Development*, translated by Louis S. Friedland & Joseph R. Piroshnikoff, New York: Lincoln MacVeagh/Dial Press, 1924, 322.

6   'According to Guyau, beauty is not anything foreign to the object itself, is not some parasitic growth on it, but is the very blossoming of that being in which it is manifest. Art is the expression of life, reasonable and conscious, which evokes in us, on the one hand, the deepest sensations of existence, and, on the other hand, the loftiest feelings, the most exalted thoughts. Art raises man from his personal life into universal life not only by means of participation in the same ideas and beliefs, but also by means of the same feelings' (Leo Tolstoy, *What is Art?* translated by A. Maude, introduction by V. Tomas, Indiana: Hackett, 1996, §3).

7   Durkheim's review of Guyau's *L'irréligion de l'avenir* appears in *Revue Philosophique*, vol. 23, 1887. See also 'The Conception of Religion' in *Emile Durkheim: Selected Writings*, edited and translated by Anthony Giddens, Cambridge: Cambridge University Press, 1972, 219–22.

8   Gabriel Tarde, *Penal Philosophy*, translated by P. Berne, New Brunswick & London: Transaction, 2001, 29.

9   See Josiah Royce, *Studies of Good and Evil: A Series of Essays upon problems of Philosophy and of Life*, New York: Appleton & Co.) 1899, 349–84 (chapter 12), and William James, 'The Moral Philosophy and the Moral Life', in *The Will to Believe*, New York: Dover, 1956, 184–216.

10 Henry Sidgwick, 'M. Guyau, La Morale d'Épicure et ses Rapports avec les Doctrines contemporaines', *Mind* 4:582, 1879.

11 G. E. Moore, 'Book Review: A Sketch of Morality Independent of Obligation or Sanction. M. Guyau, Gertrude Kapteyn', *International Journal for Ethics* 9:2, 1899.

12 G. E. Moore, *Principia Ethica*, Cambridge: Cambridge University Press, 1993, 98 (chapter II, §29).

13 Alfred Fouillée, 'Note Biographique', in *La morale, l'art et la religion chez Guyau*, Paris : Félix Alcan, 1913; Walther-Dulk, *De Guyau à Proust*, 14.

14 Namely, the *Vers d'un philosophe*, published in 1881, and *Première Année de lecture courante* (1875), *l'Année préparatoire* (1884), *l'Année enfantine* (1883), respectively.

15 Walther-Dulk, *De Guyau à Proust*, 96.

16 Guyau, *Sketch of a Morality*, 81.

17 Guyau, *Sketch of a Morality*, 84.

18 Guyau, *La morale d'Épicure*, book 1, chapter 3. References to *The Ethics of Epicurus* will be given in the text.

19 See 'Foreword' below.

20 See book 3, chapter 3 below.

21 See book 2, chapter 1 below.

22 'It would be better,' says Epicurus, 'to accept the fables about the gods than to be enslaved by (*douleuein*) the fatal necessity of the physicists. Indeed, the fable gives us the hope that we can bend the gods by honouring them, but one cannot bend necessity (*aparaitēton tēn anankēn*)' (62).

23 Pierre Hadot, *The Selected Writings of Pierre Hadot: Philosophy as Practice*, edited and translated by Matthew Sharpe & Federico Testa, London & New York: Bloomsbury, 2020, 125.

24 Guyau's thinking here develops a biological analogy: one can only understand the development and evolution of living systems by looking at the creative solutions it proposes to the environment. Every structure of the living system can be traced back to this engagement and this proactive response to the problems posed by the environment, which is what physiologist Kurt Goldstein calls the 'debate' (*Auseunaudersetzung*) between an organism and its surrounding world (see Goldstein, *La structure de l'organisme. Introduction à la biologie à partir de la pathologie humaine*, translated by E. Burckhardt & Jean Kuntz, Paris: Gallimard, 1981, 95). What we here refer to as a 'dynamic and conflictive relationship between a living system and its environment' is the fact that the development of a living system of thought is relative to its history (to time and the events it faces and the challenges to which it responds) and to its changing geographies (or to space: to its changing geographical, cultural and linguistic contexts).

25 In the light of the fact that we now have access to Kant's lectures on ethics it is necessary to reassess Guyau's positioning of Kantian ethics. Although in his published work Kant proposes an ethics based on duty and formal principles, he was more sympathetic to the philosophy of the garden than Guyau and many other commentators have suspected. For example, in his lectures Kant is keen to distinguish – like Rousseau before him – between a 'brutish Epicureanism' and a 'true Epicureanism' (Kant, *Lectures on Ethics*, translated by Peter Heath, Cambridge: Cambridge University Press, 1997, 66), and he sees Epicurus as espousing '*voluptas*' in terms of possessing a 'constantly cheerful heart' (386). For Kant, Epicurus teaches contentment with oneself and in this self-contentment is to be found an embodied wisdom. It is an embodied wisdom in that it is an embodiment of reason. For Kant, the successors of Epicurus lost sight of the morality of the system 'and pursued an ethic that was coupled only with a new enjoyment of pleasure' (387). He adds: '... they heaped up their needs, but also drew upon themselves a misery that was all the greater, the greater the want of morality' (387). Self-sufficiency has as its basis what Kant calls 'good cheer' and 'the culture of our soul'. Morality means imposing a regimen of discipline and control over oneself, a mastery and care of self.

26 See book 4, chapter 2 below.

27 Baruch Spinoza, *The Ethics*, translated by Edwin Curley, London & New York: Penguin, 1996, 69 (Part III, Preface).

28 Guyau, *Sketch of a Morality*, 212.

29 Friedrich Nietzsche, *Nachgelassene Fragmente 1884-5*, 10.7 [151].

30 Nietzsche, *Dawn. Thoughts on the Presumptions of Morality*, translated by Brittain Smith, Stanford: Stanford University Press, 2011, 251.

31 Gilles Deleuze, 'Lucretius and Naturalism', translated by Jared C. Bly, in Abraham Jacob Greenstine & Ryan J. Johnson (eds.), *Contemporary Encounters with Ancient Metaphysics*, Edinburgh: Edinburgh University Press, 2017, 250.

32 James I. Porter, 'Epicurean Attachments: Life, Pleasure, Beauty, Friendship, and Piety,' *Cronache Ercolanesi*, 2003, 33, 205–27, 212.

33 James I. Porter, 'Epicurean Attachments', 212.

34 Porter, 'Epicurean Attachments', 212.

35 Porter, 'Epicurean Attachments', 213.

36 Pierre Hadot, *Qu'est-ce que la philosophie antique?* Paris: Gallimard, 1995, 180. For this for an appreciation of Epicureanism as a teaching of living in the present, see Nietzsche, *The Wanderer and His Shadow*, translated by Gary Handwerk, Stanford: Stanford University Press, 2013, §295.

37 Hadot depicts the realization of importance of the present as the outcome of the spiritual exercise of meditation on death, which opens the perspective gratitude to the gift of existing here and now. He quotes Horace's understanding of each moment is the product of chance, an unexpected gift, that we should accept with immense gratitude (*Qu'est-ce que la philosophie antique?*, 196). Similarly, for Nietzsche: 'For the middle period Nietzsche, Epicurus is the philosopher who affirms the moment, having neither resentment toward the past nor fear of the future' (Ansell-Pearson, 'True to the Earth: Nietzsche's Epicurean Care of Self and World', in Horst Hutter and Eli Friedland (eds.), *Nietzsche's Therapeutic Teaching For Individuals and Culture*, Bloomsbury: London & New York, 2013, 111).

38 However, in *The Ethics of Epicurus,* we also find a beautiful account of the eternity that the Epicurean finds in the moment. For a closer study of the place of temporality in Guyau's reading of Epicurus, as well as his conception of eternity, see Federico Testa, 'Nietzsche and Guyau on the Temporality of Epicurean Pleasure', in Vinod Acharya & Ryan J. Johnson (eds.), *Nietzsche and Epicurus. Nature, Health and Ethics*, Bloomsbury: London & New York, 2020, 96–109.

39 Similarly, the future plays a key role in utilitarianism and in every form of utilitarian calculus, which according to Guyau is the compass that guides the Epicurean in the present.

40 We could recall Kant's phrase according to which 'the pleasure of the Epicurean is the pleasure of the sage' (Kant, *Lectures on Ethics,* 46). On the other hand, it is possible to object that the Epicurean gods play this *exemplar* role which is more important than that of the sage. According to Hadot (*Qu'est-ce que la philosophie antique?*, 190), the gods provide a vision of the 'model of wisdom', being the 'projection and incarnation of the Epicurean ideal of life', for their life consists in the enjoyment of their own perfection, of the pure pleasure of existing. See also Diogenes Laertius, *Lives of Eminent Philosophers,* X, 123; Lucretius, *De rerum natura,* II, 646–51, and III, 14–24. In his translation Strodach identifies this as the role played by the gods in Epicureanism (Epicurus, *The Art of Happiness,* translated by George Strodach, London: Penguin, 2012, 40–3). The blessedness of the gods and the possibility of achieving a godly state among men is well expressed by Epicurus in the closing of his *Letter to Menoeceus,* 135.

41 Michel Foucault, *Ethics, Subjectivity and Truth. The Essential Works of Michel Foucault (1954–1984),* volume 1, edited by Paul Rabinow, translated by Robert Hurley et al., London & New York: Penguin, 1994, 260.

Foreword[1]

On the Method Used for the Exposition of Systems

In this book we have attempted to apply the idea of evolution, which prevails in science and philosophy today, to the exposition of [philosophical] systems. From this we can derive a method that we would now like to briefly explain.

To expose[2] a system is to reproduce its various ideas, not by weakening or exaggerating them, but rather by reviving them according to the order in which one arranges them and the light one casts upon them. Exposing in this context means ordering and clarifying, which is the same, since order is the light of thought. There are only two ways to introduce order into a doctrine. First, even without knowing anything about the different doctrines that one considers, one can establish a ready-made framework and try to make the doctrine fit into it. One establishes a certain number of artificial divisions and subdivisions, which one then applies successively to the work of any author whatsoever. This procedure is the simplest one. It is used by many historians of philosophy, especially in England and Germany. They apply a method that is external to the doctrine that they want to understand and make known. Their method can be applied for analysing another philosopher and, in fact, any other philosopher. They more or less frame different systems by laying them out on the same plane, asking each author the same set of questions about the way in which they conceive matter, spirit, God, etc. Then, they look for answers in the author's work to each of the questions they have posed. They thus obtain an exact summary, a table of contents of each philosopher's thought and, more generally, of human thought as a whole. Although such a schema can be extremely useful, it ultimately gives us only an abstract version of what the author conceived as a living doctrine. If I may put it another way, it is a way of projecting different systems onto the same plane, in which nothing can be put into relief or highlighted, and there is neither height nor depth.

In addition to this external method, we hold that there is another method that has been employed by some historians but is yet to be clearly formulated. This method does not seek to give us a geometric projection of each system. Rather, it seeks to reproduce the development and evolution of each system, to observe every stage of this evolution, and each step of the author's thinking. For human thought is moving and living,[3] and there is no system that is *static*. On the contrary, [even] in [the work of] the same author, we find that each system changes and transforms itself perpetually, going from its principles to their [logical] consequences.[4] From these consequences it returns to those principles, in a perpetual movement of expansion and contraction that reminds us of the movement of life itself. The ideal goal of our method should be to replace artificial divisions and subdivisions by the natural evolution of the system in question.

The first thing to do, then, is to search for and grasp the key idea[5] of the doctrine that one wants to expose. The key idea (or ideas, for often there is more than one, which intersect) lends the system its uniqueness, its unity and its life: it is the central point to which everything is tied, and it is what one must reach first. One must neither put the key idea on the same level as other ideas [that one is considering], nor confuse it with subsidiary ones that derive from it, and that it precedes in the order of thought and probably in the temporal order also. One should rather highlight the key idea, for it is the light that will illuminate the rest of the picture, it is the very soul of the doctrine.

Once the historian possesses these principles and holds to them firmly, he can gradually deduce their consequences. In order to deduce everything that the key idea already contains, it suffices to place it in the historical milieu in which it was born, and this is revealed to him through the analysis of the texts. The historian will then consider every objection which presented itself to the author's mind, or those made by the author's contemporaries.[6] The historian will reconstruct the obstacles that the key idea has encountered. By placing it in its originally resistant *milieu*, the historian will see how the idea can overcome these obstacles and develop itself as a whole. One will see the thought of the author advancing in order to retreat, then retreating in order to advance, in an undulating movement analogous to those movements we find in the physical world, and to which modern science relates all other kinds of movement. [One can imagine] placing oneself within a system, observing its birth and gradual growth, in a process of evolution similar to that of a living being. In order to create life nature does not proceed by assembling all the different parts of the body and then artificially fusing them together. Instead, it is in one or more cells that all the others [cells] are assembled. Human thought also proceeds in this fashion. It creates one or more ideas that are initially vague. These ideas then develop, fertilized[7] by the contact with other ideas, so constituting a system conceived as a harmonious whole or an organism. Now, it is this work [of nature] that the historian's thought, if it is to be faithful to its task, must accomplish a second time.

Psychologists and novelists perform the same kind of task when they seek to portray a character. In their thought, this character is initially composed only of some prominent simple traits: it still an incomplete and formless sketch. In order to shape and develop this character, they place him within his own unique *milieu* and circumstances. On each occasion, the psychologist or the novelist predicts the choices the character will make and the direction in which he will go. Taking these primitive ideas as a point of departure, they then deduce a whole series of actions, and indeed a whole life. If their fiction is well executed and they portray the character successfully, placed in a plausible milieu and circumstances, then it becomes impossible to distinguish fiction from reality. Fiction and reality coincide insofar as they both deduce everything that was already contained within a character, as well as all the acts by means of which he necessarily manifests himself. In this way, one could reconstruct a system more or less completely by knowing its key idea, as well as the objections it has faced, and the paths through which it has deviated: from this higher viewpoint, logic and psychology become one with history. In the same way that a few traits enable us to reconstruct a certain historical figure, and just a few letters allow us to decipher a whole alphabet, so a few limbs of an animal have allowed us to reconstruct a species today extinct.

Moreover, in most cases, the historian of philosophy has abundant data at his disposal. He often has all the elements of a system. His task consists in ordering these materials well. The historian possesses all the milestones of the path, and he simply has to draw a straight line connecting them in order to indicate the trajectory of thought.[8]

Thanks to this method, which consists in reproducing the different systems in their evolution and undulation, one can solve the difficulties which hinder ordinary methods. In this way, one can explain the contradictions that one often encounters in a doctrine, contradictions which are but apparent.[9] Is there not a plurality of inclinations in systems and individuals, in thought and in action? And do not some of these inclinations tend to dominate and efface others, depending on the individual's milieu and time? If one considers the entire existence of each individual, abstracting from it time and life's evolution, one will discover a series of contradictions, at first apparently inexplicable. And yet these contradictions can be explained on reflection; they can even sometimes be understood with reference to the unity [that constitutes the individual's life], interpenetrating and cancelling each other out.[10] The same [insight] is valid for philosophical systems. To understand a philosophical system, one must inject life into it and consider the full progression of its ideas. Contradiction only appears when one divides and separates the terms of the system, when one does not articulate the different moments of thought, when one breaks the chain of its ideas. In a genuine thinker, there is always a point of junction between two ideas in which everything converges. This point is almost imperceptible, but it can be revealed in a conscientious analysis of the texts.[11]

To summarize, then, the method of historical exposition that we have just sketched rests upon the belief that the laws of life and the laws of thought are the same, that both can be understood in terms of the laws of evolution; and, therefore, [it follows that] to understand any system we must know and reproduce this evolution. Until now the history of philosophy has been conceived above all as an anatomy of human thought, but I hold that one must conceive it rather as an embryogenesis [of thought].[12] To truly understand a system, one must study its formation and growth, just as one studies the formation and growth of an organism. This formation involves two main causes whose influences converge. On the one hand, [i] there is the internal reflection that a certain fecund idea, once given, has a tendency to develop in a strictly logical sense. On the other hand, there are [ii] the circumstances, the intellectual milieu in which [this] thought is situated, sometimes blocking its development and sometimes propelling it, so forcing it to deviate from its [internal] deductive path[13] or allowing to re-establish it in its right track. By attending to these two causes, and studying their simultaneous or successive influence, the historian of philosophy will be able to understand the laws and stages that govern the system's formation. All that he needs to do afterwards is to retrace the system's formation itself: this, I contend, is his real task. The history of philosophy would then be, in its ideal form, simultaneously a work of science and a work of art. A work of science insofar as it studies thought and its laws, which is to say life in its higher manifestation. – A work of art insofar as it strives to reproduce intellectual life in its movement, its activity and its plenitude.

NOTE.[14] – Guyau wrote this book for an open competition run by the Academy of Moral and Political Sciences [*Académie des Sciences Morales et Politiques*] when he was just 19 years old. Guyau wrote the book near Paris, in Antony, but afterwards his health was so shaken that he was obliged to move to Nice. Here he printed the first edition of the book, which the Academy had crowned so brilliantly, unaware that it was the work of a very young man.

As well as a very new and original interpretation of the theories of Epicurus, including the *clinamen*, this book contains the sketch of Guyau's own moral doctrine.

Alfred Fouillée.

Notes

1 This book, which we now publish as a new edition, is based on a 1874 prize-winning dissertation [*mémoire*] for the *Académie des Sciences Morales et Politiques*. The initial version, much longer than the present one, was on utilitarianism from Epicurus to the contemporary English school. After completing that which concerned Epicurus and his immediate successors, I felt obliged to issue this work as a separate volume. Epicurus is perhaps one of those philosophers whose ideas tend to be dominant today. He is perhaps one of the most modern philosophers of antiquity, even considered so by many contemporary historians and Hellenists from Germany and England. His ethics, still misunderstood, deserves special and conscientious study. As for the second part of the original dissertation, I have published it under the title *La morale anglaise contemporaine: morale de l'utilité et de l'évolution* (1879).

Here is a kind passage from M. Caro's report [*Rapport*] of the competition, and especially of my account of Epicurus' contribution to utilitarian morality:

> The dissertation registered under No. 2, which relates to epigraph [*tò par'hēmas adéspoton;* 'that which in us is without master, ungovernable'] etc., is a work of 1,300 pages, which promises to offer the same scope of research as its dimensions, and which still holds more than it promises [...]. The author excels (it is not too much to say) in the interpretation and reconstruction of both ancient and modern theories. I can wholeheartedly bring to the attention of the Academy that this is a singularly thorough study on Epicurus, in which the author takes care to show him as a precursor to, and fulfiller of, *utilitarianism* (although this seems to be in slight contradiction with his theory of the three periods in the history of the utilitarian doctrine that he so strongly emphasizes). I will not say that the Epicurus of the author's dissertation is completely accurate, but I can say that it is an Epicurus renewed by a strength and boldness of interpretation, which is rarely seen. The explanation of the pleasures of the stomach [*ventre*] was so often levelled as a criticism to Epicurus, is, according to our author, the primary root and the physiological principle of happiness, instead of being its ultimate purpose; the transformation of voluptuousness into interest by the intervention of the idea of time; the idea of Epicurean happiness that includes the complete happiness of life, the need to exclude pain and suffering [*peine*], and (in order to bring happiness closer to the reach of all) to exclude any element that was difficult to obtain, such as wealth, luxury, honour, power; the new meaning attributed to *ataraxia*, which is not, as great authorities have claimed, a negative principle, but rather a principle of harmony; the pleasures of the soul, and a somewhat unexpected theory of moral freedom; the sovereign happiness becoming the happiness of the soul and absorbing in itself all the others; the liberating science destroying the gods and

necessity itself; finally, Epicurus anticipating the social contract with his theory of justice, all this obviously will not pass critical scrutiny without difficulty. These features are so artfully assembled into a singularly idealized picture of Epicurus, which hardly looks like the disdainful portrait that Cicero paints in the *De finibus bonorum et malorum* [*On the Ends of Good and Evil*]. For my part, I will take care not to make too much out of this boldness of exegesis which bases, for example, a scientific theory of freedom upon Epicurus' rather poor invention of *clinamen*, and which transforms it into a rational doctrine of dialectical expediency. Despite these and many other reservations, one finds in this dissertation a vigorous and clever effort to reconstruct a celebrated and powerful philosophy, supported by a large pile of texts, and it would be hard to alter even one stone of this solid edifice. I am inclined to think that this dissertation reads Epicurus through the work of John Stuart Mill. Nevertheless, the author has convinced us that, in many respects, the reappraisal of Epicurus is beginning, and that perhaps Cicero's portrait of the philosopher was too severe because he feared for the beliefs and customs of the Roman Republic.

I cite this example to give credit to Guyau's decisive originality. He is such an imperious author, who stops before no tradition or any authority in the history of philosophy, and rightly claims boldly revise the sentences that are littered before him.

M. Caro, *Comptes rendus de l'Académie des sciences morales et politiques* [*Proceedings of the Academy of Moral and Political Sciences*], vol. CII, p. 535

When publishing this dissertation, we endeavoured to strengthen our interpretations by referring to new or different texts, often by Cicero himself, that systematic detractor of Epicurus. I should add that we have written a number of new chapters: on the Epicurean theories of death, progress, piety and friendship. Other chapters were thoroughly revised and further developed, such as the one dealing with contingency in the world and man's freedom. On these points, we have found important to justify our previous opinions more completely. I believe I can no longer be accused, as our *rapporteur* has done, of attributing an excessively idealized physiognomy to Epicurus, or for having read him through John Stuart Mill or anyone else, and not through his primary formal texts. I hope to have demonstrated that the *clinamen* is not the 'poor invention' that it is usually presented as being. The texts we have assembled no longer allow, I believe, us to doubt that it was a perfectly rational and, to a certain extent, reasonable doctrine. I also would like to ask my kind *rapporteur* to *save* his final opinion about my dissertation until further notice; perhaps, after reading our book, he will benefit us by informing us of it.

2   T.N. Guyau's expression here is *exposition des systèmes*. *Exposer* in this context could also be translated as 'to explain' or 'to present'. I have chosen to stay closer to the French root, using the English verb 'to expose' and the noun 'exposition'.
3   T.N. Guyau's phrase is *mouvante et vivante*.
4   T.N. The French *conséquence*, here simply translated as 'consequence', designates what logically follows from the principles of a certain system, its derived ideas and hypotheses, or its results or conclusions. The interplay between principles and conclusions and the way they relate to Guyau's view of the life of the system is a recurrent theme throughout the book.
5   T.N. Guyau's expression is *idée maîtresse*.
6   T.N. Here, what Guyau means is the following: the historian will make objections to the philosopher's thought, reproduce the objections that the philosopher faced in his

own mind when first building his doctrine, and then the objections made by his contemporaries.

7   T.N. The French here is *fécondant*. The notion of fecundity will be pivotal in Guyau's later work.
8   T.N. Guyau's original is *marquer la marche de la pensée*.
9   T.N. Here, Guyau switches from 'systems' to 'doctrines'. He uses the term 'doctrine' to describe the material of the system, whereas the system itself is more abstract and refers to that which orders the doctrine.
10 T.N. Guyau is suggesting that the whole of an individual's life (and the same is valid for systems of thought) is a sort of zero-sum game, in which contradictions cancel each other out.
11 This only applies to our method of exposition of systems; regarding the method of assessment [and evaluation of systems], I refer to the first chapter of Alfred Fouillée's *l'Histoire de la philosophie*.
12 T.N. The French here is *embryogénie*.
13 T.N. Guyau's French here is *marche des déductions*.
14 T.N. Note added by Alfred Fouillée, Guyau's mentor and stepfather, as well as the editor of his posthumous work.

Introduction

Epicureanism in Antiquity and Modernity

The ethics of interest,[1] espoused for a hundred years by many French thinkers and today by the principal English philosophers, is far from being a historical novelty. We also know that a similar doctrine under the name of Epicureanism seduced antiquity. It was the most popular philosophy of [ancient] Greece and Rome. 'The disciples and friends of Epicurus are so many,' wrote Diogenes Laertius, 'that whole towns would not be sufficient to contain them.'[2] Plutarch claims that Epicurus' followers came from as far as Egypt to listen to their master. Bronze statues were erected in his honour. Later, when the Romans first came into contact with [the culture of] the Greek people, they were still full of their own religious beliefs, uniting the love of their fatherland with the cult of Jupiter Capitoline in their hearts. The essentially irreligious doctrine of Epicurus was the first [Greek] doctrine to enter Rome, and the first to be expressed in the Latin language. Epicureanism was then strong enough to defeat this ancient Roman religion at a stroke.[3] As Cicero notes, 'the multitude had its interest stirred and flocked around Epicurus' system in preference to any other.'[4] 'Not only in Greece and Italy,' he tells us, but 'even the barbaric world has been stirred by Epicurus' thought.'[5] When referring to the Epicureans, Cicero further reveals to us that 'the people were on their side'.[6] Indeed, most of the educated men were already on the side of the Epicureans, and did remain with them for a long time. Their adversaries, the Stoics, struggled in vain against the Epicureans and this struggle lasted for the duration of the Roman Empire. The Stoics, furthermore, could neither weaken nor defeat them, nor could they escape their influence. Seneca strongly criticized the Epicureans, although he was still nourished by [the thought of] Epicurus, who he admired and frequently quoted. He was attracted to the very doctrines he fought against. Epictetus later took up the fight against the Epicureans, railing against them with extreme violence. But his disciple Marcus Aurelius, while himself a Stoic and having the same ideas and beliefs as Epictetus, reluctantly returned to Epicurus, taking him as a model and exhorting himself to imitate him. In effect, he established a chair of Epicureanism in Athens.[7] At key moments in his meditations one recognizes the great Epicurean conceptions, which he so sincerely expressed to us, as if [these conceptions were] vaguely floating in a dream. Constantly and with some disquiet, Marcus Aurelius finds these [Epicurean] conceptions even within his own ideas, and although he confronts them with his own, his final thought is one of doubt. Lucian, a man determined to doubt, and who typically does not spare philosophers from his mockery and fierce blows, speaks of Epicurus as a 'divine man, a saint, the only one to have known the truth, who, by communicating it to his disciples, became their liberator'.[8]

Even at this time, after five centuries of struggle, we can see that Epicureanism had not lost any of its importance. The sacred aura with which the Epicureans crowned their master had not yet faded.

Epicurus' doctrine survived as long as paganism did. Epicureanism remained standing for some time even after a new belief emerged in the world. In the face of nascent Christianity Epicureanism remained as a constant temptation. Even Saint Augustine, who personifies this whole epoch, admits that he had once been inclined towards Epicureanism.[9]

When facing all kinds of religion, Epicureanism had a force of resistance that, as we shall see, surpassed all other philosophies. As a matter of principle, it rejected the miraculous[10] and the supernatural. In fact, Epicurus and Lucretius already embody the scientific and positivistic spirit of modern utilitarians, which is the reason of their strength. The practical weakness of the Epicureans when facing Christianity was the persistent emphasis on our ultimate annihilation and the reality of our death. Human beings, however, desire to be immortal. At this time people were weary of life, overwhelmed by servitude and decadence. Saint Augustine rejected a doctrine that promised him nothing more than a happy life, as did his era. Gradually the *gardens of Epicurus*, where previously sages of every nation had wandered tranquilly, and until then had been surrounded by an enchanted and ignorant crowd, became deserted for centuries. The words of the pagan master, words that each disciple learned by heart and retained in his soul as truth itself, were forgotten and effaced by more powerful words. Humankind then turned towards a new future and hastily ascended the mountain where an attainable view of heaven was shown and the doctrine of a 'single God' was preached.

Epicureanism was defeated. However, it was not destroyed. When centuries of time had exhausted the enthusiasm for the new religion, when believers became less numerous and thinkers less rare, one came to realize that earthly interests still subsisted alongside celestial ones,[11] and that they had value and were worth being taken seriously. As the centuries passed, human beings became tired of having their eyes restlessly turned to heaven, and the earth once again assumed a great importance in the people's minds. Montaigne clearly represents this epoch of transition. He was not, strictly speaking, an Epicurean but a Pyrrhonian and maintained a vigilance against the teaching of Epicurus. It is a convenient fact about Pyrrhonism that one can be Pyrrhonian while simultaneously being many other things. Scepticism does not exclude anything precisely because it rejects everything. However, it only rejects everything in theory. Given that in practice one must accept something, Pyrrhonism acknowledges only that which it wishes to. A Sceptic may get along with everyone bending before all dominant beliefs and, at the same time, be free with everybody else. An Epicurean, on the contrary, cannot be other than Epicurean – and he is an enemy to everyone who is not one. Montaigne pushed this ignominious sobriquet ['Epicurean'] far away from himself. However, in fact he was not any less an Epicurean disciple than he was a Pyrrhonian one. How many Epicurean thoughts are reborn in Montaigne, infiltrating his 'wavering' book,[12] *The Essays*! After one hundred years Montaigne's century came to be nourished by his writings and generations meditated on his book. In this 'handbook of the honest' – as it was called by a certain cardinal – what we see is not the scepticism of Pyrrho, emerging out of the meditation, but rather the ethics of Epicurus.[13]

Around the first half of the seventeenth century we observe the resurrection of the complete system of Epicureanism in both France and England. In France it was reawakened by the cautious erudition of Gassendi, and in England it was reconstructed by the rigorous genius of Hobbes. From this moment onwards, Epicurean ideas recovered their place in history, and their supporters became as numerous as they once were. Even a misanthropic and dark thinker such as La Rochefoucauld – a thinker who seems to be lost within the depths of the human soul, one who only seems to care for the finesses and curiosities of psychological analysis – is led unwittingly towards Epicurus. It is Epicureanism, combined with Spinozist naturalism, that is born again with Helvétius, d'Holbach and Saint-Lambert. It is Epicureanism that inspires all the French writers of the eighteenth century (excluding Montesquieu, Turgot and Rousseau). Then Epicureanism reappears in England, gathering in Hobbes' homeland ever more numerous *partisans*. With Bentham and Mill it assumes its definitive form which, as we will see, does not differ much from its original source. Finally, with thinkers such as Spencer and Darwin it acquires new growth. To the more or less transformed moral system of Epicurus there is added a vast cosmological system: new Democriteans provide modern Epicureans with the means to ground their ethics upon the laws of the whole world, encompassing the human being and the universe in the same conception.

To summarize, Epicureanism, so powerful in antiquity, has today regained enough force to successively dominate two of the greatest nations of Europe: in France with Helvétius and almost all eighteenth-century French philosophers; in England, with Bentham and the contemporary English school. Today, with a few rare exceptions, all English thinkers are Epicurean. Furthermore, Epicurus' influence in our own country [France], an influence that has remained considerable since the last century, shows a tendency to increase [in strength] in the face of the new Stoicism of Kant and his school. Everywhere, in theory and in practice, we find two moralities,[14] which are based on two opposing conceptions of the visible and invisible world. These two doctrines split philosophical thought and create divisions among human beings. Today it can be said the fierce half-a-millennium struggle between the Epicureans and Stoics has rekindled and is burning anew.

It seems that this battle between moral doctrines, which follows the laws of human thought, tends to increasingly occupy our minds today. Indeed, if there is something the discussion of which interests the whole of humanity, if there is something that makes us passionate, it is the moral problem. No human being's attention fails to be captured when they hear the words 'duty', 'justice' and 'rights'. Only one thing has served to divert attention from moral and social issues, relegating it to a second-rank position during a whole historical epoch, namely religious enthusiasm. Religious faith satisfies the two tendencies that define and divide human beings: that of disinterestedness and that of utilitarianism.[15] Disinterestedness [traditionally] found its object in the love of God, and in the love of men in God. Interest[16] has found its satisfaction in anticipating a future in which all could believe. Interest has also made people despise the good things of the earth to a certain extent by looking ahead to the enjoyments of heaven. Each time a religion triumphs it dampens philosophical and moral discussion, encouraging an attitude of indifference towards interests, as well as worldly duties and rights. When religious enthusiasm burns itself out, when mysteries hitherto accepted, and that had been projected as immense shadows upon the human mind, no longer serve to obfuscate problems, and when faith can no longer restrain the strongest minds, then moral and metaphysical questions can be posed once again. Only when our attention turns from temples and the heavens to questions of moral and political philosophy, only when prophets and soothsayers are forgotten, do the masses gather around thinkers who seek to show them what is present and real. It is accepted as common knowledge that the eighteenth and nineteenth centuries manifest this kind of crisis. The number of people who adhere to a strong faith appears to be decreasing, and even those who still have enthusiasm in faith no longer experience it with the same degree of intensity. This occurs in all nations, although it is especially widespread in France, as was shown by the French Revolution. It could be argued that the strength of moral sentiment that inspired the Revolution shows how religious feeling was too weak to prevent it. It is a unique historical example of a great movement in which religious feeling did not play a role. The masses were driven by purely moral and social ideas. This kind of event will undoubtedly happen again. Humanity, remaining always the same, is easy to impassion and readily driven forward by an idea. When humanity no longer finds a sufficient motive in religious beliefs, it will increasingly turn to moral and then to social ideas, which will eventually predominate and absorb everything else, including morality.

We can contend, therefore, that moral and social issues will become of vital importance.[17] They will not be limited to the abstract domain of philosophical thought but will pass into the realm of fact and action. What is more, they will become matters of life and death for different peoples. Those nations that in the past had tackled religious problems in a vicious way had frequently been surpassed and effaced by those other nations that have offered a less imperfect solution. Religious sentiment has served to give the nations in which it has strongly manifested itself a greater expansive force. The same will happen in the future with regards to moral and social feelings. Those peoples who will have more adequate notions on morality and society will have an irresistible power surpassing all others. The strength of these peoples will lie in devising the best solution to the moral and social problem facing humanity.[18]

We can now ask which one is the people, and even who is the person, that will find the solution, or that will at least be able to get close to it. If it were possible to predict the future, to determine how events will actually unfold, then the one with the knowledge of these moral and social truths could impose a direction on history, just as one can set the course of a ship when one knows where it is heading. But we no longer live in times in which one can with priestly certainty affirm where the truth lies. Absolute conviction in the correctness of one's own thinking is of the same variety as the convictions that inform religious ideas and is as fragile [and as vulnerable to critique] as they are. Today we are less willing to believe and more willing to search. We are keen to challenge our own thinking. We have seen so many ideas crumble around us, and sometimes even our own, so we no longer dare to rely on ourselves with complete confidence. Whatever we assert we are always still doubtful of and are ready to curtail our assertions. Is this bad? No, because circumspection does not prevent the fierce drive to research. If discovering the truth is a long and arduous process, we must be tireless in our pursuit of it.

When this fierce drive to pursue the truth takes possession of us, it is especially when this pursuit concerns problems regarding the behaviour of individuals and societies. In a way it is a duty to research into the question of whose side duty is on and, at the same time, on which side humanity must march. Fundamentally, the whole moral and social debate, which we have seen growing in importance, can be reduced to the debate between the partisans of interest and the partisans of meritorious virtue,[19] or between the Epicureans and their detractors. Does *duty*, strictly speaking, exist? Does *morality*[20] exist? Do we have the *merit* in doing what we think is good? – Or rather, are 'duty', 'morality' and 'merit' (as there are many reasons to believe) simply figurative expressions that humanity has taken too literally? Must we replace 'duty' with 'common interest', 'morality' with 'instinct' or with 'hereditary habit' or 'calculus'? Must we replace 'merit' in action with the 'enjoyment'[21] of the object for which we act? – Put simply, this is the very same question originally raised by Epicurus. After having traversed the centuries, and repeated like an echo by the greatest minds, this question reaches us today and demands an answer. We already know enough about Epicurean ethics and its subsequent development in history to understand the strength of its system. More often than not the strength or weakness of a philosophical doctrine can be measured by its duration and persistence. Part of humanity has long believed that life's sole purpose is interest, it has sincerely believed and courageously promoted this idea. Part of humanity still believes it and continues to support it. If this is not the whole truth one must find in it at least a large portion of the truth. Such a doctrine, therefore, deserves our most careful consideration.

Doctrines, just like individuals, have their own life. They are born, they grow, they flourish. They blossom in their youth and they mature with virile vigour. They also sometimes decline and there are some that are immortal. In order to know a doctrine, it is good to have somehow followed it in its path, to have seen its progress, and to have lived with it. How could we expect to know those doctrines which we only see *en passant*, fleetingly, in only one aspect? When we see Epicureanism unwound before us in its entirety, in all its multiple guises, only then can we hope to know what is true or false in it. Only then we can also try to judge it even though this judgement will never be without appeal. A doctrine always has a future ahead of it so that it can rise again if necessary. Neither the history of systems nor their critique is ever finished.

Notes

1 T.N. Guyau's phrase here is *morale de l'intérêt*.
2 Diogenes Laertius, *Lives of Eminent Philosophers*, Book X, Section 9. [T.N. Guyau adds the word 'disciples'. See R. D. Hicks' translation (London & Cambridge MA: Harvard University Press, 1931, 537): 'his friends, so many in number that they could hardly be counted by whole cities'.]
3 See Marcus Tullius Cicero, *Tusculanae Disputationes*, Book IV; *Academica*, Book I, Section 2; *Epistulae ad Familiares*, Book XV, 19. The first philosophical writers in Rome where the Epicureans Amafinius, Rabirius and Catius – who were extremely

mediocre writers, according to Cicero. The great poet and philosopher Lucretius appears after them.
4   Cicero, *Tusculanae Disputationes*, IV, 3. [T.N. Here, the translator's choice was to preserve Guyau's phrasing.]
5   Cicero, *De Finibus Bonorum et Malorum*, Book II, Section XV.
6   Cicero, *De Finibus Bonorum et Malorum*, Book II, Section XIV.
7   T.N. The original reads *chaire d'épicurisme*.
8   Lucian, *Alexander*, 61. [T.N. Guyau's translation abbreviates the Greek original, which in A. M. Harmon translation reads: 'Epicurus, a man truly saintly and divine in his nature, who alone truly discerned right ideals and handed them down, who proved himself the liberator of all who sought his converse' (Lucian, *Works*, Volume IV. Cambridge MA & London: Harvard University Press & William Heinemann Ltd., 1925, 253). Guyau qualifies Epicurus as a *libérateur* throughout the whole book.]
9   Augustine, *Confessions*, Book VI, XXVI, 'I used to argue with my friends Alypius and Nebridius about the limits of good and evil. Had I not believed that the soul, and the rewards we have deserved, persist after death, which Epicurus did not, I would have given the victory in my mind to Epicurus. Moreover, I used to ask, if we were immortal and lived in perpetual pleasures of the flesh with no fear of being deprived, why were we not happy?' – it was simply time that separated Epicurus from Saint Augustine. [T.N. Guyau indicates the reference incorrectly.]
10 T.N. Guyau's expression is *merveilleux*, which in this context can be associated to a rejection of divine intervention, the miraculous, as well as any kind of supernatural form of causation.
11 T.N. The contrast here is literally between the interests concerning the world 'down here' [*d'ici-bas*] and those concerning the heavens or the world 'above' [*d'en haut*].
12 T.N. Guyau's poetic adjective here is *ondoyant*.
13 T.N. The phrase '*bréviaire des honnêtes gens*' is attributed to the cardinal Jacques Davy du Perron. This reference appears in Alexandre Dumas' novel *Les Quarante-Cinq*, chapter XXXV. However, according to Aude Volpilhac ('Du bon et du mauvais usae des Essais au XVIIe siècle', *Cahiers philosophiques*, 114, 2008) one cannot find textual evidence of this phrase in Du Perron. See Gombaud de Plassac, Josias; Nicole, Pierre & Huet, Pierre-Daniel, 'Trois extraits autour de Montaigne', in *Cahiers philosophiques*, 114, 2008, p. 88; see also A. M. Boase, *The Fortunes of Montaigne. A History of the Essays in France, 1580-1669*, New York, Octagon, 1970, p. 116, note 3.
14 T.N. An alternative is 'two ethical systems'.
15 T.N. Guyau uses the French *utilitaire*, designating self-interested moral behaviour. He will further qualify this concept in the next chapters: utility will then be defined as a higher form of interest, related to unity and persistence in duration.
16 T.N. The French here is *l'intérêt*.
17 T.N. Guyau's original reads *vivante*, which could be seen as extending the vitalistic insights he put forward in the previous section. The word expresses movement, growth, proliferation and maturation.
18 T.N. In this paragraph Guyau seems to express the idea of a 'civilizational clash' in which the people who finds the solution to moral and social problems will have the advantage over others. It seems to be, on the one hand, a eulogy of progress and secularization; on the other hand, this idea seems to express a sort of social Darwinism, which brings with it a whole range of problematic presuppositions.

19 T.N. The opposition here is between *l'intérêt* and *vertu meritoire*.
20 T.N. Here Guyau uses *moralité*, which is an important distinction when it comes to the translator's choice on how to render *morale*.
21 T.N. The original is *jouissance:* in this case, the specificity of the concept and its difference with regards to 'pleasure' is made explicit. Guyau is referring to the possession and enjoyment of a desired object.

Book One

The Pleasures of the Flesh

1

Pleasure: The End of Life and the Principle of All Ethics

The positive and utilitarian character of Epicureanism:[1]

I. How Epicurus poses the moral problem: the search for the end [of life]. – Epicurus' solution: First, in all beings, nature pursues pleasure independently from reason and before reason. Force and subtlety of this naturalist argument. That Epicurus searches infallibility not in reason but rather in nature. – Second, reason, by virtue of its constitution, cannot conceive an abstract good without a sensible[2] element. The value of this argument against ancient idealism. That pleasure and pain,[3] according to Epicurus, are the only forces capable of moving beings and making them act.
II. The search for the *means* to achieve the desired end, namely pleasure. Virtue has no value except for the pleasure it procures [us]. Virtue is identical to science; how Epicurus arrives at this identity [of virtue and science]. The praise of philosophy, not in itself, but as a means to pleasure. Definition of philosophy. Thought subordinated to sensibility.[4] – A remark on ancient philosophies by Kant.

What first strikes us in Epicurus, the true founder of utilitarian ethics, is the positive and practical character of his doctrine. Aristotle said: 'Science, especially its highest forms, is the least useful.'[5] Epicurus counters this maxim. One intuits that, dedicating himself to philosophy he first asked: 'What is it for?'

This is not how we typically see the human spirit proceeding in history. As we know, peoples who begin to philosophize almost always begin with pure speculation, a confused mixture of physics and metaphysics. They think for the sake of thinking and searching.[6] It is only later, when philosophers realize that they have searched for too long and discovered too little, and when they find themselves disagreeing with one another, that they become troubled and begin to fear that they have laboured in vain.

Pyrrho and the Sceptics laughed and mocked when they grasped the contradictions and the impotence of other philosophers. The utilitarians, however, were more serious, and instead of condemning the human mind, they condemned speculation and turned their thoughts towards the *self*,[7] asserting that before pursuing absolute truth, one must search for and find relative truth and utility. This is precisely what Epicurus did in Greece. We can consider his system as an attempt to tear the human mind away from the inconsistencies of Heraclitus, Socrates, Plato and Aristotle; in a word, as an attempt to focus human thought on utility.[8] Plato searched for the truth in order to deduce the good from it. Epicurus first searched for what is good for us before searching for the truth itself. Like our modern positivists he rejects every abstract speculation and every vain subtlety. He breaks with the Aristotelian distinction between contemplative and active virtue, between the goal of thought and that of action. [Epicurus admits] No more detours in the march towards the good: he demands a unified, easy and straight path,[9] one of clarity and precision in words. He seems to loathe what our philosophers call 'metaphysics'. Nevertheless, he will be forced to do metaphysics himself, sometimes even getting carried away by it. Loyally following the development of his own system and the necessity of things, he eventually elevates himself to pure metaphysical considerations and ends up welcoming [as a friend] this kind of disinterested speculation that he began by repelling as the enemy.

I. – The first problem posed by Epicurus is the practical problem par excellence: What should we do? What is the end of our actions? What is the *end* of life?[10]

In order to solve this problem one can take two different paths: that of experience and that of rationality. According to experience, what is the end that we pursue and that all living beings around us also pursue? – According to Aristippus, the well-known predecessor of Epicurus, the end of life is said to be pleasure.[11] Epicurus repeats this, telling us: 'Pleasure (*ton hēdonēn*) is the end (*telos*) of all beings. As soon as they are born, by nature and independently of reason, they take delight in enjoyment[12] and they revolt against pain.'[13,14] This Epicurean argument contains a very subtle idea. It should not be said that in pursuing pleasure [living] beings do something evil. By what right is one entitled to blame them? It could only be done in the name of reason. But does reason have any authority here? – Reason would only have a hold on these beings if they had chosen reason in advance as their master and judge. [We could only blame living beings] if, while acting irrationally, they thought of themselves as acting rationally, or if they only took pleasure after according to a [given] *reason*. One could then oppose to it a better reason. Epicurus, however, anticipated this objection: he puts intelligence on trial, instead of letting it judge pleasure. He claims that one naturally pursues enjoyment from the moment one is born, *without reason* (*phusikōs kai chōris logou*). 'The animal,' Epicurus says, 'is inclined towards pleasure before every alteration of its nature: it is nature itself in its purity and integrity that judges within it [the animal].'[15] Relying on the ancient idea of the good as that which is according to nature, and the evil as that which goes against it, Epicurus adds: 'only nature must [be allowed to] judge what is in accordance with or contrary to itself.' In saying this, Epicurus, like several contemporary philosophers, opposes nature to reasoning, senses to thought, and most definitively he opposes the animal to the human world.[16]

The principle of this profound naturalist theory is the following: everywhere and every time nature acts without reason's calculation it cannot *be mistaken*. Where there is no reasoning, there is no error. Now, in all beings, pleasure is the object that nature pursues. It is pleasure, then, that is the *natural* end of every being. It must also be the end for the human being. The latter does by reflection that which animals do by instinct. Human beings learn from nature how to conduct their reason.

Epicurus and the Epicureans assert the impossibility of reason being able to conceive of an abstract good deprived of every sensible element, [as this would be] beyond the experience of nature.[17] Indeed, how could human intelligence, unless by error, conceive and pursue an end that differs from the one pursued by the whole of nature? According to Epicurus, an opposition between nature and intelligence cannot exist. The human being that feels and the human being that thinks are not two different beings; it is from sensation itself that thought first comes to life.[18] Is it not because we pursue pleasure and enjoy it that its *image* penetrates into us, inscribing itself within us and then becoming an *idea*? And, at the same time, is it not from the sensation of pain[19] that the *idea* of pain is born? *This is true for all our other ideas: they can all be referred back to sensations, and, consequently, either to our pleasures or our sufferings.*[20] Epicurus does not admit the existence of indifferent sensations. Ultimately, one only thinks because one has experienced pleasure or pain. Human intelligence, this complex product of sensations, is always wholly permeated by pleasure and pain: how, then, could it not naturally conceive of pleasure as desirable and pain as worthy of aversion? Every part of us coheres in this. This is one of those ideas that we could call *innate* and universal (*prolēpseis*), because such ideas have their origin in universally experienced sensations and because they found human intelligence.[21]

Every idea of this kind – every *prolēpsis* – has the property of being self-evident and clear.[22] It is enough to call it by its own name for it to be awakened within us, which is to say, it is enough for us to express it with exactitude for us to acquire full awareness of it.[23] It will be enough, then, to name pleasure and everyone will understand that it is the good. The true philosopher has here to affirm more than to reason:[24] he speaks and we discover that his word, like that of an inspired person, becomes *real, that his word had always been a reality, and that we were already there, close to the truth*. For pleasure is the truth and the good: 'it is felt'[25] and simultaneously understood. This is the point at which intelligence and sensation coincide. On a fundamental level intelligence and sensation are not two things but one. 'Simply because we have senses and we are [made of] of flesh,[26] pleasure appears to us as a good.'[27] Let us also note once again that pleasure will appear as good not only to the senses and to the flesh, but also to the mind[28] because the mind is still the senses and, ultimately, sensation and flesh. 'In truth,' writes Epicurus, 'I do not know how I could conceive the good (*tagathon*) if I was to subtract pleasure.'[29]

It is interesting to note the extent to which philosophers of the time were not able to adequately respond to Epicurus' statement: there is no other real good to [our] intelligence than pleasure. If one opposes to Epicurus only the principles of ancient philosophy, can one say that he is wrong? Even Kant agreed with him: ancient philosophy represented the good as a sensible *thing*,[30] and sometimes as an abstract and logical *idea*, almost never as personal goodness. That is what is already indicated by the impersonal and neutral term: the good.[31] The philosophers of the time expected to discover a good (*agathon*), or the good (*tagathon*), in the same way as alchemists of the Middle Ages sought to discover gold in the bottom of their crucibles. Towards the final stage of Greek philosophy, everyone proposed their own 'sovereign good', and Varro counts 288 different conceptions of it. But how can one find a good *thing* that would not be reducible to something pleasant?

Outside of active thought and of free will (if such a thing exists at all), outside of the *person*, there is no real and non-abstract good except in pleasure. But the Greek philosophers, apart from Aristotle, have scarcely admitted a free power[32] of the will, and they conceived thought in an abstract manner as something too purely logical. To designate sovereign Goodness, Plato still employed the neutral term *tagathon*. As for Aristotle's [notion of] Thought, eternally immobile, eternally immersed in its own contemplation, its supreme *act* seemed to consist in supreme inaction. This wholly intellectual consciousness, where neither willing nor a moral element could intervene, seemed empty. The ancients only had a clear conception of the sovereignly *intelligible*, which amounts to the truth, and of the sovereignly *desirable*, which amounts to happiness.[33] Their ethics was either one of intelligence or one of the senses. Therefore, when Epicurus searches for a truly real good, which is truly living and that could be accessible to everyone, and of which no one could doubt, we can understand why he rejected the doctrines of his predecessors. He exchanged in place of a distant end, half-hidden under the abstractions of metaphysical thought, a very close, sure and real end, an end [that is] universally pursued. According to Epicurus, human beings must deliberately abandon themselves to the *élan* that directs every natural being towards pleasure. Human beings must not obstruct this movement. Their intelligence must bow before nature, and not seek to bend nature to itself.

Moreover, even if one wants to live independently of pleasure, can one do so in practice? [In seeking this as a goal,] is not rationalist morality pursuing the impossible? The Stoic, for instance, while believing that he searches for suffering[34] in itself and for itself, is indeed searching for a kind of refined satisfaction: that of overcoming his suffering, and, in order to desire pain,[35] he begins by transforming it into enjoyment.[36]

Generally speaking, we cannot *desire* or *fear* anything that we cannot imagine filling us with pleasure or pain simply because desire and fear are the only forces that drag us out of a state of rest. All our actions and all our movements relate, then, to pleasure. However, that to which everything else is related and that, in its turn, is not related to anything, is the sovereign good. Pleasure is, then, the sovereign good.[37] 'We say that pleasure is the principle and the end of a happy life (*archē kai telos tou makariōs zēn*),' Epicurus writes with sincerity. 'We know (*egnōmen*) that it [pleasure] is the first and natural good (*agaton prōton kai sungenikon*); if we choose or repel anything, it is because of pleasure (*apo tēs hēdonēs*); we run towards it (*epi tautēn katantōmen*), distinguishing every good by sensation as a rule (*hōs kanoni tōi pathei pan agathon krinontes*).'[38]

II. – Now that we have established the principles, let us analyse the consequences. Considering the centrality of enjoyment, virtue, in the sense in which the common man[39] understands it, will evidently be of secondary importance. If enjoyment is an end, virtue can only be a means to this end. 'Without pleasure,' says Epicurus, 'virtues would be neither commendable nor desirable.'[40] Honesty deprived of the agreeable is nothing.[41] 'We must praise,' he says, 'honesty, virtues and other like things, if they procure pleasure; if they do not procure it, (*ean de mē paraskeuazē*) we must say farewell to them.'[42] This last hypothesis, as we shall see, is untenable for Epicurus.

Epicurean virtue is but a currency with which one procures or obtains pleasure, in the same way as we can use gold or silver to procure other things useful to life. One can be rich in virtue as one can be rich in silver. But these two kinds of wealth, if they were to be unaccompanied by anything else, would not serve human beings [in their search for happiness], any more than turning into gold everything he touched served Midas in his desire to achieve happiness.

Since virtues are the means to pleasure, it is necessary to rationally organize these means and to skilfully subordinate them to the desired end. This is the work of reason, the concern of science and of wisdom (*phronēsis*).

Epicurus will return, then, by a circuitous route to the old conception of Socrates: one cannot be virtuous without being *savant*. Virtue is identified with science, especially with the highest science, philosophy.[43]

In this way, Epicurus donates to philosophy a superb eulogy. His words to Menoeceus remind us of how Socrates responded to Callicles' reproach that he had lingered too long over his philosophical studies. Epicurus says: 'The young man should not hesitate to philosophize, and the old man should not grow tired of it! The hour has always come and has never yet passed for acquiring the health of the soul. To say that it is too soon or too late to philosophize would be to say that it is no longer or not yet time to be happy. Therefore, both old and young alike must philosophize! The former so that in growing old, he rejuvenates in the true goods and by means of his gratitude towards the past, and the latter so that he remains young even in old age on account of his confidence in the future. Let us meditate on the means to achieve happiness because, if we achieve it, we have everything, and if we lack it, we do everything to obtain it.'[44] Nevertheless, if Epicurus praises philosophy in using such enthusiastic language, we must remember that this is not because he believes that philosophy has value in itself or because it is the highest speculation of the intellect: rather, for him, philosophy has an exclusively practical end.

Indeed, as Epicurus tells us, 'the most precious thing for philosophy is *prudence* (*phronēsis*), from which all other virtues are born'.[45] It is '*temperate reason*' (*nēphōn logismos*) or, to put it differently, the art of conduct, the art of spiritual and material direction. Thus, philosophy finds its true value in practical wisdom, which it seeks to procure for us. Does such desirable wisdom have [any] value in itself? Not at all, for its value is still relative, and it would lose its importance for us if, by an inadmissible hypothesis, it ceased directing us towards the fullest enjoyments. Just as Socrates, Plato and Aristotle diminished sensibility before intelligence, so Epicurus diminishes the intellect in the face of sensibility.[46] He even borrows several of Plato's comparisons, turning them upside down. 'In the same way by which we approve the science of the doctors not in itself but because of health; in the same way we praise the art of the pilot[47] not in itself but because of its utility; so, in the same way, wisdom, this art of life, if it were not useful, would not be desired; if we desire it, it is because it is, so to say, the artisan of pleasure, the pleasure we search and seek to obtain.'[48] In brief, virtue, science and wisdom would lose all value if they were not to give rise to pleasure. From this comes Epicurus' ultimate definition of philosophy: it is not a pure and theoretical science, it is rather a practical rule of action. Much more: philosophy is in itself action, 'an *energy* that seeks to procure the blissful life[49] by discourses and reasoning'.[50]

The artist's thought has no more intrinsic value than that of the philosopher: the arts must be embraced by the pleasure they bring us. We write poems, amuse ourselves with music, in the same way one writes commentaries of authors to pass the time.[51]

As we follow the development of the Epicurean system we observe a diminishment in the value accorded to intelligence, the superior part of the soul, which according to Socrates participates in the divine: *metechei tou Theiou*. Thought and science must justify themselves by showing how they can lead us to pleasure. Our intelligence, born from our sensations, needs to be at their service or not exist at all. Here we are far from thinkers like Plato and Aristotle. Pure thought, thought without *flesh*, is, for the Epicureans, just a distant and uncoloured image, an effaced picture in which one can only glimpse the vaguest and most irresolute of lines. Bare thought, as Aristotle conceived of it, is inferior even to this sketch[52] since using relatively effaced traces our imagination can restore the picture of a face or of a body. But once the imagination is suppressed, what could still be left? 'Once the senses are taken away from man, there would be nothing left.'[53]

Most ancient philosophers, according to Kant's insightful remark, had the merit of being highly consistent with themselves; possibly more so than modern philosophers. They did not hesitate to bring to light everything that their principles contained. Once they committed themselves to a certain path they never retreated. The Epicureans exemplify this attitude. Advancing slowly, but surely, they take us from consequence to consequence, in such a way that we can only resist by challenging the very idea that founds their system.

Notes

1 T.N. At the beginning of each chapter Guyau provides a synopsis. His strategy in these summaries is that of listing the main arguments and topics of each chapter. The sentences are not explanatory, but concise points that list what the chapter will develop.
2 T.N. The French here is *sensible*.
3 T.N. The original reads *peine*.
4 T.N. Guyau's term here is *sensibilité*.
5 T.N. Guyau does not provide the reference. The passage is probably a paraphrase of Aristotle's *Metaphysics* (volume 1, translated by W. D. Ross, Oxford: Oxford University Press, 2020), Book A.
6 T.N. That is the Aristotelian definition of philosophy, as a pure theoretical activity that has its end in itself. See Aristotle's *Metaphysics*, Book A. Guyau seems to be revising Aristotle's idea, by saying that philosophy begins as abstract and speculative and develops towards practical concerns and utility.
7 T.N. le *moi*.
8 This means that it would be a mistake to picture Socrates as an utilitarian, or as a predecessor of Epicurus; he is above all a logician and a rationalist; in effect, his ethics rests upon the identification of the rational and the useful [*utile*], but not on the absorption of the rational by the useful; Socrates' ethics is, at least in what concerns its highest principles, clearly opposed to the ethics of Epicurus. (See Fouillée, *La philosophie de Socrate* [Ouvrage couronnée par l'Académie de sciences morales et politiques. Paris: Librairie philosophique Ladrange, 1874]).

9 '*O apertam et simplicem et directam viam!*' ['Here is indeed a royal road to happiness – open, simple, and direct!'], Cicero, *De finibus*, I, XVIII, 57, 18). See also Epicurus' *Letter to Herodutus*.
10 One knows that Epicurus' most important work is his treatise *Peri telous* (*On the end* or *On the goal of life*), to which Chrysippus the Stoic responded by another treatise, *Peri telōn* (*On the ends*). Probably, in his *De finibus*, Cicero borrowed a lot from Crysippus' *Peri telōn*.
11 T.N. The French here reads *plaisir*. Aristippus was a disciple of Socrates, who claimed that pleasure is the ultimate goal of existence. He is known as the founder of Cyrenaic school, which would later be known and criticized by its hedonism, empiricism and sensualism.
12 T.N. The original reads *jouissance*.
13 T.N. The French *peine* is a more general concept than the English 'pain', the French *peine* can refer to trouble, suffering, toil, but also to the domain of sanction and penalty.
14 Diogenes Laertius, *Live of Eminent Philosophers*, X, 129, 137. – We translate these texts ourselves.
15 '*Idque facere depravatum, ipsâ naturâ incorruptè integrè judicante. Necesse est, quid aut ad naturam aut contra sit, a naturâ ipsâ judicari. Ea quid percepit aut quid judicat, quo aut petat aut fugiat aliquid, praeter voluptatem et dolorem?*' ['One thus acts to the extent one is not perverted, under the influence of non-corrupted and healthy judgement of nature herself. Now, what does it perceive, what does it judge, in function of what does it search for or do anything, if not by pleasure and pain?'] (Cicero, *De finibus*, I, IX, 30).
16 T.N. The passage seems to suggest the contrary: namely that Epicurus opposes the setting up of clear-cut distinctions between these domains. There is, however, a way in which one could make sense of this passage. When commenting on the opposition between the human and animal world, Guyau seems to be referring to how we typically understand these terms; the human world seems to refer to a convention of what it means to be human (as being outside the order of nature and superior to it). Guyau seems to be indicating that Epicurus reveals the existence of a conventional opposition only in order to challenge it (i.e. privileging nature over reason, sensibility over thinking, etc.). This is explained in the following paragraph: nature does not make mistakes, it is only the intervention of our thinking that introduces error ('Where there is no reasoning, there is no error').
17 '*Negent satis esse, quid bonum sit aut quid malum, sensu judicari, sed animo etiam ac ratione intelligi et voluptatem ipsam per se esse expetendam et dolorem ipsum per se esse fugiendum*' ['They deny that it is enough to judge by sensation of what is good and of what is bad, but they say that one also understands by intelligence and reason that one must seek pleasure for itself, and that pain must be avoided in and by itself'], Cicero, *De finibus*, I, IX, 31.
18 '*Quidquid porro animo cernimus, id omne oritur a sensibus*' ['All that which we later perceive by intelligence comes originally from the senses'], Cicero, *De finibus*, I, XIX, 64. – *kai gar epinoiai pasai apo tōn aisthēseon gegonasi* ['and, indeed all notions are born from the sensations'], Diogenes Laertius, *Lives of Eminent Philosophers*, X, 32.
19 T.N. Here Guyau uses the French *douleur*.
20 T.N. The French here is *peines*.
21 '*Aiunt hanc quasi naturalem atque insitam in animis nostris inesse notionem ut alterum (voluptatem) esse appetendum, alterum (dolorem) aspernandum sentiamus*' ['They say

that there is a natural and inate notion in our souls, which makes us feel that one (pleasure) should be desired and the other (pain) avoided'], Cicero, *De finibus*, I, IX, 31. By a 'natural and innate notion' Cicero understands the Greek *prolēpsis* ('anticipation' or 'preconception'). See the definition of 'anticipation' or 'preconception' in Diogenes Laertius, *Lives of Eminent Philosophers*, X, 33: 'Anticipation or preconception is a notion, or a general conception stored in the mind, which is to say the recollection of an external object often presented to us.'

22 *Enargeis eisin ai prolēpseis* ['Preconceptions are self-evident'], Diogenes Laertius, *Lives of Eminent Philosophers*, X, 33. This clarity and certitude that characterizes the *prolēpsis*, it borrows it from sensation. The *prolepsis* is but the imprint [or engraved mark] (*tupos*) of a sensation, an image, a lively recollection or memory of a sensation (*mnēmē*). See Sextus Empiricus, *Adversus Mathematicos*, VII, 203.

23 See the beginning of Epicurus' *Letter to Herodotus*.

24 '*Negat opus esse ratione . . . satis esse admonere*' ['He denies that one must [give] reasons . . . It is enough to admonish or remind'], Cicero, *De finibus*, I, IX, 30.

25 '*Sentiri hoc, ut calere ignem, nivem esse albam, dulce mel*' ['To feel that fire burns, that snow is white, that honey is sweet'], Cicero, *De finibus*, I, IX, 30.

26 T.N. chair.

27 *Aisthēsin dei echein kai sarkinon einai, kai phaneitai hēdonē agathon* ['It is enough to possess [the capacity of] sensation and to be made of flesh, and pleasure will appear as a good'], Plutarch, *Against Colotes*, 1122a.

28 T.N. *esprit*.

29 Diogenes Laertius, *Lives of Eminent Philosophers*, X, 6. '*Ou gar egōge echō ti noēsō tagathon, aphairōn tas hēdonas . . .*' Athenaeus, f, VII (translated in the text).

30 T.N. That is to say that which exists to our senses.

31 T.N. *le bien*.

32 T.N. *pouissance*.

33 T.N. *bonheur*.

34 T.N. *peine*.

35 T.N. *douleur*.

36 One can note that, according to several chapters of the *De finibus*, the Epicureans, feeling the need of grounding their moral doctrine upon psychological analysis, prefigure the ingenious analyses of feelings [or sentiments] that will be later proposed by Hobbes, La Rochefoucauld, Helvétius and the contemporary English school. They were aware of how their system could strengthen these [analyses of the] 'geneses' of moral sentiments. '*Haec ratio late patet*' ("This argument is largely [self-]evident'), says Epicurus in Cicero's *De finibus*. The praise that on offers to courage, the merit one gives to ethics, all this is overthrown by analysis: '*totum evertitur*' ([*De finibus*,] I, X, 36). There is in these words a sort of anticipation of the later developments of the Epicurean doctrine, which found and support it upon psychology.

37 Diogenes Laertius, *Lives of Eminent Philosophers*, X, 128, 129.

38 Cicero, *De finibus*, I, XIII, 42: '*Et appetendi, et refugiendi, et omino rerum geredarum initia proficiscuntur aut a voluptate aut a dolore . . . Quoniam autem id est vel summum vel ultimum vel extremum bonorum, quod Graeci* telos *nominant, quod ipsum nullam ad aliam rem, ad id autem res referentur omnes, fatendum et sumum esse bonum jucundè vivere*' ['The first principles of desire, aversion, and of action in general, come either from pleasure or pain . . . Now, that which the Greeks call *telos* (the end), that is to say the highest, ultimate or most final of goods, is that to which all things are

referred [or reduced], but which does not refer back to anything else, one must admit that this good is to live pleasantly'].

39 T.N. *le vulgair*.
40 Cicero, *De finibus*, I, XIII.
41 Cicero, *De finibus*, II, XV.
42 Epicurus *apud* Athenaeum [*Deipnosophistae*, or *Banquet of the Learned*], XII, 67. *Timēteon to kalon kai tas aretas kai ta toioutotropa, ean hēdonē paraskeuazē ean de mē paraskeuazē, chairein eateon* (translated in the text). See Seneca, *Epistles*, 85, 18: '*Ipsam virtutem non satis esse beatam vitam, quia beatum efficit voluptas quae ex virtute est, non ipsa virtus*' ['Virtue itself is not enough for achieving a happy life, since it is the pleasure that virtue brings that makes one happy, and not virtue itself'].
43 There is nothing surprising about this agreement of systems apparently as divergent as Epicurean sensualism and Socratic rationalism; as long as the good is conceived as an end exterior to us, and appears as essentially rational, beautiful or agreeable, rather than simply moral, then an act of will and a straight intention are no longer enough for attaining it; one can make mistakes, taking a merely apparent pleasure for a real one, or a real evil for a real good; intention does not matter much, success is everything. Now, it is better to possess knowledge in order to be successful [in our search for the good]. The only remedy to everything that is not moral and voluntary evil but mere *error* or intellectual evil [*mal intellectuel*] is science: this is why Epicurus and Socrates agree in recognizing the need for science and its identity with virtue. Socrates, however, places the good – which he sees from a neutral and impersonal viewpoint – in science itself. Epicurus, by contrast, subordinates science to a more concrete and palpable good: pleasure. Epicureanism is, in this sense, the Socratic theory turned upside down. Epicurus could, therefore, accept Socratic ideas on several points, as did also his predecessor Aristippus, Socrates' disciple. Among other things, Epicurus seems to agree with Socrates on the distinction between *eupraxia* (the good attained via causal knowledge and with the certitude of science) and *eutuchia* (or the good attained by chance). See Plutarch, *Against Colotes*, 15, 4.
44 *Mnēte neos tis ōn mellētō philosophein, mēte gerōn huparchōn kopiatō philosophōn*, Diogenes Laertius, *Lives of Eminent Philosophers*, X, 22 (translated in the text).
45 [footnote 23, p. 64]. *Philosophias to timiōteron huparchei hē phronēsis, ex hēs ai loipai pasai pephukasin aretai*, Diogenes Laertius, *Lives of Eminent Philosophers*, 132, 138, 140 (translated in the text).
46 T.N. Here the sense is of proportion: Epicurus diminished the intellect before sensibility in the same ways as Socrates diminished sensibility before the intellect. Guyau will later refer to Epicureanism as a form of 'Socratisme rétournée', something like 'Socratism turned upside down'.
47 T.N. *l'art de tenir le gouvernail* – the art of holding the rudder.
48 '*Sapientia non expeterentur, si nihil efficeret; nunc expetitur, quod est tanquam artifex conquirendae et comparandae voluptatis*' ['One would not search for wisdom if it was without effect; but one strives for wisdom because it is like an artisan who searches and obtains pleasures'], Cicero, *De finibus*, I, XIII, 42. – *Dia de tēn hēdonēn kai tas aretas aireisthai, ou di' hautas, hōsper tēn iatrikēn dia tēn hugieian* ['It is for the sake of pleasure that one chooses virtue, rather than for [virtue] itself, in the same way one chooses medicine for the sake of health'], Diogenes Laertius, *Lives of Eminent Philosophers*, X, 138. See Plutarch, *Against Colotes*, 17, 3; see also Alexander of Aphrodisias, *De anima*, 156b.

49 T.N. *la vie bienheureuse*.
50 Sextus Empiricus, *Adversus Mathematicos*, XI, 169. *Tēn philosophian energeian einai logois dialogismois ton eudaimonia bion peripoiousan* (translated in the text).
51 *Agogēn diagōgēn* ['Culture is an amusement'], Diogenes Laertius, *Lives of Eminent Philosophers*, X, 138.
52 T.N. Here *esquisse* refers to the 'effaced image' of the previous sentence.
53 '*Detractis de homine sensibus nihil reliqui est*', Cicero, *De finibus*, I, IX, 30 (translated above).

2

Fundamental Pleasure: The Stomach[1]

The origin of all pleasure: the *flesh*. Comparison between the value of different pleasures. Epicurus measures the value of different pleasures according to the *necessity*. Opposition between Epicurus and Socrates, who measured the value of things according to their *generality*. – What is the fundamental pleasure? – The stomach, the root of every good according to Epicurus, and the object of philosophy according to Metrodorus. The true meaning of these usually misunderstood expressions. Analogy between contemporary naturalist conceptions and Epicurus' principle.

After having considered the relations of the [ultimate] end of man, that is pleasure, to virtue, science and prudence, which are all merely means of achieving it, let us now analyse the idea of pleasure itself. What is the content of this idea according to Epicurus? There are different kinds of pleasure. Can we distinguish pleasures that are honest from those that are shameful? Those that are beautiful from those that are ugly?

Epicurus did not acknowledge anything higher than pleasure, and so could not admit without contradiction any rule that would impose on pleasure a beautiful or ugly character, or one of baseness or elevation. All enjoyment is, therefore, good, simply because it is enjoyment.

When questioned about the meaning of these terms – pleasure, enjoyment, voluptuousness[2] – Epicurus replied without hesitation: these are all forms of sensuous pleasure,[3] pleasures of the *flesh* (*hēdonē tēs sarkos*). He recognized no other [pleasure]. Epicurus was the first Greek philosopher to pronounce this expressive word.[4]

This is how Epicurus enumerates the pleasures without which he 'cannot conceive any idea of the good': the pleasure of taste, hearing, sight, and the pleasures of Venus. Apart from these pleasures there is no true enjoyment and, therefore, no true good.[5]

Now, all other goods can be reduced to these three or four. Let us now classify them in order to, as much as possible, bring them into a unity.[6]

Concerning the pleasures of sight and form (*tas dia morphēs*), we can say aesthetic feeling is not absent from them. The pleasures of hearing are even purer, they touch our soul intimately. Are not these pleasures produced by a simple vibration, by a simple movement of atoms? Now, movement is perhaps that which is less material in matter. Thus, Epicurus finds that the pleasures of form and sound are not dense enough, not sufficiently filled with matter.[7] He cannot place these pleasures on the same level as others. To see and to hear are complex modes of enjoyment. As they develop, they become spiritualized and they lose their aspect of brute, physical necessity. We can choose between these different modes of enjoyment, selecting one to be an end while excluding the other. They do not provide the kind of unity to which human thought tends; a unity that, once known, excludes every choice. The pleasure of taste (*tas dia chulōn*) has more the characteristics of raw brutality, where we can still dispense with flavours. For Epicurus, we must find something that we could not do without, something *simple* enough to be *necessary*, something base enough to be an *exclusive* end.

When, in his definitions, Socrates assigned each thing its place and rank, he took their generality as the criterion of their value. For him, wisdom consisted in classifying objects by kinds, both in thought and action, *logō kai ergō dialegein kata genē*.[8] For Socrates, each good could be more or less good, more or less useful, according to its generality. The sovereign good was nothing other for him than the universal. Indeed, since he considered everything from a rational perspective, he found in the general the reason for the particular, and in the superior the reason for the inferior. Concerning the investigation into the different modes of pleasure, Socrates evidently assigned a greater value to the pleasures procured by our eyes and ears than to the other bodily pleasures, because he believed that these pleasures were more general, as well as more extensive than the others. In the pleasures of sight and hearing, he found both everything that exists in the inferior pleasures and other features that could not be reduced to these pleasures, such as the aesthetic feeling and thought. He affirmed, for instance, that the pleasure of sight is better than the pleasure of touch, because the former is an enlargement of the latter. Epicurus, by contrast, opted for a completely sensible point of view instead of a rational and intellectual one, and thus arrived at quite a different conclusion.[9]

That which is first in the intellectual order becomes last in the sensible order. In the sensible order, we always have to move from an inferior pleasure to a superior one, from very strict particular pleasures to more general ones. In this type of progress, or of ascendant dialectics, every step[10] achieved would not be possible, could not even exist in fact, without a prior one. In this sense, the inferior precedes the superior and supports it; the inferior is the condition for the superior and is more *necessary* than it. Thus, Epicurus, when attempting to reduce or refer all pleasures to a single principle, should aim at the less comprehensive of pleasures, at a pleasure that would be, in itself, already so narrow [and limited] that it could not be reduced any further. Now, which pleasure is the most necessary on account of the fact that it has the least dignity,[11] without which all others would not exist, but while it could exist without them? The pleasures of the ears and eyes are still superfluous,[12] since they are superior. The pleasure of the mouth (*dia cheilōn* or *chulōn*) is not yet the first of goods: one can do without the mouth, which chews food as long as we have something that digests it. This is the stomach – which is at the same time the organ of life, and the organ of every pleasure. 'The principle and the root of all good,' Epicurus writes with precision, 'is the pleasure of the stomach, *archē kai riza pantos agathou hē tēs gastros hēdonē.*'[13]

The pleasure of the stomach is good; indeed, it is at the *root* of every sensible pleasure. Modern naturalists in France and England willingly concurred with the doctrine of the Greek philosopher. Epicurus does not want to say that nutrition gives rise to perfect enjoyment. Enjoyment *blossoms* so to say, but nutrition is the seed[14] of enjoyment, its *root* (*rhiza*), its principle and *beginning* (*archē*). In a similar way

Democritus says that the sense of touch is the principle of knowledge, although he does not claim that it constitutes the supreme knowledge. The pleasure of the stomach is the narrowest kind of pleasure, but the most solid, and the foundation for all other pleasures. The pleasure of the stomach supports all sensible life, and consequently, following the Epicurean doctrine, is the ground of all good. 'Wise and excellent things,' Epicurus stresses, 'are related to this kind of pleasure.'[15] It does not follow from this that only this kind of pleasure constitutes wisdom and the good, nor that Epicurus stops short at saying that it is the supreme end. No, it is not the supreme end but is rather the necessary condition of any other pleasure and any other end. It is the germinal principle,[16] for Epicurus, from which all voluptuousness is born and all goods emerge.

It is to the 'pleasure of the stomach' that one can reduce[17] all the others. If it is through it that we can explain all other pleasures, just like one explains all bodies by an aggregation of atoms, it is also in it [the 'pleasure of the stomach'] that we can find the primordial principle of the science whose object is the good or pleasure itself; this science is philosophy. Indeed, as soon as one identifies the good with pleasure, with the moral end and with sensible interest, one is led to the following conclusion: the pleasure of nutrition, developed, enlarged, diversified in a thousand ways, eventually turns into other pleasures, such as taste or sight. This is the subject of ethics. In the same way, Metrodorus, when explaining his master's ideas, gives Epicurus' thought a new paradoxical form, writing: 'It is in the stomach that reason conforming to nature finds its true object (*peri gastera ho kata phusin badizōn logos tēn apasan echei spoudēn*).'[18] This is a very clear thought when compared with the previous one. Most interpreters mistakenly consider the words of the disciple only, before understanding those of the master. Gassendi does not say a word about these important passages, which shows that he had a less vigorous and less systematic mind than Epicurus. Brucker, favourable to Epicureanism, also tries to challenge its authenticity. But its authenticity is *a priori* evident: it is a perfectly logical consequence of Epicurean principles; it is a necessary, if not definitive, moment[19] in the thought of Epicurus, just as it is for all empiricist and utilitarian philosophers. Is not the pleasure of living the principle of all pleasure? Consequently, is this not the pleasure of renewing and constantly replenishing our lives? Is not the principle of all interests the interest to live and consequently to preserve the most immediate means of life, which is nourishment? We can say, therefore, with Metrodorus, that any utilitarian philosophy – as that of Hobbes, Helvétius, Bentham and Stuart Mill[20] and [just as well as] that of Epicurus – finds its final *object* in the stomach (*spoudēn peri tēn gastera*).

On this topic let us recall the conclusions of Herbert Spencer and contemporary English philosophy. According to Spencer, our sciences, our arts, our civilization, all these complex moral and social phenomena that constitute human existence, can ultimately be reduced to a certain number of feelings and ideas. These feelings and ideas are to be referred back to primitive sensations, to the data of the five senses. The five senses are reduced to touch, and Democritus was right to say: 'all our senses are modifications of touch.' Finally, touch itself probably originated in the phenomena of integration and disintegration that are the basis of all life, and that distinguish organic matter from inorganic matter. Therefore, integration and disintegration, concentration and dispersion of forces, assimilation and dissimilation, are the primitive phenomena that we discover, and the source from which stem all other phenomena. This is the 'germ' and 'root' of all life and all science.[21]

Notes

1. T.N. The French here is *ventre*, which has a wider meaning the English 'stomach'.
2. T.N. The French here is *volupté*. Although this term could also be translated as 'pleasure', especially considering the Latin *voluptas*. Our choice preserves the Latin root common to the French and English terms.
3. T.N. *plaisir sensible*.
4. See Félix Ravaisson, *Essai sur la Métaphysique d'Aristote*, II, 94 [Paris: Librairie de Joubert, 1845], and Eduard Zeller, *Die Philosophie der Griechen* [Leipzig : R. Reisland, 1882]. [T.N. Guyau is referring to the word *sarkos*.]
5. Diogenes Laertius, *Lives of Eminent Philosophers*, X, 6; Athenaeus [*Deipnosophistae*, or *Banquet of the Learned*], VII, VIII, XI; Cicero, *Tusculanae Disputationes*, III, XVIII; *De finibus*, II, III; Plutarch, *Non posse suaviter vivi secundum Epicurum*, 4, 5.
6. T.N. *ramener à l'unité*.
7. T.N. Guyau is sketching a contrast between spiritualized, almost immaterial, pleasures and the roughest and most concrete and material form of pleasure, to which nothing is added, and which has no complexity or variety: only the simplest pleasure could be a unified principle and the root of all others, only this simplest form of pleasure could be completely necessary in nature. Guyau is then showing how Epicurus thinks that the pleasures of sight and hearing are not good candidates for this place of radical priority: they are not *material* enough, they can be delicate and can be detached from strict physical necessity as they develop. The contrast here is between the complexity and refinement of sight and hearing, on the one hand, and the simplicity and brutality of mere nutrition, the satiety of the stomach, on the other.
8. See Fouillée, *La philosophie de Socrate*, volume 1 [Paris : Librairie philosophique Ladrange, 1874].
9. T.N. Epicurus arrived at an opposite conclusion, *conséquences opposes* in the French original.
10. T.N. The French here is *degré*, which could also be translated as a stage, degree or level.
11. T.N. Here the French reads *parce qu'il a le moins de dignité*. It is rather strange to affirm that the most necessary pleasure is so *because* it is the one which has least *dignité*. One could say that it is the most necessary because it is the least dignified, the least complex, the one which has nothing else added to it. Its necessity comes from the fact that it is the most simple and ordinary.
12. T.N. Potentially odd sounding in English, 'ears' and 'eyes' are here employed in order to clearly render the parallelism Guyau proposes with the 'mouth' and 'the stomach' in the following sentences. The intention here was to preserve the relation, of fundamental importance in the original, between each particular kind of pleasure and its corresponding organ.
13. Athenaeus [*Deipnosophistae*, or *Banquet of the Learned*], XII, 67, [Guyau exceptionally adds the page number or the edition he consulted] p. 546.
14. T.N. *germe*.
15. Athenaeus [*Deipnosophistae*, or *Banquet of the Learned*], XII, 67: *ta sopha kai peritta eis tautēn echei tēn anaphoran* (translated above).

16 T.N. *germe féconde*.
17 T.N. The French here is *ramener*, which in this context can mean both 'reduce' and 'refer back to'.
18 Athenaeus [*Deipnosophistae*, or *Banquet of the Learned*], VII, 2; Cicero, *De natura deorum*, I, 40; Plutarch, *Non posse suaviter vivi secundum Epicurum*, 4, 10; 5, 1; 16, 9. – Heinrich Ritter, *Histoire de la philosophie*. Translated by Clément-Joseph Tissot [Paris: Librairie philosophique de Ladrange, 1835–6], III, 379: 'A doctrine that focuses on nature must only be concerned with [or must only care about, *avoir soin*] the stomach.' This imprecise claim gives a fully practical dimension to an originally theoretical maxim: one cannot render the Greek word *spoudēn*, which has a very wide range of meaning, as the French *soin* [or the English *concern* or *care*], which has a narrower range.
19 T.N. Here the idea is that of a logical moment, a moment in the process of argumentation and formation of the system.
20 T.N. Guyau uses 'Stuart Mill' when referring to John Stuart Mill (1806–73). From here onwards I will simply use 'Mill'.
21 Herbert Spencer, *Principles of Psychology*, [London: Longman, Brown, Green and Longmans, 1855,] §39, and Théodule Ribot, *La psychologie anglaise contemporaine* [*L'école expérimentale*. Paris: Librairie philosophique de Ladrange, 1870].

3

The Rule of Pleasure: Utility. – Happiness, The Sovereign Good

I. The rule of pleasure: *Utility*. – Introducing the consideration of future pain into the consideration of present pleasure. The idea of time combined with the idea of pleasure. The point where the divergence between Epicurus and Aristippus begins. How this divergence marks the birth of *utilitarian ethics*.[1]

II. *Happiness* as the achievement of pleasure and as sovereign good. – Opposition between Epicureanism and Cyrenaism. The superiority of Epicurus. First, emphasis on intelligence; the ideal of order and harmony in happiness. Second, emphasis on freedom: the possibility of choice between different pleasures and of extinguishing the force of a present pleasure through the thought of happiness to come. Third, emphasis on beauty and morality.

We have descended as deeply as possible into the Epicurean system, penetrating its foundations. Nevertheless, after such a dialectical descent,[2] thought aspires to rise and re-ascend. Now that we firmly grasp the first ring of the chain with which Epicurus strives to link virtue and pleasure, let us examine in turn all the intermediary rings.[3] How can we, from the lowest pleasure, the pleasure of the stomach, accede to moral sentiment and to the dignity of the sage that Epicurus strives to preserve in his system?

I. – Until now, the focus of our analysis of Epicurus' system has been pleasure, the only end of desire. We now need to introduce another element that everyone must count as part of reality: pain.[4]

Any pleasure whatsoever is good in itself (*kath' heautēn*):[5] this is the principle of utilitarian philosophy. How could an enjoyment, considered in itself, or even in relation to its antecedents, be an evil? Thus, for Epicurus, it is useless to consider the sequence of circumstances, including just or unjust acts that *precede* the enjoyment of a pleasure. It is useless to examine the ways in which enjoyment is obtained. Enjoyment simply exists, this is enough. Because it exists, it is good. Because it exists, enjoyment is an *end* in itself and it makes all means to it *good*.[6]

Once the consideration of the past is discarded, we can turn our attention to a consideration of the future. Now, if every pleasure and every means to pleasure is good, we cannot say the same for all consequences of this pleasure. Intemperance, for instance, produces illness.[7] This example shows that the idea of pain produces a drastic change in the idea of pleasure. Epicurus is left with a choice between two alternatives: [i] insisting on the claim that every kind of pleasure is good and an end, not only in itself, but also in relation to its consequences; or [ii] conceding that one must not will only an actual, present pleasure, but that one must also will the greatest sum of future pleasures. Here, a huge difference between Epicurus and the old Aristippus emerges: the two systems up until this point have developed in harmony.

Aristippus has reduced all pleasure to the actual instant. Who knows if any of us even has a future? Only the present is ours.[8] Let us enjoy it without calculating too much. We must circumscribe the idea of our life within very narrow limits so as to enjoy all the fugitive instants that pass before our eyes as easily and completely as possible. [According to Aristippus], we must abstract duration and succession from pleasure. We must forget the pain that enjoyment sometimes drags along after itself. We must also forget that, according to Plato, pain sometimes also drags behind enjoyment. Instead of pursuing a single end – namely the total sum of future pleasures, which is to say pleasure to which one adds the abstract element of time – let us pursue as many particular ends as there are particular pleasures.[9] The sovereign good is not pleasure or happiness [in the singular], but numerous pleasures. 'The *end* differs from *happiness*: *telos eudaimonias diapherei*. In effect, the end is the partial pleasure that we gleam from all fading moments, whereas happiness results from an assemblage of partial pleasures, to which one adds those of the past to those of the future. For Aristippus, partial pleasure is virtue itself. Happiness is nothing in or by itself, but it is only composed by many partial pleasures.'[10] In this sense, Aristippus' doctrine of pleasure aims to establish multiplicity and variability in themselves as the end for human beings. Every action must be considered apart from others, abstracted from the other actions, and it must be allotted its own particular goal, namely the particular pleasure that will result from it.[11] Therefore every possible fixed point (*hōrismenon*) to which one could link an indefinite series of actions is eliminated. Movement and perpetual change (*hēdonai en kinēsei*) reign outside ourselves in the [realm] of pleasures that we ought to desire. We are therefore obliged to reflect this external change within ourselves, to make our will as mobile and transitory as the pleasures our will desires. We must scatter our will between thousands of ends, without being able to connect all those dispersed fragments of happiness that constitute life into any overall unity (*ek tōn hēdonōn merikōn sustēma*). The foresightedness that could guide actions by subordinating them to a superior end appears to Aristippus as a kind of servitude. Nevertheless, he does not realize that by wishing to become independent of the future he becomes a slave of the present. He does not realize that within the small republic[12] that we are, harmony, the common pursuit of one and the same end throughout time, produces a freedom that is greater than the disorderly surging of the passions, one against another.[13] To limit our will to the present, to preclude it from looking forwards or backwards, to prevent it, in a word, from finding itself in the past and from projecting itself into the future, is this not the same as suppressing all its freedom of action? It is just like abolishing all of intelligence's clairvoyant aspects by surrounding its viewpoint from the front and the back with the night. It is to make every action opaque, as if one did not want to look at one's own actions and to see the past that has produced them, or the future that they will [help to] bring about. Shortsighted intelligence and an unstable will, which constitute the subtle theoretical ideal and also the coarse practical ideal of Aristippus and his disciples, cannot satisfy the human being who aspires to constantly surpass the limits of the present and to possess these two things: unity, on the one hand; fixity [or stability], on the other.

This is something that Epicurus understood, and it is important for us to note the changes that the introduction of the idea of the future produced in his doctrine of pleasure, which in other respects is so similar to that of Aristippus.

The first outcome of this idea is a classification of the different forms of enjoyment. Aristippus claimed that all pleasures were equivalent: voluptuousness,[14] he said, cannot differ from voluptuousness, and the word *pleasant* does not admit of comparisons.[15] Epicurus, however, finds a very simple way to establish degrees between different forms of enjoyment. Instead of considering them in themselves he invites us to consider them in relation to their consequences, in relation to one's whole life.[16] It is evident that there are many pleasures that are followed by pain, a pain which is sometimes stronger than the pleasure itself. We should abandon these kinds of pleasure, we should pass over them (*huperbainomen*)[17] to search for less dangerous pleasures beyond them.[18] The sage begins, above all, by imposing self-consistency as a law on himself. He extends his thought towards the future in order to prevent it from contradicting itself. He aims to govern his desires in order to prevent them from turning against themselves, his aim is to stop them from producing pain and evil as, in their heedless and thoughtless impetus, they strive towards voluptuousness and the good.[19] Thus, those pleasures that in Aristippus' doctrine are variable and multiple, which drag the soul along haphazardly, are viewed very differently in Epicurus' system. In the Epicurean system we see these pleasures naturally arranged with a view to an end, an end that is not different to [the pleasures] themselves, once stripped of foreign and inferior elements. From a logical point of view progress is evident: the will does not scatter or divide itself between them; one can see, over time, a unity that one is pursuing and that one hopes to attain.

We must pay attention to the moment when the ideas of Epicurus and Aristippus begin to diverge and depart from one another. For in this very moment a new doctrine is born and manifests itself for the first time, a doctrine that will play a significant role in the history of moral philosophy. From the moment when pleasure instead of being considered as an immediate end is fertilized by the idea of time, then an ultimate and final end is announced as a goal and ideal for one's life as whole.[20] Pleasure, then, assumes a new name and the doctrine of *voluptuousness* becomes the doctrine of *utility*.

II. – We have previously seen a certain means–end relationship established by virtue, on the one hand, and pleasure, on the other. Now, an analogous means–end relationship will be established between the pleasures themselves. As Epicurus likes to repeat, each pleasure is a good in itself and by itself, *di' autēn or kath' autēn*. However, if one compares the good that some pleasures contain with the evil that they produce, it is wise to reject them as imperfect means, as bad instruments. Even if they are good in themselves they cease to be *ends* in themselves. This is the apparent contradiction that Epicurus and all the utilitarians accept.

One can even go further: in the same way that certain pleasures produce pain, certain pains produce pleasure; if one rejects the former, why then would one not opt for the latter? 'Every pain is an evil, however not every pain should always be avoided: *algēdōn pasa kakon, ou pasa de pheuktē aei*.'²¹ Furthermore, sometimes we must endure pains, even long-lasting ones, *polun chronon hupomenein*, on the condition that they are followed by superior pleasures. One can clearly see the distance that separates the Epicurean and the Cyrenaic systems. To summarize his thought Epicurus uses the following formula, which is a subtle but faithful expression of the utilitarian doctrine: 'We can make use of a good in certain moments as if it were an evil, and conversely, we can make use of an evil as if it were a good.'²²

How is it possible to clearly distinguish between pleasure and pain, good and evil, in our thinking if we confuse them in action? You promise me this pleasure if I suffer that pain; but how can my mind establish a fair scale to ascertain the precise weight of the pleasing and displeasing sensations that you promise me? How can I see which one prevails over the other? In addition to this, I can only imagine those sensations that are in the present moment. This is why before comparing them I must construe them with the aid of the data of experience, and also with the efforts of understanding. The slightest error in measuring and calculation could make me joyful or sad, and in certain cases could impact upon my life as a whole. This explains the fundamental importance of intelligence in utilitarian doctrine. Here, intelligence still functions as a means. Nevertheless, without this means one cannot achieve one's end. Not only is the task of human thought, *dianoia*, and wisdom, *phronēsis*, to direct all actions of human beings towards pleasure, but they should also organize pleasures themselves and, what is more, pains, with a view to [attaining] supreme pleasure. In this way, human actions are improved and elevated.²³ Moreover, Epicurus' eloquent praise of philosophy or wisdom now seems to be better justified. Indeed, what could be more important than the *art of measuring things together*,²⁴ *summetresis*, of embracing in the same glance of the eye those things that are useful and harmful, *sumpherontōn kai asumphorōn blepsis*?²⁵

Now, from this new level to which the Epicurean doctrine had led us in its ascending path, let us go back and examine the path through which we have travelled. Even if one was to maintain that Epicurus' ethics does not provide us with the *ideal* or a [conception of the] good superior to ourselves, at least it confronts us with something that is superior to the present, a good that surpasses and encompasses all particular goods, and so gives us a *whole*.²⁶ Therefore, utilitarian ethics grants a place to that sentiment that Aristippus wanted but could not efface: the tendency to surpass every particular object, every end which is not *final*, which ultimately means *infinite*. Indeed, considering present pains or pleasures Epicurus' utilitarian doctrine provides us with a certain freedom with respect to these pains and pleasures: we can look beneath or beyond them, and we can extinguish them by the idea of a superior pleasure. Each of these tendencies and passions that appear as a master over and within us when considered solely in the present moment, we are able to master them once we connect them to the whole of our lives (*ho holos bios*). We are free to pursue or restrain a passion or tendency in accordance with the distance with which we view it.²⁷ Equally, it can be said, when there is more freedom within us there is also more order and harmony. The passions do not collide anymore in an indescribable turmoil.²⁸ Just like the atoms of Epicurus have space before them to effect their spontaneous movements in an eternal order, so, too, the instincts and passions of the soul have *duration* in front of them: if restrained, imprisoned, they would erupt in revolt; however, when they are spread over time they cool down. When they are no longer hindered by obstacles, they cease to trouble one another.

When we see the future open up before us without some fixed end point,[29] we are left with only one thought: to prepare and organize everything with a view to *happiness* over the course of this whole lifetime. This is the task of wisdom.[30] *Happiness* is the new element in the doctrine of pleasure. Aristippus could not see in life anything but independent instants of enjoyment and pieces of happiness (*hē kata meros hēdonē*). Only Epicurus was able to pronounce the word ['happiness'] in its plenitude, and he did not stop there. For him, to be happy (*eudaimōn*) is not enough; he also wants the sage to be *blessed* (*makar*).[31] The ancient poets reserved this divine name for the inhabitants of the heavens, and when they said 'the *blessed*' (*hoi makares*), their listeners should search beyond the earth, the indwelling of mutable happiness and good fortune (*eutuchia*), and beyond man, who is only happy through the capricious will of good and bad demons (*eudaimonia, kakodaimonia*), and thus find in the heavens of supernatural beings [those] to whom they could ascribe the word '*blessedness*' (*makaria; makariotēs*) without contradiction. However, Epicurus brings heaven to earth and the happiness of the gods to human beings: the sage is the one who is truly blessed.[32] The life of the sage is the living realization of happiness.[33]

Just as Epicurus' conception of ethics is more complete and richer than that of Aristippus, it is also more beautiful and more moral. From the aesthetic point of view is there not beauty in this rational disposition of life in which the parts are subordinate to the whole? Isn't there beauty in the fact that this happiness, while it replaces pleasure and fulfils it, also and at the same time purifies it? Life, then, becomes a canvas of undetermined lines and contours in which the sage, this 'artist of happiness', groups his future emotions, placing some in the foreground, some in the background, choosing which emotions he brings to light and those upon which he throws shadows and casts into oblivion.[34] The sage contemplates and admires this artwork, which is simultaneously beautiful and rational. Like other artworks its end is not outside of itself, but rather it is its own end and its own good. 'Fortune has but little hold on the sage: the greatest and most important things for him have always been, are, and will be directed by reason for the whole duration of his life.'[35]

The person who forgets the supreme end of nature, which is happiness, and turns towards particular ends contradicts himself: in effect, he can only search for pleasure. However, if this pleasure brings with it a pain that is stronger than the pleasure itself, he would have sought pleasure in his mind but found pain in his action. 'If you do not on every singular occasion refer each of your actions to the end prescribed by nature, but instead of this in the act of choice or avoidance swerve aside to some other end, your acts will not be consistent with your reasoning.'[36]

Notes

1 T.N. The French here is *morale utilitaire*.
2 T.N. *dialectique descendante*.

3   T.N. The metaphor for the philosophical system is here the concrete image of the chain, different rings of a chain, the *anneaux de la chaîne*.
4   T.N. *douleur*.
5   Diogenes Laertius, *Lives of Eminent Philosophers*, X, 129: *Pasa oun hēdonē dia to echein phusin oikeian agathon* ['Every pleasure is a good since it has an appropriate nature']; X, 141: *Oudemia hēdonē kath' eautēn kakon* ['No pleasure is in itself an evil'].
6   Epicurus agrees on this point with Aristippus. *Hē hēdonē agathon, kan apo aschēmonestatōn genētai* ['Pleasure is a good, even when it comes from the most shameful acts'], Diogenes Laertius, *Lives of Eminent Philosophers*, II, 88.
7   T.N. *maladie*.
8   *Monon hēmeteron esti to paron* ['Only the present is ours'], Claudius Aelianus, *Varia Historia*, XIV, 6.
9   T.N. For Aristippus there are many ends for human beings – as much as there are particular or partial pleasures in each particular moment.
10 Diogenes Laertius, *Lives of Eminent Philosophers*, II, 417.
11 *Tou men holou biou telos ouden hōrismenon etaxan hekastēs de praxeōs idion huperchein telos, tēn ek tēs praxeōs periginomenēn hēdonēn* ['They claimed that there is no determined end goal for the whole of life: each action has its own particular end, the pleasure that results from action'], Clement of Alexandria, *Stromata*, II, 417.
12 T.N. The French here reads *petite république*.
13 See Cicero, *De finibus*, I, XVIII, 57: '*Neque enim civitas in seditione beata esse potest, nec in discordiâ dominorum domus, quò minùs animus a se ipse dissidens, secumque discordans, gustare partem ullam liquidae voluptatis et liberae potest*' ['For a city prey of sedition cannot be happy, not more than a house where discord reigns among the masters; even less so can a soul in conflict with itself and subjected to discord enjoy a free and limpid pleasure']. See also XVIII, 43: '*Cupidates non modò singulos homines, sed ... totam etiam labefactant saepe rem publicam*' ['Passionate desires are not content with only ruining men individualy ... they often also ruin the entire republic']. These are ideas that the Epicureans borrowed from Plato.
14 T.N. *la volupté*.
15 Diogenes Laertius, *Lives of Eminent Philosophers*, II, 87.
16 T.N. Or to 'the whole of one's life', *l'ensemble de la vie*.
17 T.N. the Greek, *huperbainomen*, means also 'to exceed'.
18 Diogenes Laertius, *Lives of Eminent Philosophers*, X, 129.
19 '*Nec enim satis est judicare quid faciendum non faciendumve sit, sed stare etiam oportet in eo, quod sit judicatum ... Qui ita frui volunt voluptatibus, ut nulli propter eas dolores consequantur, et qui suum judicium retinent, ne voluptate victi faciant id quod sentium non esse faciendum, ii voluptatem maximam adipiscuntur praetermittendâ voluptate*' ['It is not enough to judge what to do and what not to do, but it is important to persevere in one's judgement ... Those who wish to enjoy pleasures without suffering any of the painful consequences of these pleasures, and who retain their [faculty of] judgement and avoid being seduced by pleasure into courses that they perceive to be wrong, attain the highest pleasure by forgoing pleasure'], Cicero, *De finibus*, I, XIV, 47, 48.
20 T.N. Guyau's expression is *pour la vie entière*.
21 Diogenes Laertius, *Lives of Eminent Philosophers*, X, 129.
22 Diogenes Laertius, *Lives of Eminent Philosophers*, X, [129–]130: *Chrōmetha tō men agathō kata tinas chronous hōs kakō, to de kakō toumpalin hōs agathō* (translated above).
23 T.N. Guyau is slightly ambiguous here: he says that human actions are enhanced and elevated when informed by wisdom and knowledge. Moreover, he also seems to

indicate that human thought and wisdom acquire greater importance when it comes to organizing the means to achieve supreme pleasure.
24 T.N. *mesurer ensemble les choses*.
25 Diogenes Laertius, *Lives of Eminent Philosophers*, X, 130.
26 T.N. *un tout*.
27 T.N. In the original one finds an interesting analogy between time and space in this passage: if we look into the distance (in relation to the actual moment), i.e. towards the future, or even if we look to the moment from a distant perspective (the perspective of our whole lifetime), then we can master our passions.
28 '*In animis inclusae inter se dissident atque discordant*' ['[The pleasures] enclosed in the soul, are in conflict and disagreement with each other'], Cicero, *De finibus*, I, XII, 44.
29 T.N. *sans terme fixe*. It is important to stress that the term 'end' here does not express finality, but the chronological and/or spatial end: the point of arrival. In this particular passage, Guyau's statement seems to neglect the centrality of death in Epicureanism. For his analysis of the issue of death, see the third chapter of book two below.
30 *Hē sophia ta pragmata paraskeuazetai eis tēn tou holou biou makariotēta* ['Wisdom prepares and arranges things for the happiness of a whole life']. [T.N. Guyau does not provide the reference here; he could be quoting Diogones Laertius, *Lives of Eminent Philosophers*, X, 148. An alternative translation to *l'oeuvre de la sagesse* – the 'task of wisdom' above – would be the more literal 'the work of wisdom'.]
31 T.N. In Guyau's French we read an interplay between *heureux* and *bienheureux*, the latter is literally a superior state, which is marked by the '*bien*', literally, 'good'. It is the adjective form of 'beatitude'. The distinction stems from the difference between the Greek ideas of happiness (being *eudaimonos* or *heureux*, happy) and beatitude (being *bienheureux*, or reaching a divine state of blessedness or blissfulness, being *makaros*).
32 T.N. *le vrai bienheureux*.
33 *Zēsē hōs theos en anthrōpois* ['He will live as a god among men'], Epicurus, *Letter to Menoeceus*, final part.
34 T.N. The metaphor here is painting: the sage is like a painter, an artist of happiness. Guyau here offers his own version of the idea of life as a work of art and aesthetics of existence in this passage.
35 Diogenes Laertius, *Lives of Eminent Philosophers*, X, 144: *Bracheia sophō tuchē parempiptei, ta de megista kai kuriōtata ho logismos diōkēke kai kata ton sunechē chronon tou biou dioikei kai dioikēsei* (translated in the text above). The Didot edition reads *brachea tuchē* ['few things happen by chance to the sage'], an ingenious but non-necessary correction, and one which would be mistaken if one refers back to Cicero (*De finibus*, I, XIX, 62) who literally translated it as *exiguam fortunam* ['little fortune'].
36 *Ouk esontai soi tois logois hai praxeis akolouthoi* (translated in the text), Diogenes Laertius, *Lives of Eminent Philosophers*, X, 144 [T.N. The correct reference seems to be X, 148 (§25)].

4

Desire – The Ultimate End of Desire: Rest, Enjoyment of Self[1]

Is happiness achievable? Or is the desire that pursues it always frustrated? The importance of this question for an ethics that seeks to make the sovereign good accessible to all. On the contradiction that seems to appear in every utilitarian doctrine between the end to pursue, which is pleasure, and the means to achieve it, which are effort, anguish[2] and suffering. How Epicurus solves this difficulty.

I. *Classification of desires.* How Epicurus banishes voluptuousness,[3] refinement, and variety of pleasures. The only pleasure that remains is nourishment. Bread and water. – Objections: The void[4] of Epicurean happiness.
II. *Highest goal of desire* and final essence of happiness: *ataraxia.* – Distinction between 'pleasure in movement'[5] and 'constitutive pleasure'. – The sovereign good is the absence of trouble. – Is not the absence of trouble a form of rest and sleep similar to death, as some interpreters of Epicurus believed? On how the absence of pain[6] reveals the bliss that characterizes the harmony and health of a being. – That the highest or supreme pleasure is the most independent, and how the part of the sentient subject[7] is larger, and that of the sensed object is smaller.

Epicurus elevates the utilitarian doctrine beyond the ethics of pleasure. Multiple objections will force it to further clarify and develop itself.

First, in proposing that human desire has an end one must also demonstrate that such an end is achievable. Nevertheless, in several circumstances, happiness can escape the grasp of human beings. Nothing is easier than to find pain; we do not even have to search for it. All we need do is stay still and wait, and pain comes by itself. As for pleasure, in certain cases, it is completely out of reach. For example, the chained slave cannot enjoy the pleasure of being free. In other cases, when it is possible to reach pleasure, one needs the means to do this, means which, to a greater or lesser extent, imply a series of troublesome efforts. Labour, tension of the will, and tension in the muscles – to put it simply, the effort and toil (*ponos*), which the Stoics designated as the highest good, and which the Epicureans conceive as an evil, appears on every side, especially when one wishes to banish it.

It is quite possible that the very pursuit of happiness can elude us if we pursue it through means that are excessively troublesome. There is an opposition in Epicurus' doctrine, as often in every utilitarian doctrine, between the given end and the means to achieve it. Every end should be achievable with the help of a particular means, without the means producing change in the end itself.[8] For instance, if I take the mountain summit to be the end of my walk, the summit remains fixed and elevated [above the path] regardless of the path I take in order to arrive at the summit. In this case, the end is *exterior* to me. But, when the end is *interior*, if instead of choosing to reach the summit I set as the goal of my efforts the pleasure of reaching the top, then I must not consider the end in isolation but also the means to achieve it. This is because the toil and trouble that I will endure in order to climb the mountain could have an impact on the very pleasure that I pursue. Nevertheless, even in this example, the end preserves a certain independence with regard to the means employed to reach it: I will always experience a certain pleasure in reaching the summit, regardless of any preceding labour, pain or trouble. But what happens if, instead of regarding a particular pleasure as an end, like that of reaching a mountaintop, one follows Epicurus in regarding the sum of pleasures – past and present – in a whole life as the end? This is a very complex goal that requires an even more complex means. To attain such a goal, would it not be necessary to expend a certain amount of effort and trouble greater than the total sum of pleasure that one pursues? Could the benefits of such a pursuit ever compensate its expenses?

This is why in order to make happiness available to all Epicurus is constrained to exclude from it all the elements that are difficult to obtain, such as wealth, luxury, honours, power. To allow easier access to the supreme end he gradually extricated every material element from his conception of pleasure. In his willingness to give more space to pursuing pleasure freely, he gives also more space to morality.

I. – 'Of our desires,' says Epicurus, 'some are natural and necessary, *phusikai kai anankaiai*; others are natural, but non-necessary; others, finally, are neither natural nor necessary, but are due to vain opinion, *para kenēn doxan*. By natural and necessary desires Epicurus means those which bring relief from pain, such as drinking when thirsty; while by natural and non-necessary he means those which merely add variety to voluptuousness, *poikillousai*, but do not remove any pain, such as refined dishes; by desires that are neither natural nor necessary he means the desire for crowns and the raising of statues in one's honour.'[9] One notes the importance of this division of desires, which was already outlined in Plato and Aristotle. Among desires, only those that are both natural and necessary, those that bring suffering when not satisfied, are those to which the sage should listen at all times. While those desires are the most pressing for happiness, they are also the least demanding. Once the sage appeases them, as one appeases Cerberus by throwing him a honey-covered loaf,[10] the sage's life can continue without trouble. As for the desires which result from empty opinions, *doxai kenai*, Epicurus, who like Socrates and Plato is an enemy of variable opinion, wishes to banish these desires completely. Finally, those other desires that exist between the two extremes, those that arise from nature but do not necessarily constrain us [i.e. natural and non-necessary desires], one must judge when to satisfy them and when to reject them. This judgement is the work of practical wisdom, *phronēsis*, of temperate reason, *nēphōn logismos*, and it is a very important feature of utilitarian doctrine. This kind of desire is indeed good and easy to alleviate, *eudiachutoi*. The sage accepts this form of desire with reservations, never eagerly wishing to satisfy it, because this very eagerness could suddenly change it into a necessary desire, and produce in him a kind of servitude with regards to them.¹¹ One must always be vigilant when it comes to this kind of desire, never loosening the reins, [except] with the condition of tightening them again soon, in such a way that the superfluous never becomes the necessary.¹²

One concludes from this that happiness becomes easily accessible to everyone. At the same time, the idea of happiness is purified of the material element of *voluptuousness*, that is to say, happiness is purified of the refinement and variety in pleasure, *poikilma*.¹³ Pleasure does not need to be refined or embellished; its natural beauty is enough. As Epicurus says, 'pleasure in the flesh admits of no increase once the pain caused by need¹⁴ has been removed; after that it only admits of variation, *poikilletai*.'¹⁵ Nevertheless, this variation in the forms of pleasure does not correspond to any greater intensity of enjoyment, therefore this variety [in pleasure] does not offer desire a firm or lasting attraction. Variation is not indispensable in achieving the desired end, namely the total happiness of a life.¹⁶ Only one condition is necessary for the presence of happiness: only the object that is absolutely necessary to sensible life,¹⁷ and that is food.

Here we return to where we began, to the 'pleasure of the stomach' which, as we know, is the principle and the root source of every good. The pleasure of the stomach appears, therefore, as the indispensable means to [achieve] the supreme good. If one attains this pleasure, one attains everything. Even though it is the most necessary pleasure, it is also the least rare one. As Epicurus says, could one not [simply] search for nourishment, such as sufficient food and drink to maintain life? One can do this without trouble, especially in the pleasantly warm Greece where our philosopher lived, at a time when poverty was not yet widespread. Very well, this is enough for happiness. Give Epicurus barley bread and water, and he will 'rival Jupiter in happiness' (*kai tō Dii huper tēs eudaimonias diagōnizesthai*).¹⁸ Bread and water: that is the wealth of nature. 'Nature's wealth at once has its bounds and is easy to obtain; but the wealth of vain fancies and opinions recede into an infinite distance (*eis apeiron ekpiptei*).'¹⁹ These are remarkable words, and a response to certain objections against the ethics of interest. The pleasures of vain opinions are as elusive as the opinions themselves, and the instability of *doxa*, which Plato compared with the moving statues of Daedalus,²⁰ is also the distinctive character of the enjoyments it produces. Ambition, for instance, grows the more we gratify it; it is a sort of artificial hunger that one excites by satiating, that one deepens indefinitely in attempting to fulfil. It consists in pursuing an object that is animated by the movement of ambition itself, an object that ambition distances from us while we seek to reach it, and which finally disappears into infinity, *eis apeiron ekpiptei*. According to Epicurus, however, nature has greater foresight than opinion, as it never excites desires that it cannot satisfy with little expenditure (*hōrismenos kai euporistos*). Against these desires, characterized by complete fixity, unalterable principles of happiness, one cannot employ the same objections that one employed to [address] the variability and instability of the passions.

Let us now note the point in the continuous development of the Epicurean system at which we have arrived. The kind of pleasure that is really desirable seems not to differ from the sensations produced by strictly satisfying a need. Aristippus portrayed human beings as assaulted by innumerable desires. Epicurus, by contrast, frees human beings from these desires, only positing two pleasures: eating and drinking. But is not a void then produced in human life? How could we fulfil the temporal interstices that separate pleasures from one another? Hunger and thirst are ceaselessly being extinguished – which is why they are ceaselessly being reborn. Would this movement also extinguish all enjoyment? Epicurus wished to liberate us from physical needs. However, since he did not place true happiness above these very needs, has he not, in the very attempt to deliver us, simultaneously deprived us [of the very possibility of happiness]? Two pleasures sown by an avaricious hand across the infinite succession of duration: this is what appears to be left of happiness! At least Aristippus tried to fill the interstices that separate instants of pleasure. He crushed every desire and every pleasure against one another in the narrow space separating the past and the future. It is possible that he was attempting an impossible task. Perhaps Socrates was right to compare, half jokingly and half seriously, [Aristippus] to the wretch that, according to the myth, is hidden at the bottom of the Orcus[21] and brought back to earth by him, who eternally tried to fill a pierced barrel. It seems as if Epicurus did even less than Aristippus' disciples: he does not even try because he recognizes himself as powerless, and instead of filling the insatiable barrel he takes it out of the water and leaves it resting on dry land.

II. – To counter these objections, Epicurus modifies his theory again, taking it in an unexpected direction. Following him, let us attempt a psychological analysis of the kind of desires to the satisfaction of which the utilitarians linked enjoyment. We have examined these desires only from an external perspective, classifying them according to their [level of] exigency and necessity. We must now penetrate deeper in their intimate essence to discover the unique tendencies that are hidden beneath their diversity.

Aristippus referred every enjoyment and, more generally, every sensation to movement: pain to rough movements, pleasure to gentle ones. Rest, which invariably follows every movement, and which separates these movements from one another, is non-enjoyment,[22] the absence of pain or pleasure, the void.

Epicurus' analysis aimed at very different outcomes.

He does not deny that movement is how pleasure begins. But every movement has a goal. Would not rest, the opposite of movement, be the goal of those movements that produce pleasure? Indeed, when an organism is repaired by nourishment, recovering the atoms it had lost, there is an equivalence between loss and expense, and so rest takes place.[23] [When this happens] there is an absence of trouble or suffering (*aponia*)[24] and [a presence of] health (*hugieia*). However, as soon as the organism exhausts its reserves of force, this equilibrium is disturbed. Then, pleasure ceases, which was not different, perhaps, from this very equilibrium. Pain begins with change and movement, which are the rupture of this state of equilibrium.

Nevertheless, our nature responds to this pain, to this movement that is directed against us from the outside, by moving in the opposite direction: this is desire. Aristippus also referred to desire as a form of movement. But there is nothing 'gentle' or pleasant in desire itself; rather, it becomes so only once it has been satisfied. Is it not, the Epicureans ask, only when desire is satisfied, that is, when everything returns to rest, that equilibrium is re-established, and that appeasement takes place? Is it not then that the absence of pain and trouble[25] begins? Thus, at the beginning and end of all desire, one finds rest. The value of movement depends on the rest that precedes it or that follows it. Movement only takes place with a view to rest: it is an intermediary state, a moment in which the lost pleasure was not yet fully recovered.

Therefore, rest is far from being, as Aristippus thought, non-enjoyment and the void. According to Epicurus, the opposite is true.[26] As soon as pain[27] is absent, pleasure is present.[28] Pleasure immediately fills the void that pain[29] creates, in the same way that air fills the space that water leaves when it flows out of a vase. Aristippus, therefore, was wrong to identify a middle ground between pleasure and pain, moments in which we would be simultaneously free of every suffering and deprived of every pleasure, instants of insensitiveness,[30] instants of void within life. Epicurus rejects Aristippus' hypothesis as contradictory: for the sentient being,[31] the absence of every pleasure and every pain, that is, all sensation, is impossible: 'This very state, that seemed to some an intermediary state as it would (hypothetically) be deprived of all pain, constitutes not only a pleasure, but supreme pleasure. Every sentient being, in effect, in any way that it is affected, is always necessarily either in pleasure or in pain.'[32] The dilemma is inescapable: either pleasure is suppressed and we have pain; or pain is suppressed and, then, how could we not have pleasure? There are no gaps in the happiness of life. The only void is the instant taken by anguish.[33] Nevertheless, this void can never be absolute. Indeed, pain is never pure:[34] on the one hand, the pain that is most intense is also the shortest in duration; on the other, the pain that is less intense and more persistent is often forced to give space to pleasure. According to Epicurus, not even the pain of a lingering illness can eliminate pleasure entirely. Pleasure, by contrast, generally eliminates pain as soon as it [pleasure] appears. All things considered, lingering illnesses contain more enjoyment than painful suffering.[35] That which we regard as the greatest evil cannot entirely destroy happiness. In order for one to be happy, it is enough not to always suffer; and how short, in sum, are moments of suffering when compared to the totality of life! Happiness, therefore, no longer has anything inaccessible about it: one always finds it within oneself[36] once trouble and pain disappear.

Epicurus constantly returns to this idea, and his insistence proves the importance he attaches to it. Diogenes Laertius demonstrates this in his book *Peri Haireseōs kai Phugēs* (*On Choice and Refusal*), as well as in his treatises *Peri Telous* (*On the End*) and *Peri Biōn* (*On the Ways of Life*), and finally in his *Letter to the Philosophers of Mytilene*, by constantly differentiating the *pleasure of movement*, which is but the remedy to a certain pain, which comes to 'tickle the senses',[37] from the true and pure pleasure, which is stable and *constitutive*, *katastēmatikē*. Less exclusive than his predecessor Aristippus, he simultaneously admits these two forms of pleasure. Without doubt inspired by Aristotle,[38] however, and following the natural trajectory of his own thought, he clearly subordinates the transient, intermediary *enjoyment* that is produced by movement to the enduring and definitive pleasure that is produced by rest. 'The end[39] of the grandeur of pleasures,' he says, 'is the exemption (*hupexairesis*) of everything that causes suffering.'[40] If this is the highest pleasure, it is also the most final:[41] to preserve ourselves in the greatest rest possible, that is to say, in the most complete inner equilibrium, in the most complete harmony, this is the final goal of all of our efforts.

Since that is the sovereign good, the worst evil will then be [inner] turmoil,[42] the disorder produced by the intervention of every exterior cause. To avoid evil and to desire the good, this is what we want.

Indeed, we do not desire this good as something foreign or strange [to us], as something out of our reach; it is within us, it is naturally and immediately produced once the causes of trouble are suppressed. That which we desire is simply the suppression of these causes. We, therefore, have Epicurus' words: 'The end is not to suffer in one's body and not to be troubled in one's soul' (*telos einai mēte algein kata sōma mēte tarattesthais kata psuchēn*) ... We do everything in order not to suffer and not to be troubled.'[43] It is the absence of suffering that makes enjoyment appear. *Aponia* and *ataraxia* are very efficacious means to happiness. They give us happiness as soon as they are given: 'Since the moment when the health of the body and the ataraxy of the soul are born within us, as soon as the storm of the soul is pacified, being does not have to march as if towards the pursuit of something it lacks (*endeon ti*), it does not have to search for anything else that would *fulfil* (*sumplērōthēsetai*) the good of the soul and of the body (*to tēs psuchēs kai to tou sōmatos agathon*).'[44]

We conclude then that the sovereign pleasure and the sovereign good is the absence of pain and trouble, *aponia*, *ataraxia*; it is rest itself and tranquillity, *katastēma*.

Should we believe, following most critics,[45] that Epicurus understood absolute imperturbability to be a state similar to sleep and death? – The idea of trouble, which Epicurus strongly conceived and developed, has its natural principle in the idea of *harmony*. One can only disturb that which is harmonious, and one only fears turmoil and trouble because one wishes to preserve harmony. The last word of Epicureanism, therefore, should not be *aponia*, the absence of pain,[46] but rather the conservation of pleasure: it is with a view to conserving pleasure that we must avoid every change, every movement coming from the outside. It is to preserve pleasure that we must reduce ourselves to [a state of] imperturbability regarding the outside. This imperturbability is itself only a means – indeed, an infallible one – with the help of which one preserves oneself, one maintains oneself, one persists in being and in the harmony of being.

To summarize, the good according to Aristippus consists in moving, in changing oneself, running from pleasure to pleasure, enhancing past enjoyment with a new enjoyment. In contrast, to possess the good, Epicurus says, is to rest immobile in oneself. Instead of concerning oneself with gaining [new *enjoyments*] we need to make every effort not to lose anything. It is to restrain and restrict all the fugacious and superficial enjoyments to just one, an indestructible and profound one, which is an enjoyment of life itself. The good, then, is serenity. It is important to note that Aristippus, not wanting to hear about time and duration, consequently ends up assimilating every pleasure with perpetual movement and change, consequently subjecting these pleasures to time. By contrast, Epicurus, who wanted to maximally organize and dispose in the best possible way the whole of life, past, present and future, ends up escaping time, by searching in the core of every pleasure that which lasts and stays the *same*. Aristippus' final precept is: change, that is, live in time. Epicurus' precept is: remain the same, that is to say, live, as much as it is possible, outside of time.

To express the ineffable enjoyment that Epicurus experiences when elevating himself above what is accidental and variable, he finds the word *euphrosunē* insufficient. The etymology of this term is *eu-phrēn*, and it expresses a fortunate disposition of the soul, a sort of fugitive chance.[47] He situates the *euphrosunē* among the inferior pleasures of movement. Additionally, he even demotes to a second rank the *chara*, that is to say, the joy, elation, that has its source in movement (*kata kinēsin*) and in the tension of muscles or energy (*energeia*). The only really profound pleasure is *constitutive pleasure*, which is, as we have seen, the one that engenders the absence of pain and trouble: *aponia* and *ataraxia*.[48] The Epicurean sage does not rejoice himself, rather he *enjoys*.[49] – If Epicurus excludes everything that appears to imply movement and change from happiness, he does not limit himself to express his conception negatively. First, the term *hēdonē katastēmatikē* (*stable and constitutive pleasure*), which constantly appears in his writings, expresses something different from the absence of *trouble* and absolute imperturbability; it seems to designate a pleasure that is at the same time stable and profound, inherent in our nature, in our sensible *constitution*. Epicurus employs another term which is even more positive, *eustathes katastēma sarkos* (*stable constitution of the flesh*). We have seen him employing another expression that is not less striking: *sumplērōthēsetai to tēs psuchēs kai to tou sōmatos agathon* (*will fulfil the good of soul and body*). This plenitude of good cannot be the void defining insensibility. Epicurus uses words like *pistis bebaios, pistōma bebaiotaton,* which are anything but negative: the unshakable assurance of the sage is not the *laisser-aller*[50] of apathy. We will see him speaking elsewhere of the courageous struggle of the sage against fortune, *tuchē antitattesthai*. How could this conscious struggle be considered as that passive and empty resignation, which is so often attributed to the Epicureans? Finally, another strongly positive term that is employed by Epicurus confirms our interpretation: it is the term *hugieia*; that is, the healthy and good proportionate state of the being as a whole, body and soul, in order and harmony. This is undoubtedly the happiness that the Epicurean sage finds within himself once he has eliminated all trouble.[51]

This happiness, which is born from moral and physical health, from unaltered harmony, is a delicate, subtle and profound pleasure, which the Cyrenaics did not understand; they even called it true 'sleep', or even real 'death'.[52] This sort of pleasure is what Epicurus calls sovereign voluptuousness,[53] attributing to it a very particular feature: its independence.

By deeply analysing the very idea of pleasure, Epicurus realized that exterior things do not play the most important role in it. He realized that the dominant role belongs to sentient beings[54] themselves. It is we ourselves who produce our pleasure, much more than [exterior] things.[55] That which comes from outside is pain; in this case, we feel our activity blocked by an [exterior] obstacle.[56] The greater importance we accord to the role of the *object*, less important becomes the role of the *subject* of sensation. Pain is, therefore, dependence and subjection. In the pleasure of *movement* (*hēdonē en kinēsei*) the role of activity is already more important. It is activity which moves towards the desired object and seeks to possess it. But if we suppress this object and keep the sentient subject,[57] will pleasure also be suppressed? If pleasure is essentially the deliverance from obstacles and independence, if it comes above all from within ourselves, then it can only increase once we suppress every object. Being only has to fold upon itself. It is from itself, from its own conscience, that it takes up a [superior] pleasure, which is simultaneously more profound and more independent: 'From the moment when we are freed from pain, we enjoy the deliverance itself and exemption from every kind of constraint.'[58] To live in freedom, in rest and harmony with oneself, to have the inner feeling that one lives, this is supreme pleasure, in comparison to which all the others are but so many changing forms. Forever the same, this pleasure can exist independently and subsist above all others.

Notes

1. T.N. The original French here is *la jouissance de soi*.
2. T.N. As explained in the 'Note on the Translation', I have adopted a contextual approach to translating the wide and polyvalent *peine*.
3. T.N. *la volupté*.
4. T.N. This phrase could be rendered as *emptiness*. Rival schools criticized Epicureanism for its empty conception of happiness.
5. T.N. Here the French is *le plaisir en movement*, i.e. kinetic pleasure.
6. T.N. *douleur*.
7. T.N. A more literal translation of *sujet sentant* would be 'the subject of sensation' or the 'subject who feels'. The word 'sentient' in this phrase expresses a being's capacity of sensation.
8. T.N. That is to say: the means used to achieve such end should not change or disfigure the end pursued.
9. Diogenes Laertius, *Lives of Eminent Philosophers*, X. 149.
10. T.N. The French is *gâteau au miel*. In Virgil's Aeneid, Sybil throws Cerberus a loaf laced with honey and herbs to induce sleep, enabling Aeneas to enter the underworld, and so apparently for Virgil – contradicting Hesiod – Cerberus guarded the underworld against entrance.
11. T.N. Guyau means, perhaps, that they will appear to us as necessary (i.e. in the opinion we hold about them or in the way in which we represent our relationship to them), as opposed to a change in the nature and status of the desire itself, which would represent a contradiction of one of the important Epicurean premises regarding the classification of desires and pleasures.
12. T.N. For Epicurus these desires do not change but our perceptions of them (and their status as natural and necessary, for example) might change.
13. As we know, most of the time, *hēdonē* cannot be translated as *voluptuousness* [*volupté*] or *voluptas* because these terms express an idea that is very sensual [*sensuelle*]. Remarkably, the Latins did not have a term for the Greek word *hēdonē*. This still vulgar people could not distinguish between voluptuousness [or sensuousness, *volupté*] and pleasure [*plaisir*]. This is why the Epicureans criticized the Latin language, which annoyed Cicero (*soleo subirasci*). See Cicero, *De finibus*, II, IV, 12.
14. T.N. *besoin*.
15. Diogenes Laertius, *Lives of Eminent Philosophers*, X. 144. *Ouk epauxetai hē hēdonē en tē sarki, epeidan hapax to kat' endeian algoun exairethē, alla monon poikilletai* ['Pleasure does not increase in the flesh once the suffering due to lack is supressed, it only varies'].
16. T.N. The French phrase here is *le bonheur total de la vie*.
17. T.N. *vie sensible*.

18 [Joannes] Stobaeus, *Sermones* [or *Anthology*], XVIII, 30; Clement of Alexandria, *Stromata*, II [p. 415, in Guyau's edition].
19 Diogenes Laertius, *Lives of Eminent Philosophers*, X 144.
20 T.N. See, for example, Plato's *Euthyphro*, 11c–e.
21 T.N. Orcus is a Roman figure associated with the underworld: 'In Roman popular belief Orcus was the spirit that presided over death, barely distinguishable from Hades itself as the realm of the dead. He appears in funerary paintings in Etruscan tombs as a bearded, hairy giant. Gradually this spirit was absorbed into the Greek pantheon and Orcus was used as another name for Pluto or Dis Pater' (Pierre Grimal, *A Concise Dictionary of Classical Mythology*, edited by Stephen Kershaw, translated by A. R. Maxwell-Hyslop, Oxford & Cambridge: Basil Blackswell, 1990, 312). On the figure of the 'pierced barrel', see also Johann Jakob Bachofen, *Myth, Religion, and Mother Right: Selected Writings of J.J. Bachofen*, translated by Ralph Manheim, Princeton: Princeton University Press, 1967, 62. The image also appears in Plato's *Gorgias*.
22 T.N. Literally: *non-jouissance*.
23 T.N. This seems to be a typographical error. Perhaps Guyau meant 'between expense and gain or assimilation'. It is also important to note the introduction of the physical doctrine of atoms, gain and loss of atoms, to explain pleasure, and to justify via physics the importance of rest for ethical life. Differently from Aristippus, Epicurus thinks that rest is not void or emptiness.
24 T.N. I have chosen the phrase 'absence of trouble and suffering' to convey the wide semantic field of the Greek word *aponia*, which Guyau renders as *absence de peine*. One could think of this state as one of freedom from pain, exemption from toil, and as a condition of relaxation and non-exertion. Like the French *peine* the Greek *ponos* expresses both the idea of toil, effort and work, and the notion of suffering, distress, preoccupation, trouble and pain.
25 T.N. Here, again, Guyau refers to the Greek *aponia*.
26 See Diogenes Laertius, *Lives of Eminent Philosophers*, X, 128–36; Cicero, *De finibus*, I, x; II, ii–x.
27 T.N. *peine*.
28 'In omni re doloris amotio successionem efficit voluptatis', Cicero, *De finibus*, I, 10 (translated above).
29 T.N. Here Guyau uses *douleur*, which has a narrower scope than *peine*, closer to the English 'pain'.
30 T.N. *insensibilité*.
31 T.N. Again, *être sentant*.
32 '*Itaque non placuit Epicuro medium esse quiddam inter dolorem et voluptatem: illud enim ipsum, quod quibusdam medium videtur, quum omni dolore careret, non modo voluptatem esse, verum etiam summam voluptatem. Quisquis enim sentit, quaemadmodum sit affectus, eum necesse aut in voluptate esse aut in dolore*' ['This is why Epicurus thinks that there is no intermediate state between pain and pleasure: because that which seems to some as an intermediary state, when every pain ceases, is not only already pleasure itself, but supreme pleasure. Anyone that happens to feel any feeling whatsoever is affected either by pain or pleasure'], Cicero, *De finibus*, I, 38. This is how this sentence reads in all manuscripts [of the *De finibus*]; we believe we are able to reject all the corrections regarding the terms *videtur* and *careret*, proposed by all editors, from Orelli to Boeckel. See our own edition of the first two books of the *De finibus* [Cicero, *Des suprêmes biens et des suprêmes maux* (followed by *Éclaircissements*

relatifs à l'histoire de l'épicurisme, by Jean-Marie Guyau), translated by Regnier Desmarais, edited by Jean-Marie Guyau, Paris: Librairie Charles Delagrave, 1875].

33 T.N. *peine*.
34 T.N. Pain is never found in a pure state, it is never an absolute state.
35 Diogenes Laertius, *Lives of Eminent Philosophers*, X, 140.
36 T.N. The French phrase here is *au fond de soi*. Thus, happiness appears as our natural, underlying condition. Guyau's choice of words here expresses a particular interpretation of Epicureanism.
37 *Titillare sensus*. This is Epicurus' phrase, which had great impact on Cicero, who loved to repeat it.
38 See Aristotle, *Metaphysics*, I, 100ff.
39 T.N. The French *le terme* here designates both the point of arrival and the ending point.
40 *Horos tou megethous tōn hēdonōn hē pantos tou algountos hupexairesis* (translated above); see Cicero, *De finibus*, I, XI, 37, 38, 39. '*Non modo voluptatem, verum etiam summam voluptatem*' ['Not only pleasure, but supreme pleasure'].
41 T.N. The qualification *le plus final* here means the kind of pleasure that is more properly an end.
42 T.N. *trouble*.
43 Diogenes Laertius, *Lives of Eminent Philosophers*, X, 128, 131.
44 Diogenes Laertius, *Lives of Eminent Philosophers*, X, 128.
45 Mainly, Félix Ravaisson.
46 T.N. The French here is *peine*, see note above.
47 T.N. *hasard fugitive*.
48 *Hē men gar ataraxia kai aponia katastēmatikai eisin hēdonai, hē de chara kai euphrosunē kata kinesin energeia blepontai* ['indeed, the absence of trouble and pain are stable and constitutive pleasures, whereas joy and delight are regarded as in act and motion'], Diogenes Laertius, *Lives of Eminent Philosophers*, X, 136.
49 T.N. Guyau here proposes an interplay between the words *réjouit* and *jouit*. As mentioned in the translator's introduction, *jouir* has a wide and ambiguous meaning in French, denoting a corporeal enjoyment, usually related to taking pleasure in or from something: tasting it, using it, possessing it; it can also designate sexual pleasure in its climax.
50 T.N. *Laisser-aller* here designates the act of letting go, close to indifference.
51 Félix Ravaisson (*Essai sur la Métaphysique d'Aristote*, II, 105, 106) seeks to refer [or reduce] *hugieia* and *aponia* to the mere absence of peine and trouble. Having this identification [of *hugieia* and *aponia*] as his starting point, this is Ravaisson's conclusion: 'The goal of wisdom and the art of living is, according to Epicurus, to reach a point where one *no longer feels anything* ... Epicureanism finds sovereign good in a state of *absolute impassibility*, which is an *abstraction*, a *negation*, in a word, *nothing*.' – Impassibility in relation to the exterior, maybe; but inner insensibility? – The [Epicurean] texts we have quoted prove the opposite. Ataraxia is, without any doubt, the negation of all that which is foreign to [a certain] being; but what is left is the being itself, which affirms itself in face of the exterior: the ineffable enjoyment of intimate harmony – spiritual and material – is this an *abstraction*, is this *nothing*? It seems much more logical to refer, by finding support in [Epicurus'] texts, *aponia* (the absence of *ponos*, pain or suffering) and *ataraxia* (the absence of trouble or turmoil) to *hugieia* (health) than to reduce, without a clear reason, *hugieia* to *aponia*. Epicurus does not say anywhere that the absence of pain [*peine*] constitutes pleasure all by

itself. He rather says that 'pleasure is *perceived* as soon as all pain is subtracted [*enlevée*],' *percipitur omni dolore detracto* (Cicero, *De finibus*, X, xi, 37). Epicurus' originality in relation to his predecessors – Aristippus, on the one hand, and Hieronymus, on the other – is precise to have denied the existence of a purely negative or neutral state, in which one would only find absence of pain: Epicurus this intermediate state, this *medium quiddam* (Cicero, *De finibus*, I, 38); it is not, therefore, turning it into his ideal. That which also helps refuting Ravaisson's position is the consequences that he extracts from his hypothesis: 'If the end goal of happiness is not suffering or perceiving any pain, doesn't this mean that what is most desirable for man is to die – and, what is more, to never have come into existence in the first place?' (*Essai sur la Métaphysique d'Aristote*, II, 113). – We will [later] see the verse of the poet that Ravaisson mentions attacked by Epicurus himself. – Moreover, Ravaisson writes, 'Pleasure is nothing but the end of pain, and whenever pain comes to an end only by means of death itself.' – Believing that Epicurus did not see these consequences or simply accepted them means attributing to him incredible naivety and absurdity. Let us look, by means of contrast, to a text by Epicurus: 'Death is indifferent to us, because *all good and all evil reside in the action of feeling*, and death is the privation of sensibility: *mēthen pros hēmas einai ton thanaton, epei pan agathon kai kakon en aisthēsei, sterēsis d' estin aisthēseōs ho thanatos*' (Diogenes Laertius, *Lives of Eminent Philosophers*, X, 124). How could one [after reading this passage] still defend the thesis according to which Epicurus thought that insensibility and negation found in *sterēsis* (*privation*) consisted in achievement and perfection, or the *sumplērōsis* (*plenitude*) of the good? Neither insensibility nor death are good for Epicurus, and he clearly responds to all those who attribute this idea to him.

52 Diogenes Laertius, *Lives of Eminent Philosophers*, II, 89; Clement of Alexandria, *Stromata*, 417.
53 T.N. *volupté*.
54 T.N. *être sentant*.
55 T.N. Guyau's idea is that we are the active agents producing our pleasure, and not exterior things that we usually attribute causal role in our pleasure.
56 '*Dolor, id quo offendimu*' ['Pain, this is what offends us'], Cicero, *De finibus*, I, 38.
57 T.N. *sujet sentant*.
58 '*Quum privamur dolore, ipsâ liberatione et vacuitate omnis molestiae gaudemus . . . Gaudere nosmet omittendis doloribus, etiam si voluptas ea, quae sensum moveat, nulla successerit*' ['When we are liberated from pain, we enjoy [*gaudemus*] this very liberation and the absence of all other trouble . . . We enjoy ourselves as soon as pain leaves us, even if we feel none of those pleasures which move sensibility'], Cicero, *De finibus*, I, xi, 37; I, xvii, 56.

Book Two

The Pleasures of the Soul

1

Intellectual and Moral Serenity – Science, Opposed by Epicurus to the Idea of Miracle

I. The pleasures of the soul are superior to those of the body, encompassing simultaneously the present through enjoyment, the past through the memory[1] of enjoyment, and the future, through the anticipation of enjoyment. – New transformation produced in Epicurus' system by the introduction of the idea of *duration*.

II. Obstacles to the pleasure of the soul: trouble produced by the ignorance of the exterior world and by the superstition that derives from this ignorance. – On superstition in Epicurus' epoch. – That paganism was not the cheerful[2] and benign religion that one usually imagines. Epicurus as the 'liberator'[3] of human beings from the chains of religion. – Analogy with the struggle of modern utilitarians against the religion of their time. – Epicurean 'physiology', or the research for the natural causes of phenomena. – Epicurean logic places the criterion of truth in the experience of the senses.[4] – The victorious science of the gods.

We have already seen how the idea of *duration* transformed Epicurus' doctrine. The same idea will provide him with the means to move from the pleasure of the senses to the pleasure of the mind,[5] without, however, establishing an irreducible difference between the mind and the senses.

I. – Up to this moment we have considered life as a succession of pleasures and pains distinct from one another. It seems that at a given moment there can only be either pleasure or pain, and that each one of these sensations at the moment when it exists excludes the contrary sensation: for instance, one cannot enjoy the pleasure of being satiated and, at the same time, suffer from hunger. Pleasure, excluded by pain, cannot encompass the whole of life as Epicurus wished. In order for pleasure to fill our life, it would be necessary to totally expel pain, or at least to associate it with an enjoyment, making the two coexist, and making the most intense sufferings bearable by mixing them with pleasure.

So long as we hold on to the body, to the 'pleasure of the flesh' itself, it is undoubtedly impossible that a pain could ever coexist with its contrary pleasure. Why? Because the body lives only in the present, having only an actual existence: it either suffers or enjoys, that is all. However, to this life confined in the present let us open the [doors of the] past and [of] what is to come. In this case, everything suddenly changes, because at the same time that I suffer I remember a pleasure that is contrary to that suffering, and beyond it I expect that pleasure: this is a feeling of a different nature that takes place within us. It is, so to speak, the *pleasure of pleasure*. This pleasure, born from other pleasures, is not like the others that are dependent on exterior circumstances: it suffices for me to have enjoyed it once to have apprehended pleasure in the core of my being. This pleasure will pass, but its immortal image forever fixed in my thought will still appear as seductive long after the pleasure has disappeared. Its living remembrance will excite in me a living hope, and the union of this recollection and this hope, of this past and this future, will be able to secure my happiness. To *remember* and to *hope* are two new ideas introduced into the utilitarian doctrine. Until now, it has been possible to confuse the pleasures of the body with those of the soul;[6] but from now on this will be impossible: the pleasure of the soul is the pleasure that allows us to enjoy both the past and the future and that, coexistent with the most violent pains in the body, can supersede them. Therefore, the flesh and the mind can be differentiated: the former suffers or enjoys only the present instant (*dia to paron monon*); the latter suffers and enjoys the present, the past and the future (*kai dia to parelthon kai to paron kai to mellon*).[7] Thus, in the same way that the pain of the mind is much more cruel than that of the flesh, so the enjoyment of the flesh is much less gentle than that of the mind. Here, and one more time, the disagreement between Epicurus and Aristippus is accentuated.[8]

Moreover, the pleasure of the mind for Epicurus, as in general for all sensualists, is not a kind of pleasure completely apart from the others; it consists in nothing else but the pleasure of the flesh more or less modified by the idea of present and future. It is at the same time memory (*mnēmē*)[9] and anticipation (*protopatheia*).[10] It is also, if you will, an association of ideas. This pleasure is something that surpasses sensible pleasures, it is a semi-possession of the future.[11]

Once these premises are posed, a logical transformation occurs in Epicurus' doctrine, a doctrine which is as much in movement as its object. Since the pleasure of the soul is superior to that of the body, and the same is valid for the pain of the soul, it is then these pleasures and these pains that we should now investigate. Henceforth, we must reflect upon not only the utility of the body, but also the interest of the soul.[12] The real goal is still *aponia* [absence of pain], *ataraxia* [absence of trouble] and *hugieia* [health]; however, it is to the soul that we should relate these words. The ataraxy of the soul is superior to the absence of suffering in the body since it grows and is nourished simultaneously by its past, present and future. The mind, which was at the beginning nothing but a means for the body, reassumes its role as the real goal: the anguish or the pleasures of the mind have something of infinity and of the 'eternal' within them. Duration opens up before them: and what a 'great increase' (*permagna accessio*) they bring to the pains and pleasures of the body![13] What does the present sensation become when faced with imagination and thought, which have infinity as their object and domain? The sovereign good is the happiness of the soul.

In the same way that a thousand obstacles were opposed to happiness in the sensible realm, where we have been placed until now, is it not the case that we will also see the emergence of new obstacles in the intellectual realm, and into which we now probe?

We have tried to avoid trouble [or turmoil] in the functions of the body; let us now try, with Epicurus, to repel the even more dreadful *trouble* which afflicts the soul with misery.[14] Here, Epicureanism will reveal one of its most original aspects.

II. – The first cause of trouble for the mind is its ignorance of the external world. – In what ways and in which order are the phenomena that take place around us linked! This is the question that man has posed in every epoch of history. Now, there are two answers to this question. The first subjects all phenomena, and consequently the sentient being itself, to one or many powerful and capricious deities: the will of such gods, unpredictable and unavoidable, is the master of all things, and allots to each being the series of goods and evils that will constitute its happiness or misfortune; this is the hypothesis common to all religions. The second hypothesis, instead of subjecting the events to such arbitrary powers, encompasses them in immutable laws: everything is part of a chain; around us and within us we find an inexorable necessity, to which nothing ever escapes, in which everything could be predicted in advance, in which the place of each thing and each being is fatally fixed in such a way that it can neither escape nor be replaced by another thing or being. The latter is the hypothesis of Fate, of Necessity, of universal determinism, a hypothesis that was strongly adhered to by ancient theologians, as well as by Plato, the Stoics, Spinoza, Leibniz, Kant and, in our days, by almost every scholar and a considerable number of metaphysicians.

Let us start with Epicurus by examining the first hypothesis, which is the background of religious beliefs. We will then be able to understand Epicurus' struggle against the religion of his time, a struggle which will find its analogy later in history in the struggle of the utilitarians and modern positivists against the religion of their century.

Still in his youth Epicurus used to go with his mother, who was a magician by metier, to read the lustral formulas at the homes of the poor. Initiated in this way in the practices of superstition, he experienced a deep contempt towards them, seeing in them the biggest obstacle to a happy life.[15]

Today we mistakenly represent the religions of antiquity: we depict them with gay colours, when in fact, in the time of Epicurus, they still retained their terrible aspects. Originally, human thought ignored the various distant causes of phenomena, placing causality in the phenomena themselves. Human thought attributed to every object that it encountered a good or a bad will; the human being projects onto plants, animals and nature as a whole the intelligent power that he feels within himself. After he has become encircled by [those projections of] *himself*,[16] and after having transferred his own powers outside of himself, he returns to himself through reflection but is no longer able to find himself. In fact, his freedom has disappeared and the circle of good and bad wills that he has traced around his own will tightens around him, confines him, and thus he feels enslaved. The religion that man has himself created now subjects him to omnipotent and capricious masters, who are especially terrible because he cannot see them, and even more invincible because he is unable to anticipate their blows.[17] What, then, are we to do against these phantoms that religion has populated the world with? They can make a man happy, but they can also deprive him of happiness; he is nothing, they are everything; for him there is nothing left but subjection and the attempt to influence these unknown and probably inflexible gods though humility and prayers.

If the will of these gods were not the object of conjecture, if there were not a means to predict it, then at least one would be able to enjoy a partial freedom given by ignorance: since I have the perspective of being punished independently of what I do, the result is that I do whatever I want; thus, I can preserve my independence and 'ataraxy'. But things are not like that. If we cannot absolutely predict the conduct of the gods as it concerns us, we can at least speculate about [their behaviour], and so to a certain extent influence it. In addition, we can make conjectures about their behaviour through the art of divination and the science of auguries, which inform us of the relationship between certain phenomena and the will of the gods. We can even modify this will to a certain extent through offerings and sacrifices, which establish a certain relationship between our actions and the will of the gods. In this way the science of happiness becomes the science of the signs that announce or the acts that conjure the will of the gods.

Now, there is nothing more variable than these signs: every external object has its language, a language that is often contradictory in which these objects speak to us and threaten us. The omens are multiplied around us, and life becomes a perpetual apprehension.[18] Even after having filled the altars and their priests with gifts, even after having accomplished all the expiations and instructions required to make a single instant of pleasure and be forgiven by the gods, man is still not able to reach tranquillity. At the moment when he thinks he holds happiness in his hands, or that he is close to it, he can suddenly see on the wing of a bird that flies above him, happiness blurring and disappearing just to his left.[19] No place on earth, no moment of life can allow man to subtract himself from the despotic caprice of the gods. Even death itself, which the philosophers considered as a deliverance, appears for popular religion the beginning of a new and even more severe slavery. Fear of hell is far from being a modern idea; it had an even more terrifying aspect in antiquity because it had a more indeterminate character. In antiquity people thought that some among them were undeniably doomed. However, only a few positively believed that there were chosen ones, and even fewer would dare to count themselves among them. One feared future life even more than death itself.[20] So, human hope could not point a way out, neither in the present nor in the future. The demands of the gods were boundless; the rites that ruled life and encompassed every action formed a sort of tyrannic code, contrasting the social and political freedom of that period. The etiquette that ancient monarchs imposed upon those who frequented their court, and lived in the presence of kings, and that even used to dictate the number of steps forwards or backwards and that used to prescribe the measure of reverences to each dignitary and indicate the precise moment when one should kiss the queen's dress, all of this pales into insignificance when compared to that other kind of etiquette that the ancient religions demanded of every human being living and dying in the presence of the gods. The least significant act of negligence could irritate a deity to eternity. If, as has been claimed, a look from Louis XIV killed Racine, one can also imagine what might have become of a devout believer when the ire of the gods was directed at him.[21]

It is necessary to know all the thoughts that still today assault the superstitious soul, so as to be able to represent what might have been the life of superstitious people from earlier times. In those times, superstition was supported and encouraged by religion itself, being a part of the beliefs of the State. For instance, Cicero himself had the title of soothsayer.[22] At the ultimate point of superstition the devout ones ended up fearing the gods so strongly that they envied the atheists and, according to Plutarch, one could even become an atheist out of fear.[23] Fear, after having created religion, was also responsible for its destruction. Plutarch, like Cicero, distinguished between the superstitious religion and the true religion, but this very distinction proved difficult to make. Even if we suppose it was possible, only the philosophers, or those who prided themselves on being philosophers, could make that distinction. All other men were prey of that 'ulcer of conscience', as Plutarch called superstition, to this 'fever', this 'fire that devours the soul', to this 'servile abjection'.[24] Indeed, no master can be more tyrannical than the master that one gives to oneself, and it was not a pleasant thing to serve the gods.

Let us add to this that the gods, providers of happiness for the human beings, were concerned about not giving it to them in excess. All primitive religions attributed to the gods a certain sentiment of jealousy. This is why Socrates, with his Greek subtlety, so easily demonstrated that sometimes it is a misfortune to be happy. You believe yourself to be happy? You are a fool! – yells Solon with all his ancient wisdom – You cannot know but in death, at the moment in which you cease to be, if you have been happy or not!

In the pagan conception, not only was each man a slave of divinized chance, but human beings, even when uniting and grouping themselves and helping one another, could not acquire any greater freedom. On the contrary, we can say that these groupings, and the accumulation of so many particular superstitions, produced a common servitude. Many large bodies – armies, cities and nations – became linked by the 'tight knots of religion', to employ Lucretius' phrase.

More than any other ancient philosopher, with the exception of his disciple Lucretius, Epicurus felt the discomfort of these tight knots of religion. The Cyrenaics, Theodorus and Euhemerus,[25] had already attacked the gods of paganism. They often employed logic as their sole weapon, but logic alone, especially when it hides forms of impiety, is insufficient to overthrow beliefs so deeply rooted in the human heart. Epicurus was more than a logician: he knew how to speak to the heart and to awaken in his disciples, as a way of fighting the tendency to superstition, an even stronger tendency: the tendency to freedom. Not only did he want to persuade,[26] but he also wanted to liberate; he assigned himself the task of the liberator.[27] What is more, and as we will see later, it was with a certain form of piety that he sought to challenge the blind piety of the masses. He used to say: 'Impious is not he who abolishes the gods of the vulgar, but rather he who attributes to the gods the opinions of the vulgar.'[28]

Now, what is the procedure Epicurus adopts to accomplish this liberation of humanity and to achieve peace of mind for those who are 'oppressed by religion'? – Superstition, he holds, comes from ignorance:[29] the vulgar,[30] without knowing the causes of phenomena, place divine will behind these phenomena; but the savant, who seeks to penetrate the causes (*aitiologei*) [of phenomena], observes the domain of the arbitrary recede. Everything is explicable to him, and everything is linked in a regular way. Consequently, every object of terror is dissipated.[31] The more he knows the less he is subject to fear; this is because he will not need to substitute supernatural and frightening powers for the actual forces of nature. For Epicurus, as well as for Lucretius, this means that science is the direct enemy of religion. Moreover, since religion is the direct enemy of our independence, of our *ataraxy*, science, particularly natural science (*phusiologia*), becomes a necessary means to the achievement of happiness. Science is emancipation: 'Ataraxy, he says, is the emancipation from all those opinions (*hē d' ataraxia to toutōn pantōn apolelusthai*)... If we apply ourselves to know these events from which *trouble* and fear are born, we then discover the true causes (*exiaitiologēsomen orthōs*) and we emancipate ourselves (*kai apolusomen*), since we know the causes of meteors and of all the other unpredicted and perpetual events that bring the most horrifying fear to the rest of men.'[32]

One can find the same appreciations of science as offering the emancipation of humanity in utilitarian ethicists and among a number of contemporary thinkers, including Herbert Spencer. Epicurus was the first to apprehend the opposition between the scientific spirit and the religious spirit; he has the merit of having sensed the struggle between them, which in later times was to become even more intense.

[With this conception of science], the role accorded intelligence in the Epicurean system becomes even more important [than initial appearances suggest]. Epicurus no longer simply understands by the word *science* a science of measurement[33] (*summetrēsis*), or simply a wisdom of conduct (*phronēsis*). On the contrary, he extends the use of the term. All physical and natural sciences become important to know, not only because they offer an evident and immediate advantage over ignorance, but because they provide the sage with *ataraxy* and a stable confidence (*ataraxian kai bebaion pistin*).[34] Undoubtedly, the sciences are ultimately of value because of the happiness they can procure for us, and Epicurus insistently subordinates them to a superior end: utility. But the sphere of utility is constantly being enlarged, and one can, without exiting it, advance further and further.

From *physics* or *physiology* one can pass to logic or *canonic*; in order to distinguish the true from the false, and what is real from what is illusory in natural phenomena, one must have a criterion of true and false. Now, this criterion can only be provided by logic, and thus, it simultaneously supports physics and ethics.[35]

Epicurus' logic is original in many aspects, and deserves, as Lange noted,[36] a specific appreciation, but it is not one that we can develop here. Let us emphasize, however, the extent to which it is strictly connected to ethics. In this regard, Epicurus prefigures the contemporary positivists by rejecting all modes of intuitive knowledge of the truth, making the truth something essentially sensible and subjective. According to him, the truth is to be found in the same place as the good. Now, we have found the principle of the good in sensation, it is also there that we find the rule of truth.[37] Sensation is true and irrefutable; it is the irreducible fact. What could ever refute a given sensation? Another sensation of the same kind? But such a sensation would have equal force. Perhaps another sensation of a different kind? But such a sensation would refer[38] to a different set of objects. Perhaps reason? But reason in its entirety comes from sensation.[39] The senses can never be convinced of error.[40] Error is only born when we interpret our sensations, and we add our own conjectures to them (*opinatus... addimus*).[41] Indeed, Lucretius enumerates the errors that we often commit when our opinions go beyond the precise data given to us by the senses; so long as we remain in the domain of the senses we are sure of grasping absolute truth. In sum, the truth is felt as the good, the true is but one aspect of the good. The good is the sensation as it affects us in a pleasant or painful way[42] (*pathos*); the truth is sensation as affecting us purely or simply (*aisthēsis*); it is sensation abstracted from its attractive or repulsive character.

Thus, in the same way that the Epicurean seeks to eliminate the fear of the supernatural through physics, he will equally liberate himself through logic from the hesitation that is generated by the sentiment of error and doubt. It is important to remember that in Epicurus' time the sceptics were really powerful and tormented ancient thought. In these circumstances, it was necessary to protect oneself against doubt, just as it was essential to protect oneself against faith: Epicurus' logic achieves this goal.[43] It strives to establish certitude on the secure ground of sensation; it gives science a positive object, namely the sensible fact; it aims at showing that thought is not vain, and that one can affirm with all confidence so long as one affirms nothing other than the sensations. On this point, contemporary positivists agree with Epicurus: John Stuart Mill's logic reaches no other conclusion than that of Epicurus. The weakness of Epicurus' theory is that, owing to the fact that science was in a primitive state in his day, one could not clearly distinguish sensation itself from the illusions of the senses, such as are produced during sleep or vigil. From these conditions derive obvious errors whose consequences we will deal with later.

After showing the possibility of science, and consolidating the ground upon which to go forwards, Epicurus diligently applies himself in the pursuit of scientific explanations for every natural phenomenon. We know that he read and meditated on the works of Democritus, antiquity's greatest physicist. 'Without Democritus' example,' Metrodorus said, 'Epicurus would not have been able to advance towards wisdom.'[44] Since Epicurus has clearly understood the rewards and utility of natural science in dissipating the superstition that comes from ignorance, it seems that he then turns its study with boundless confidence and as towards liberation. 'The obstacles,'[45] says Lucretius with the double enthusiasm of the poet and the scientist, 'irritate his courage with great fieriness; he is impatient to break open the close-barred gates of nature. Thus, his ardent strength of soul has prevailed; he advanced beyond the walls of the world, gleaming from afar, and he travelled through immensity with his mind and his heart.'[46] Lucretius makes us witness Epicurus' supreme appeal addressed to reason so as to pacify imagination. The poet will then explain what the philosopher demanded exactly from science: 'Whence victorious he returns bearing his prize, the knowledge of what can come into being, and what *cannot*, in a word, how each thing has its powers *limited* and has its deep-set boundary mark.[47] Therefore, religion is now in her turn cast down and trampled underfoot, while we in our victory are exalted as high as heaven.'[48] In the struggle that Epicurus undertakes against the gods, like a 'new Titan', science and reason (*ratio*) are deployed as the main weapons, and it is only through them that he will achieve his independence, as well as the independence of humanity. In the external world around us Epicurus places powerlessness (*quid nequeat oriri*), only to find supreme power[49] within us.[50] He wishes to understand everything, and through this knowledge to limit all things (*finita potestas*);[51] he wants to perceive at the core of every phenomenon this secret boundary forever enclosed (*alte terminus haerens*), which cannot be crossed and against which the will of the gods is dispelled. In short, he strives to establish around the sage a sort of impassable barrier, by which, tranquil and sheltered from every storm, and trusting his reason to contain his imagination, he will be finally able to enjoy a felicity[52] free of turmoil[53] and with an unshakable confidence: *ataraxia kai bebaios pistis*.

However, at the very moment when Epicurus thinks he has found the happiness he has looked for for so long, it once again escapes him. Imagination, it is true, has been reduced to impotence; but it is now replaced by reason. The problem now is that reason, in its turn, will heavily oppress human beings with a new and even more dreadful domination. While, on the one hand, imagination varied and contradicted itself, reason, on the other hand, always consistent with itself, will show us the immutable necessity that rules the world and encompasses our lives. What is the goal of the science of Democritus and the 'physicists' if not to link each thing with one another, revealing to us, in this eternal harmony, an eternal mechanism? When confronted with this infinite chain of causes, which he himself is bound up with, will the human being not feel even more agitated, even more troubled than before?

Notes

1 T.N. The French here is *souvenir*, which could also be translated as 'memory'. An alternative English translation is 'recollection', which I have avoided because of the possible Platonic meaning it could also imply.
2 T.N. The French here is *riante*, literally 'laughing'.
3 T.N. I have preserved the French root, quite literally: *libérateur*.
4 T.N. The original here reads *expérience sensible*.
5 T.N. An alternative translation for the French *esprit*, which Guyau employs here, would be the English 'spirit', since 'mind' seems to have a more immediate epistemological connotation. Even if the pleasure of the spirit involves knowledge, the emphasis here is on that which contrasts the senses. Since the French term designates both, I will in most cases use the English term 'mind', occasionally choosing 'spirit', indicating it in the footnotes. It is important to stress that in the context of Epicurean materialism, 'spirit' evidently does not have the theological connotation sometimes attributed to it in the English language.
6 T.N. The French here is *âme*.
7 Diogenes Laertius, *Lives of Eminent Philosophers*, II, 137.
8 Athenaeus [*Deipnosophistae*, or *Banquet of the Learned*], XII, 63; Diogenes Laertius, *Lives of Eminent Philosophers*, II, 89; 137; [see also] Cicero, *De finibus*, I, and Pierre Gassendi, *Animadversiones* [in *Librum X Diogenis Laërtii, qui est de vita, moribus, placitisque Epicuri*, Lugduni: Barbier, 1649], 1200.
9 T.N. The French here is *souvenir*, which could also be rendered as 'recollection' or 'remembrance'. One should not, however, associate this notion of *mnēmē* to a potential Platonic tone that the word 'recollection' carries in translation. 'Remembrance', on the other hand, carries a somehow mournful tone, which would not do justice to the power of *mnēmē* in Epicurean philosophy. I have, therefore, chosen the more neutral 'memory', which indicates both the faculty or capacity of remembering and the thing remembered.

10 Clement of Alexandria, *Stromata*, II, 417.
11 T.N. Guyau's remarkable formula here is: *une demi-possession de l'avenir*.
12 T.N. *l'intérêt de l'âme*.
13 Cicero, *De finibus*, I, xvii, 55.
14 T.N. The French here is *peine*.
15 Diogenes Laertius, *Lives of Eminent Philosophers*, X, 4. See also Pierre Bayle's entry on Epicurus [in his *Dictionnaire historique et critique*, Rotterdam: Reinier Leers, 1697].
16 T.N. Guyau's subtle French expression is difficult to capture: man has surrounded himself with *others of himself* [*d'autres lui-même*], reflections or projections of himself; that is to say, he has projected his own powers onto exterior objects, no longer recognizing his own nature and power in what he projects. The argument is close to those employed by Feuerbach and the young Marx when discussing alienation and estrangement. Guyau was a reader of Feuerbach, whom he associated with the Epicurean tradition (see, for instance, book 2, chapter 3).
17 T.N. In the sense that we are never ready for what they reserve to us.
18 Stobaeus, *Sermones* [or *Anthology*], 98; Plutarch, *On Superstition* [in *Moralia*].
19 T.N. It is the idea of a sign of bad fortune: the example is the bird flying over his left.
20 See Lucretius, *On the Nature of Things*, I, 108 [the refence here seems to be rather 110–11]; Cicero, *Tusculanae Disputationes*, I, 5; Plutarch, *On Superstition*, 30.
21 See Plutarch, *On Superstition*.
22 T.N. *augure*.
23 See the last part of Plutarch's *On Superstition*. [See also Constant] Martha, *Le poème de Lucrèce* [*morale, religion et science*, Paris: Librairie Hachette, 1869].
24 Cicero writes: '*Superstitio quâ qui est imbutus, quietus esse nuquam potest*' ['He who is imbued with superstition can never find rest'], *De finibus*, I, xviii, 60. Superstition, being essentially [a form of] trouble and a disquiet of the soul, should have appeared as even more dreadful to the Epicureans, who searched above all for calm and ataraxy.
25 Diogenes Laertius, *Lives of Eminent Philosophers*, II, 86, 96; Plutarch, *De Iside et Osiride*, 23 ; Cicero, *De natura deorum*, I, 23.
26 T.N. the French is *dépersuader*, which means convince of the contrary, to break the persuasion effected by the opposite opinion: here to break superstitious beliefs through freedom.
27 In the eyes of all his disciples and acolytes, as for Lucretius, Torquatus and Velleius, as well as for the sceptic Lucian, Epicurus is the 'liberator'. – '*Philosophiae servire, libertas est*' ['To serve philosophy is freedom'], Epicurus cited by Seneca, *Epistles*, 8.
28 Diogenes Laertius, *Lives of Eminent Philosophers*, X, 123. *Asebēs d' ouch ho tous tōn pollōn theous, anairōn, all' ho tas tōn pollōn doxas theois prosaptōn* (translated above in the text).
29 Cicero, *De finibus*, I, xix, 63.
30 T.N. Guyau recurrently uses this term [*le vulgaire*] to designate the common man, the layman, the ignorant or the common herd. I have opted for 'the vulgar' in order to preserve the French root. This figure of the vulgar should be understood in opposition to the sage, the savant or the scholar.
31 Cicero, *De finibus*, I, xix, 63: '*Rerum naturâ cognitâ levamur superstitione . . . non conturbamur ignoratione rerum, e quâ ipsâ horribiles existunt saepe formidines*' ['Through the knowledge of nature we are cured or relieved of superstition . . . We are not troubled by ignorance, from which horrible fears often emerge'].
32 Diogenes Laertius, *Lives of Eminent Philosophers*, X, 82.
33 T.N. *science de mesure*.

34 Diogenes Laertius, *Lives of Eminent Philosophers*, X, 85. – The physics of Epicurus is far from always having been well understood (on this point, see Paul von Gizycki, *Enleitende Bemerkungen zu einer Untersuchung uber den Wert der naturphilosophie des Epikur*, Berlin: Gärtners Verlag, 1884). Epicurus' physics undoubtedly has its naivety, but it is less naive than Aristotle's cosmology. Let us point to an inaccuracy in the work of Zeller, who believes that Epicurus admits a celestial origin of man: Zeller reads very literally a passage by Lucretius (*On the Nature of Things*, II, 991), when its merely metaphorical sense is well made clear in the lines that follow it (see also Lucretius, *On the Nature of Things*, II, 1153; V, 793).

35 For Epicurus, logic was a part of physics, and even its necessary complement: *eiōthasi to kanonikon homou tō phusikō suntattein* ['They usually place canonic at the same level as physics'], as Diogenes says [*Lives of Eminent Philosophers*, X, 30] (see also Cicero, *De finibus*, I, xix). The only goal of logic was to ground the possibility of science. Epicurus fiercely rejected all forms of vain subtlety, all scholasticism. On this point, he was in direct opposition to the Stoics, friends of subtlety of thought, and to the Cyrenaics, who emphasized the important role of logic and who despised as vain and empty Epicurus' physical research (see Diogenes Laertius, *Lives of Eminent Philosophers*, II).

36 Friedrich Albert Lange, *Histoire du matérialisme et critique de son importance à notre époque* [*Geschichte des Materialismus und Kritik seiner Bedeutung in der Gegenwart*, 1866], translated by B. Pommerol, Paris: Reinwald, 1877, 85.

37 *Kritēria tēs aletheias einai tas aistheseis kai prolēpseis kai pathē* ['The criteria of truth are the sensations, anticipations or preconceptions, and the affects'], Diogenes Laertius, *Lives of Eminent Philosophers*, X, 31. – The term *pathē* designates sensations inasmuch as they affect us agreeably or painfully. As for *prolēpsis*, or anticipation [or preconception, representation or mental scheme], this term designates the memory or recollection of several similar sensations (Diogenes Laertius, *Lives*, X, 33), the common impression (*tupos*) that they leave in our soul, which is like a faithful image of the sensations to come. By means of the *prolēpsis* we can in a way perceive sensations in anticipation [or in advance] (*prolambanein*). Thus, past, present and future are connected: the *prolēpsis*, which is to say sensation at the same time extended and anticipated, is the condition of all research and reasoning (Diogenes Laertius, *Lives*, X, 33; Sextus Empiricus, *Adversus Mathematicos*, I, 37; XII, 21). One could say that Epicurean anticipation [*prolēpsis*] has become in our epoch the principle of induction of British philosophy (see John Stuart Mill, *Logique* [Guyau probably refers to Mill's *A System of Logic, Ratiocinative and Inductive, being a connected view of the principles of evidence and the methods of scientific investigation*, London: John W. Parker, 1843].

38 T.N. Guyau uses the French verb *juger* ('to judge'). A literal alternative here would be: 'these two sensations *judge* different sets of objects.'

39 Diogenes Laertius, *Lives of Eminent Philosophers*, X, 3: *Pasa gar, phēsin, aisthēsis esti kai mnēmēs oudemias dektikē* (146) ['Every sensation is deprived of memory']; Sextus Empiricus, *Adversus Mathematicos*, VIII, 9.

40 Plutarch [Pseudo-Plutarch], *De placitis philosophorum*, 4, 9: *Epikouros pasan aisthēsin kai pasan phantasian alēthē tōn de doxōn tas men alētheis, tas de pseudeis* ['According to Epicurus, every sensation and representation are true: by contrast, some opinions are true and others false']. See Sextus Empiricus, *Adversus Mathematicos*, VIII, 63ff; Epicurus *apud* Diogenes Laertius, *Lives of Eminent Philosophers*, X, 147.

41 Lucretius, *On the Nature of Things*, IV, 350 and ff [T.N. the passage seems rather to be 380 onwards; see also IV, 478, which seems even more adequate to the idea he (Guyau) is explaining].
42 T.N. This is a strange formulation. It is clear that the good is sensation inasmuch as it affects us in a pleasant way. However, it is not clear why Guyau adds the potentially painful [*douloureuse*] aspect of sensation to this sentence. Perhaps Guyau meant: the good is sensation affecting us in a pleasing – and not in a painful – way.
43 See Lucretius, *On the Nature of Things*, IV, 350 and 470; see also Cicero, *De finibus*, I, xx, 64. [T.N. Guyau's view of the sceptics does not seem to consider sceptic philosophical therapy, the therapeutic value of *epochē*, and their emphasis on tranquillity: the sceptic's aim was not to produce trouble through doubt, but to purge our opinions producing tranquillity and ataraxia, through *epochē*, the suspension of judgement.]
44 Plutarch, *Against Colotes*, 3.
45 T.N. He seems to be referring to the obstacles encountered in the study of natural phenomena.
46 Lucretius, *On the Nature of Things*, I. [T.N. In his translations of Lucretius, Guyau privileges philosophical content over poetic form. The complete reference here is I, 60–70].
47 [Lucretius, *On the Nature of Things*, I, 64]: '... *Finita potestas denique cuique / Quânam sit ratione, atque altè terminus haerens. / Quare*, etc.' (translated above).
48 Lucretius, *On the Nature of Things*, I [T.N. Guyau does not provide the full reference, which is I, 75–7. I have consulted and adapted W. H. D. Rouse's translation here. Both the Rouse (Cambridge MA & London: Harvard University Press, 1992 [1924]) and the Stallings (London: Penguin, 2007) translations use the word 'superstition' in this passage ('Therefore Superstition is now cast down'; 'Therefore it is the turn of superstition to lie prone'). Guyau's translation from the Latin is more accurate, since the term employed by Lucretius in I, 78 is *religio* (rather than *superstitio*): '*quare religio pedibus subiecta vicissim obteritur, nos exaequat victoria caelo*' (78–9).
49 T.N. *puissance*.
50 T.N. Guyau refers to the state of impotence or powerlessness to which ancient religions reduced human beings when they attributed to external forces (such as the forces of nature and the gods) power over our lives. For Guyau, Epicurus' critique of superstition inverts this logic: outside us, he finds an absence of power, because we are source of the power that we see projected onto the natural world. Guyau's description here seems close to Feuerbach's or Marx's analyses of alienation.
51 T.N. The Latin suggests he wants to limit the power of everything else. In this context, Epicurus wants to show the limits of the power of exterior events upon us in order to reveal our own power upon ourselves and the world. Guyau's phrase is *tout limiter*.
52 T.N. I have stayed close to the French here, by rendering *félicité* as 'felicity', so as to differentiate it from the French *bonheur*. An alternative here would be 'bliss'.
53 T.N. *trouble*.

2

Freedom – Contingency in Nature, the Condition of Human Freedom

On the profound sentiment, in Epicurus and Lucretius, of the determinism of nature, and the search for a principle that escapes necessity.

I. Epicurus' original position on the issue of freedom. The meaning of his doctrine, which has not been well understood until now: solidarity between the human being and the world; spontaneity in things as the condition of human freedom. – First cause of movement: the collision.[1] Reworking of Democritus' ideas about movement; that every movement is but the effect of an inexorable or *fatal collision*. That the exterior necessity of the *collision* presupposes *weight*,[2] a sort of interior necessity. – The second cause of movement: *weight*. That weight itself presupposes spontaneous and free movement. – The third cause of movement: *spontaneity*; Epicurus as Maine de Biran's predecessor. Psychological analysis of spontaneous movement in Lucretius; contrast between forced movement and voluntary movement. Effort. Contrast between the swiftness of the commands of the will and the resistance of the organs. Induction by which Epicurus extends to the seeds of everything, or the atoms, the same power[3] of spontaneous movement. The true meaning of the power [of the atom] to swerve by itself or *clinamen*. Attempt of a cosmological explanation via the *clinamen*. The first cause is, according to Epicurus, spontaneity. – First consequence of the Epicurean conception: *infinity of worlds*. Their birth and dissolution. – Second consequence: *human freedom*. That this freedom is not foreign or superior to nature, but it rather has its origin and its principle in nature itself. Texts by Lucretius, Cicero and Plutarch. That the apparent or real absurdity, often reproached in the Epicurean conception of the *clinamen*, exists in the very conception of freewill. – Carneades' objection to the Epicureans: Carneades as a predecessor of the Scottish thinkers.[4]
II. That spontaneity, after having contributed to the production of the world, does not disappear from it; rather, according to Epicurus, it persists, introducing the element of contingency into the world. – Distinction between *miracle* and *spontaneity*.
III. Epicurus' fight against logical determinism. – Propositions on the future. – The divinatory science[5] refuted by Epicurus. Objections against Stoic fatalism. – The *responsibility* founded on freedom by Epicurus.

IV. The true meaning of the Epicurean *chance*. – The sage's struggle against fortune. – Memory, the work of human will, according to Epicurus; the memory of past pleasures as a means of compensating for present pains. Identity of happiness and freedom for the sage.

V. The truth that emerges from Epicurus' doctrine: one must conceive the world and man under the same category; one must not admit for one what one rejects in the other. If determinism governs the world, it must then also govern man. In order for the human being to be free, it is also necessary for there to be the seeds of a similar freedom in everything.

We have seen how Epicurus, after having fought against the religious idea of providence or of divine caprice, finds himself confronted by the scientific notion of necessity. It is against this idea that he will now engage in a new struggle. This part of his system is still little known; it is the most original and important part of the system, and it reminds us, in several respects, of contemporary doctrines.

'It would be better,' says Epicurus, 'to accept the fables about the gods than to be enslaved by (*douleuein*) the fatal necessity of the physicists. Indeed, the fable gives us the hope that we can bend the gods by honouring them, but one cannot bend necessity (*aparaitēton tēn anankēn*).'[6] As we have seen, Epicurus had a lively sentiment of the effect that the notion of scientific determinism produced on the human spirit, especially because the rival school of Zeno founded its doctrine on this universal chain of causes and effects. On the other hand, Democritus the physicist, Epicurus' predecessor and master, also claimed that 'everything is made in the world according to necessity'. After having overthrown the gods of paganism, Epicurus sees rising before him the unknown and mysterious god to whom the ancient theologians subjected Jupiter himself. This sombre God was the son of Chaos and Night and sat immobile at the bottom of Olympus. He was represented with no eyes, because he could not see those he crushed. In this depiction his head was crowned with stars, for his power extended as far as the heavens go. This divinity represents the fatal force of nature, and contrasts with the powerless efforts of human will. This [divinity and this force] is what Epicurus tries to overthrow – an even more dreadful divinity whose power extends over to everything at the same time, within and outside us, including our own thoughts and actions. To imagine the gods above everything means to subject oneself to them. However, to explain everything, including oneself, by necessary reasons that exclude our personal power, is to do even more: it means to suppress oneself. The choice we are presented with is between the absolute power of eternal gods or the absolute power of eternal laws. The conclusion we reach is that the human being is powerless, and everywhere encounters the same obstacles that prevent the attainment of happiness. How could one find 'a principle that is able to break with the bonds of fate and that would serve to prevent cause following from cause *ad infinitum*?'.[7] This is how the Epicureans come to pose the problem: it is the ever-pending question of freedom or fatalism, of contingency or universal necessity.

I. – Placed between the pagan gods and the necessity of the Stoics and Physicists, Epicurus saw that there was only one side to take. If every being naturally had a spontaneous power within itself, instead of borrowing it from outside, a spontaneous power from which every being could derive its own movements, would it not then escape from the universal chain of causes and effects? Could nature be conceived both without the gods and without necessity?

For a long time, and in spite of Socrates and Plato, the vulgar[8] placed in man a power[9] that under the form of free will would appear to an external observer as mere chance. However, no one thought of attributing a similar power to beings that are inferior to the human being, so introducing contingency in nature as in humanity. Epicurus attempts to do that, and by doing so, he opens up a completely new [philosophical] path. It is above all on this point that he could truthfully claim that he did not owe his philosophy to anyone but himself.[10] He wanted to destroy both necessity and the power of the gods. Cicero, Lucretius and Plutarch will tell us, in the most formal way, that Epicurus' main hypothesis, that of the spontaneous power of 'swerving'[11] inherent in beings, aims at making possible, and preserving, the power we have over ourselves, in short, our freedom: *hopōs to eph' ēmin mē apolētai*.[12]

In order to build this unique theory of the world Epicurus begins by partially accepting Leucippus' and Democritus' atomistic doctrine. Nevertheless, with respect to their conception of the primitive chaos, he introduces an important change. Democritus considered every movement to be the result of a fatal collision (*plēgē*) and an equally necessary new development and bouncing of the atoms emerging from this collision (*palmos, apopalmos*).[13] Epicurus denies that every movement has its sole origin in the transmission of another movement through through collision or propulsion.[14] Indeed, according to Epicurus, this doctrine, besides implying a contradiction (admitting a movement prior to movement itself),[15] introduces everywhere an absolute necessity: *panta kat' anankēn ginesthai*.[16] Collision, according to Epicurus, is but an ulterior effect that presupposes a prior movement. What can the principle of this movement be then? – To find it, it is first necessary to pass from the outside to the inside, from external violence (*externa vis*) to internal impetus.[17] The latter is not different from weight. 'Weight,' says Lucretius, 'prevents everything from being the result of *collisions* as if by an external violence: *Pondus enim prohibet ne plagis omnia fiant, Externa quasi vi*.'[18] Weight is, then, already the cause of an internal movement, less visibly material, whereas fate, if it still exists, becomes inherent in the very nature of beings, and seems to acquire a more spontaneous character, if not a really free one.[19]

However, this second explanation of movement [i.e. weight] seemed to Epicurus to be insufficient because it presupposes the idea of a necessary law. Weight, indeed, has a determined direction according to an invariable law; the line it follows is subjected to mathematical theorems. If the atoms were animated only by this force, they would be carried [away] in parallel to one another with the same speed for all eternity, 'all things would fall like drops of rain into the deep void: *Imbris uti guttae caderent per inane profundum*'.[20] This hypothesis arrives and stops at a purely mechanical point of view, according to which necessity could be represented by the straight line: the principles of things [i.e. the atoms], driven by weight, would eternally persevere in the motion initiated, as long as another force does not intervene by abruptly curving the rigid straight line that the atoms trace throughout space. But where could this force be found? – Here, Epicurus appeals to inner experience: he searches within the human being for the principle of movement that, when transposed to the core of all things, would provide the explanation being sought.

The observation that serves as a starting point for Epicurus is the one according to which we distinguish within ourselves two kinds of movement that are impossible to confuse, namely constrained and spontaneous movement. *Being moved* [by something else] is not all that there is; we also know by experience that we are *self-moving*. We notice the former by means of a very different feeling from the one that reveals the latter to us. 'It is from the mind's will[21] that movement proceeds; from there it is then distributed throughout the body and limbs. And this is not the same as when we move under the impact of some blow propelling us, ceding to superior external forces or when capitulating to a violent constraint. For in this case it is evident that all the matter in our bodies is moved and dragged despite our own efforts until the point when this matter is curbed[22] in our limbs by the will. Do you see, then, that although an exterior violence propels us, forcing us to move against our will, dragging us and hurrying us headlong,[23] there is something in our breast that can fight against it and so become an obstacle to it?[24] On account of its command[25] the matter is also often mobilized throughout the limbs and through the joints of the body: when propelled forward it is restrained and brought back into its place, settling back into rest.'[26]

A second factor to be considered, when reflecting upon the opposition between voluntary movement that is characterized by effort, and the fatal [or necessary] movement of the organs, is, according to the Epicureans, the difference between the immediate impetus[27] of the will and the slower execution of this impetus in rebellious matter: all animate beings exemplify duality. 'Do you not see also, when [at the races] the starting gate swings open, that the eager force of the horses cannot burst forth as quickly as the mind itself desires? For all the mass of matter must be stirred together through the whole body and called upon in every limb, so that once stirred together, it may be able to follow the impetus of the mind.'[28]

These are the facts of inner experience invoked by Epicurus; these facts compel us to unexpectedly see him as a predecessor of Maine de Biran.

Now, from these observable facts, and by means of an induction founded on the principle of causality, Epicurus proceeds to a consideration of the universe as a whole. The key principle is that nothing exists without a cause, and nothing can come from nothingness. Thus, the power which is within us must have its cause and must be found in the seeds of all things, within the 'seeds of life' or atoms. One should not represent the atoms as something inert and dead, but as carrying within them the power[29] to move. 'Therefore, one must admit that in the seeds of all things there must be, in addition to weight and collisions, another cause of movement and from which our own innate power arises: because we know that nothing can emerge from nothingness.'[30]

According to Epicurus, there are decidedly three intimate and deep causes of movement: [1] *collision*, which is simultaneously exterior and necessary; [2] *weight*, which is interior but still seems to be necessary; finally, [3] the *will*, which is at one and the same time internal and free, *libera voluntas*.[31] This will manifests itself through the power of the swerving movement, which enables it to deviate from the line or the necessity that moves it. It is, in a word, the power of inclining itself in motion. This a power that in the eternal seeds of everything assumes the form of a spontaneous declination, escaping every predetermination of time and place. 'Weight prevents everything from being the result of *collision* as if by an *external* force; however, what keeps the soul from having in itself an internal necessity for everything it does, and from being constrained to passively suffer from everything, is the imperceptible swerve of the atoms, concerning which it is not possible to determine either time or space.'[32]

Having considered psychology let us now return to cosmology. In the ideal origin of things, as we know, the atom fell into the void by virtue of its weight. Not far from it, other atoms fell, equally solitary. If necessity had continued to impose this eternally equal movement on the atoms, the world would not have come into existence: necessity would have been infertile. However, we now know through experience that there is 'another cause of movement, which is neither collision nor weight'. Furthermore, since 'it is from the seeds of everything that the innate free power[33] is given to us', it follows that the principle of this power must be originally situated in the atom itself. The atom can then draw from itself the movement that will make possible for it to approach other atoms. Through this power, and by spontaneously tearing itself away from necessity, the atom will be able to rouse itself from itself and its isolation, and at this point the creation of the universe takes place.[34] If necessity were the master of all things, there would be nothing other than a chaos of atoms being dragged through the void. The first self-effectuated movement, originated in being itself, marks the origin of the cosmos. From the straight line that the atom traced throughout space, and that was like a representation of necessity, the atom deviates spontaneously, *sponte sua*, without any intervention from another force, without intersection with any other line: this is a deviation which is subtle, imperceptible, infinitely small.[35] As long as deviation is produced, however subtle and slight, this new line, barely drawn, marks the emergence of a power inherent in being itself, of a 'new cause of movement in the universe' or, could one ask, the emergence of life? To have the power of self-movement is to be alive. This line, which will gradually complicate itself, will initially form within the void a first sketch of geometrical figures, a first harmony, which is the abridgement of all the harmony in the universe.

When expanding their curved trajectories throughout 'the depths of the void', the atoms end up meeting, encountering and touching one another. 'Palpitating' under the collision they vibrate and bounce until they become entwined with one another.[36] Having, then, conquered the space that separated them (*to diorizon hekastēn atomon*), they become obstacles to the fall of other atoms. The latter are held up on their way, and come to augment an already formed body, which is the kernel[37] of a new world. The void is then populated by strange forms, and worlds are born. Once the regular harmony of these worlds is produced, it makes us believe mistakenly that everything is governed by primordial necessity.

On the basis of this understanding it is no longer necessary to have recourse to a *deus ex machina*, a superior and supernatural cause, to explain [the coming into being of] the universe. Such a cause would become a tyrannical power weighing upon human beings. It is possible to explain the world without making reference to gods or to an ordering – and consequently necessary – intelligence. Space is infinite, and the atoms are infinite in number. Time, which opens up before them, is also infinite: with these three infinites[38] how could anything be considered impossible? Moreover, how is it that the spontaneous force existing in each atom could not have sufficed to organize the finite world before our eyes? The Epicureans do not retreat when confronted with the idea of the infinite,[39] unlike many modern partisans of the notion of universal contingency, who share the same aversion regarding the notions of *infinity* and *necessity*. By contrast, Epicurus sees infinity as the guarantee of human freedom and of the spontaneity in everything that exists. It is the very infinity of combinations in infinite space and time that makes useless the hypothesis of a divine intelligence, of a preconceived plan which is fatally followed, of a world of Ideas pre-existing the actual world and making it necessary. The initiative of the atoms can replace the agency of a creator; the spontaneous will of the atoms, which will become freedom in man, can replace the reflected will of a demiurge or of providence.

The first outcome of this Epicurean conception is that it enlarges our appreciation of the world. If the world were created by a divine will, this inscrutable will could just take all things from nothingness and only that which it wanted; that is to say, this will would only give birth to the one world it had chosen, and surrounded by a belt of stars and suns. However, if the world is in some way a product of infinity it must be infinite in itself.[40] By suppressing the idea of a divine creator Epicurus and Democritus logically anticipate and move towards a modern conception of the world, and to which recent astronomical discoveries have led us. If our earth is the product of the work of atoms, then 'why do all the other atoms placed outside of it, remain idle?'[41] Nature is as fertile as it is grand. Everywhere in space life bursts forth. 'To say that there is but one world in infinity,' wrote Metrodorus, 'is like saying that a vast field exists only with the aim of producing one cob of corn.'[42] Instead of only one world there are [multiple] worlds, just as there are multiple atoms, and to infinity. 'I see them forming within the void,' says Lucretius enthusiastically. These worlds, these orbs, *terrarum orbes,* have their own inhabitants; they consist in large bodies that develop just like ours, and that die in the same way as ours in order to give space to other bodies. Each day worlds die and worlds are born in infinite space; it is a perpetual evolution followed by a perpetual dissolution.[43] Epicurus was not less emphatic about the idea of the dissolution than that of the spontaneous formation of worlds, and to this topic Lucretius often returns. A world which would remain eternally the same would have a *divine* character; one would be led to worship it as the ancient worshipped the stars. Such a world would become for us the object of superstitious fear, and present us with a new sort of destiny. On account of his perseverance in expelling from the world every form of the divine Epicurus finds himself in the company of those contemporary scholars who consider the course of events to be produced independently of any organizing god. For their part modern scholars have been able to find in Epicurus the germs of their own ideas. Long before Lamarck, Lucretius spoke about the successive trial and error (*tentando, experiundo*) by which the elements endeavour to combine among themselves and find a stable combination. And, long before Darwin, it was also Lucretius who spoke of the existence of species now long disappeared, simply because they were not able to employ enough strength, cunning and agility to defeat their adversaries, and so reproduce over the centuries. Long before Spencer, he spoke of a development of worlds resembling the development of individuals, a development leading to old age and death. Finally, it is with Lucretius that we find clearly expressed for the first time, and scientifically formulated, the idea of a progress by which humanity is able to advance step by step towards what is best, *pedetentim progreditur.*

A second consequence of the Epicurean theory is that the human being is formed in the same way as the world by the spontaneous rapprochement of life's principles, and derives from the world everything he is. Man is made in the image and after the likeness of the world,[44] and thus there is nothing supernatural about him. What are we if not a mere union of atoms, and of very subtle atoms, more capable of swerving, and more conscious of the inner impetus[45] by which we move ourselves? Our very freedom, far from being superior to nature, has its origin in it and is the achievement of nature's essential spontaneity. If this were not the case we could neither explain the power that we all claim to possess to choose between two different opposing directions, taking ourselves freely to where our will conducts us, *quo ducit quemque voluntas*, nor could we explain the power of tearing ourselves away from the burden of habits and acquired tendencies. 'If a new movement is always born from a preceding one within a necessary order, if the seeds of all things in swerving did not produce a principle of movement which brakes the chains of necessity, and prevents cause from following cause ad infinitum, from where, then, could there emerge in living beings on earth this free power[46] that is wrested from fate? It is through this power that we can go where our will leads us. We, too, swerve in our movements, and in such a way that the moment in time or place cannot be determined in advance; rather we effect this movement according to what our mind desires. Undoubtedly, it is one's will which is the principle of one's action, and it is from this will that the movements irradiate to our limbs.'[47]

One notes that unity reigns in Epicurus' conception: not only is the world self-sufficient, but it also sufficiently explains man and the freedom he feels within himself. Nature and the human being are solidary and connected to such an extent that we will not find in one of these anything absolutely new with regards to the other and that would be lacking in the other: if we want to recognize a principle of freedom and spontaneity within us, then let us not entirely subtract this very principle from everything else. One cannot claim a special place for the human in relation to necessity and say it reigns around us, but it does not reign within us. 'Epicurus acknowledges,' Cicero writes, 'that he wouldn't have been able to set limits to fate had he not taken refuge in the hypothesis of the swerve of atoms.'[48] 'It is,' he explains, 'through the spontaneous movement of swerving that Epicurus thinks it is possible to avoid the necessity of fate. He puts this hypothesis forward because he feared that if the atom were always carried by its natural and necessary weight, *we would not have any kind of freedom*; because the soul would then be moved in the same manner, that is to say, it would be constrained to move by the movement of the atoms. The author of the atomic theory, Democritus, preferred to accept the view that all events are caused by necessity, rather than to deprive the atoms of their natural motions.'[49] Democritus and Epicurus are both equally logically consistent; the former, admitting necessity everywhere in the world, will also place it in the human being; the latter, admitting freedom within the human being, was also compelled to introduce an element of contingency into the world. The true disagreement between Democritus and Epicurus stems from this question: Are we free or not? – and more generally: Is there spontaneity or absolute necessity in everything? It is in relation to this that the alternative between spontaneous swerve and necessary movement is referred; and this is the moral problem that Epicurus transposes to the origin of things, making it the problem of creation itself.[50]

Neither Epicurus nor Lucretius dissimulate the extent to which they shocked [common] opinion when proposing the idea of a spontaneous swerve. Cicero asks: 'What is this new cause in nature by means of which the atom swerves?'[51] Indeed, it is simply incomprehensible to suppose that, without physical or mathematical determination, without a necessary force coming from the outside or placed within, the atoms deviate or swerve in a way that escapes every calculation. At a first glance, the 'physicists' seem to have an advantage in what regards atoms, straight and curved lines, taken as purely geometrical notions; but this is not the case, according to Epicurus, because when reflecting upon ourselves we reclaim the freedom that we deny to all other beings. If one admits *arbitrium*[52] within us, will we then restrict it to ourselves? When there is no sufficiently strong reason that determines us to necessarily accomplish a certain action, we presuppose a sufficiently powerful will that is able to direct itself. If one does not see any contradiction here, one should also not see any contradiction in the movement of living atoms where there is absence of exterior and apparent cause. If one assumes that our little [inner] world is a source of living will and movement, why would the vast world that surrounds us be only a huge and inflexible mechanism?

With this skilful way of posing the problem, Epicurus expects to remove from his answer everything that at first glance seems to be absurd or contradictory: absurdity, if there is any, is transposed to the notion of free will. Given the apparent necessity of every phenomenon, on the one hand, and the apparent freedom of will and movement, on the other, it is impossible to avoid the conflict between these two contradictory powers. It is necessary to accept one and reject the other. Moreover, according to Epicurus and Lucretius, the choice is not a dubious one, because we feel our own freedom of will and movement, whereas in the case of phenomena we can just speculate about their necessity.

When Epicurus confronted his contemporaries with this choice, they sought to escape it. One finds in Cicero's *De fato* an interesting passage on this topic. According to Cicero, Carneades said that the Epicureans could have defended their thesis [on freedom] against Stoic determinism without having to make recourse to the idea of the swerve of the atoms. 'Because they taught that there could be a voluntary movement of the soul, it would have been better to defend this point without introducing the swerve, whose cause they could not exactly determine; in defending this principle they could have easily withstood Chrysippus.'[53] Carneades blames the Epicureans for having transposed the problem of freedom to the [whole] universe, instead of simply restricting it to the human being. They could have argued that the human being is free without placing this freedom of movement within the atom: they should have said that the atom and the human being move themselves both in virtue of their own *nature*, without exterior or antecedent causation, and thus putting nature in the place of necessity or freedom. 'To agree that there is no movement without a cause is not the same as to say that everything happens by antecedent causes,[54] for our will does not have *exterior* or *antecedent* causes. We use, therefore, mere ordinary language when we say that it is "without cause" that we want or do not want something, since we take these words to mean [that we do or not do something] without an exterior or antecedent cause, rather than without *any* cause at all. In the same way when we say that a vase is empty we are not speaking as the physicist, who denies the void, but we want to say, for example, that the vase is without water, wine or oil; in the same way, when we say that the soul moves without cause, we are actually saying that it moves without an antecedent or exterior cause, and not absolutely without cause.[55] One can say of the atom, since it is moved throughout the void by its own weight, that it moves without cause because no cause intervenes from the outside. But in order not to be mocked by the physicists, if we wish to say that anything happens without cause we should make a distinction and say that the very nature of the atom consists in being moved by its own weight, and that this is the cause by which it moves the way it does.'[56] By this ingenious introduction of the idea of *nature*, Carneades believes he escapes the idea of necessity without the need to invoke the idea of a spontaneous swerve of the atoms; according to him, the atom moves neither by the intervention of an exterior cause nor because it spontaneously deviates from its course: it moves because this is its nature. 'In the same way, when considering the voluntary movements of the soul, one should not look for exterior causes, because voluntary movement has in itself this nature of being under our power, of obeying us, and this is not without a cause: nature itself is the cause of this action.'[57] Therefore, through the idea of *nature*, that is to say, of a cause that would neither be properly free nor necessary, Carneades expects to reconcile the regularity of movement in the universe and arbitrary freedom in the human being.

Nevertheless, Carneades' subtle argument (which Bayle admires) could not convince the Epicureans: is it not just fine words to invoke nature as a cause, maintaining that this cause does not have a necessary character? Would it not surreptitiously revive the notion of necessity it was trying to discard? Carneades believes that if the atom's nature consists in being moved by its own weight, then the atom would escape [the action of] exterior causes and, therefore, also escape necessity. To this Lucretius replies by distinguishing two types of necessity that equally instil fear within us: the first is exterior necessity, *externa vis*, the other is internal, *necessum intestinum*. Because weight is *natural* (*gravitas naturalis*), does this mean it is less necessary (*necessaria*)? If necessity only rules the movement of the atoms, why would the movements of our soul escape it? From where could come this new nature of movement, which according to Carneades' expression would be 'under our power and that would only obey us'? Is not our soul composed of the same elements as the rest of the universe? Could they be an exception to the common law of the universe? In this debate it is Epicurus who seems to be the most logical. To say the least, it is interesting to note the extent to which the Epicureans and the whole of antiquity were concerned with the idea of freedom.

II. – A new question is then posed. It seems impossible to dispute that Epicurus was the first in antiquity to place contingency at the heart of nature, and to explain by its spontaneous movements the formation of the world, thus legitimizing the existence of human freedom. However, one generally believes that contingency, placed by Epicurus in the origin of things, existed only at the origin and then disappeared, subsequently giving place to necessity. Once the world is produced, once the machine is constructed, why wouldn't it work all by itself? Why would we need to invoke any other force than necessity itself? The 'chain of destiny' that Lucretius speaks about was broken once, as we say, by 'a twist of fate'. It is possible that this could have happened; later, however, was not the chain restructured, ring by ring, encompassing the universe once again? According to this hypothesis, Epicurus would have introduced the 'swerve' in nature only as a sort of dialectical expedient and he would have been eager to remove it as soon as possible.

To confirm this hypothesis of an absolute and universal determinism, which comes after [an initial] contingency in the world, one invokes a passage in which Lucretius, fighting against the idea of divine creation, argues that no being can in fact emerge from nothingness, and that in order for it to be born it needs a pre-existing seed and certain determined conditions (*certis*).[58] Thus, says Lucretius, the rose does not pop out of nothingness, a harvest crop does not suddenly appear yellowing on the surface of the earth, the child does not become a man in just one day. Nothing comes out of nothingness, and all beings come from a seed which develops over time in a determined way. Besides, he adds, this seed must be appropriate to the individual that must come out of it; because beings are not generated under random, indeterminate conditions and by chance (*incerto partu*): neither the body nor the trees can produce fruits of every kind, fish cannot be born on earth, herds do not fall from the skies, man is not formed in the bottom of the sea, for 'every being is born from determined seeds' (*seminibus quia certis quidque creatur*).[59] It is on [Lucretius'] repeated use of the word *certus* when referring to the seeds of organisms that one grounds the conclusion that in the Epicurean system, after the indeterminacy of the first cause, there would come an immutable determination of effects. This would amount to saying that the vast universe obeys now and will eternally obey the laws of necessity. It would also mean that that swerve would be incapable of breaking any ring of this causal chain after its first occurrence.

Such a conclusion seems to go beyond anything that we find in Lucretius' own thought. Do the philosophers, who in our own day rightly or wrongly admit, like Epicurus, the contingency of the universe, believe that because of this contingency an apple tree could produce an orange, or that an orange tree could produce an apple? Do they believe that an atom all by itself could produce what requires a certain determined combination of [many] atoms, or that a man all by himself could engender a family or a city? Believing that the universe in its first principles is not subject to absolute necessity is different from believing in the sudden derangement of all laws and all their natural consequences. The initial spontaneous movement cannot be *calculated* or *determined* in advance (*nec tempore certo nec regione loci certa*), but the combinations of movements, once produced, can be calculated and determined, and they constitute a definite matter that things require in order to be born (*materies* certa *rebus gignundis*).[60] The idea of the miraculous or the marvellous is what Epicurus and Lucretius seek to attack. We know that they have a deep aversion both towards the miraculous power[61] of divinity and the rational power of necessity. It is these two powers that they want to supress. To introduce in [the realm of] phenomena enough regularity so that miracles could not find space, and enough spontaneity so that necessity loses all its absolute, primordial and definitive character: this is the twofold goal that the Epicureans pursue. Let us examine how they seek to do this.

Against the idea of the miracle Epicurus and Lucretius invoke the very nature and form of the atoms, which explain the ineffaceable differences between them. The atom cannot change its nature in the same way that human beings cannot abandon their human nature. It follows from this that in order to form any [possible] body it is not enough to randomly associate atoms of every kind. A specific and determined seed is required, in which we find a certain number of atoms of a given kind already gathered together. Then, in order for this seed to develop, it must encounter in space atoms whose nature is analogous to its own [atoms], and it must then assimilate them. If the seed does not encounter those atoms it will be stopped in its development, and so it will perish. If it encounters those atoms, however, it will develop by assimilating them [to its own structure]; it will grow, although slowly, for it cannot find in just a single encounter all the elements and materials that it requires. Thus, time becomes the condition and the factor of development for every being. Therefore, no capricious power can make completely new beings appear suddenly in the world; in the same way, it cannot make the world emerge out of nothingness. Creation and the miracle are equally impossible. All the fables of pagan religion, in which the gods resurrect the dead, or metamorphose [into] other living beings, are suppressed as a result of this insight. Celestial or earthly phenomena, in which one used to see the direct manifestation of the ire or mercy of the gods, lose their meaning. When Lucretius sought to demonstrate how Epicurus succeeded in defeating religion and the gods, he said that he did so by instructing us about 'what can be engendered, and what cannot, by which reason each thing has a delimited power and meets a limit that is deeply attached to it (*alte terminus haerens*)'.[62] Therefore, Lucretius' words are especially directed against religious ideas and against any divine intervention in the universe. According to him, the objection to the supernatural[63] derives from the determinate organization and regular development of bodies. Here one finds a remarkable idea. Not every science seems to be equally hostile to religion. Indeed, the opposition between science and religion seems to be clearer in the case of physiological sciences. This is because the genesis of organisms, in which heredity and time play a key role, decidedly excludes any appeal to a supernatural power, as well as any magical creation of beings; if a *fiat lux* seems still admissible, the idea of a *fiat homo* or *fiat lupus* makes us smile.[64] The first preserves a certain sublime appearance, whereas the ridiculous nature of the latter is readily visible. The less a science is abstract, the more it is incredulous.

Now, from the fact that Epicurus sought to destroy the marvellous and the miraculous,[65] does it follow that, after the chance event of the first swerve, he posited the necessity of everything? Does it follow from the fact that there are no gods acting upon the world that there is no freedom or spontaneity anywhere in the present? Nothing authorizes us to think that this corresponds to Epicurus' thinking.

We know that, according to Epicurus, what explains and somehow initiates the freedom of the human being is the spontaneity of movement within the atom, its power to swerve or decline. Why would this power, which introduces contingency into the universe, disappear completely after the formation of this universe? Why, after producing the world by their spontaneous movements, would the atoms remain idle, to quote Lucretius' expression? Would they not contribute to new progress by constantly 'attempting' 'new combinations'? The texts we have previously examined do not provide us with any positive answer regarding this hypothesis. On the contrary, wherever the Epicureans speak about the swerve of the atoms, they consider it not as a past event, as a twist of fate, a fortuitous exception that took place one time never to be repeated again, but rather as a very real power[66] that is conserved by the atoms and the individuals that are formed by the union of these atoms. For Lucretius, the human being employs this power every day. One must not forget the important text: 'We swerve in our movements, not at a *predetermined* space or time, but to where our mind takes us.'[67]

Declinamus item motus, nec tempore certo
Nec regione loci certa, sed uti ipsa tulit mens.[68]

As we have seen, the same power is found in other living beings (*animantibus*).[69] Finally, perhaps this power is not foreign even to inorganic bodies, or at least to their fundamental elements. Evidently, says Lucretius, the heavy bodies that we see falling do not follow, in their fall, an oblique direction; but can one say 'that they do not swerve or deviate at all from the perpendicular line? Who could even discern it?'

Sed nihil omnino recta regione viai
Declinare, quis est qui possit cernere sese?[70]

In this sense, we cannot rely on the apparent testimony of our senses. Thus, following this slightly naive conception, even before our eyes, and even within the lowest assemblages of matter, spontaneity could still find its place, if not in the mass of the body, then at least within the elements [that compose it]. It could even manifest itself by a real, albeit imperceptible movement, by a perturbation whose effect would only appear in the long run. Everywhere we find atoms, in exterior objects as well as in ourselves, we can find to a higher or lower degree the latent power that breaks necessity; and because outside the atom there is nothing but the void, absolute and elementary necessity cannot reign anywhere. The free power that the human being possesses exists in every element of things, in lower or inferior degrees, but always ready to be awakened and to act should it encounter favourable combinations, such as those that result in the *living being*, the *animal* and the *human being*.

Is it the case that Epicurus, when placing in all things an element of spontaneity, also placed in them a sort of miracle, thus returning against his better judgement to the conception of a marvellous power similar to that of the gods? No. Epicurus had always believed that it was possible to reject the idea of miracle while at the same time defending the hypothesis of the swerve of the atoms that was so dear to him. For there to really be miracles two conditions must be fulfilled: first, one must suppose the existence of powers[71] outside of nature; second, one must suppose that these powers are powerful enough to modify an ensemble of phenomena according to a preconceived plan. By contrast, the spontaneity of the atoms is a power[72] placed within beings, within their atomic elements, and not outside of them. On the other hand, this power[73] is exercised only in one motion, and it can only surpass the necessary laws of mechanics (ulterior and derivative laws) at one specific point and in a completely imperceptible way. Finally, the spontaneous movements of the atoms find a limit in the laws of their combination. The movements that are specific to certain atoms, including those of living beings, cannot have durable results in the universe except by accumulation. They cannot hinder the march of things. Spontaneity, if it exists, must take place within nature [and its processes]. Thus, according to Epicurus, we do not really disrupt the laws of nature when, by a decision of the will that is impossible to predict in advance (*non certa*), we determine ourselves in this or that direction, when we take this or that path.[74] The miracle, on the contrary, is in direct and formal opposition to nature: it is a violent interruption of the progression of things. For instance, to suddenly provoke a comet or a meteor,[75] it would be necessary to disrupt an ensemble of phenomena, to make a series of movements converge to a certain particular point, and in a way that would be absolutely contrary to nature. The power[76] of the gods would then be completely inimical to nature and this is the reason why Epicurus and Lucretius so fiercely combat it. Spontaneity, by contrast, proceeds, follows and completes nature, preventing it from being a mere mechanism incapable of the best and subject to an inexorable fate. It is because of this that Epicurus preserves spontaneity [in his philosophy]. It is undoubtedly not possible to attribute to Epicurus very precise theories regarding this subject. What is certain is that he wanted to counterbalance the necessity of a chain of causes (*ex infinto ne causam causa sequatur*) without deranging the order of the universe, at least perceptibly.

III. – In the same way that Epicurus fought against physical determinism, he equally aimed to destroy the sort of logical determinism that is based on the axiom according to which between two contradictory propositions one is necessarily true and the other false. Applying this axiom to propositions regarding future actions, the Stoics maintained that it is necessarily true or false that I will or will not accomplish a certain action, and from this they concluded that the action itself was necessary. On the contrary, according to Epicurus, between two contradictory propositions regarding a future event, neither one nor the other, considered in particular, is true: this is because if one of the two was true one could immediately predict the decisions of free will, and as a result free will would be suppressed.[77] The different events are not, then, as the Stoics supposed, mere consequences and diverse aspects of an eternal truth preceding the fact itself; rather, there is truth only regarding what has already occurred. For example, it *is not* true today that Epicurus will be alive tomorrow, but it could *become* true.[78] According to Epicurus, a certain contingency seems to lie at the heart of everything, and truth itself arises from this [contingency].[79]

The art of divination or prescience that attempts to predict[80] the future is, therefore, rejected: the future remains open to spontaneous power, to life, to our will; the future is what will emerge from indetermination, which persists even in the present, actual determination. The art of the soothsayers is unsustainable: *mantikē anuparktos*.[81] One can neither derive prognostics from the flight of birds nor from all those phenomena that the ancient augurs so patiently observed. How could we possibly believe, Epicurus asks, that the departure of animals from a certain place is regulated by a god that then strives to fulfil this prophecy? Not even the animals would want to be subdued by this foolish fate; even more so when there are no gods to establish it.[82] – It is not only a superstitious belief that Epicurus fights here when he rejects divination, it is – still and always – the idea of fate or necessity. Until Epicurus, all antiquity, philosophers included, more or less strongly believed in destiny and fate, and believed therefore in prescience and divination. The Stoics formally accepted it; for them everything was connected, concurring and conspiring so that it should be possible for the inspired soul to apprehend future things within present things, to read the future in the simplest events, even in the apparently most insignificant one. However, if we suppress both the realm of necessity and that of the divine, then divination, this belief upon which the life of the ancients was largely grounded, disappears immediately. We know the passage of *De natura deorum* in which the Epicurean Velleius derides the Stoic's triple faith in providence, fate and divination: 'If a god resides within the world as its governor, maintaining the course of the stars and of the seasons, conserving order and the regular process of change in things, and keeping an eye on land and sea to guard the interests and lives of men, why, what a bondage of sad and laborious business is his! Like the tragic poets, being unable to bring the plot of your drama to a conclusion, you have recourse to a god ... And so you have saddled us with an eternal master, whom we are to fear day and night. Who would not fear a god who foresees everything, who thinks of and notices all things, and deems that everything is his concern and curiosity? Whence an outcome of this is first of all your doctrine of necessity or fate, which you call *heimarmenē*. Everything that happens is the result of an eternal truth and an unbroken chain of causation: but what value can be assigned to a philosophy that thinks that, as do old women, and the ignorant among them, everything happens by fate? And then comes your doctrine of *mantikē*, which the Latins call divination. If we believed you, we would become superstitious, and we should be the devotees of soothsayers, augurs, oracle-mongers, seers and prophets. But for us, liberated from superstitious terrors by Epicurus, we do not fear the gods in any way...'[83]

Epicurus tried to destroy physical and logical determinism, but he does not stop there: he also riles against what we could call moral determinism, that is to say the doctrine which negates responsibility and regards praise and blame as lies.

The idea of responsibility, of personal value, without the need to think of exterior punishment or reward, is in general foreign to utilitarian systems. Epicurus, however, considers freedom as the highest utility and conceives of it as the definitive condition for the attainment of happiness. He could, therefore, not avoid freedom's natural corollary [viz. responsibility], which appears not to be consistent with the first idea of the system [viz. pleasure or utility]. 'Necessity,' he writes to Menoeceus, 'which some consider to be the master of all things, can actually be reduced to chance and to our own personal power of agency.'[84] The exterior events that are not primitively subjected to a necessary law, but rather to spontaneous causes whose effects we cannot predict, are attributed to chance. Our inner events, which are not subject to any necessary law, but have freedom as their cause, are attributed to our personal power. 'Indeed,' says Epicurus, 'on the one hand, necessity is *irresponsible*; chance, on the other, is *unstable*; whereas freedom has *no master*, and blame, as much as its contrary (praise) naturally accompany it.'[85]

Thus, because we are *sans maître*,[86] and since we are independent of everything that is not ourselves, blame and praise cannot be referred to anything above us, that is to say, they can neither be referred back to chance nor to necessity; they can only be attributed to the *self*.[87] By attributing an intrinsic value to freedom, Epicurus seems to want to exceed [the terms of] his own moral system. If he wrests freedom from fate, as Lucretius says, it is not only in order for freedom to advance independently towards pleasure, but it is also so that freedom, in its very independence, finds the first and final pleasure – that which we cannot even properly call a pleasure, namely the sentiment of a personal value, praise and dignity.

The good in question here, according to Epicurus, is no longer something irresponsible (*ananke anupeuthunon*), or unstable as in the case of chance (*tuche astaton*); it is rather an immortal good, which, when joined with other goods, makes them as immortal as itself. Thus, after having opposed the meritorious freedom of the sage to fate and chance, Epicurus adds: 'In this way you will live as a god among men. For how could the man that lives in the midst of immortal blessings resemble a mortal being?'[88]

IV. – The texts we have analysed so far can help us to understand the true sense, still obscure, that Epicurus attached to the word *chance*. He tried to preserve, at one and the same time, according to Plutarch, chance in [the realm of] nature, freedom within the human being, and the moral consequences to be extracted from his theory of the *clinamen*.

First, for Epicurus chance is not the complete absence of causality since, as we know, nothing takes place without a cause, nothing comes from nothingness: it is this principle that encourages Epicurus to extend[89] his insight from our will to nature. For him, chance is not freedom itself, as it was often taken to be. Epicurus poses these two notions in parallel, *chance* and *freedom*, without ever confusing one with the other (*ha men apo tuchēs, ha de par' hēmas*): *certain things are produced by chance, others by our making*.[90] Chance, in effect, is exterior, whereas freedom is interior. Chance is the way in which things appear to us and in their relationship with us: it is the unforeseen, the indeterminable, which takes place in an undetermined time and place. This unforeseen [event], however, is the result of a cause that hides itself underneath chance: '*In seminibus esse aliam, praeter plagas et pondera, causam motibus, unde haec est nobis innata potestas*: there is in the atoms another cause of movement beyond collisions and weight, it is from this [cause] that our innate power stems.'[91] This cause, operating at the foundation of reality is, as we have already seen, the inherent spontaneity of movement within the atoms. Chance is but the form in which this spontaneity reveals itself to us. With respect to ourselves that which constitutes us is [our] power[92] over ourselves and the freedom of movement and will: *to eph' hēmin*. This is how we can explain the following passage from Plutarch: Epicurus presupposes 'the slightest possible swerve of an atom, and that alone, is [enough] to produce the stars, living beings, chance, and to prevent freedom from being destroyed:[93] – *atomon parenklinai* (spontaneity of declination or swerve) ... *hopōs tuchē pareiselthei* (exterior chance that is the form of this swerve) *kai to eph' hēmin mē apolētai* (inner freedom which is the sentiment that expresses it). The *tuchē* and the *to eph' hēmin* are two modes of a spontaneity fundamentally identical to that which Epicurus says the fate of the physicists refers back to.

However, this exterior chance, once manifested, becomes *fortune*, a hostile power,[94] against which we must know how to protect our freedom through ethics. Fortune is not, indeed, an absolutely invincible and invariable power, such as destiny or fate was taken to be. If chance is changeable and variable, hope is always possible and, even more than possible, it is always demanded. Rather than counting on a chance event to correct another, it is better to count on ourselves and on that which depends on us: *ha par' hēmas*. This is because nothing absolutely unfortunate, no irremediable misfortune, no inflexible fate can impose itself upon us, externally or internally. Nature cannot rule over us in an absolute way, and we are the ones who should try to rule it by means of our own will. The sage, who otherwise would have been reduced to desperation and inertia when facing the absolute aspect of necessity or divine caprice, will find his strength confronting chance, that is to say spontaneity, a power which is not as terrible as the unknown, but which he knows because he himself possesses it. He will, then, train himself and stand up as a combatant against chance (*antitaxesthai*),[95] and he will fight against it in close hand-to-hand combat: a noble fight in which the sage, certain of his superior freedom, is confident about his final triumph. On this issue the Epicurean rivals the Stoic.[96] The future does not trouble him: how could he care about what may happen to him? If it is something bad, he will avoid it, by swerving, by freely tearing himself, his thought and his will from it, [or even] by separating himself from the world through voluntary death when necessary.

Fortune and chance have so little dominion over the sage that, as Epicurus says, it is better to be unfortunate with reason (*atuchein eulogistōs*) than to be fortunate without reason (*eutuchein alogistōs*).[97] Fortune adds neither evil nor good to the total sum of happiness, but only the beginnings of great goods and great evils.[98] In other words, chance gives better or worse tools to the sage. However, this 'labourer of happiness'[99] adds to the imperfect instruments given by chance the ability of his own hands, equally making use of both. He seizes each instant of duration as it presents itself to him, as well as every sensation that it brings along with it. These sensations brought to the sage by [the flux of] time are ones that time itself cannot carry away because the sage captures them through memory,[100] keeping them eternally under his gaze. Memory for Epicurus is a work of the will: one can always choose not to forget. For the sage, who knows how to remember, the present is without sorrow, the future without apprehension or fear, and the past without regret. On the contrary, with regards to this past, from which his memory brings him all his enjoyments, and from which it will subtract all his pains, he experiences not only a negative and passive feeling, but rather a true sentiment of gratitude, of recognition (*charis*).[101]

Chance brings to the sage the most fearsome things: suffering, sickness, torment; but even when he is placed under torture, even if he is thrown into the burning 'brazen bull of Phalaris', he will remain free, independent, untroubled. He will seek assistance in fortune itself, by remembering the goods that fortune had previously given him, and 'anticipating' those which it will give him in order to efface the sensation of the evils that it currently produces.[102] The Epicurean, by retreating into himself, and seeking the best things that he lived in the past, will find there a force of resistance against the obstacles of the present life, [a force] which is no weaker than that of the Stoic: he will be happy.[103] 'O Chance,' as Metrodorus wrote, 'I'm not vulnerable to your blows; I've closed all the paths that could take you to myself!' The soul of the sage is, then, free, serene, satisfied with itself and everything else. When pain comes, and in order to avoid it, it will suffice for the sage to make use of this *clinamen*, which is found in several degrees in the reflected wisdom of the human being, as well as in the blind spontaneity of the first elements [i.e. the atoms]: it will be enough for the sage to simply move backwards or forwards, a free retreat into the past or a free impetus[104] towards the future; he will swerve away from pain, he will escape from it as the atom escapes from fate; then he will withdraw, tearing himself away into the most inalterable stillness and the sweetest imperturbability. Thus, the sage, since he is free, is someone with 'no masters' (*adespotos*); this is why he lives 'among immortal goods' (*en athanathois agathois*); [with the figure of the sage] the spontaneous swerve has become virtue and happiness.[105]

V. – In the Epicurean conception of freedom, as it has been laid out in this chapter, the most salient and original point to be gleaned is the solidarity that can be established between man and world. Usually, the partisans of free will are far from conceiving man and the world under the same kind: freedom appears to them rather as a divine power,[106] superior to nature, and not as a power borrowed from nature itself and to be found in nature's elements. Today, we are still led to believe that the question of freedom is an exclusively human question, as something that concerns only ourselves; we are encouraged to withdraw into our inner self and discuss as an activity of leisure whether we are free or not. We easily imagine that the whole universe is subjected to fate, without thinking that our freedom, if it exists, will be affected and diminished by this fact. But we could also ask with Epicurus: Where does this freedom come from? '*unde est haec, fatis avolsa, potestas?*' How could it have been born and subsist in a world absolutely governed by necessary laws? Would we not, then, be strangers in this world? Would we have fallen from the sky, like Vulcan?[107] If this was the case, it would be necessary to suppose the existence of a Jupiter, a god, a master, and we would then return to the kind of slavery that Epicurus wished us to overcome. No, every cause is a natural cause, and given that 'nothing comes out of nothingness', our freedom comes from nature itself. It is interesting to see Lucretius invoking in favour of the idea of a spontaneous swerve of the atoms the famous axiom *ex nihilo nihil* ('nothing comes out of nothingness'), [a principle] which precisely we have seen so many times being mobilized against this hypothesis. According to Lucretius, that which is found in the effects is already present in the causes: if we have, then, spontaneous movements, it is because, in every elementary cause of movement, there can be a degree of spontaneity. If we are truly free to take ourselves in a thousand directions, then, every part of our being, each part that forms our being by assembling with other parts, must possess in germinal form an analogous power, more or less pervasive and conscious, and only limited by determinate combinations. Epicurus thus denies [the idea of] absolute inertia, if not in the entire realm of matter, at least in its primitive elements. It is a sort of dynamism – still rudimentary – that he adds to the pure and simple mechanism of Democritus.

As we have seen, Epicurus' adversaries tried to escape from the dilemma he posed to them: – [the choice between] spontaneity within things or the necessity within the soul; – but it is doubtful that they succeeded. Today, the same dilemma presents itself to us. Indeed, nature is not a completely heterogeneous whole; we have within ourselves something of the animal, the animal something of the vegetal, and the vegetal has in itself something of the realm that precedes it; and all these beings, in turn, must have something in common with the human being: 'Everything is in everything,' said the phrase of the ancients.[108] If there was only one molecule, one single atom in the universe, in which the germs of spontaneity would not be present in any degree, then freedom would not be possible for us: all beings are in a relation of solidarity. Conversely, if human freedom exists it cannot be absolutely foreign to nature, it must be sensed in nature, and gradually emerge from within it. The shadows have in themselves something of the light of the day: if the night was completely dark it would be eternal. In a word, for man to be considered free everything around him must tend towards freedom and possess the same germ of freedom within its elementary atoms. Everywhere Epicurus' spontaneity allies itself to the fatal collisions of Democritus was a way of organizing the universe.[109]

It remains to be investigated whether or not this universal spontaneity, and this element of variability introduced in the universe, agrees with the theories of modern science centred on the equivalence of forces and the mechanical laws of evolution. It is a question that we cannot examine here. We have simply attempted to search for the true sense of one of Epicurus' main theories, aiming to show its historical importance.

Notes

1 T.N. The French term here is *choc*.
2 T.N. *la pesanteur*.
3 T.N. *puissance*.
4 T.N. With the term *Écossais*, Guyau is especially referring to the thinkers of the Scottish Enlightenment.
5 T.N. I have preserved Guyau's choice of words. Perhaps a more correct phrase would be 'divinatory art', which would allow for the contrast with science (discussed in the previous chapter).
6 Epicurus quoted by Diogenes Laertius, *Lives of Eminent Philosophers*, X, 134. [T.N. Hicks' translation reads slightly different from Guyau's: 'It were better, indeed, to accept the legends of the gods than to bow beneath that yoke of destiny which the natural philosophers have imposed. The one holds out some faint hope that we may escape if we honour the gods, while the necessity of the naturalists is deaf to all entreaties.']
7 Lucretius, *On the Nature of Things*, II, 255: '*Principium quoddam quod fati foedera rumpat, / Ex infinito ne causam causa sequatur* (translated in the text). Let us stress that the word *fate* (*fatum*), as defined here by Lucretius, is a synonym of [the word] *determinism*, which we employ today.
8 T.N. Here, again Guyau uses *le vulgaire*, a common expression in philosophical French at the time. The vulgar used as a noun covers a wide semantic field, designating ordinary people or laymen, but usually with a negative connotation: those who are not philosophers, or those have unjustified opinions, coarse manners, or those who are ignorant.
9 T.N. *puissance*.
10 Diogenes Laertius, *Lives of Eminent Philosophers*, X, 13.
11 T.N. Guyau uses the term *déclination* to refer to the Epicurean notion of *clinamen* or *parenklisis*. This notion is usually translated in English as 'swerve' or 'swerving'. In this passage I have chosen the latter, for it designates a power of effecting a certain action.

A fully literal option to Guyau's French would be 'declination', but one could also think of the capacity of the atom to 'deviate'.

12 Plutarch, *De sollertia animalium*, 7 [in *Moralia*]. See below.
13 Simplicius, *On Aristotle's Physics*, 96; [Pseudo-]Plutarch, *De placitis philosophorum*, I, 23.
14 T.N. The French term is *impulsion*. Guyau is here referring to the concrete physical process of propulsion, when one thing pushes another (not in the more vitalistic sense of impulse, drive or impetus). Guyau expresses here a physical idea, explaining that all movement cannot have its origin only in the shock of a certain body with other moving bodies that would move it – by 'pushing' it forwards; in short, he is describing a derivative form of movement (and claiming that this cannot be the only source of movement for a physical body).
15 Aristotle, *De caelo*, III, 2.
16 Diogenes Laertius, *Lives of Eminent Philosophers*, IX, 45.
17 T.N. Again, *impulsion*
18 Lucretius, *On the Nature of Things*, V, 288 [T.N. The quote seems to actually come from II, 290–2]. This conception of a movement transmitted to atoms by weight was, for a long time, the target for objections to the Epicurean school. Since Cicero, one reproaches Epicurus the naivety of admitting a top-down movement, and consequently a 'top' and a 'bottom' [*bas*] in infinite space. However, a text by Epicurus shows that he was not that naive. 'Up' [or 'top'] [*haut*] and 'down' [or 'bottom'] [*bas*] are conventional terms that designate, according to Epicurus, two opposite directions of movement within an infinite space. *Hōst' esti mian labein phoran, tēn anō nooumenēn eis apeiron, kai mian tēn katō, an kai muriakis pros tous podas tōn epanō to par' hēmōn epi tous huper kephalēs hēmōn topous aphiknētai, ē epi tēn kephalēn tōn hupokatō to par' hēmōn katō pheromenon. Hē gar holē phora ouden hētton hekatera hekatera antikeimenē ep' apeiron noeitai* [In Hicks' translation: 'Hence, it is possible to assume one direction of motion, which we conceive as extending upwards *ad infinitum*, and another downwards, even if it should happen ten thousand times that what moves from us to the spaces above our heads reaches the feet of those above us, or that which moves downwards from us the heads of those below us. None the less is it true that the whole of motion in the respective cases is conceived as extending in opposite directions *ad infinitum*']. (Diogenes Laertius, *Lives of Eminent Philosophers*, X, 60). Thus, 'up' [or 'top', *haut*] and 'down' [or 'bottom', *bas*] designate, for Epicurus, a relative state, as the words right and left, big and small, high and low. That which remains unsustainable is the hypothesis that attributes to primitive movement no more than *two* possible directions.
19 T.N. This is a relatively a strange claim by Guyau. The translator is careful not to correct his arguments. However, he seems to be claiming that *fatalité* seems to become more spontaneous and even free, which seems paradoxical. A possible way to explain this would be to say that if there is necessity, it is the necessity of the freedom of beings. From a different perspective, one could say that weight is an internal principle of movement, but not yet *free* movement itself.
20 Lucretius, *On the Nature of Things*, II, 219. [T.N. More precisely, the quote seems to be II, 222]. Epicurus and his disciples admitted and clearly expressed the law according to which every body, independently of its volume, falls with the same speed though the void. See Diogenes Laertius, *Lives of Eminent Philosophers*, X, 61. Lucretius, *On the Nature of Things*, II, 230.
21 T.N. The French here is *volonté de l'esprit*. I have chosen the word *mind* because in Lucretius' Latin one reads *mens*.

22 T.N. Lucretius' Latin here is *refrenavit*.
23 T.N. This is Rouse's expression for the Latin *praecipitesque rapi*.
24 T.N. I have chosen to render the last clause very literally, for in French Guyau uses *se dresser en obstacle* (the Latin is *obstareque*), therefore the image is that of the obstacle; Rouse's choice is 'something strong enough to fight against and *resist it*'.
25 T.N. The Latin here is *arbitrium*.
26 Lucretius, *On the Nature of Things*, II, 269: '*Ut videas initium motûs a corde creari, / Ex animique voluntate id procedure primum, / Inde dari porro per totum corpus et artus. / Nec simile est ut quum impulsi procedimus ictu, / Viribus alterius magnis magnoque coactu: / Nam tum materiam totius corporis omnen / Perspicuum est nobis invitis ire repique, / Donicum eam refrenavit per membra voluntas / Jamne vides igitur, quanquam vis extera multos / Pellit et invitos cogit procedure saepe / Praecipitesque rapit, tamen esse in pectore nostro / Quiddam, quod contra pugnare obstrareque possit: / Cujus ad arbitrium quoque copia materiai / Cogitur interdum flecti per membra, per artus / Et projecta refrenatur, retroque residit?*' (translated in the text). [T.N. Here, again, I have chosen to translate Guyau's French translation, for it presents some important terminological differences with regards to other existing translations, such as the idea of violence (not present in Stallings' or Rouse's translations, for example). The singularity of Guyau's translation of this passage might explain why he considered necessary to reproduce the whole Latin passage in the footnote.]
27 T.N. The French here is *élan*.
28 Lucretius, *On the Nature of Things*, II 263–8: '*Nonne vides etiam patefactis tempore puncto / Carceribus, non posse tamen porumpere equorum / Vim cupidam tam desubito, quam mens avet ipsa? / Omnis enim totum per corpus materiai / Copia conquiri debet, concita per artus / Omnes, ut studium mentis connixa sequatur*' (translated above).
29 T.N. *puissance*.
30 Lucretius, *On the Nature of Things*, II, 283: '*Quare in seminibus quoque idem fateare necesse est / Esse aliam, praeter plagas et pondera, causam / Motibus, unde haec est nobis innata potestas: / De nihilo quoniam fieri nil posse videmus*' (translated above).
31 Lucretius, *On the Nature of Things*, II, 256.
32 Lucretius, *On the Nature of Things*, II, 288: '*Pondus enim prohibit ne plagis omnia fiant, / Externâ quasi vi: sed ne mens ipsa necessum / Intestinum habeat cunctis in rebus agendis, / Et devicta quasi cogatur ferre patique, / Id facit exiguum clinamen principiorum / Nec regione loci certâ, nec tempore certo*' (translated above in the text) [T.N. The passage seems to be II, 290. I have based my translation on Stallings]. Cicero completely agrees with Lucretius when he writes: '*Epicurus declinatione atomi vitari fati necessitatem putat: itaque tertius quidam motus oritur extra pondus et plagam quum declinate atomos intervallo minimo, id appellat* elachiston' ['Epicurus thinks that the necessity of fate is avoided by the swerve of the atom; and so in addition to gravity and shock there arises a *third form of motion*, when the atom swerves in a minimal space [or interval] (termed by Epicurus *elachiston*)'], *De fato*, X.
33 T.N. *libre puissance*.
34 T.N. Guyau uses the word 'creation', but it seems that the notion of *production* would be more appropriate, since the atoms pre-exist all other entities, and are eternal substances, which means that their encounters through deviation and *libre puissance* would characterize production of worlds and entities (rather than creation).
35 Lucretius, *On the Nature of Things*, II, 243: '*nec plus quam minimum*' ['not more than minimal']; Plutarch *De animae procreatione in Timaeo*, 6: *akares* ['infimal']; Cicero, *De*

finibus, 19:'*perpaulum, quo nihil posset fieri minus*' ['so small that nothing smaller can be thought of'].

36 Diogenes Laertius, *Lives of Eminent Philosophers*, X, 43: *Epi tēn periplokēn keklimenai* ['They fall into an association']; Cicero, *De finibus*, I, vi, 19:'*ita effici complexiones et copulationes et adhaesiones atomorum inter se*' ['This is how associations [or combinations, *complexiones*], joining together and intertwining of atoms among themselves, take place'].

37 T.N. *noyau*.

38 T.N. *ces trois infinis*.

39 Except with regards to the idea of the divisibility of bodies ad infinitum; that is for them a fully physical question, a question of facts. According to Epicurus, the atoms, even if they were mathematically divisible, would still be factually indivisible and unbreakable [in reality], because they are completely solid (*individua proper solidatem*) ['indivisible because of their solidity']. See Lucretius, *On the Nature of Things*, I, 486: '*Sed quae sunt rerum primordia, nulla potest vis / Stringere; nam solido vincunt ea corpore demum*' ['But that which constitutes the first principles of things, no force can / Separate them into pieces; they are victorious because of their solid body'].

This absolute solidity of atoms comes, as we know, from the fact that 'they do not participate in the infinite void': *atomos ametochos kenou*. Whereas all other bodies are constituted of both void and solidity [*plein*], being also composed and therefore dissoluble, the atom is, by contrast absolutely solid [or filled, *plein*], and it is completely invulnerable to the penetration of forces that could dissolve it: this solidity of the atom is what makes it eternal: *Agennēta, aidia, aphtharta, oute thrausthēnai dunamena oute diaplasmon ek tōn merōn labein out alloiōthēnai* ['They are not generated and are also eternal and indestructible; they can neither be broken nor assume new forms from their parts, nor can they be transformed'], Stobaeus, *Eclogues* [*Physical and Moral Extracts*], 306 [Guyau quotes a page number from the edition he consulted and identifies it as 'Heer'. He is probably referring to a 1792 edition annotated by Arnold Hermann Ludwig Heeren, *Ioannis Stobaei Eclogarum physicarum et ethicarum libri duo. Ad codd. mss. fidem suppleti et castigati annotatione et versione latina instructi ab Arn. Herm. Ludov. Heeren*, Göttingen: Vandenhoek & Ruprecht, 1792].

40 [Pseudo-]Plutarch, *De placitis philosophorum*, II, 1: *Dēmokritos kai Epikouros kai ho toutōn mathētēs Mētrodōros apeirous kosmous en tō apeirō kata pasan peristasin* ['Democritus, Epicurus and their disciple Metrodorus maintain that there is na inifity of worlds in the infinite [space], in every Direction . . .']; Cicero, *De finibus*, I, vi, 21: '*infinito ipsa quam* apeirian *vocant*' ['the infinite itself, which they call *apeiria*'].

41 Lucretius, *On the Nature of Things*, II, 1055:'*Nil agere illa foris tot corpora materiai*' (translated in the text).

42 [Pseudo-]Plutarch, *De placitis philosophorum*, I, 5.

43 Cicero, *De finibus*, I, vi, 21:'*innumerabiles mundi, qui et oriantur et intereant quotidie*' ['The innumerable worlds that are born and die every day']. – Lucretius, *On the Nature of Things*, III, 17 & ff.; II, 1075.

44 T.N. Guyau uses creationist vocabulary to signify a non-creationist idea: man is produced and structured according to the same principles as the rest of the world.

45 T.N. *élan*.

46 T.N. *libre puissance*.

47 Lucretius, *On the Nature of Things*, II, 251:'*Denique, si semper motus connectitur omnis / Et vetere exoritur semper novus ordine certo. / Nec declinando faciunt primordia motûs / Principium quoddam, quod fati foedera rumpat. / Ex infinito ne causam causa*

sequatur: / Libera per terras unde haec animantibus exstat, / Unde est haec, inquam, fatis avolsa potestas, / Per quam progredimur quô ducit quemque voluntas? / Declinamus item motus, nec tempore certo, / Nec regione loci certâ, sed uti ipsa tulit mens. / Nam, dubio procul, his rebus sua cuique voluntas / Principium dat; et hinc motus per membra rigantur' (translated above in the text).

48 Cicero, *De fato*, 20: '*Qui* aliter obsistere fato fatetur se non potuisse, *nisi ad has commentitias declinationes confugisset*' (translated above).

49 Cicero, *De fato*, 10: '*Epicurus* declinatione atomi vitari fati necessitatem putat ... *Hanc Epicurus rationem induxit ob eam rem, quod veritus est ne, si semper atomus gravitate ferretur naturali ac necessariâ*, nihil liberum nobis esset, *quum ita moveretur animus, ut atomorum motu congeretur. Hinc Democritus auctor atomorum accipere maluit, necessitate omnia fieri, quàm a corporibus individuis naturales motus avellere*' (translated above; I have used the H. Rackham translation). – Cicero, *De natura deorum*, I, 25: '*Epicurus, quum videret, si atomi ferrentur in locum inferiorem suopte pondere,* nihil fore in nostra potestate, *quod esset earum motus certus et necessarius, invenit quo modo* necessitatem effugeret ... *Ait atomum, quum pondere et gravitate directo deorsus feratur, declinare paullulùm*' ['Epicurus realized that if the atoms [only] fell downwards by the effect of their own weight, [then] *nothing would be under our power*, since their movement would in that case be certain and necessary; he then invented a means to *avoid necessity* ... He says that the atom, while propelled downwards by means of its own weight and gravity, also very slightly deviates [from its path]'].

50 T.N On Guyau's use of the term 'creation', see notes 34 and 44 above.

51 Cicero, *De fato*, 20.

52 T.N. *arbitre*, or the capacity for free choice, deliberation and action.

53 T.N. Guyau does not provide a reference for this quote.

54 T.N. *causes antécédentes*.

55 Cicero, *De fato*, XI. This is the argument used by Clarke, Reid, Cousin and Jouffroy, who, as we can see, have not significantly contributed to this question.

56 T.N. Guyau provides no reference.

57 '*Acutiùs Carneades, qui docebat posse Epicureos suam causam sine hâc commentitiâ declinatione defendere. Nam quum docerent esse posse quemdam animi motum voluntarium, id fuit defendi melius, quàm introducere declinationem, cujus praesertim causam reperire non possunt: quo defenso, facile Chrysippo possent resistere. Quum enim concessissent motum nullum esse sine causa, non concederent omnia quae fierent fieri causis antecedentibus: voluntatis nostrae non esse causas externas et antecedentes ... De ipsâ átomo dici potest enim, quum per inane moveatur gravitate et pondere, sina causâ moveri, quia nulla causa accedat extrinsecùs. Rursus autem, ne omnes a physicis irredeamur, si dicamus quicquam fieri sine causa, distinguendum est, et ita dicendum, ipsius individui hanc esse naturam, ut pondere et gravitate moveatur, eamque ipsam esse causam cur ita feratur. Similiter ad animorum motus voluntarios non est requienda externa causa: motus enim voluntarius eam naturam ipse in se continet, ut sit in nostrâ potestate, nobisque pareat, nec id sine causâ, ejus enim rei causa ipsa natura est*' ['Carneades was more sublte, and taught that the Epicureans could sustain their cause [viz. their idea of causality] without [committing to] this idea of an imaginary swerve. Indeed, since they taught there could be a certain [form of] voluntary movement, it would have been better [for them] to simply defend this idea than to introduce this [idea of] swerve, of which they cannot, however, find the cause: by means of this defence, they could have easily resisted Chrysippus. Now, even if they conceded that that there could not be a movement without cause, they could not concede that all that

happens does so as an effect of antecedent causes: there are no external or antecedent causes when it comes to our will ... Moreover, one can say that the atom itself, when it is moved through the void by the effect of its weight and gravity, is moved without cause, since no cause acts upon it from outside. By contrast, in order to avoid the mockery of physicists if one says that something happens without a cause, one must rather draw a distinction, and say that the nature of each atom consists in being moved by its own weight and gravity, and that that is the cause by which it moves in this particular way. In the same way, no exterior cause is required for the voluntary movements of our soul: for voluntary movement has itself a nature that consists in being under our power and obeying our command, and this is not the same as an absence of cause, since the cause in this case is nature itself'] (Cicero, *De fato*, XI).

58 Lucretius, *On the Nature of Things*, I, 170.
59 Lucretius, *On the Nature of Things*, I, 170; in the same way, 173: '*Atque hac re nequeunt ex omnibus omnia gigni. / Quod certis in rebus inest secrete facultas*' ['It is for this reason that everything can be born of everything: / Because the is a distinct potentiality in determinate things']; also 189: '*Ominia quando / Paulatim crescunt, ut par est, semine certo*' ['All beings when they / grow little by little, as it is convenient, from a determinate seed']; and 204: '*Si non materies quia rebus reddita certa est / Gignundis,e quâ constat quid possit oriri*' ['It is only because a determinate matter is given to everything / At their birth, from which what can emerge is determined'].
60 T.N. Guyau's interpretation is that the first movement cannot be predicted, but once movement is produced, regular laws of association operate, which is clear in the fact that things need a determined kind of matter to be produced, and this follows regular laws. Guyau's point is showing that admitting contingency and *clinamen* does not presuppose the complete disruption of the laws of nature. The second point is showing that contingency is integrated in nature in such a way that the *declination* or *swerve* does not represent a miracle, nor the interruption of nature's laws or functioning.
61 T.N. *puissance*.
62 T.N. The author does not provide a reference for this quote. It is Lucretius, *On the Nature of Things*, I, 75–79.
63 T.N. *merveilleux*.
64 T.N. Let there be light, let there be man, and let there be [a] wolf, respectively.
65 T.N. Or, less literally, the 'supernatural'. The French is, again, *merveilleux*.
66 T.N. *puissance*.
67 T.N. Here, as in previous occurrences, Guyau translates the Latin *mens* as *esprit*.
68 T.N. Latin quote in the original, translated in the previous sentence.
69 Lucretius, *On the Nature of Things*, II, 263.
70 Lucretius, *On the Nature of Things*, II, 243.
71 T.N. *puissances*.
72 T.N. Here, *pouvoir*.
73 T.N. Again, *pouvoir*.
74 We know the analogous doctrine of Descartes, and the opposed theory of Leibniz.
75 T.N. The sentence is hypothetical: 'If a god, for instance, wants to provoke the fall of a comet.'
76 T.N. *pouvoir*.
77 Cicero, *De fato*, 9. Cicero responds to Epicurus using an argument that is analogous to the one regarding *premonition*, by Thomas Aquinas and Bossuet: the theologians have not added anything to Cicero.

78   Cicero, *De natura deorum*, 25, 70; *De fato*, 16, 37; *Academica*, II, 30, 97. On this point, Zeller approves Epicurus to a certain extent ([See Zeller's] *Die Philosophie der Griechen* [Leipzig : R. Reisland, 1882]).
79   T.N. Guyau's argument is that, for Epicurus, truth depends on the contingency of events and becoming; truth is open to the unfolding of events in the world and does not precede it.
80   T.N. Guyau's expression here is *lier*. This is probably a typographical error, since in the next page he uses the verb *lire* ('to read') in the same context. The art of divination *reads* the signs of things to come in things present.
81   Diogenes Laertius, *Lives of Eminent Philosophers*, X, 135.
82   Diogenes Laertius, *Lives of Eminent Philosophers*, X, 135 (especially the end of Epicurus' *Letter to Pythocles*).
83   Cicero, *De natura deorum*, I, 20. [T.N. Note that, in his translation, Guyau operates selections in the original text].
84   T.N. Diogenes Laertius, *Lives of Eminent Philosophers*, X, 133.
85   Diogenes Laertius, *Lives of Eminent Philosophers*, X, 133: *Dia to tēn men anankēn anupeuthunon einai, tēn de tuchēn astaton, to de par' hēmas adespoton, hō kai to mempton kai to kai to enantion parakolouthein pephuke* (translated above).
86   T.N. Literally, without masters.
87   T.N. *moi*.
88   Diogenes Laertius, *Lives of Eminent Philosophers*, X, 135.
89   T.N. The concept of induction is probably not appropriate here, but this is the expression Guyau is using: *induire de notre volonté à la nature*.
90   See Stobaeus' texts, which confirm our interpretation and show that Epicurus does not confuse the freedom of choice (*proasiresis*), which is proper to man, and chance (*tuchē*), which only exists outside ourselves: *Epicouros (prosdiarthoi tais aitiais tēn) kat' anankē, kata proairesin, kata tuchēn* ['Epicurus differentiates that which is produced by necessity, that which is the product of a deliberate choice, and that which happens by chance'] (Stobaeus, *Eclogues* [Heeren edition], I, 206). Sextus Empiricus wrote, in the same terms: *Ta men tōn ginomenōn kat' anankē ginetai, ta de kata tuchē, ta de kata proairesin* ['Some events are produced by necessity, others by chance, and others still are due to a deliberate choice'] (Sextus Empiricus, [Guyau does not provide the reference for the work quoted, he is most likely referring to *Adversus Mathematicos*] 345. See also [Pseudo-]Plutarch, *De placitis philosophorum*, I, 20; Galen, c. 10 [the editors could not identify Guyau's reference to Galen].
91   Lucretius, *The Nature of Things*, II, 285 [T.N. Guyau slightly modifies the quote].
92   T.N. *pouvoir*.
93   Plutarch, *De sollertia animalium*, 7.
94   T.N. Here and in the next two occurrences of the term 'power', we translate *puissance*.
95   Diogenes Laertius, *Lives of Eminent Philosophers*, X, 120.
96   Diogenes Laertius, *Lives of Eminent Philosophers*, X, 122, 135, etc.
97   Diogenes Laertius, *Lives of Eminent Philosophers*, X, 135.
98   *Tas archas tōn megalōn agathōn ē kakōn* (Diogenes Laertius, *Lives of Eminent Philosophers*, X, 135; translated above in the text).
99   T.N. *ouvrier de bonheur*.
100 T.N. *souvenir*.
101 See the beginning of the *Letter to Menoeceus*. One has proposed *chara* (joy, delight) instead of *charis* (recognition, grace, gratitude, goodwill), but that is a prosaic substitution; it is also a misinterpretation, since Epicurus places *chara* among the

inferior *pleasures of movement*, which he despises. – '*Grata recordatio*' ['grateful memory or recollection'], Torquatus says in the *De finibus*.
102 T.N. In this description, Guyau shows how the sage, although unable to control fortune, can master it.
103 Diogenes Laertius, *Lives of Eminent Philosophers*, X, 218; Cicero, *Tusculanae Disputationes*, V, 26; Plutarch, *Non posse suaviter vivi secundum Epicurum*, 3.
104 T.N. *élan*.
105 Mr [Theodor] Gomperz, the learned professor at the University of Vienna, discovered in Naples an unpublished fragment of Epicurus' *Peri phuseos* (*On Nature*) on the theory of the will [*théorie de la volonté*]. This peculiar fragment in no way invalidates the texts we have analysed; on the contrary, Epicurus maintains that 'one addresses us warnings [*avertissements*] because the cause of our actions resides *within ourselves and in our primitive and fundamental constitution* [*constitution primitive*], and not in the fatal influences of the milieu or in the accidents of chance' (*Comptes rendus des séances de l'Académie de Vienne*, t.LXXXIII, p. 87).We recognize the old objection to determinism, deducted from the inefficacy of warnings and threats: the determinists targeted here are undoubtedly the Stoics. The fragment analysed does not concern the key, and the ultimately original, feature of the Epicurean theory, [namely] the relationships of the human will to atomic swerve.
106 T.N. *puissance*.
107 T.N. Vulcan is the Roman equivalent of the Greek god Hephaestus.
108 T.N. Or 'everything-in-everything'. Guyau refers here to one of the key ideas of Presocratic philosopher Anaxagoras.
109 The chapter we have just read was firstly published in July 1876 in the *Revue philosophique*. This is Mr [Charles-Bernard] Renouvier's assessment of our work in his *Critique philosophique*: 'It is a study worthy of attention, with a competent analysis, supported by very well explained texts, of one of the most interesting issues of philosophy, and one of the most neglected and, we could even say, unjustly despised ones. The author highlights the way in which Epicurus understood free will and chance, and defined their relationship, by considering them not only or essentially in the human being but also in the atoms. The derided idea of atomic *swerve* is clearly brought to light [by Guyau]. We only lament that the fact that Mr Guyau has not sufficiently distinguished, at least linguistically, between *spontaneity*, which is fully reconcilable with natural determinism (forced determination by each nature in which it is produced) and pure *freedom*, ambiguous in its acts, undetermined with regards to its effects inasmuch as they are not actual or actualized. The author's conclusion is weakened by this terminological confusion – although he had clearly fixed the meaning of free will and chance in the Epicurean school, in opposition to the deterministic freedom of the Stoics. – Nonetheless, Guyau's is a very bold conclusion!
  As a matter of fact, it is the boldest conclusion that we have ever read. Modern science, by suppressing the dividing lines once clearly separating the mineral, vegetal realm, and the animal and human realms, has established a real solidarity between all beings: from this solidarity between beings and this unity of the universe we believe it is possible to draw two conclusions: either determinism *envelops* mankind and world, or indeterminism *is to be found* in all its constitutive elements. If we limit ourselves to admit in the elements of things a spontaneity as the one conceived by Leibniz, making it one with necessity itself, it will be henceforth impossible not to place an identical necessity within the human being. Therefore, we must choose. The

human being surely differs a lot from other beings in nature. However, between freedom and necessity we find not only mere difference, but rather opposition and contradiction. We cannot pass from one to the other. Thus, if we place in the human being a freedom 'undetermined with regards to its effects', we must also make of this freedom the very core of things. Now, such a freedom is no longer mere spontaneity, it is indetermination [*indétermination*], contingency: it is impenetrable [or unfathomable]. And this impenetrability [...] is what essentially constitutes it. At the origin and core of things we should therefore place indeterminism, contingency and, for an external spectator, chance. Yet human freedom, which many philosophers accept, clearly escapes reason; since if one could give reasons for an action considered free, this action would be then referred back and reduced to the necessary predominance of a reason, and would thus fall back into the domain of determinism: for to explain something it to determine it. Thus, freedom is essentially a non-rational power [*puissance*], a power of being indifferent with regards to reason. Moreover, freedom is not properly speaking a power of *deliberation*, since the truly rational deliberation is nothing but an attempt to scientifically determine the best motive [for action], that which would be the most determined, the one about which one could completely give an account, and finally the least free (in the ordinary sense of the term). Free will resides in the blow of a *decision*, in the *action* abruptly stemming from the core of being, in a *motion* which detaches itself from every other exterior movement, neither mechanical nor logical, nor rational, and so timidly conscious that many philosophers, such as Kant, have denied the reality of its consciousness. If we do not hesitate to place, by an at least apparent contradiction, a power such as free will in a rational being, we do not see why we hesitate to place it within non-rational beings. One must take this thought to its last consequences. Malebranche has said – Kant and Schopenhauer have repeated it – that freedom is a mystery: why would the human being have privilege over mystery? Moreover, if *one supposes that this mystery exists*, why not place it at the core of being itself? It seems to us that Epicurus was right, since he wanted to break the 'chain of causes', and for not deriving of the apparition the human being in the world this apparent exception to the world's order, which he thinks stems of the world itself. From a logical point of view, his doctrine seems perfectly justifiable to us: it is more consistent than many modern doctrines. Does that mean it is the ultimate truth? Is *indeterminism* a more exact and faithful representation of the core of things than determinism? That is a whole different question. We have no intention of solving this problem here, we only aim at developing it. If one criticizes us for being extreme and concluding absurdities, our reply is that absurdity is without any doubt contained in our premise, and it is more productive to become aware of it: we prefer philosophers who want to be completely absurd to those who want to be just half absurd: they at least have the merit of being logical. If we are only dealing with hypotheses, we absolutely prefer the Epicurean [hypothesis] *clinamen* to the vulgar free will reserved to human beings.'

Mr Renouvier later returns to this interesting issue (*Critique philosophique*, 9th year, t. 1, no. 8) and defends the idea that Epicurus had escaped our dilemma – universal determinism vs. universal spontaneity. In order to do this, according to Renouvier, it was enough for Epicurus to represent freedom as the outcome of a particular combination of atoms, as a property or faculty proper to the human being, of which we can find no trace in the constitutive elements of human mind considered individually; this property or faculty is only created by their rapprochement: 'we know the use that all doctrines of this kind make of the virtue of combinations'. We answer that a convinced partisan of free will cannot represent it as the outcome of a combination, as a simple property or a derived faculty. Free will can only be primitive [i.e. original and primary]. Once we admit the chain of causes and effects in nature, we cannot concede that this chain, because of a simple combination, will destroy itself in human beings, generating its opposite, and that the outcome of the set of mechanical causes is to produce an effect without mechanical cause. Free will cannot be a matter of combination because it is not a matter of *quantity*. We cannot even say that it constitutes a new *quality* introduced in nature. No, it is a power without analogy or precedent: it is an absolute. And as Mr Renouvier himself admits, an absolute cannot be produced through combination, but rather by an authentic creation. Thus, if freedom is really the monopoly of man, it would have to have been created *ex nihilo* within him, thanks to an even more striking miracle than those of faith, since it would be a miracle without author. This miracle would still be highly analogous to Epicurus' *swerve*, it would still be an exemption from the mechanical laws of movement (and, what is more, from the laws of thought itself). And this kind of *swerve* would happen without atoms, in the void and through the void.

3

Tranquillity in the Face of Death. – Epicurean Theory of Death, and its Relation to Contemporary Theories

I. Ancient ideas of death in Epicurus' time. Conception of death by analogy with sleep. Belief that there is a vague consciousness in death as with the sleeping person. The tomb conceived as a sort of dwelling or residence. [Idea] that the underworld of the ancients is a kind of expanded tomb. The horror that these ideas about death caused to the ancients. Comparison with our modern ideas on death.

II. That the fear of death, according to Epicurus, is not rational but simply an effect of the imagination. That death in itself is not an evil. Should the time that will pass after our death frighten us more than the time that elapsed before our birth? Comparison between Epicurus' doctrines and those of Schopenhauer, Strauss, Büchner, Bentham, de Bain, etc. – How Epicurus is led to a unique and curious theory: happiness is independent of duration, and immortality itself would not increase our happiness. Analogy between this theory and Feuerbach's [theory].

III. If death is not to be feared, should it be desired? Hegesias of Cyrene as a predecessor of the modern pessimists. Opposition between Epicurus and Hegesias. That death is neither an evil nor a good. On the cases in which the sage can, exceptionally, resort to suicide. – The death of Epicurus and his last letter.

IV. Originality of Epicurus' doctrine. That many objections made to his doctrine do not refute it. [That] from the perspective of the doctrine of pleasure, Epicurus' theory of death is much more coherent than is usually thought. Reasons why the Epicurean can, to a certain extent, face death without fear. – The sole condition under which immortality would be possible. – [That] there are *two* different ways of fearing death, and that Epicurus was wrong in not distinguishing them.

As we already know, the dominant idea in Epicurus' philosophy is the idea of emancipation, of moral and intellectual liberation. However, as soon as the human being is delivered from the [power] of the gods of the fable and the fate of Democritus, he finds himself still in the presence of a final and ultimate necessity, the most unavoidable of all, that of death. To liberate the human being from the fear of death: this will then be the supreme objective of Epicurus' doctrine. 'There is nothing terrifying in life,' he says, 'for he who knows that there is nothing terrifying in the privation of life.'[1]

Epicurus' theory of death can be seen as the most remarkable effort that was ever made in order to liberate the human mind from all fear of dying, excluding the belief in immortality. When, three centuries after Epicurus, Christianity appeared and strongly affirmed the afterlife and resurrection, the Epicurean theories on death were abandoned. In our days, when Christianity has lost much of its strength, one is no longer satisfied with the idea of immortality and with the groundless affirmations of religion. [Presently,] when the Epicurean conception of the universe reappears in the sciences and seems, until further notice, closer to the truth, it is important to study the attitude towards death that the ethics of happiness acquired with Epicurus, examining whether the criticisms made against our philosopher are at all serious, and then to determine the precise point on which his theory appears to be insufficient. By taking this path, we will reveal more than one analogy between the doctrines of Epicurus and those of Schopenhauer, Strauss, Feuerbach and other contemporary thinkers.

I. – In order to understand the true meaning of the Epicurean doctrine, one needs to get rid of the ideas that Christianity has somehow inculcated in everyone regarding the topic of death. In the fear of death imagination has the same share as reason. According to Epicurus, imagination is the main cause of this fear, especially because the imagination of the ancients was especially overexcited concerning death, and in this respect very different from ours.

Considering the images offered by the poets and religious traditions, one may speculate that the first peoples represented death by an *induction*, an analogy taken from sleep.[2] Now, even the deepest sleep is not completely deprived of feeling. The ancients represented death, then, as accompanied by a vague sensibility, and that is why they made death the object of a very particular dread. Following Lucretius' exposition of the Epicurean doctrine, 'man cannot remove himself from life, he cannot completely abandon his being [or existence], to separate himself from this body lying down on earth; he imagines that this body is still himself, and that standing beside his corpse, he continues to animate it with his own sensibility.'[3] Thus emerges the fear, about which Lucretius talks, of being devoured by vultures or wild beasts, of being buffeted by the waves, or simply to feel oneself oppressed under the weight of the cold stone of the tomb.[4] Hence the respect to very precise burial rites that, if neglected, could bring the eternal misfortune of the dead person. Hence also the care in preparing close to the tomb, in the *culina*, the food that should placate the dead's hunger. If one neglected to bring him his food, the dead person would come out of his grave, and one would hear him moaning in the night.[5] The same idea of there being a vague consciousness after death would, throughout its development, give rise to a conception of immortality. If death is a sort of sleep, a kind of lethargy, why wouldn't it be followed by a more or less complete reawakening? 'Our friend Lazarus is asleep,' said Jesus about his disciple from Bethany, immobile in his tomb. This phrase resounded in every human mouth, way before it was said by Jesus, and one asked oneself when Lazarus would stand up and walk. However, one should not believe that for the majority of ancient peoples[6] this problematic life to come would in any way be more desirable or preferable than the present life. Far from it. First, this future life is hardly imaginable outside of the tomb. For the living it is difficult to suppose that the dead could be able to move away from that place where they had placed them with their own hands, where they have seen the dead for the last time, where they have entombed them with their arms, their clothing, their horses, and sometimes their wives, the place where the living took milk and honey to the dead so that they could nourish themselves. In this way, for most religions, the abode of the dead is the earth. We have possibly not sufficiently remarked until now that the underworld is not different from an enlarged tomb. The dead can move there, whereas they were still and immobile in the tomb, and this is basically the only difference.[7]

Let us add that death was conceived as an eternal sojourn in the subterranean night, and popular imagination will soon populate this darkness with the most terrifying phantoms. Clearly then, as in our own day, there were incredulous people who laughed at Cocytus, the Acheron, of Cerberus and Tantalus; but the crowd always feared these chimeras. In the temples, as well as inside houses, there were paintings representing infernal tortures, and one looked at them with terrified eyes.[8] 'Superstition,' Plutarch says, 'makes fear last longer than life itself, attaching to death the imagination of everlasting evils; once it reaches the end of every toil and trouble, our imagination is persuaded that it should begin to suffer others that will never end.'[9] Plutarch adds that, for his part, he would rather be Epicurean than superstitious. Even in our days, when religious fears have lost most of their force, one knows to what extent the horror of infernal punishment frightens a great number of people. In certain countries, like the United States of America, where religious faith is much more robust than in Europe, especially France, this terror often produced nervous incidents and provoked epileptic attacks in whole congregations. Nevertheless, after Christianity, believers only experience a vague fear towards eternal punishment, which is combatted and mitigated by the hope of eternal rewards. They know that heaven is open to the elected or chosen ones, and they hope to be among them some day. In ancient religions, on the other hand, the hope of *heavens* did not exist, or it was very vague. Perhaps some heroes, such as Hercules or Bacchus, and certain triumphant figures, had the merit of taking a place up there among the gods; but the rest of the disordered ordinary mob buried under the earth would live there forever away from daylight, and if among them there were some more intensely chastised, some more unfortunate than others, one could ask oneself if there was anyone [among them who could be said to be] *fortunate*. Thus, according to Cicero's expression when exposing the Epicurean system, the idea of death weighed upon the ancient world as the mythical rock weighed upon Tantalus. Christianity produced a real revolution by transporting the dwelling of the elected from the underworld to heaven. Christianity provided the human imagination with a new path. By lifting the stone of the tomb, until then enclosed upon the dead, it opened our eyes to a day brighter than the ones we enjoyed during our lives. One feared until then that dying involved descending under the earth and into the night. Henceforth, one believed that it was – at least for the elected – to ascend into the light. A blissful life had appeared after the life 'down here',[10] and earthly existence, which until then seemed to offer supreme happiness at the expense of the horror that the existence in the underworld inspired, now suddenly appeared as despicable.

In Epicurus' time nothing could announce this revolution. Death is the universal object of popular fears; or, rather, which is truly remarkable, one fears death less than the future life represented by religion. In the long run a tenacious association of ideas was constituted between the afterlife, the horror of the tomb, the subterranean life, and the phantoms with which [our] imagination populates the night. One cannot imagine death as being peace and rest instead of unrest and torment: one cannot believe in a full, complete annihilation. The Epicurean, who could think of himself as 'entirely dead', was an object of the secret envy of the superstitious who believed in the underworld.[11] Nowadays, from the perspective of the faithful, death is, following Pascal's reasoning, a throw of the dice in which one can lose everything, but in which one can also win everything. For the ancients one could only lose. For them, the afterlife was a threat and could not be a promise. Epicurus' doctrine suffers from the impact of this ancient conception; it will establish as its goal the alleviation of this primitive fear of death.

II. – For Lucretius, the fear of death has such a strong power that it would be the principle of every negative passion in the human being.[12] It is to this fear that an attentive analysis refers ambition, envy, avarice, baseness: according to him, all these vices come from the exaggerated importance that we attribute to life and to the things of life. It is certain that the fear of death is essentially corrupting: we would all have a more perfect life if we were not always afraid of losing it.

Now, why do we fear death and why do we try to avoid it at all costs? If we are to believe Epicurus, this fear is always an ingenuous one; we suppose, following the vulgar common belief, that something of ourselves remains in death, and it is this something that brings us disquiet, it is what awakens our imagination, casting phantoms before our eyes. Today the fine English psychologist Bain is not too far away from Epicurus in his belief that when it comes to death it is especially the thought of the unknown and the night of the tomb that terrify us. 'The fear of death,' says Bain in his analysis of emotions, 'is the ultimate manifestation of superstitious fear. What all the emotions produced by the fear of death have in common is the fear of an unknown future into which a being is introduced. Death's darkness and obscurity is likely to strike us with terror. It is the deepest midnight gloom that human imagination is able to picture.'[13] If, on the contrary, according to Epicurus, we reacted against these superstitious ideas and persuaded ourselves that death is nothing real and, so to speak, nothing living, if we understood that death is for us the dissolution of all life and complete annihilation, how, then, could we have any reason to fear it? There is nothing dreadful in that which is not anything by itself. Destruction is simply rest. The Cyrenaics, in their theory of pleasure, made of rest the middle ground between voluptuousness and sorrow. Epicurus, on the other hand, filled with enjoyment and happiness the very instants of apparent inaction in which life is sown, and admitted only one middle term between pleasure and pain, that of a state of complete indifference: that is, the supreme rest of death itself.

'Death is nothing for us,' says Epicurus in his *Maxims*, 'because that which is once dissolved is incapable of feeling, and that which does not feel anything is nothing to us.'[14] He then develops this idea in the letter to Menoeceus, where he writes: 'Accustom yourself to believe that death is nothing to us, for good and evil imply the capacity to feel, and death is the privation of this capacity; therefore, a correct knowledge that death is nothing to us prevents the mortal character of life from precluding enjoyment; and it does this not by presenting us with the perspective of an unlimited time, but by taking away the desire for immortality.'[15]

As one notes, Epicurus' reasoning is based on the very principle of his system, namely that the good is pleasure and that evil is suffering. Once this principle is rigorously admitted, the first consequence that Epicurus extracts from it follows logically. Not being[16] does not imply either pleasure or pain, and consequently, there is neither good nor evil for that which has ceased to exist. But Epicurus also extracts a second consequence from this principle, extending this reasoning to that which still exists: he speaks to the living as if they were already dead. When he tells us, 'death [in] itself is not an evil,' we could respond to him as Bayle does: 'It is enough to be deprived of the life I love so well.'[17] Taking Epicurus' argument to its ultimate consequences we would be led to maintain that it is useless to turn away from a precipice; for once one falls, one will no longer suffer, and when one has not fallen, one does not yet suffer. This is close to what Epicurus states in the following passage, full of Greek subtlety and that would have charmed Gorgias or Protagoras: 'When we are, death is not present, and when death is present, we are not. It is nothing, then, either to the living or to the dead, for with the living it is not and the dead exist no longer.'[18]

According to Epicurus, death is not an evil the moment when it arrives, rather it can only become an evil to the imagination that foresees it. 'Foolish, therefore, is the man who says that he fears death, not because when it [death] is present it will trouble him, but because it troubles him in the prospect of it; that which does not bring trouble when present can only affect [us], when still to come, by a vain opinion.'[19]

Our future, Lucretius adds, should not worry us any more than our past: Is it not a fact that nothingness precedes us? Don't we have death [before we have] life?[20] 'Can you see how past eternity, the one which was before we were born, is indifferent to us. It is the mirror in which nature shows us the future time that will be after our death. Is there anything dreadful in that? Anything sad? Is it not a state of tranquillity, stronger than that of sleep?'[21] In our days, this Epicurean argument has been reproduced by Schopenhauer. Like Epicurus, Schopenhauer attributes a great importance to the topic of death, because 'death is the true inspiring genius, or the muse[22] of philosophy'; or, yet further, according to him, if our fear of nothingness was reasonable, we would equally have to worry about the nothingness that has preceded our existence and the one that must succeed it. Because in both cases it is still nothingness. I am horrified about an infinitude *a parte post* which will be without me, but I find nothing horrifying about an infinitude *a parte ante* which had been without me.[23] The fear of death is, both for Schopenhauer and Epicurus, something which concerns the imagination rather than reason, and the philosopher must break free of it.

Thus, both what is 'beyond' and 'below'[24] life are equally closed to our fears and desires. We must divert our gaze from this new infinity that seemed to present itself to us, the infinity of time. The idea of a limitless duration, at least when we want to apply it to our life, is only a vain and hollow opinion, just as the idea of Necessity, or that of divine Caprice: Saturn should not trouble us any more than Jupiter or Destiny. Epicurus, when arguing that immortality is impossible, hastily concludes that it is not desirable.[25]

On this point, Epicurus' theory is remarkably analogous to the modern doctrine of [David Friedrich] Strauss, according to which immortality would be rather something to fear than something to desire. Strauss partially employs Epicurus' terms. 'He who is not swollen with pride,' he says, 'knows how to appreciate the humble measure of his faculties, and is grateful for the time given him to develop them, but does not aspire to an increase that would go beyond this earthly life; the perspective of eternity would frighten him.'[26] Büchner endorses the same opinion: according to him, humankind personified in the legend of Ahasuerus the instinctive fear that it experiences when faced with the idea of an immortal life.[27]

According to Epicurus, every desire that does not have its confirmation in nature itself should be suppressed. The desire for immortality (*ho tēs athanasias pothos*) must, then, disappear from within us, as should many others, such as the desire for wealth and honour: it is about this desire that one should say that it 'falls into the indefinite' (*eis apeiron ekpiptei*). The sage does not envy the alleged happiness of immortality any more than he envies the crowns given to the poets or the statues erected to the conquerors. 'He does not rely upon future things; he looks forward to them.'[28] He does not worry about the number of days that the unknown future reserves [to] him. 'We must remember that the future is neither wholly ours nor wholly not ours, so that neither must we count upon it as quite certain to come, nor despair of it as quite certain not to come.'[29]

However, in order to justify the desire for immortality and the fear of death from the perspective of Epicureanism, one could reply: If the good is pleasure, and if pleasure is shortened and interrupted by death, the good is then diminished; death, on the other hand, even if it is not an evil in the absolute sense of the word, is always a lesser good. It is, then, a legitimate object of aversion for the being who tends to the greatest good. Immortality, by contrast, and if one perceives it as the perpetuity of enjoyment, will be a legitimate object of desire.

It was, no doubt, in response to this kind of argument that Epicurus conceived one of his most original and most paradoxical doctrines.

According to this doctrine, not only can we be fully happy independently of the future, and independently of immortality, but immortality itself would not increase our happiness: happiness is a self-sufficient, complete whole. 'Epicurus denies that duration could add anything to the happiness of a life, and that a voluptuousness would be inferior if enjoyed in a brief span of time than if it were everlasting ... He places the sovereign good in pleasure, and yet he says that no greater pleasure would result from a lifetime of endless duration than from a limited and moderate period.'[30] What really matters with regards to enjoyment is not its duration, but rather its intensity. The truest enjoyment and the most perfect life (*pantelē bion*) exist for and by themselves, regardless of time. 'Unlimited time and limited time afford an equal amount of pleasure, if we measure the limits of that pleasure by reason.'[31] There is, therefore, a plenitude and an interior superabundance in enjoyment, which makes it independent of time as of all the rest: true pleasure carries infinity within itself. What does it matter if the life of the sage is limited? Considered in itself his life is as happy as divine and eternal life, and Epicurus can 'compete in happiness with Jupiter himself'.[32]

Epicurus' doctrine elevates happiness above time, condensing it somehow in a limited duration without subtracting from it any of its inestimable value. In our time, this doctrine was taken up by a contemporary German philosopher who, as Epicurus, denied personal immortality: we speak of Feuerbach. It is interesting to compare the arguments by which both Epicurus and Feuerbach seek to demonstrate that immortality is vain. 'Each instant,' the German philosopher writes, 'is a fulfilled and complete existence of an infinite importance, satisfied in itself, with an unlimited affirmation of its own reality.'[33] It is the same idea, translated into a metaphysical language, that Epicurus expresses when he says: 'Time, be it limited or unlimited, contains an equal pleasure.' Lucretius, as well, wrote: 'If the pleasures poured into your soul as in a bottomless vase were not drained and wasted in vain, why, as life's satiated guest, don't you leave it?'[34] Feuerbach adopts this image from Lucretius: 'Every moment is a drink that drains to the dregs the cup of immortality, the cup that, like the magic goblet of Oberon, always refills itself on its own.'[35]

Feuerbach's doctrine is based on a particular conception of time and eternity. Eternity would not consist of an infinite extension in duration, but it would rather be the infinite intensity of life; it could be found, then, concentrated somehow in every instant of existence. 'Eternity,' he says, 'is force, energy, action and victory.'[36] Instead of these metaphysical theories inspired by Hegel, Epicurus invokes a practical example. 'In the same way that the sage chooses his food not merely and simply the larger portion, but the more pleasant, so he seeks to live a life that is the most pleasant and not merely that which is longest.'[37] Feuerbach gives a more aesthetic example: 'The musical tones,' he says 'even if within time, are, because of their meaning, outside and above time. The sonata that they compose is also of short duration; one cannot play it eternally; but is it long or short? What would you say of the person who, while one plays it, would not listen to it, but count, taking its duration as the basis of his judgement, and, when the other listeners seek to express their admiration by precise words, would only find the following words to characterize it: it lasts a quarter of hour? Undoubtedly, to call him a *fool* would be too weak an adjective for this man. How, then, should we name those who believe that they can judge life by saying it is limited and transitory?'[38] By means of this comparison between life and a sonata, which is up to us to make sublime, whereas death is eternal silence, Feuerbach attacks, as does Epicurus, the religions and philosophies of his time that wish to reduce life to nothingness, and to make nothingness more desirable than life: 'That with which one says nothing, thinks nothing, determines nothing, is it anything different than nothingness? How could we name those who reduce the reality of life to nothing? They call themselves Christians, pious men, rationalists, and even philosophers; you can call them fools, insane, and affirm until your last breath the reality and the truth of this life.'

This supreme affirmation, as we will see, is that which Epicurus utters when dying.

III. – If we should not fear death, it does not follow, according to Epicurus, that we should desire it. One should not push his doctrine so far as to believe that its aim is to preach the disgust of life and the renunciation of existence. On the contrary, we know that death supresses the faculty of feeling; [we also know that] the senses are the condition of pleasure, and that pleasure is the only end of beings. Thus, a thing that is not a pleasure cannot be an end in itself. As Seneca says, Epicurus does not reproach any less those who aspire to die than to those who fear death.[39] 'The sage,' Epicurus writes, 'does not fear not living, and life is not a burden for him.'[40]

It is on this point that Epicurus is radically opposed to a famous philosopher of his time, Hegesias, whose doctrines recall those of our modern pessimists. Hegesias was Aristippus' indirect disciple, and his starting point and principles were analogous to those of Epicurus, namely that pleasure is the only good.[41] However, according to Hegesias, this good is rarely found in its plenitude. Frequently, following his argument, hope drags disappointment along with it, enjoyment produces satiety and disgust. In life the sum of misery and pain[42] is superior to that of pleasures, and nowhere happiness exists or is realizable: *anuparktos hē eudaimonia*.[43] To look for happiness, or even just pleasure, is something vain and contradictory, because we will always find a *surplus of misery*.[44] It is thus to that that we should strive, that is, to avoid pain; and for this there is only one means: to make oneself indifferent to pleasures and to what produces them,[45] to weaken sensibility and to annihilate one's desires. Indifference and renunciation are the only palliative for life. Even if amended in this way, life is not more desirable than death; those who are weary of life can then heal themselves [of it]; life is as worthy as a death, and death worth the same as life: *hē zōē kai ho thanatos hairetos*. Because of this, Hegesias was called *Pisithanate* or 'counsellor of death'. Many listeners[46] rushed to him, and his doctrine rapidly spread. At his call, convinced disciples took their own lives. King Ptolemy was struck by Hegesias' doctrine and, fearing that this disgust with life would become contagious, he closed down Hegesias' school and sent the master into exile.

Hegesias' doctrines remind us of the contemporary systems of Schopenhauer and his disciples.[47] Hegesias' doctrine occupies in relation to Epicureanism the same position that Schopenhauer's philosophy occupies in relation to the English utilitarian school. It is curious to note how, in two different epochs, two different schools, one claiming that pleasure is the goal of life and that this goal can be attained; the other, claiming that pleasure is, after all, the most positive goal of life, nevertheless claims that this goal is out of our reach, and that the wisest thing to do is to practise a sort of ascetic renunciation. Hegesias and Schopenhauer have a common point: both of them took inspiration from Indian ideas. Schopenhauer referred to himself as a modern Buddhist. Hegesias, on the other hand, has lived at a time when Asia and Europe were put in relation by the conquests of Alexander. The gymnosophists had amazed the Greek army; Calanus voluntarily set himself on fire in front of the assembled soldiers, like Hercules, this god of the Greeks, and while dying he uttered prophetic words. Undoubtedly, the old beliefs of the Orient, when placed in contact with the Greek *genie*, acquired a new strength, and a sort of fermentation had begun in the minds, which would make itself felt in the philosophical schools. Hegesias' doctrine was perhaps a sort of synthesis, and probably an unconscious one, between Buddhist and Cyrenaic ideas.

In any case, Epicurus protests against this doctrine with great energy. In this protest, one could see Bentham or one of his disciples responding to the modern pessimists. 'What an insanity,' he wrote, 'to run towards death by disgust of life, when in fact it is your way of life[48] that forces you to envy death!'[49] And elsewhere: 'What can be more ridiculous than to invoke death when it is the fear of death that poisons our life!'[50] Finally, he wrote to Menoeceus: 'The worst (among our adversaries) is he who repeats the verses of the poet: – The first good would be not to have been born at all; the second, to traverse the gates of Hell as quickly as possible.[51] – If he is convinced of what he says, why then doesn't he leave this life for good? For that is always possible, if he is firm and resolute after reflection. But if he speaks out of mockery, then he jokes about things that are not the object of jokes.'[52] One will find this *ad hominem* argument a little inconclusive. It is not, however, that easy to respond to it. Let us add that a better critique of pessimistic doctrines can be extracted from the very core of the Epicurean system: according to Epicurus, when life does not encounter exterior obstacles and trouble, it is always, in itself, enjoyment: pleasure is thus conceived as constituting the core of existence's weft. Trouble [or pain][53] is but a momentary suspension of this state of well-being, a transitory agitation after which everything returns to rest. Life is a deep source from which pleasure stems continuously: to live ultimately means to be happy, and these two things are one for the Epicurean sage. If an unexpected misfortune arises, or an incurable disease, or anything in relation to which our will feels impotent; if, by a rare exception nature reserves to us a surplus of trouble and pain over pleasure, then there is always for us a way not to be unhappy: it is the moment to employ the heroic remedy advocated by Hegesias, and to know how to die. To die is sometimes *useful*. Not of course because death would be a sort of good in itself; but we know that it is not in itself an evil. On the other hand, we also know that life can become an evil under certain circumstances: it is thus evident that when faced with this choice between unhappiness and nothingness the latter is preferable. Similarly, we sometimes prefer suffering with the aim of achieving the [higher] pleasure it will produce: suffering, although bad in itself, becomes thus a relative good. Even more so death, which is not an evil in itself, can become a good when it suppresses a sum of evils which is superior to the total sum of goods: 'It is an evil to live in deprivation; however, to live in deprivation is by no means a necessity.'[54] – 'If pains are tolerable, let us endure them; if they are not, let our soul, like in theatre, leave the stage of this life that no longer pleases us.'[55] This withdrawal must not be premature, but rather the result of reasoning and reflection: the sage knows how to assess the pros and cons of this choice. Furthermore, Epicurus has considered in advance the several infirmities that could befall him and has traced a [plan of] conduct for each case. If, for example, the philosopher becomes blind, he will nevertheless continue to live with no regrets; this is because the privation of sight does not imply a positive form of suffering, all pleasure can arise through the other senses; besides has not the sage always, in Lucretius' words, the inner light of his thought? This thought, always serene, knows how to preserve its tranquillity in the face of death, and can nevertheless make use of it, only as long as with firm determination and reflection, as a means for happiness. The Epicurean, like the Christian, but with a very different goal, has death under his eyes and prepares himself for it, anticipating it in thought. 'Which way is better,' asks Epicurus, 'that death comes our way or that we ourselves go in its encounter?'[56] And Seneca, when commenting on these words, adds: 'To think of death is to think of freedom ... A single chain holds us back, and that is the love of life ... Without entirely breaking this chain, one must loosen it to such an extent that, at our call, it will not be an obstacle or a barrier that prevents us from doing right now what we will must do sooner or later.'[57]

As we know, Epicurus had given both the precept and the example of 'ataraxia' in the face of death: in his painful sickness (he had kidney stones) he displayed a courage that the Stoics themselves exhorted us to imitate. Marcus Aurelius wrote in his *Meditations*, telling himself: 'Imitate Epicurus. Epicurus says: When I was sick, I would not speak with anyone of the sufferings of my body; never, he says, have I mentioned it to those who came to visit me. Rather, with them I always discussed my habitual subject, the nature of things; I tried to understand how thought, although in communication with these sorts of movement that affect the body, can be immune to trouble, dwelling in the enjoyment which belongs to it. Moreover, he says, I did not give others the chance to become proud on the basis of the idea of the importance of their help. Even then, my life was happy and tranquil. Imitate therefore Epicurus.'[58]

Epicurus' final letter has been preserved for us. It reads: 'Epicurus to Hermarchus, greeting. I write you these words having had a happy day, which will also be the last; nothing could increase the intensity of the suffering I experience; however, in face of all these pains of the body, I have disposed and brandished (*antiparetatteto*)[59] the joy of the mind which came from the memory of my inventions. To give a new sign of the devotion which from your youth up you have displayed towards myself and towards philosophy, [I charge you] to protect the children of Metrodorus.'[60] – One knows that Metrodorus, Epicurus' inseparable friend, had died before him: Epicurus' last thought was for this friendship.

As one notes, Epicurus wanted to be happy until the end: he possessed an obstinacy of happiness as others possess an obstinacy of virtue or science. This obstinacy also has its nobility; there is something grand in this perseverance to triumph over pain [and sorrow],[61] on this supreme call on the past to compensate present pain, in this desperate affirmation of happiness of life in the face of death. It is not always easy to persuade oneself that one is happy; for that, an unshakable willpower is required. And since to persuade oneself that one is happy is to a great extent the same as being happy, Epicurus could by himself make real this utopia of happiness which he dreamed of for the sage. Like Socrates, he died smiling; the difference is that Socrates nourished the beautiful hope of immortality and, turning his eyes away from life, he saw in death only a form of healing. Epicurus, by contrast, died with his face turned to this existence that he left, condensing his entire life in his memory to oppose it to the death that approached him; in his thought, he saw the depiction of a last image of his past which was about to disappear; he contemplated it 'with gratitude', with no regrets and no hope; then everything suddenly disappeared at the same time: past, present and future – and he finally rested in eternal annihilation.

IV. – We will not fully appreciate the doctrine that Epicurus teaches through his deeds and words. We shall only aim to summarize in a few words what in our view constitutes its historical value and originality.

It is easy not to fear death when one believes in a blissful immortality. In this regard, the courage of the first Christians, for example, is not surprising. Every religion has its martyrs, and one has equally shed blood for errors and for truth: the contempt for death inspired by a religion is no doubt an appropriate marker for measuring the degree of faith that this religion inspired among its adherents, but not its degree of truth. On the contrary, to preserve man's independence and courage in the face of death, while at the same time discarding every superstition, is indeed a fully original enterprise, and one that Epicurus has not entirely failed to accomplish. As La Rochefoucauld said, 'Neither sun nor death can be looked at with a steady eye.' But Epicurus did look at death with a steady eye, without fear and without hope; and he attempted to show that he could limit life without troubling it.

Epicurus' theory of death has not always been [well] understood, and a certain number of objections that one can address to it, never actually reached it. 'Death in itself is not [an] unfortunate [event],' Lactantius said, challenging Epicurus, 'it is the access to death that is unfortunate.'[62] Bayle, in his subtle articles on Epicurus and Lucretius, remarks: 'The Epicureans cannot deny that death arrives when a man is still able to feel. It is thus something that concerns man, and from the fact that the separate parts no longer feel, they [i.e. the Epicureans] have wrongly inferred that the accident that separates these parts is not felt by the man who dies.'[63] In these objections, one seems to mistake death itself, that state of he who no longer lives, for what popular language calls 'an unfortunate quarter of hour'. One must, however, clearly distinguish these ideas. For many, death is but a painful operation, before which one retreats with the same fear as when faced with a chirurgical operation. In this case, it is mistaken to say that one fears death; for it is not death but pain that one fears. One simply lacks courage. Now, no philosophy, and Epicurus' doctrine no less than others, can give someone that very practical virtue of courage. The suffering that usually accompanies death is a fact that Epicurus did not wish to deny, and this fact is considered in his philosophy like every other [fact]. According to him, the final pain is susceptible of the same forms of alleviation as all the others; it only demands the deployment of courage. Once one has suffered the pain, a new period will open up for us: complete insensibility, the annihilation that, according to Epicurus, is not be feared, neither by the courageous nor by the pusillanimous man, nor by any sensuous being whatsoever. From the perspective of sensibility, death is not an evil, since it is the extinction of sensibility itself; from the point of view of intelligence, it is also not an evil, since it is part of the logic of nature. Existence is, for Epicurus, a whole that one must accept in the way it is, in its relative perfection; it is a work of art, a sort of poem which one embellishes by extending. 'The sage,' Epicurus says, 'does not compose poems, he lives them.'[64] The diverse parts of his life are in harmony with each other and mutually presuppose one another: youth tends towards adulthood, and the latter towards old age; old age leans forwards towards death. One cannot straighten out life, which is completely inclined towards its end: it is better to die with grace in order to die with pleasure. According to Lucretius, present beings must pass life on to their successors, and this torch must pass from hand to hand, so that its flame can shine with all its radiance; blood must never stop flowing: it must eternally circulate in the veins of great Nature. The Epicurean, not being able to do otherwise, will then be resigned to death, whose necessity he understands. He will submit to it as one must submit to all acts imposed by nature: his death will display the tranquillity of that which is inevitable.

From the point of view of the doctrine of pleasure pure and simple, Epicurus' theory is highly consistent. The Epicurean can peacefully view death simply because he does not put life at the service of a superior ideal. Since the pleasure that life can give him is limited in quantity, he can empty this life as a goblet, becoming weary of it as he enjoys it, becoming disgusted with it when he exhausts all its sensations. For those who seek only pleasure and interest in life, death would not be as much of an evil as it is to those who seek to accomplish a disinterested work. Among all primitive nations, in which people often only think and care about enjoying[65] life, for whom pleasure is the supreme good, where eating and drinking are the sweetest things [in life], one has little or no fear of death; one gladly offers oneself to it, without worry. Life appears as an entertaining game, without anything serious or grave about it; nothing about it weighs upon your spirit and paralyses you, nothing about it is sacred or respectable.

Similarly, childhood is the age in life when one attributes the highest importance to pleasure and pain, when disinterestedness does not last long, when it is difficult to devote oneself to something for long; when it is first of all necessary to nourish oneself, to move, in a word, to live: the child is naturally an Epicurean. Now, children experience fear as everyone else, and perhaps even more, the 'bad fifteen minutes';[66] however, for those who are not afraid of brief suffering, death itself is not dreadful. That is perhaps what explains the relative frequency of suicides among children, although their scope of reasons for taking their own lives is narrower than that of adults; – statisticians and moralists[67] are indeed astonished by this frequency.

Life, in most cases, has a very different importance for the adult person. Rightly or wrongly, the adult seeks in life something other than present or even future pleasure.

There are few strongly persuaded Epicureans. Every man, even the humblest, posits a goal in life; and this goal, in itself more or less humble, suffices to arouse in him a courageous energy that takes him beyond the obstacles of existence. This same virile determined energy, this will to win, recedes in front of death as before an invincible obstacle. Every human life originally attaches itself to a work,[68] which it seeks to accomplish and to perfect, and it is because of this work that it fears death. This one lives and works for his family, the other for an idea. People dedicate themselves to ideas more frequently than one thinks. One finds them everywhere, in all classes; what is really rare are those who work for the right idea. And nonetheless this idea, whatever it may be, explains the whole existence of the person who conceived it. Let us add that our very life is a sort of superior work, which one wants to make complete and beautiful. Our past efforts engage us; we do not want them to be in vain. The adult is not like the child, who only faces the future and can diminish its importance. On the contrary, the adult has a whole past upon which he must count, and that drives him forwards.

To explain the fear of death, Pascal stressed: 'One dies alone.' That is not completely accurate: only the fully persuaded Epicurean could die alone; every man carries with him a great memory of affections, a whole world of impersonal thoughts and generous desires, which he cannot decide to simply abandon; this is what constitutes his strength in life, his sadness before death. If one were in a state of complete moral solitude, one would die happily, as did our ancestors the Gauls. The more one is courageous and strong, the less one fears the suffering which accompanies death. Nevertheless, one can still fear death itself, which does not reach you alone, but annihilates the will that aims for the best, and the work you have begun. The grandeur of 'art' makes us think, as did the old Hippocrates, about the brevity of life. When life is conceived as a persevering effort, as a struggle to attain the good and the beautiful, then this struggle can only be meaningful if it has triumph as its goal; now, death comes to abruptly prevent this goal from being realized. Nothing can be more disheartening than to die in a defeat, or when the outcome of the combat is still uncertain. By contrast, soldiers die happily when they see that victory is theirs: they then say that they have not lost their lives in giving it.[69]

Those for whom life is but a game and an amusement can, without contradiction, see it come to an end without grief. One cannot eternally amuse oneself. If one only lives superficially, one gets tired of it; if one lives life in its depths, one becomes attached to it. As for the Epicurean, he does not become attached in this way.

By a natural law every prolonged pleasure is followed by disgust. Lucretius makes Nature tell the man who is afflicted by the thought of death: 'Do you think that I would invent yet another new pleasure for you? There is nothing else. Everything is always the same.'[70] This ultimate monotony of existence is a new reason that justifies the Epicurean indifference towards death.

Generally speaking, one could say that in nature every being whose life has no other end than enjoyment is necessarily destined to die; every being that has itself as its sole centre of thought and will is destined to see this centre being displaced one day – then, its will and thought will be meaningless and will be reduced to nothing. Those who only exist for themselves cannot exist forever, or nature would be halted in its evolution. Only disinterestedness, supposing that it is possible, could make immortality possible.

If, on the contrary, the human being has no other end than his own pleasure, following Epicurus' thought, then he is destined to annihilation, and he can only come to terms with this fact as a consequence and condition of his present life. This very life, as Lucretius says, is a sort of continuous death; one sees oneself dying at each instant, in seeing a pleasure and an enjoyment dying at every instant. Sleep, which necessarily interrupts the series of pleasures, amounts to death writ small. Death is then an integral part of life, such as it is conceived by the Epicureans; it is a habitual thing, which has nothing dreadful beyond what we project onto it. From the perspective of intelligence, death is rational and even useful; for sensibility, it is nothing.

In short, there are two different forms that fear of death can assume, which Epicurus has not distinguished: a childish and lazy fear, in which imagination plays the key role; and an intellectual and virile fear, in which reason plays the main role, and which is in reality more the disinterested horror[71] of death than a real fear. Epicurus has shown the vanity of the first, but not of the second. Surely, one must not return to the ancient religion overthrown by Epicureanism, and one must instead banish from the idea of death everything dreadful that the imagination of the first peoples attributed to it. The underworld is a conception which derives from this life; as Lucretius remarks, it is down here that we find Tantalus and Sisyphus.[72] We must not forge chimeras and populate the future with the evils of the present. Fearing to be punished by an exterior power is childish; demanding a reward like a mercenary is not a dignified thing; but, on the other hand, one can ask not to perish, one can desire, without counting on it becoming a reality, an existence that would be a progress in relation to this one; one could think that death is a step forwards rather than a sudden interruption in the development of being. One can hope not to lose, as in a shipwreck, all the interior wealth one has gathered, but to traverse death taking with oneself the world of generous thoughts and will that one has created in oneself. Here, the path to metaphysical hypotheses and utopias remains open. From the viewpoint of Epicureanism, hope is a form of consolation that one must not suppress. Had Epicurus lived in our day, when the idea of immortality tends to become more cheerful and *celestial*, perhaps he would not have attacked it as openly as he did; perhaps he would prostrate himself before it just as he did in the temples of the gods. This belief is a source of happiness that one must not disdain. As for those who do not agree with all the Epicurean ideas, they will always be led, despite Epicurus' idea, to place some ulterior thought of hope beyond death. Those who are disinterested, or who believe themselves to be so, have more reasons to trust in nature's justice; the *I* that has sufficiently enlarged itself would have the right not to perish.[73]

Notes

1. Diogenes Laertius, *Lives of Eminent Philosophers*, X, 125: *Outhen gar estin en tō zēn deinon tō kateilēphoti gnēsiōs to mēden huparchein en tō mē zēn deinon* (translated in the text).
2. T.N. See, for example, Plato's *Apology* 40d, where Socrates advances the hypothesis of death as a 'dreamless sleep'. See also Plato's *Phaedo* 71c.
3. Lucretius, *On the Nature of Things*, III, 890.
4. Lucretius, *On the Nature of Things*, III, 890 – This formula, used in Greek and Roman funerals, 'May the earth be light upon you,' originally did not have anything metaphorical about it. It expressed a widespread feeling among a great number of peoples, and which is found in all its naivety in savage tribes. The Guaranis, for example, are careful to see that the earth does not weight too heavily upon the dead; the Amerindians of Peru unearthed their dead parents, whom the Spanish had buried in their churchyards, claiming that they would suffer from being in the crowded space beneath the flagstones. Among the Tupis, with a completely different intention, and graceless towards the dead, one tightly ties the limbs of the dead in order to prevent them from escaping their tomb and tormenting the living. The women of Matiamba throw the body of their dead husbands in the water, so as to submerge their soul and liberate them from all jealousy. The Abyssinians abandon their criminals to wild beasts, in order to annihilate them both in this life and in the next. The Chinese attach such great importance to being buried in their homeland in order to be able to wake up there one day that, if they happen to migrate to California, it is with the condition that their dead bodies will be returned to their Celestial Empire. Mr [Herbert] Spencer, in his *Principles of Sociology* [London: Williams and Norgate, 1876, three volumes], mentions the Inca Atahualpa who, when sentenced to death, has agreed to become a Christian, in order to be hanged instead of dying at the stake, for he believed that, if he was burned to death, he would no longer have the possibility of resurrection. In our own days, in 1874, Lincoln's bishop – reasoning, as Spencer remarks, just like the Amerindian warrior – preached against cremation, which tends, according to him, to weaken human faith in resurrection.
5. See Fustel de Coulanges, *La Cité antique* [*étude sur le culte, le droit, les institutions de la Grèce et de Rome*, Paris: Durand, 1864; English translation by Willard Small: *The Ancient City: A Study on the Religion, Laws and Institutions of Greece and Rome*, Boston: Lee & Shepard, 1877] – Still today, in certain places in Germany, one goes to sleep early in All Saint's Eve, leaving dinner served for the poor souls on the table.

6   T.N. Guyau uses the expression 'primitive peoples'.
7   One should recall, on this topic, Ulysses' descent to the underworld in the *Odyssey*. The underworld is a dark, low and cold place; the dead crave sunlight, and sadly think about those who live on the earth above their heads and are happily able to contemplate it. But not only the culprits, the lazy and cowards are condemned to darkness and suffering; the 'good and brave' have a similar fate; there is not much difference between them. The conception of the Elysian Fields is posterior and relatively recent. Upon all men the imagination of ancient and primitive peoples extends the shadows of the tomb; even when the dead sometimes return and ascend to the surface of the earth, haunting the dwelling place of the living, it is at night, in dark hours – a darkness similar to that of the underworld.
8   Plautus, *Captivi* [*The Captives*], V, 4, i.
9   Plutarch, *De superstitione* [*On Superstition*], 4.
10 T.N. *d'ici-bas*.
11 Plutarch, *On Superstition*, 31. Philosophers thought of comforting those who had lost someone dear, by teaching them that there is no future life and that consequently the mourned person enjoyed an eternal rest (Martha, *Le poème de Lucrèce* [*morale, religion et science*, Paris: Librairie Hachette, 1869]). In Rome, in Seneca's time, a young man died; because of the purity of his mores, he merited joining, still a child, a collegiate of priests. Seneca wrote to his mother, Marcia, consoling her: 'Think that there are no ills to be suffered after death by the one you lost; these beliefs that render the underworld terrible to us are mere fables; no darkness threatens the dead, no prisons, no blazing streams of fire, no river of oblivion, no judgement court, nor accused; and in this new freedom so unfettered there are no new tyrants. All these things are the fancies of the poets, who have terrifed us with groundless terrors ... a great and everlasting peace has welcomed your son' (Seneca, *De consolatione ad Marciam*, 19, V). If we replace Seneca's thought by one of a contemporary philosopher, and Marcia by the pious mourning mother of a young priest of our days, these words become very strange. Generally, it is precisely to these priests and faithful believers that a religion promises the highest destiny after death. Pagan religion, however, promised so little to its followers that in comparison the complete annihilation could appear preferable.
12 Lucretius, *On the Nature of Things*, III, 31.
13 Alexander Bain, *The Emotions and the Will* [London: John W. Parker and Son, West Strand, 1859, p. 86]. [T.N. In order to preserve Guyau's interpretation of the passage I have translated Guyau's translation of the English original. Guyau's quote is not a literal translation, but rather a paraphrase of Bain's original, presenting important differences, which I believe are important to preserve in order to understand Guyau's reading and interpretation of Bain's passage. This is how the original 1859 English edition reads: 'The Fear of Death is naturally the crowning manifestation of the feeling under discussion. Still the aspect of the last enemy is so exceedingly different in different circumstances, that the sentiment produced has little of a common character. The one fact of the situation is the unknown future that the being is ushered into. The loss of life's pleasures, interests, and relationships is felt according to the value set upon these; the darkness of the shadow of death is essentially calculated to strike terror. That is the deepest midnight gloom that the human imagination can figure itself; and from that quarter emanate the direct forms of apprehension and dread.']
14 Epicurus *apud* Dioegenes Laertius [*Lives of Eminent Philosophers*, X, 139], Second Maxim: *Ho thanatos ouden pros hēmas; to gar dialuthen, anaisthētei; to de anaisthētoun, ouden pros hēmas* (translated in the text above).

15 Dioegenes Laertius, *Lives of Eminent Philosophers*, X, 139. – In the fragments preserved by Diogenes Laertius, Epicurus does not formulate arguments against the immortality of the soul. Lucretius, however, gave us a remarkable summary of the Epicurean argumentation. According to the Epicureans, experience shows that body and soul have a parallel and solidary existence; they are born, develop and grow old together, and they must die at the same time; every cause acting upon one also acts upon the other; sickness, delirium, lethargy, drunkenness are all felt both in soul and body: 'For all substance that can be troubled and altered will necessarily be destroyed and is deprived of immortality if it is exposed to the action of a superior cause' (Lucretius, *On the Nature of Things*, III, 483). The life of the soul, like that of the body, depends solely upon the degree of [the action of] destructive forces; when the latter prevail, death takes place.

16 T.N. *ne pas être*.

17 T.N. Guyau refers to Bayle's *Historical and Critical Dictionary* [second edition, volume 3, 1776, entry on Lucretius, p. 927]: 'The love of life is deeply rooted in the heart of man; and this is a sign that it is considered as a very great good: from whence it follows, that death is feared as a very great evil, merely for robbing us of this good. What signifies it, against this fear, to say, *You will feel nothing after you are dead? Will you not quickly be answered, It is enough to be deprived of a life I love so well; and if the union of my body and soul is a state which belongs to me, and which I passionately desire to preserve, it cannot be pretended, that death, which breaks this union, is a thing which does not concern me*. Let us conclude, that Epicurus and Lucretius' argument was not just, and could only be conclusive against the fear of pain in another world.'

18 Diogenes Laertius, *Lives of Eminent Philosophers*, X, 125: *Oute oun pros tous zōntas estin, oute pros tous teteleutēkotas* (translated above [T.N. I have followed Hicks' translation]).

19 Diogenes Laertius, *Lives of Eminent Philosophers*, X, 125: *Ho paron ouk enochlei, prosdokōmenon kenōs lupei* (translated above).

20 T.N. This argument echoes Plato's 'cyclical argument' in the *Phaedo* (70d–72d).

21 Lucretius, *On the Nature of Things*, III, 985.

22 T.N. French *Musagète*, which could actually refer to *Apollon musagète*, or Apollo, 'leader of the muses'.

23 Arthur Schopenhauer, *Die Welt als Wille* [*und Vorstellung*], volume 2, chapter 41; volume 1, book 1, §4 [*The World as Will and Representation*, volume 1, translated by Judith Norman, Alistair Welchman and Christopher Janaway, Cambridge: Cambridge University Press, 2010; volume 2, 2018]. Lucretius and Schopenhauer's argument is clearly sophistry, since infinite 'nothing' only terrifies us to the extent that it interrupts our existence and arrests the impetus of our will. Now, one thing is the 'nothing' that precedes our birth and leads to our existence; a completely different things is the 'nothing' that comes to suddenly suspend our existence. One finds consolation more easily in the fact of not having always possessed a good than in being doomed to lose it.

24 T.N. *l'au delà* and *l'en deçà*.

25 Diogenes Laertius, *Lives of Eminent Philosophers*, X, 124: . . . *Ouk apeiron prostitheisa chronon, alla ton tēs athanasias aphelomenē pothon* ['without adding to it an infinite time but subtracting from it the thirst for immortality'].

26 David Friedrich Strauss, *The Old Faith and the New: A Confession* [translated by Mathilde Blind, second edition, London: Asher & Co., 1873, p. 149]: 'He who does not inflate himself is well aware of the humble measure of his capacities, and while grateful for the time allowed him for their development, makes no claim for its prolongation

beyond the duration of this earthly life; nay, its eternal persistence would fill him with dismay.'

27   Bentham has expressed analogous ideas in his book *The Influence of Natural Religion on the Temporal Happiness of Mankind* [Amherst: Prometheus Books, 2003; Bentham originally published this book under the pseudonym of Philippe Beauchamp (London: R. Carlile, 1822)].

28   Cicero, *De finibus*, I, xix, 62: '*Neque pendet ex futuris, sed exspectat illa*' (translated above).

29   Diogenes Laertius, *Lives of Eminent Philosophers*, X, 129: *To mellon, oute hēmeteron oute pantōs ouch hēmeteron* [T.N. I have used Hicks' translation, where the passage appears under X, 127].

30   Cicero, *De finibus*, II, xxvii, 87–8: '*At enim negat Epicurus ne diuturnitatem quidem temporis ad beatè vivendum aliquid afferre, nec minorem voluptatem percipi in brevitate temporis, quàm si illa sit sempiterna . . . Quum enim summum bonum in voluptate ponat, negat infinito tempore aetatis voluptatem fieri majorem quàm finite atque modico*' (translated above). See also *De finibus*, I, xix, 63.

31   Diogenes Laertius, *Lives of Eminent Philosophers*, X, 45: *Ho apeiros chronos isēn echei tēn hēdonē kai ho peperasmenos, ean tis autēs ta perata katametrēse tō logismō* (translated above) [the passage is actually X, 145].

32   [See] Stobaeus, *Florilegium*.

33   T.N. Guyau does not provide references. His version seems to be a paraphrase rather than an actual quote: 'Every moment of life is fulfilled being, is of infinite significance, exists for its own sake, is posited by itself, is self-satisfied, complete, and saturated plenitude of reality, is unrestricted self-affirmation' (Feuerbach, *Thoughts on Death and Immortality*, translated by James A. Massey, Berkeley & Los Angeles: University of California Press, 1980, p.171).

34   Lucretius, *On the Nature of Things*, III, 930 & ff.: '*Nam si grata fuit vita anteacta priorque, / Et non omnia, pertusum congesta quasi in vas, / Commoda perfluxere atque ingrata interiere, / Cur non, ut plenus vitae conviva recedes, / Aequo animoque capis securam, stulte, quietem?*' (translated above. Guyau does not translate the last verse quoted: 'And why, foolish man, not resting calmly, with a tranquil soul?').

35   T.N. Here, again, Guyau does not provide the reference for his quote: Feuerbach, *Thoughts on Death and Immortality*, 171.

36   T.N. I have decided to stay close to Guyau's French translation of Feuerbach by rendering the French *force* as the English 'force'. The English translation by James Massey reads: 'Eternity is power, energy, active deed and triumphant victory' (*Thoughts on Death and Immortality*, 172).

37   Diogenes Laertius, *Lives of Eminent Philosophers*, X, 126: *Houtō kai chronon ou ton mēkiston, alla hēdiston karpizetai* (translated above in the text).

38   T.N. Guyau's does not provide the reference here. In Massey's translation (Feuerbach, *Thoughts on Death and Immortality*, 172): 'The tone is tone only because it is the negation of passing away in passing away, only because it is not merely temporal but, in its temporality, is determinate, meaningful, time-negating tone. Indeed, the tone is short or long. But is it nothing more than its length? This sonata, in which the individual tones are short or long, passes away; it will not be played for all eternity. But, I ask you, what would you call someone who, while the sonata was being performed, did not listen, but only counted, who separated the length of the tone from its content, who, in this separation, took the temporality to be his object, and, when the sonata was over, made the fifteen minutes that it took to be played into the predicate of his

judgement concerning the sonata, and, who, while other people, overcome with admiration at its content, sought to catch its significance in exact words, characterised the sonata as a quarter-hour sonata? Wouldn't you assuredly find the predicate *fool* too affirmative to define such a person? Then how should one call those who take transitoriness to be a predicate of this life, who believe that they say something, that they pass a judgement on this life, when they say that it is temporal, it is transitory?'

39 Seneca, *Epistles*, 24, 22: '*Objurgat Epicurus non minus eos, qui mortem concupiscunt, quam eos qui timent*' ['Epicurus upbraids those who crave, as much as those who shrink from, death'].
40 Diogenes Laertius, *Lives of Eminent Philosophers*, X, 126: *Oute phobeitai to mē zēn; oute gar auto prosistatai to zēn* (translated above).
41 Diogenes Laertius, *Lives of Eminent Philosophers*, II, viii, 93.
42 T.N. *peines*.
43 Diogenes Laertius, *Lives of Eminent Philosophers*, II, viii, 94.
44 T.N. Or a surplus of pain, *peines*.
45 Diogenes Laertius, *Lives of Eminent Philosophers*, II, viii, 96.
46 T.N. *auditeurs*.
47 T.N. Could Guyau be referring to Nietzsche's *Birth of Tragedy*? *The Ethics of Epicurus* is from 1874 and *The Birth of Tragedy* is from 1872, so that could be the case – at least from a merely chronological point of view. Fouillé, however, claims that Guyau did not know Nietzsche's work. See Alfred Fouillée, 'The Ethics of Nietzsche and Guyau', *International Journal of Ethics*, 13, 1, 1902, 13–27.
48 T.N. *genre de vie*.
49 Epicurus *apud* Seneca, *Epistles*, XXIV ['Despising Death'].
50 Ibid. – Lucretius develops his master's thought (*On the Nature of Things*, III, 79 & ff.): '*Et saepe usque adeo, mortis formidine, vitae / Percipit humanos odium lucisque videndae, / Ut sibi consciscant moerenti pectore lethum, / Obliti fontem curarum hunc esse timorem*' ['And suddenly such is the hatred towards life and to the sight of light / That one develops because of the fear of death / That one chooses death with a sorrowing heart, / Forgetting that this very fear is the actual source of their worries'].
51 T.N. We read here the wisdom of Silenus, which Nietzsche mentions in his *Birth of Tragedy* (§3), quoting Sophocles' *Oedipus at Colonus* (1224 & ff.). See Friedrich Nietzsche, *The Birth of Tragedy & The Case of Wagner*, translated by Walter Kaufmann, New York: Vintage Books/Random House, 1967, 42.
52 Diogenes Laertius, *Lives of Eminent Philosophers*, II, 92: *Ei de mōkōmenos, mataios en tois ouk epidechomenois* (translated above).
53 T.N. *peine*.
54 Epicurus *apud* Seneca, *Epistles*, XII, 10: '*Malum est in necessitate vivere; sed in necessitate vivere, necessitas nulla est*' (translated above).
55 Cicero, *De finibus*, I, xv, 49: '*Si tolerabiles sint dolores, feramus; sin minus, aequo animo e vitâ, quum ea non placet, tanquam e theatro, exeamus*' (translated above).
56 T.N. Guyau provides no reference for this quote.
57 Epicurus *apud* Seneca, *Epistles*, XII.
58 Marcus Aurelius, *Meditations*, IX, 41.
59 T.N. Terence Irwin, in his *The Development of Ethics* (volume 1, Oxford: Oxford University Press, 2007, 273), translates *antiparetatteto* as 'was set up against' (see note 50).
60 Diogenes Laertius, *Lives of Eminent Philosophers*, X, 122 [T.N. In Diogenes Laertius, this letter appears not as addressed to Hermarchus, but to Idomeneus (X, 22)] – See Cicero, *De finibus*, XXX, 96 [in Cicero, the letter is addressed to Hermarchus].

61 T.N. Here, again, the French is *peine*.
62 Lactantius, *Institutiones Divinae*, III, 17.
63 Bayle, *Historical and Critical Dictionary*, 'Lucretius'.
64 *Poiēmata energein, ouk an poiēsai* (translated in the text above).
65 T.N. *jouir*.
66 T.N. *le 'mauvais quart-d'heure'*, a painful but brief experience.
67 T.N. The term 'moralists' here preserves the French root; however, in this case, it could sound ambiguous given the historical connotation of *moralistes* in the French context; one should think of the ethicist or the scholar of morality.
68 T.N. *œuvre*.
69 T.N. *perdre leur vie en la donnant*.
70 Lucretius, *On the Nature of Things*, III, 944 & ff.
71 T.N. *horreur desintéréssée*
72 Lucretius, *On the Nature of Things*, III, 1058.
73 T.N. Here, Guyau is referring to a process by which one goes beyond oneself through disinterestedness.

Book Three

Private and Public Virtues

1

Courage and Temperance. Love and Friendship. The Genesis of Friendship. The Conduct of the Sage in Human Society

That virtues, according to Epicurus, are simply practical means to attain the human ideal, namely happiness in serenity and freedom.

I. Private virtues. – *Courage* is related to foresight[1] and resignation. – *Temperance*. – That this virtue is the core of Epicureanism and all utilitarian ethics.
II. Social virtues. – Epicurean theory of *love*. – Its conformity to ancient ideas. – Its analogies with Stoicism and Christianity. – *Friendship*. – Its practical utility according to Epicurus. – The new pleasure that is born from friendship itself. – Genesis of friendship for Epicurus: how we can come to love our friends *as* we love ourselves. – Comparison of a page by Cicero and one by Bentham. – On the predominant role that friendship acquires in the Epicurean system. – Why Epicurean virtue is fundamentally sociable. – Ultimate insufficiency of Epicurus' theory of friendship. – How this theory is transformed by his successors, by means of an evolution that is often not well understood. – 1. Friendship founded in a mutual pact. – 2. Friendship founded on habit. – New genesis of friendship, which recalls the complex analyses of John Stuart Mill and Alexander Bain.
III. The conduct of the Epicurean in relation to free men and slaves. – Epicurean amiability.[2] – Disdain of honours, political abstention. – Disdain of riches combined with the care for a certain comfort.[3] – Epicurus' coin [*as*]. – Must the sage beg?

We have analysed Epicurus' conception of happiness as a whole. We have followed the movement that gradually elevates Epicurus' [thinking] from the pleasures of the stomach towards the serenity of spirt, and the self-conscious freedom that affirms itself even in face of death. After having thus reconstructed the Epicurean ideal, we still need to look for the means by which the human being can partially realize this ideal in practice. Whatever these means may be, if they are efficacious, they will be legitimate: as we know, to be happy is in and by itself to be virtuous. Would Epicurean virtue, which is [nothing but] an effect of and means to attain happiness, be at odds with the common [conception of] virtue, which is typically considered as an end in itself? Could interest and duty coincide in our conduct? This is the new problem that is now posed [to us]. We now approach the practical part of the Epicurean doctrine, which is not any less interesting than its theoretical part. In order to defend his system until the end Epicurus will have recourse to a peculiar theory of human society that can appear decidedly modern.

I. – Let us first analyse the private virtues, which are to a certain extent the principle of all the others.

The main virtue that antiquity admitted, and the virtue to which all the others referred, is courage. Now, courage resonates with the Epicurean doctrine and, in a certain sense, constitutes it. For what is courage if not the absence of trouble in face of life's events? And what is the absence of trouble, [what is] ataraxia, if not the very ground of happiness and the goal which the Epicurean doctrine pursues? No one could be more courageous than the sage because no one would be less vulnerable to the objects of fear than him. If we believe Epicurus, there would be no fear within the sage because there would be no dangers for him. After all what could he fear? Death? He does not think of it as an evil. Suffering? He is able to make all suffering vain [and needless]. Moreover, the Epicurean will not assume the theatrical pose that the Stoic assumes when facing suffering. In torture he will be allowed to shout and cry with no shame.[4] However, from this one should not conclude that he is afraid. Other men cannot disturb the calm of the Epicurean any more than the bolts of lightning of Jupiter or the nails of destiny: if they envy or despise the Epicurean, he will overcome their hatred, their envy and their contempt through his reason (*logismō periginesthai*).[5]

This courage, which consists not in confronting dangers but in withdrawing from them, this art of sheltering oneself from the events, is a common feature to all utilitarian doctrines: for them, it is more a matter of having *foresightedness* and resignation than it is a matter of having *courage*; for Epicurus it is even more a matter of having *confidence*. This judicious and, so to say, wise courage is not a product of chance, and it does not come *ready made* from nature: it is produced, says Epicurus, by reasoned knowledge[6] concerning matters of true utility, *logismō tou sumpherontos*.[7]

Will not the sage be temperate and sober? This is a delicate question; if the evils despised by courage are not real evils, the goods to which temperance must attach itself are for every utilitarian real goods.[8] Nevertheless, one can still say that temperance is an essential virtue in the Epicurean system because the end for Epicurus is happiness, and not this or that particular pleasure. Now, in order to attain happiness, one must reject pleasures that drag pain after themselves and are contradictory with themselves and with the reason of those who pursue them. In every doctrine which is not of pleasure but of utility, temperance and moderate calculation (*nēphōn logismos*) are fundamental virtues.[9]

Standing above these two virtues [*courage* and *temperance*], one finds the *practical wisdom* that produces and moderates them. This wisdom is one with reason and philosophy.

II. – If virtue and interest agree with each other in the private domain, can we say the same when it comes to the social domain?

Let us first consider the virtues which are purely affective. If the greatest evil is *trouble*, which passion could be said to be more capable of bringing *trouble* to the soul than love? The sage will therefore avoid love as an irremediable evil. Epicurus and Lucretius distinguish here two things: the passion itself and the physical need. The need, which is 'natural and necessary', must be satisfied; the passion of love sung by the poets, on the other hand, has nothing natural or rational about it: it amounts to a psychological illusion. Ultimately, love is nothing else, says Lucretius, than a tendency to give the loved object all the perfections, divinizing it, which is absurd. Love is a sort of unconscious cult, a sort of religion, a form of superstition, which must disappear [just] like all the others. In what concerns marriage, it brings with it innumerable worries:[10] in order to avoid the hassles of the household, the sage will generally not get married, and will not have children. According to Epicurus, there can be exceptions to this rule.[11]

The Epicurean theory of love conforms to ancient ideas. The Stoics are mistaken when they reproach Epicurus for wanting to extinguish society by preventing the sage from having children. First, one can see that this idea is not absolute. Second, it is addressed more to the accomplished Epicurean, the sage, who represents more of an ideal than a real type: indeed, a great number of Epicureans got married. Metrodorus had children, and on his deathbed Epicurus recommended Hermarchus to take care of them. Moreover, some Stoics, strangely enough, advise their sage to avoid marriage. Epictetus, who vigorously attacks Epicurus, hardly speaks differently from him: 'Behold,' he says, 'if the Cynic gets married, he will have to do certain things for his father-in-law, to fulfil certain duties towards the relatives of his wife, and also towards his wife. And there he is consequently absorbed by the care of his sick relatives and by the need of earning money. Put aside all the rest, he must have at least a vase to warm up the water for his child, and a basin to wash him; he will need, for his wife, a woollen blanket, a bed, oil, a cup; and, as a result, his baggage is augmented! And I am not mentioning other occupations that distract him from his role. He becomes as busy as a monarch whose time is dedicated to watching over humankind.'[12] One can see, then, that for the ancients philosophy is [a] jealous [activity] and demands total dedication. With Christianity this advice against marriage and shared life increases rather than diminishes. We know the enormous amount of work carried out in the ancient world by a movement that drew thousands of the strongest and best-tempered souls to a life of solitude. One believed oneself to be closer to God by isolating oneself, and ecstasy replaced love. Christianity, of course, was more harmful to marriage than Epicureanism had ever been. The [Early] Fathers of the Church are surprisingly in agreement with Epicurus on this point. The great Saint Jerome in his desert meditates about Epicurus and proposes him as an example to the Christians. In his metaphorical style, he writes: 'his works are full of fruits, herbs and abstinences.'[13] Christians and Epicureans had the same fear of love; but the causes of this fear were different: the latter feared risking their happiness, the former feared forgetting their God. The practical outcome was the same for both doctrines.

If the heart of the sage ought to banish love, would the same apply in the case of friendship? Will the sage want to withdraw completely into himself, will he be [completely] self-sufficient? Nestled within his wisdom, and despising the anger and ire of his fellow beings, will he also despise the benevolence of their friendship? Not at all: friendship is too useful to be neglected. Friendship is like a 'field to be sown', from which one will reap the harvest. 'Of all the goods which are procured by wisdom to ensure happiness throughout the whole of life, by far the most important is the acquisition of friendship.'[14] To find a friend is to find protection against all the vicissitudes of life: we know that the Epicureans aided each other in [times of] public misfortune.[15] A friend is a supporter,[16] someone who fights on your side in the struggle against fortune, and on whom you can always count. Friendship, by augmenting confidence, also augments ataraxia and happiness.

Up to this point interest and friendship seem to agree with one another. However, many difficulties arise: in friendship one is not limited to receiving, but one must also give. Friendship thrives on hardship[17] and effort, mutual sacrifice, and sometimes even devotion. It is an exchange where, by a very singular law, each one makes the effort to give in retribution more than what one has received, and, somehow, to lose instead of gaining.[18] From this still exterior perspective in which we are placed it seems that for the Epicurean the advantages of friendship will be outweighed by its losses. Epicurus is then led to a more penetrating analysis of friendship, searching beyond exterior profits, for a more intimate and profound enjoyment that justifies it.

This enjoyment that the doctrine of personal utility has to acknowledge is the pleasure of loving. 'As anger, jealousy and the marks of contempt are opposed to pleasure; in the same way, friendship not only assures but also *produces* pleasure, equally for our friends and ourselves.'[19] Thus, a new advantage is added to the exterior profits of friendship. Having a friend is a pleasant thing, not only because of the favours he offers, but for the very fact that he loves us. We can, then, reach out to him and love him in the same way that we seek for everything that gives us pleasure. 'Friendship begins with need;[20] but it can only be sustained through experiencing the joys of a life in common.'[21] However, let us note that we will love our friend for our own pleasure, not for his; for our own sake, not for his.

Hence, a profound vice persists in Epicurean friendship. The friend is not another *I*,[22] to whom we would attach ourselves in a disinterested way: he is always a humble servant of our *self*,[23] he is an instrument for us. Given this, how do we re-establish equality in friendship? How to gradually suppress this relationship of means and end that is established between my friend and myself? By which subterfuge can I eliminate this *self*, which, after having given birth to friendship, must now disappear so as not to annihilate it? This is the peculiar problem posed to the Epicureans, a problem that they perfectly understood, a problem that deeply tormented them and to which they proposed different solutions at different times.

The Epicurean needs friendship, and friendship itself requires disinterestedness in order to survive. Here lies the main difficulty. But why couldn't the Epicurean be temporarily disinterested after all? Disinterestedness will be for him a simple means; but he uses it as he does any other thing with a view to his own happiness. 'Without friendship we cannot, in any way, have solid and lasting happiness; *but we cannot preserve friendship if we don't love our friend like we love ourselves*: then this result is produced within friendship, and thus friendship is closely linked to pleasure. We enjoy our friends' joy as our own, and similarly, we suffer from their pain.'[24] In this passage, in which Epicurus prefigures the contemporary English school's [theory of the] 'genesis of sentiments', one sees friendship, initially based on interest, being modified by the action of interest itself, so tending towards disinterest. Epicurus concludes: 'It is because the sage will always have for his friends the same feelings he has for himself; and every trouble that he takes on for pursuing pleasure for himself, he will take on to pursue pleasure for his friend.'[25] In addition, in friendship 'it is more pleasing to do good than to receive it.'[26]

It is remarkable that in his theory of friendship Epicurus expresses exactly the same ideas that Bentham will reproduce twenty centuries later. In effect, after taking egoism as his starting point, Bentham later comes to recognize that enjoying sympathy and affection is inseparable from happiness, so they should be pursued. Now, one can only obtain the affection of others by displaying[27] one's affection towards them, and one can only display affection through actions in which there is a portion of sacrifice of one's egoism. If it is to preserve itself, egoism needs to sacrifice itself to a degree. This is a strong argument to which the two authors were led to by the force of logic. 'How,' asks Bentham, 'can a man be happy except by obtaining the friendly affections of those on whom his happiness depends? And how can he obtain their friendly affections except by convincing them that he gives them his own in exchange? And how can he best convince them, but by *giving them these friendly affections in reality*; and if he gives them in reality, the evidence will be found in his words and deeds.'[28] It is not enough for egoism to simulate affection. The most credible affection is the one that is most real, and what one emulates is never as good as what one really experiences. Therefore, egoism should strive to experience a genuine affection. In this way, Epicurus and Bentham overcome the enormous gap that separates one*self* from another *self*.[29]

When Epicurus introduces friendship into his system it is not in order to relegate it to a second rank, but rather to give it a genuinely honourable place. His conception of friendship is, moreover, very delicate, and more modern than ancient. Friends, he says, must be united to a point of putting their goods at each other's disposal.[30] However, they should not, as Pythagoras recommended, place them in common. This forced community would engender mistrust rather than free friendship.[31] According to Epicurus, the influence of friendship governs the whole of life and subordinates it. What is more, friendship even seems to extend beyond the limits of life: with a friend at his side the sage will not look upon death with diffidence. 'It is the same thought,' Epicurus says, 'that inspires us with confidence that no evil is eternal or even long-lasting, and that shows us that in this limited time of life, friendship's aid is the most useful.'[32] Friendship, like virtue, is a means to happiness, but it is such an efficacious means that it merges with happiness itself. 'Just like virtues, friendship cannot be separated from pleasure... That which we have said of the virtues, namely that they are always linked to pleasures, should also be admitted of friendship.'[33] Friendship, virtue, happiness are, ultimately, three different aspects of the same thing: to be loving is to be happy, and to be happy is to be loving.

From this perspective friendship appears to us as such an elevated good that, compared to it, everything else seems to be of no value. All our joys somehow depend on the life of our friend, which becomes very precious to us, even more precious than our own life. The friend's absence, which typically weakens the ties of ordinary friendships, does not have the same effect on the sage: 'Only the sage will keep over his friends, present or absent, an equal benevolence.'[34] Finally, the death of a friend, this eternal absence, appears to us as something more dreadful than our own death: in friendship, is it not that the best part is with who dies first? 'The sage will give his own life for that of his friend, if necessary'.[35]

It is now possible to explain the notorious friendships of the Epicureans, this life in common, these numerous disciples and confidants that, as Diogenes says, 'entire villages could not contain.'[36] There was among all these hearts, in the words of the ancients, an agreement, a perfect harmony: *conspiratio amoris*, as Cicero writes. Epicurus' family gave the example: 'It was a wonderful thing,' says Plutarch, 'the way in which his brothers were affectionate towards him.'[37] Metrodorus, his disciple, became for Epicurus another of *himself*;[38] they never left each other. In the Louvre we can find a marble statue that represents Epicurus and his inseparable friend side by side. During the siege of Athens by Demetrius, Epicurus nourished all his disciples who have stayed close to him.[39] This tradition of friendship was propagated in his school more than in any other. In Greece many used to quote the beautiful examples of Epicurean friendship.[40] In Cicero's dialogue, Torquatus notes that even if one refers back to the time of Theseus it is hard to find more than three well-known pairs of friends. Friendship is given limited space in the ancient fables, which means that it had an even smaller place in real life. 'But how numerous are the groups of friends that Epicurus gathered in his house, which nevertheless was not big! (...) This is still today the habitude of the Epicureans.'[41] Loyalty in friendship is one of the key qualities which Cicero and Seneca recognize in Epicureanism. They lived in a sort of mutual solidarity, analogous to that of the first Christians; they aided each other in times of public adversity; and not only would they celebrate together Epicurus' birthday every year, but they would also gather every month for shared meals.[42] For centuries, no other sect of antiquity presented such concord and such intellectual and moral cohesion.

As one can see, one cannot reproach Epicurus and the Epicureans for not holding friendship in high esteem. They praised it and practised it more than their adversaries, the Stoics. If one posits happiness as the goal of one's conduct, as opposed to virtue, one is able to better appreciate one's personal insufficiency and the need to rely on others [for achieving it]. Virtue is not diminished when in solitude. That is why in the Stoic there is more magnanimity but also more harshness and asperity; the Epicurean, on the contrary, is essentially sociable and, in him, amiability and kindness[43] compensate the true strength of the soul. The only thing that takes away the importance of this tenderness is to think that it has as its principle the pursuit of personal happiness. As Epicureanism progressed, one was able to better perceive this contradiction between the elevated character of friendship and the somewhat base origin that Epicurus attributed to it. For the Roman Epicureans the thought of their master pointed to an ideal that was too beautiful not to be pursued, and too elevated to be entirely referred to the concerns of interest. They held that at the apex of things and at the highest point of friendship there resided a complete disinterestedness and a genuine love of others and not only of oneself. Cicero indicates several times this break that takes place in the Epicurean field. The theory of friendship must have been very important for the Epicureans, to the extent that it led them to significantly modify [this aspect of] the master's original doctrine.[44]

How, though, is it possible to reconcile friendship conceived of as something truly disinterested with a principle of interest? This is a most difficult task. The Epicureans have recourse to an idea that the master himself had expressed and upon which his theory of justice is founded: this is the idea of a mutual pact, of a more or less tacit contract that would serve to regulate human relationships. When they applied this conception to friendship the Epicureans believed they could find in it a certain kind of pact effected precisely against egoism. 'Some of us maintain that there is a sort of pact of sages, which oblige them not to love their friends less than they love themselves: we understand that this is possible; we often see many examples of it, and evidently nothing is more appropriate than this union in order to make life happy.' 'Some Epicureans,' says Cicero, 'state that the sages make a vow of having towards their friends the same feelings they have towards themselves.'[45]

Here we have a new theory of friendship that Cicero carefully distinguishes from that of Epicurus.[46] This theory does not violate the principles of Epicureanism: human beings are still considered as agents moved by personal interest; only the most enlightened among them, the 'sages', are able to understand the superior beauty of friendship and engage themselves in realizing it in their conduct with one another. They forbid in advance every return towards the self,[47] and amidst a harshly egoistic nature they [choose to] swear affection and devotion to one another. Don't they swear in the same way, says Cicero, 'to love justice, moderation and all the other virtues, without return[48] and for themselves?' The Epicureans could reply that such a commitment is beyond their power since they cannot change human nature in its core; in practice they can only neglect it; their will can contradict nature but without ever silencing it. Nevertheless, the main defect of this friendly pact imagined by the Epicureans is that it does not really have any obligatory character. If one asks what its *raison d'être* is the answer cannot be other than the search for happiness, and there can be, then, no other reason for its duration. Interest, which has originally formed the pact, will be able to suddenly break it.[49]

The Epicureans found themselves constrained to search for a third solution to this problem, a third way to link a friend to another without supposing any profit. The will of each of the friends that they previously invoked is not a definite guarantee since, despite all the pacts in the world, the will can always be retracted. One should find something less variable than the will, a more tenacious link, and the Epicureans thought they had found it in habit. This is what, according to Cicero, these very *subtle* men (*satis acuti*) imagined, and we can see how similar their theory is to that of our modern 'associationists'.[50] 'The first encounters and the first rapprochements, as well as the desire to establish links of friendship, undoubtedly find their reason in personal pleasure; but as soon as the progress of habit produces intimacy, it is then that love blossoms, to the point where one cherishes one's friends only for their own sake, without taking any advantage from this friendship. Indeed, if we have the habit of becoming attached to places, temples, cities, gymnasiums, to a land, to our dogs, our horses, our games, through the habit of the exercise or pursuing [those things],[51] how easier and more just it is for us to develop this attachment with regards the habitual society of men?'[52] In this much misunderstood passage the Epicureans remain faithful to their master's spirit. They do not contradict themselves as some have believed; they only summon an observed fact, namely that an object or a being that we initially loved by virtue of something else we now come to love only by virtue of itself, and from being a mere means they ultimately become ends [in themselves] to us. The contemporary

English school will stress this very same fact of observation;[53] it will explain this fact by the association of ideas and will make it the basis of its theory of morality. Virtue, according to Mill and Bain, becomes precious to the habitually virtuous person because of the same phenomenon which makes the avaricious one feel attached to his gold. One should surely not look for such refined 'beginnings'[54] in the Greek or Roman Epicureans. However, in its primordial simplicity the Epicurean theory rests upon the same facts on which rests the English theory. The Epicurean theory explains these facts almost in the same way through the notion of habit. According to the Epicureans, asking why one becomes attached to one's friend is the same as asking why one attaches oneself to one's dog or horse, and for the two cases the answer is absolutely the same. That which makes beings precious to one another is the habit of living and acting in common, and owing to this fact a certain mutual and intimate habituation[55] (*consuetudo*) takes place, and as a sort of adaptation. Bring any two beings together through a shared interest and in the long run, whoever these beings are, and supposing there is no instinctive repugnance between them, the *rapprochement* itself will end up producing a union. When hunting with a dog one may well end up loving it; in living with one's friend we will end up becoming attached to him. This will be especially so when we are considering a man rather than a dog, since a man is more capable of responding to the affection that is offered to him.

This third theory could still be criticized for being incomplete and for considering friendship as something too passive, making it part of a broader mechanism of interest and habit. What is more one can reproach it for not distinguishing between things and persons, between human beings or hounds and horses. Nevertheless, this theory represents a progress over the ideas of Epicurus since it makes a remarkable effort to account for 'the love of the other for the sake of the other'. Finally, it attests to the work that was already done in ancient thought on these important issues. The Epicureans conclude as follows: 'Not only does one not preclude friendship when placing the sovereign good in pleasure, but without pleasure one could never establish friendship among human beings.'[56] Indeed, following Epicureanism, we know that pleasure and pain are the only two motives that move human beings, and they alone can make human beings look for [one another] and find one another.

III. – Epicurus recommended friendship between single individuals. Additionally, he recommended by his precepts and by his actions friendship between *all* human beings among themselves. Diogenes tells us of the piety he displayed towards his parents, his benevolence with his brothers, and his gentleness with his slaves.[57] Although it is occasionally necessary to punish the latter (*kolasein*), one also needs to show mercy (*eleēsein*) and forgive those who prove their good will (*sungnōmēn tini hexein tōn spoudaiōn*).[58] We know that Mus was both Epicurus' slave and disciple. According to Diogenes, Epicurus' kindness towards human beings in general was extraordinary (*anuperblētoi chrēstotētes*), and his benevolence was without comparison (*anuperblētos eugnōmosunē*). In addition, his philanthropy was universal (*katholou hē pros pantas autou philantrōpia*).[59] It is interesting to note how since its beginnings the utilitarian doctrine has assumed these colours of philanthropy, which can be seen in the work of its modern representatives such as Bentham, Owen and Mill.

If the sage must seek to win the affection of his fellow men, he must not be unduly concerned about their admiration. 'I have never wanted to please the people,' said Epicurus, 'because what I know is not of their liking, and I know nothing about that which is.'[60] He wrote to one of his companions of study: 'We are to one another [something] like a big theatre.'[61] The sage, then, will not look for honours.[62] Power[63] and royalty are only goods 'according to nature' when they can protect us against the attacks of others; otherwise they are actually evils. Before desiring the splendour of life one ought to desire its security (*asphaleia*), which is more useful.[64] Thus the sage will love life in the countryside more than in the city, and he will avoid public festivities and crowds.[65] 'The moment when one needs to retreat into oneself is when one is forced to mix with the crowd.'[66] It follows that the sage will not get involved in the affairs of the republic; he will live unknown, abstaining and retiring into himself: *lathe biōsas*. We know how fiercely Cicero combatted this doctrine of political abstention, which was then common, and for very different reasons, to the Epicureans, the Platonists, and even to the majority of the Stoics. But the troubles of the city and the calm of the Epicurean sage cannot coexist: the true city of the sage is his happiness. Epicurus, who in his theory of friendship emphasized the more or less temporary self-oblivion, did not want to comprehend or admit political disinterestedness.[67]

After honour Epicurus deals with wealth. The sage, as we know, needs only bread and water in order to be happy: 'he despises the pleasures of luxury, certainly not in themselves, but because of the trouble [and pain] that follow them.'[68] 'Frequently the acquisition of wealth,' says Epicurus, 'is a change in our experience of miseries and not the victory over our misery. Do you wish to become rich, Pythocles? Then do not add [anything] to your wealth, but remove desires.'[69] 'Poverty according to the laws of nature is a great fortune.'[70] We know that Epicurus and his disciples were a living example of this wise poverty.[71] As Diogenes Laertius shows, 'their lives were of great simplicity and excessive sobriety; just a little bit of wine was enough for them; and the first sip of water satisfied them.' In a letter Epicurus tells a friend: 'Send me a little pot of cheese from Kythera, so that I may fare sumptuously when I like.'[72] Writing to Polyaenus on a different occasion he boasts of spending less than one *as*[73] for his food, while Metrodorus, who was less advanced than him, had to spend the whole *as*.[74] Nevertheless, it is strange that even in its beginnings utilitarianism – [conceived] as a moral economy that makes of life a *bourse*[75] and of happiness wealth – did not attribute any importance to material gain when it attributed so much importance to moral gain. Thus, Epicurus, while maintaining that the sage does not need [material] wealth, advises him not to despise it and to take care of his fortune, providing for his old age.[76] Would not the person who is able to do without wealth be the one who could better enjoy it?[77] In this way the sage will profit from his wisdom and save, managing his affairs properly.[78] He should not beg as did the Cynics, and he will aim to be self-sufficient.[79] Overall, it seems that Epicurus' conception of the happy life is more modern and seems also to have more genuine dignity than the ragged wisdom of Antisthenes.

Even today the Epicurean will live in a similar fashion to every other human being and not fail in the fulfilment of his social duties. He may even get married and have children; he will certainly have friends, and he will be benevolent towards his servants, indeed he will be benevolent towards everyone. Despite it representing a danger for his *ataraxia* he will not be able to remain completely indifferent to other people's affairs, to honours, wealth or public esteem: his *self*[80] will live, then, as much as possible in harmony and sympathy with others.[81] Apart from the deep devotion and self-sacrifice without ulterior motive – which is indeed rare – interest can explain and can produce most of the external acts of what we could call the affective life. This is because, ultimately, there is a community of ends (*sunteleia*) and a community of interests between human beings that encourages them to join their efforts towards the attainment of a shared goal, and so compels them to provide [each other] with mutual help.

However, when interests exceptionally diverge instead of converging, who will be able to judge them? Who will be able to end or prevent the conflict that ensues? Do we now appeal to justice? If this is the case it must mean that there is a principle of action that is superior to interest. However, we know that according to Epicurus this is impossible. We must then analyse the notion of justice, which among all moral notions is the one that can hardly be reduced to mere interest. The Epicurean theory of justice, founded on a social contract, is just as interesting to study as the theory of friendship. Examining this theory will provide us with a set of interesting analogies with the modern theories of Hobbes and Rousseau.

Notes

1. T.N. The French here is *prévoyance*.
2. T.N. *aménité*.
3. T.N. By using the French word *aisance*, Guyau also refers here to a material form of comfort, a certain material affluence.
4. Diogenes Laertius, *Lives of Eminent Philosophers*, X, 118.
5. Diogenes Laertius, *Lives of Eminent Philosophers*, X, 117.
6. T.N. *connaissance*.
7. Diogenes Laertius, *Lives of Eminent Philosophers*, X, 120.
8. T.N. The apparent inconsistency is that the evils are not real evils; the goods obtained by temperance are real goods.
9. Diogenes Laertius, *Lives of Eminent Philosophers*, X, 132.
10. T.N. *soucis*.
11. St Jerome, *Against Jovinianus*, I, 48: '*Epicurus raro dicit sapienti ineunda conjugia*' ['Epicurus rarely says that a sage should marry']. Diogenes Laertius, *Lives of Eminent Philosophers*, X, 119. Lucretius, *On the Nature of Things*, 118–20; 142 [T.N. Guyau seems to be quoting rather IV, 1233 & ff.] – This is also Democritus' opinion.
12. Epictetus, *Discourses*, III, 22, 70 & ff. [T.N. That is to say, he would become as busy with the care for others as a monarch is with the care for his subjects].
13. St Jerome, *Against Jovinianus*, I, 191; II, 8.
14. Diogenes Laertius, *Lives of Eminent Philosophers*, X, 148: *Hō hē sophia paraskeuazetai eis tēn tou holou biou makariotēta, polu megiston estin hē tēs philias ktēsis* (translated above). – See also Philodemus, *De vitiis*, IX, col. 24.
15. Diogenes Laertius, *Lives of Eminent Philosophers*, X, 10.
16. T.N. The French *soutien* allows for different translations related to support, help, aid; but it is also a crutch: Guyau's sentence could also be employing it in this sense.

17 T.N. Again, the French here is *peines*.
18 T.N. The beauty of this sentence in the original relies on the fact that *gagner* means both gaining and winning. The friend, in seeking to give more than he receives, also seeks to lose instead of winning (and gaining or profiting).
19 Cicero, *De finibus*, I, xx, 67: 'Atque ut odia, invidiae, despicationes adversantur voluptatibus, sic amicitiae non modo fautrices fidelissimae, sed etiam effectrices sunt voluptatum tam amicis quam sibi' (translated above).
20 T.N. *besoin*.
21 Diogenes Laertius, *Lives of Eminent Philosophers*, X, 120.
22 T.N. *un autre nous-mêmes*.
23 T.N. *moi*.
24 Cicero, *De finibus*, I, xx, 67: 'Quod quia nullo modo sine amicitiâ firmam et perpetuam jucunditatem vitae tenere possumus, neque vero ipsam amicitiam tueri, nisi aequè et nosmetipsos diligamus, idcirco et hoc ipsum efficitur in amicitiâ, et amicitia cum voluptate connectitur. Nam et laetamur amicorum laetitiâ aequè atque nostrâ, et pariter dolemus angoribus' (translated above).
25 Cicero, *De finibus*, I, xx, 68: 'Quocirca eodem modo sapiens erit affectus erga amicum, quo in seipsum, quosque labores propter suam voluptatem susciperet, eosdem suscipiet propter amici voluptatem' (translated above).
26 Plutarch, *Non posse suaviter vivi secundum Epicurum* 1100 [T.N. The reference seems to be actually 1096–7].
27 T.N. Guyau's expression is literally 'to give testimony of one's affection'.
28 [Jeremy] Bentham, *Deontology or the Science of Morality* [manuscript edited by John Bowring, volume 1, London: Longman, Rees, Orme, Browne, Green & Longman, 1834], p. 19. See also [Bentham,] *An Introduction to the Principles of Morals and Legislation* [New Edition Corrected by the Author, London: W. Pickering, 1823], ch. xi, Human Dispositions in General.
29 T.N. *le large intervalle qui sépare un moi d'un autre moi*.
30 T.N. *Bien*, here, designates good things, qualities, as well as property and possessions.
31 Diogenes Laertius, *Lives of Eminent Philosophers*, X, 11: *Apistountōn einai, oude philōn* ['it characterises me who do not trust each other rather than friends'; in Hicks' translation (X, 11): 'such a practice in his opinion implied mistrust, and without confidence there is no friendship'].
32 Diogenes Laertius, *Lives of Eminent Philosophers*, X, 148: *Hē autē gnōmē tharrein t' epoiēsen huper tou mēthen aiōnion einai deinon mēde poluchronion, kai tēn en autois tois hōrismenois asphaleian philias malista katidein einai sunteloumenēn* (translated above). – See also Cicero, *De finibus*, I, xx, 68.
33 Cicero, *De finibus*, I, xx, 66[–8]: 'Ut enim virtutes, sic amicitiam negant posse a voluptate discedere ... Quaeque de virtutibus dicta sunt, quemadmodum eae semper voluptatibus inhaererent, eadem de amicitiâ dicenda sunt' (translated above).
34 Diogenes Laertius, *Lives of Eminent Philosophers*, X, 118: *Monon charin hexein ton sophon philois kai parousi kai apousin homoiōs* (translated in the text).
35 Diogenes Laertius, *Lives of Eminent Philosophers*, X, 121.
36 Diogenes Laertius, *Lives of Eminent Philosophers*, X, 9: *Tosoutoi to plēthos ōs mēd' an polesin holais metreisthai dunasthai* (translated above).
37 Plutarch, *De fraterno amore* [On Brotherly Love, in *Moralia*], 16.
38 T.N. *lui-même*.
39 Plutarch, *Demetrius* [in *Lives*], 45 [1–3].

40 V. Maxim., I, 8, 17 [T.N. Guyau seems to be referring to Epicurus' *Vatican Sayings* or to the *Principal Doctrines*; the editors could not identify this particular reference, especially since it is supposed to provide examples of Epicurean friendship.]
41 Cicero, *De finibus*, I, xx, 65: '*At vero Epicurus unâ in domo, et eâ quidem angustâ, quam magnos quantâque amoris conspiratione consentientes tenuit amicorum greges! quod fit etiam nunc ab Epicureis*' (translated above). – This friendship did not exclude frankness [*franchise*], if we believe in Philodemus (*Papyrus Herculanensis*, 15, 72–3; *Peri parrhēsias* [*On frankness*]).
42 Cicero, *De finibus*, II, xxxi, 101; V, 1; Pliny, *Naturalis Historia* [*Natural History*], XXXV, 2.
43 T.N. *l'aménité et la douceur*.
44 Cicero, *De finibus*, I, XX, 66: '*Tribus ergo modis video a nostris esse de amicitiâ disputatum. Alii, quum eas voluptates, quae ad amicos pertinerent, negarent esse per se ipsas tam expetendas, quam nostras expeteremus, quo loco videtur quibusdam stabilitas amicitiae vacillare, tuentur tamen eum locum seque facilè, ut mihi videtur, expediunt ... Sunt autem quidam Epicurei timidiores paulò contra vestra convicia, sed tamen satis acuti, qui verentur ne, si amicitiam propter nostram voluptatem expetendam putemus, tota amicitia quase claudicare videatur*' ['I see that our [Epicureans] have treated frindship in three ways. Some of them defend friendship even though they deny that the pleasures that regard our friends are as desirable to us as the ones which affect us. This doctrine is thought by some critics to undermine the foundations of friendship, but I believe its supporters can easily justify it ... There are also those Epicureans who, although being a little more shy [when defying] your invectives, are still sufficiently perspicacious and fear that, if friendship were to be sought only for the sake of pleasure we can extract from it, it would be crippled altogether'].
45 Cicero, *De finibus* I, xx, 70: '*Sunt autem qui dicant foedus esse quoddam sapientium, ut, ne minus quidem amicos quam se ipsos diligant. Quod et fieri posse intelligimus, et saepe quidem enim videmus, et perspicuum est nihil ad jacunde vivendum reperiri posse, quod conjunctione tali sit aptius*' ['There are also those who say that there is a sort of pact among sages of not loving their friends less than they love themselves. We understand that this is possible, and we effectively often see it, and it is clear that one cannot find anything more likely to allow for an agreeable and pleasant life than this [from of] association']; II, xxvi, 83: '*Posuisti etiam dicere alios foedus quoddam inter se facere sapiens, ut, quemadmodum sint in se ipsos animati, eodem modo sint erga amicos: id et fieri posse et saepe esse factum et ad voluptates percipiendas maxime pertinere*' ['You have claimed that others say that the sages celebrate pacts among them animated by the same feelings towards their friends as they feel towards themselves: this, you said, was possible and in fact had often occurred, and it was highly conducive to the attainment of pleasure'].
46 Cicero, *De finibus*, XXVI, 82: '*Attulisti aliud humanius horum recentiorum, nunquam dictum ab ipso illo (sc. Epicuro)*' ['You quoted another and more humane argument of more recent Epicureans, which was never uttered by the master himself (that is, by Epicurus)'].
47 T.N. This is an ambiguous expression in the French original, and it could potentially designate both the interdiction of profiting from friendship, and the interdiction of converting one's attention to oneself in friendship. Both meanings seem to go against the utilitarian characterization of friendship.
48 T.N. *salaire*.
49 Cicero, *De finibus*, II, xxvi.

50 T.N. Quite literally *associationnistes*.
51 T.N. Guyau's translation is more literal: exercises and hunting.
52 Cicero, *De finibus*, I, xx, 69: '*Primos congressus, copulationesque, et consuetudinum instituendarum voluntares fieri propter voluptatem; quum autem usus progrediens familiaritatem effecerit, tum amorem efflorescere tantum, ut, etiamsi nulla sit utilitas ex amicitiâ, tamen ipsi amici propter seipsos amentur. Etenim si loca, si fana, si urbes, si gymnasia, si campum, si canes, si equos, si ludicra, exercendi aut venandi consuetudine, adamare solemus, quanto id in hominum consuetudine faciliùs fieri potuerit et justius?*' (translated in the text). – This passage is very controversial and interesting, as the philosophical theory it contains, and the slightest modification of the text, even if it does not alter the thought underlying it, disfigures it. Following Back (*ad Cic. leg.*, 463 [the editors could not identify this quote]), Baiter reads it as follows: *equos ludicrâ exercendi aut venandi consuetudine*, a lesson contrary to [that of] the manuscripts, which all have *si* before *ludicra*. Boekel reads *consuetudines* and inserts *si* before *exercendi*, which equally contradicts the manuscripts; moreover, the sentence read in this way does not have a plausible sense, and amounts to the following: – If we love (in themselves) the habit of exercise and hunting, we can equally love our friends in [and by] themselves; – can someone say that we love exercise in and by itself rather than because of the physical well-being that results from it? The only option in accordance with the manuscripts is the one by Madvig: '*Si equos, si ludicra exercendi aut venandi consuetudine adamare solemus*'; however, one should not render *ludicra exercendi* as the 'pleasure of exercise'. It seems to us that we can obtain a more satisfactory version, both from the point of view of philosophy and grammar, by placing *exercendi aut venandi consuetudine* between commas, interpreting the sentence as follows: 'If we are accustomed to becoming attached to places, temples, cities, gyms and to the land (*or* the Field of Mars), as well as to dogs, horses, certain games and the habit of exercising or hunting (in these places, cities, etc., or with dogs, etc.), then how much more easily and justly could this effect (namely becoming attached by habit) be produced in the habitual society [or intercourse] of men?' – Chapter xxvi of book II confirms our interpretation: '*Quum autem usus acessisset, tum ipsum (amicum) amari per se*' (Cicero, *De finibus*, II, xxvi: 'When habit is added, one loves one's friend in and by himself' [or 'when habit grows we love our friend for his own sake']).
53 T.N. The French here is *fait d'observation*; it can indicate means an empirical fact, something widely accepted by experience.
54 T.N. *genèses*.
55 T.N. The French *accoutumance* encompasses: becoming accustomed to something, familiarization, acquaintance, mutual adaptation or habituation, as well as addiction and dependency.
56 Cicero, De finibus, I, xx, 70: '*Quibus ex omnibus judicari potest, non modo non impediri rationem amicitiae, si summum bonum in voluptate ponatur, sed sine hoc institutionem amicitiae omnino non posse reperiri*' (translated above).
57 Diogenes Laertius, *Lives of Eminent Philosophers*, X, 10.
58 Diogenes Laertius, *Lives of Eminent Philosophers*, X, 119.
59 Diogenes Laertius, *Lives of Eminent Philosophers*, X, 10.
60 Seneca, *Epistles*, XXIX.
61 Seneca, *Epistles*, XXIX.
62 Diogenes Laertius, *Lives of Eminent Philosophers*, X, 120.
63 T.N. Here understood as the attribute of he who 'commands', *commandement*.
64 Epicurus *apud* Diogenes Laertius, X: maxims 7 e 8.

65 T.N. A tension emerges in Guyau's argument if we look at Diogenes Laertius, *Lives of Eminent Philosophers*, X, 120: 'He will take more delight than other men in state festivals.'
66 Epicurus *apud* Seneca, *Epistles*, XXV.
67 Diogenes Laertius, *Lives of Eminent Philosophers*, X, 140, 119, 121. See also Philodemus, *Papyrus Herculanus* [*Volumina Herculan.*, Guyau], *Peri rhētorikēs*, col. 14: *Oude chrēsimēn hēgoumetha tēn politikēn dunamin autēn kath' autēn* ['We do not think that political power is useful in itself']. – For an exception that recalls Aristippus, Epicurus allows the sage to court the monarch, 'flatter in order to correct' (*epicharisesthai tini epi tō diorthōmasti*).
68 Stobaeus, *Sermones*, XVII, 30.
69 Seneca, *Epistles*, XXI.
70 Seneca, *Epistles*, XXI. The Epicurean Philodemus also says *Philosophō d' esti ploutou mikron* ['The philosopher has but little wealth'] (*De vitiis*, IX, col. 12).
71 T.N. *pauvreté savante*.
72 Diogenes Laertius, *Lives of Eminent Philosophers*, X, 10–11.
73 T.N. '*As*' was a Roman coin. The word seems anachronistic or displaced in the Greek context (the ancient Greek currency was the *drachma*). A possible answer for this is that the quote comes from Seneca.
74 Seneca, *Epistles*, XV.
75 T.N. This term has multiple meanings in French: from purse to stock exchange, but they are related to the economic meaning of the analogy Guyau proposes here.
76 Diogenes Laertius, *Lives of Eminent Philosophers*, X, 119–21: *Ktēseōs pronoēsesthai kai tou mellontos* ['He will have foresight regarding his property and his future'].
77 Epicurus *apud* Seneca, *Epistles*, XV.
78 Diogenes Laertius, *Lives of Eminent Philosophers*, X, 120: *Chrēmatisesthai all' apo monēs sophias aporēsanta* ['He will make money if need be, because of his wisdom'] – Philodemus, *De vitiis*, IX, col. 12, 27, 40.
79 Diogenes Laertius, *Lives of Eminent Philosophers*, X, 120.
80 T.N. *moi*.
81 T.N. *les autres moi*.

2

Justice and Social Contract

Natural justice boils down to civil law by the Sophists, the Sceptics and Democritus. – The state of the question in Epicurus' time. – Points to be elucidated. – That the goal of human society is interest, according to Epicurus; that it is formed by the mutual consent of each one of its members. – First conception of the pact or *social contract* as clearly expressed by Epicurus. – That justice has contract as its principle, and that it only exists between contractors. – In which sense injustice is an evil. – That justice can vary to a certain extent, according to place and time. – Approximation between Epicurus' words and a page from Bain. – The Epicurean social ideal.

Before Epicurus the sophists had already attacked the idea of justice. We know how vigorously Plato makes Callicles speak against the alleged natural law, superior and anterior to human laws in the *Gorgias*. The true natural law, the law of the strongest, the criterion according to which one judges actions in nature, is that of force. In the city, this force was passed on to the hands of the law. However, if one respects the legislator's prescriptions, one is still respecting force, before which one bows, and not justice. Pyrrho and the sceptics, after the sophists, defended the same cause. Pyrrho said that in nature there was nothing beautiful or ugly, just or unjust. After all, if justice was natural how could one explain the diversity of laws? Pyrrhonians gathered carefully the majority of the contradictions observed among the customs[1] and beliefs of several peoples, and they made of these contradictions one of their favourite arguments against natural moral law. Finally, Democritus, whose books exercised great influence on Epicurus, also denied [the existence of] natural justice. In short, this is the situation of this question by the time of Epicurus: 1) there is no natural law; 2) civil laws were established by force and became respectable through the influence of habit.

Nevertheless, in this substitution of natural right by civil law carried out by the sceptics, two highly important elements were still missing: first, every force has a goal, an end exterior to itself; which end does this social force that gives birth to right[2] pursue? The sophists did not pay enough attention to the end pursued, but rather stressed the means employed, namely force. However, this means is not enough to entirely explain the formation of society. Moreover, [we must note that] force is not equally accepted by those who are constrained by it, and by those who exercise it, and therefore it has little chance to last. Even from the mechanical perspective, a force must be intense in order to produce a lasting effect; and it will only preserve its intensity if it does not encounter too many obstacles in its way. Now, which obstacle should social force avoid in order to preserve its intensity and thus endure? Is it not the secret rebellion of the souls upon which it is imposed? In order to complete the sceptic's theory of social justice, raising it to a higher level that creates trouble to its adversaries, one must first make explicit what is the end towards which social force aims, that is, what is the *purpose* of society?[3] Second, there is a need to understand how individual forces are organized and grouped around a social force so that its exercise meets with the least possible number of obstacles. Epicurus in antiquity, and Hobbes in modernity, were the first thinkers to solve the issue in a utilitarian way. They invoked the interest of each one of its members as the end of society and, as a means for its organization [they posited] mutual consent, that is the mutual acceptance of burdens with a view to the common enjoyment of profits; in a word, the social pact.

'Natural right,' explicitly says Epicurus, 'is not different from a pact of utility by means of which we mutually refrain from harming one another.'[4] One notes how ancient is the conception of society as a kind of contract of assurances, whose end is the reciprocal guarantee, not of rights,[5] but of one another's interests. Epicurus thought that a reflection on the conduct of the utilitarian sage towards his fellow men was not enough. He attempts to understand the very nature and the end of society, and to ground both social and individual life only upon interest. 'Justice is not something valuable in itself; it can only exist through mutual contracts, and it is established everywhere where there is reciprocal engagement of not harming and not being harmed.'[6] This is why when there is no society there is no right: 'Where there are beings who cannot make contracts with an end to mutually not harm or be harmed, there is nothing just or unjust. The same is valid for peoples who did not want or could not make this kind of contract.'[7]

Furthermore, one must not believe that one acts for the sake of others when consenting to the social pact. Each one was only concerned with himself, his own personal protection, and evidently his own interest: 'The laws are established for the sages, not in order to prevent them from committing injustice, but rather in order to prevent them from suffering it.'[8] Nevertheless, by a marvellous reciprocity one finds that each one, when thus protecting himself from others, also protects everyone from himself. Would not the same punishment that threatens those who want to dispossess me[9] turn equally against me if I wanted to dispossess the other contractors? If I were to do this, my action would not be bad, for I would have acted according to my own interest. However, alongside the profit obtained from this action I would meet the correspondent penalty.[10] Evil resides in this penalty, and in this sanction resides moral obligation.[11] Indeed, 'injustice is not an evil in itself, but it is so because of fear; for one is never sure if his injustice will escape the gaze of those who punish this sort of action.'[12] That is why, without the guardians of justice and public peace, there would be no justice and no peace.

One could say, however, that the fear of the law could only hold back the culprit if he was sure of being caught and punished. Could he not expect precisely never to be discovered, or to elude every suspicion, or to escape to every investigation? – Certainly, Epicurus replies, it is *possible* for him to escape his punishment; but this possibility can never be a *realized* fact until after his death.[13] Only he who knew the future would feel free to commit injustices because he would know in advance that they would escape human justice; and not only could he [commit these unjust acts], but he should do so if committing them were to bring him a happy life. According to Epicurus, however, since no one knows the future, and our condition is one of doubt, it is better to abstain from [committing] injustice: 'It is impossible for he who secretly violates any article of the social contract celebrated among men to feel confident that he will escape punishment,[14] even if he has already escaped ten thousand times; for right until the end of his life he is never sure he will not be detected.'[15] For all his life the culprit lives in uncertainty, expectancy and anxiety. 'The just man enjoys the greatest peace of mind, while the unjust is full of the utmost disquiet.'[16] But is not trouble the worst of evils? The sage will, therefore, guard himself from committing injustice, in the same way that he guards himself from intemperance; because things that are goods in themselves can become great evils because of their consequences.[17]

As we can see, it is impossible to reproach Epicurus' logic regarding this issue: interest is the only rule for individuals and nations.[18]

We can now understand the reason why Pyrrhonians and the adepts of a dogmatic morality fight one another without ever being capable of reaching mutual understanding. The former could see in customs and laws of peoples nothing but diversity and contradiction, while the latter had seen only harmony and unity. According to Epicurus, both are right: that which is universal is the search for the greatest interest possible; and since a certain number of interests (for instance, that of not killing, of not enslaving, etc.) is the same for everyone, it follows that the articles of the tacit contract that protect those interests will be more or less the same for all men. On the other hand, there is a great number of interests that vary from one epoch to the other, and one land to another. In this case, the laws inspired by those interests will be variable and particular. On an initial glance, the partisans of dogmatism appear to be right; but if one looks again a little more closely, they are obviously wrong: '*Taken generally*, justice is the same for all, for there is something useful in mutual society'[19] (and also in the laws that are the immediate conditions of this society); 'however, *taken in particular*, from its different places and conditions of application of whatever kind, it results that a thing is not just for all.'[20] The ideas that Epicurus expresses here are exactly the same as those of the English utilitarians, so on this point his [modern] disciples did not do anything different and basically reproduced the doctrine of the ancient master.[21]

Once it has been established that the good is simply the interest of society sanctioned by the law, when the law no longer represents this interest, can it be said it continues to represent justice? Should one blindly conform to it, without any hope of progress? Epicurus' answer is negative and nevertheless he cannot be mistaken for a sceptic. The law does not derive its value from the mere fact of being law and force, but rather because it is a means to the realization of the greatest utility: 'Among the things considered just that which is recognized as useful to the needs of mutual society is thereby stamped as just, independently of it being the same for all or not; and in case any law is made and does not prove advantageous for mutual society, then this [law] no longer has the nature[22] of being just (or "justice").'[23]

There is, then, according to Epicurus an infallible criterion – more infallible than the alleged voice of conscience that the partisans of natural law defend – a criterion with which it is possible to judge justice itself: it is the *sumpheron* (*useful*), superior to *nomos* (*law*). Nevertheless, as interest varies, and in order to not lose sight of it, one must appeal to experience: if the institutions that one believed to be just are recognized as harmful *in reality* (*ep' autōn tōn ergōn*), then they cease to be just, regardless of whether they have an ancient or recent origin. The origin is irrelevant when the end ceases to be public interest. The justice of one particular time is not the same as the justice of another. One must employ past and future tenses when approaching justice; one must admit that some things were once just and are not anymore; as well as that things that are not just now but may well be so in the future.[24] Epicurus could say with Pascal: 'right[25] has its epochs; the entry of Saturn into the Lion marks to us the origin of such and such a crime.'[26]

Despite the changes that the Epicurean doctrine brings to the soul of the social organism, it apparently does not change anything in the body of this organism. What difference does it make if, as Epicurus holds, injustice is not an evil in itself? The matter is not injustice in itself but social injustice. Hence, the sage must keep himself from [the acts and sufferings of] social injustice if he is to preserve his inner peace and ataraxia. Only then will he be able to enjoy a complete happiness and his life, fulfilled with this happiness, will be perfect in its kind. His life will not be one that fears a death that, despite shortening its duration, can never take away life's prize:[27] 'Those who master the art of securing the absence of trouble, especially with regards to their neighbours, live happily with one another and nourish a very solid trust; they entertain the most perfect intimacy and if one of them comes to die a premature death they would not be afflicted as if by a sad thing.'[28]

According to Epicurus, the social ideal consists of a strong union of all the contractors in mutual trust, in a form of happiness where everyone would have their share, and which everyone would enjoy at once.[29] This ideal is far from being that of a primitive and natural state of man. [On the contrary, a]ccording to Epicurus, as according to Hobbes, man in the natural state is man's wolf. Without contracts or laws, claimed Metrodorus, we would devour one another. One could, of course, reproach Epicurus for too quickly transforming wolves into sheep. Undoubtedly the Epicurean sage, who has extinguished all violent desire and troubling passion within himself, will be able to judge that the observance of the social contract is more useful for him than its violation. Unfortunately, however, the Epicurean society[30] is not formed exclusively of sages. For those who are not sages, will social force be sufficient for making conventional justice, born from a pact of interests, something respectable and inviolable? This difficulty appears in Epicureanism as in every other utilitarian system, and I do not propose to discuss its merits here.[31]

In short, in his doctrine of individual and social virtues, and especially in the theory of friendship and justice, Epicurus sought to prove a thesis that we can locate at the basis of every utilitarian doctrine, namely the identity between interest and that which one calls virtue or duty. Without being ends in themselves, virtues are infallible means with a view to the supreme end; [and this] in such a way that, [even] if the sage sometimes hesitates and asks himself where his true interest is, he can always walk without fear in the direction of virtue. This path leads him straight to happiness, 'it runs there.'[32] Epicurus formulates his system of conduct, in accordance with the results of the previous analyses, in the following way: 'Virtue is inseparable from pleasure, but everything else (for instance, wealth and glory) is separable from it because they are perishable ... One cannot live happily if one does not live in a prudent, wise and just way; [however,] one cannot live in a way that is prudent, wise and just if one does not live happily.'[33] In other words, wisdom and justice are a guarantee of happiness; and happiness is a proof of justice and wisdom.

Notes

1 T.N. The French here is *moeurs*.
2 T.N. The French here is *droit*. In order to be consistent with the French original here, I would choose law for *loi* and right for *droit*. The meaning of *droit* here is the system of laws, the set of laws (and not having rights or a right to something).
3 T.N. 'reason' or 'cause'; the French expression is *le pourquoi*. Guyau asks why society exists.
4 Diogenes Laertius, *Lives of Eminent Philosophers*, X, 150: *To tēs phuseōs dikaion esti sumbolon tou sumpherontos eis to mē blaptein allēlous mēde blaptesthai* (translated in the text above). [Hicks' translation is slightly different: 'Natural justice is a symbol or expression of expediency, to prevent one man from harming or being harmed by another.']
5 T.N. *droits*.
6 Diogenes Laertius, *Lives of Eminent Philosophers*, X, 150: *Ouk ēn ti kath' heauto dikaiosunē, all' en tais met' allēlon suntrophais, kath' hopēlikous dēpot' aei topous sunthēkē tis huper tou mē blaptein mēde blaptesthai* (translated above).
7 Diogenes Laertius, *Lives of Eminent Philosophers*, X, 150: *Hosa tōn zōōn mē ēdunato sunthēkas poieisthai tas huper tou mē blaptein allēla mēde blaptesthai, pros tauta outhen estin oude dikaion out' adikon. Hosautōs de kai tōn ethnōn hosa mē ēdunato ē mē ebouleto tas sunthēkas poiesthai* (translated above).
8 Epicurus *apud* Stobaeus, *Sermones*, XLIII, 139: *Hoi nomoi charin tōn sophōn keintai ouch hina mē adikōsin, all' hina mē adikōntai* (translated in the text). The true *sages*, according to Epicurus, have no need of restrictive laws for themselves; wisdom alone restrains their desires and, consequently, also their actions, and prevents them from colliding with others.
9 T.N. The sentence should be understood as follows: 'those who seek to disposes or deprive me of my rights and/or resources'. *Dépoullier* here designates the act of depriving or stripping someone of something.
10 T.N. The French here is *peine*; here used in the sense of (juridical) sanction.
11 T.N. Guyau will later criticize this idea in his *Esquisse*. See Guyau, *Sketch of a Morality Independent of Obligation and Sanction*, translated by Gertrude Kapteyn, London: Watts & co., 1898 (especially first and second books on the 'equivalents of duty').
12 Diogenes Laertius, *Lives of Eminent Philosophers*, X, 151: *Hē adikia ou kath' heautēn kakon, all' en tō kata tēn hupopsian phobō, ei mē lēsei tous huper tōn toioutōn ephestēkotas kolostas* (translated above). [Hicks' translation is slightly different: 'Injustice is not in itself an evil, but only in its consequence, viz. the terror which is excited by apprehension that those appointed to punish such offences will discover the injustice'].
13 T.N. The idea here is the following: for as long as the criminal is alive, punishment is possible. Escaping punishment is never an accomplished fact, since one can always still be caught and punished.

14 Hicks, here, has 'remain undiscovered'.
15 Diogenes Laertius, *Lives of Eminent Philosophers*, X, 151: *Ouk esti ton laphra ti poiounta hō sunethento pros allēlous pisteuein hoti lēsei, kan muriakis epi tou parontos lanthanē; mechri gar katastrophēs adēlon ei kai lēsei* (translated in the text).
16 Diogenes Laertius, *Lives of Eminent Philosophers*, X, 144: *Ho dikaios ataraktotatos, ho d'adikos pleistēs tarachēs gemon* (translated in the text).
17 T.N. See book 1, chapter 3.
18 Nevertheless, in addition to the exterior advantage linked to observing [or abiding to] justice, one must also bear in mind other moral considerations. The virtue of justice realizes not only exteriorly [*au-dehor*], but also within the individual himself, a form of harmony and an interior justice, which produced the equilibrium of desires and passions; 'by its own strength and it nature it soothes the soul;' injustice, on the other hand, and only by its mere presence (*hoc ipso, quod adest*), brings trouble to the soul (*De finibus*, I, XVI, 50). Taking this principle as his starting point, Epicurus came to recommend justice independently of its social consequences, and to prevent us from committing injustice even if it were to remain hidden and undiscovered. His disciples seem to have insisted above all upon this point of his doctrine. Philodemus, for example, recommends that we abide to the *spirit* rather than the *letter* of the law, to be just 'with pleasure, and not by necessity, and to be so with confidence and not with disquiet' (*De rhetorica*, Volumina Herculan. [*Papyrus Herculanensis*], v. a. col. 25: *Meth' hēdonēs, ou di' ananke, kai bebaiōs, all' ou saleuomenōs* [translated above]).
19 T.N. Hicks chose the term 'intercourse'; Guyau uses *société*.
20 Diogenes Laertius, *Lives of Eminent Philosophers*, X, 151: *Kata men to koinon, pasi to dikaion to auto (sumpheron gar ti hēn en tē pros allēlous koinōnia); kata de to idion, chōras kai hosōn dēpot' aition, ou pasi sunpetai to auto dikaion einai* (translated in the text).
21 'It would appear,' Bain writes following Epicurus, 'that in the rules suggested by public and common necessities, there is a certain uniformity, because of the similarity of situation of all societies; in the rules founded on men's sentiments, likings, aversions, and antipathies, there is nothing common, but the fact that some one or more of these are carried to the length of public requirement, and mixed up in one code with the more imperative duties that hold society together' (Alexander Bain, *The Emotions and the Will*, London: John Parker & Son, 1859, 301).
22 T.N. This word could seem strange here, but it reflects the Greek original: *tou dikaiou phusin*. This reflection prefigures Guyau's ideas regarding the non-universality of laws in the *Sketch of a Morality Independent of Obligation and Sanction*.
23 Diogenes Laertius, *Lives of Eminent Philosophers*, X, 152: *Ean te nomothētai ti, mē apobainē de kata to sumpheron tēs pros allēlous koinōnias, ouketi touto tēn tou dikaion phusin echei* (translated in the text above).
24 Diogenes Laertius, *Lives of Eminent Philosophers*, X, 153.
25 T.N. *le droit*.
26 T.N. This is quote from Pascal, *Pensées* [*and Other Writings*, translated by Honor Levi, Oxford: Oxford University Press, 1995, 23], §294: 'Three degrees of latitude reverse all jurisprudence; a meridian decides the truth. Fundamental laws change after a few years of possession; right has its epochs; the entry of Saturn into the Lion marks to us the origin of such and such a crime. A strange justice that is bounded by a river! Truth on this side of the Pyrenees, error on the other side.'
27 T.N. The French *prix* covers a wide semantic filed; it could also be understood as award, worth, value and importance.

28 Diogenes Laertius, *Lives of Eminent Philosophers*, X, 154. [T.N. Compare with Hicks' translation: 'Those who are best able to provide themselves with security against their neighbours, being thus in possession of the surest guarantee, passed the most agreeable life in each other's society; and their enjoyment of the fullest intimacy was such that, if one of them died before his time, the survivors did not lament his death as if it called for commiseration.']
29 T.N. The English *all would enjoy at once* does not fully capture the French *tous jouiraient à la fois*, which has a much stronger connotation implied in the verb *jouir* and in the noun *jouissance*. Guyau's expression suggests that the contract is a way of organizing *jouissance*, so as to assure that all could *jouir*; in this sense, the contract assures my pleasure while also assuring the pleasure of the other (see conclusion of book 4).
30 T.N. This is a tricky expression (*la société épicurienne*), because it could mean both 'the Epicurean [idea of] society' and the 'Epicurean society', that is, the Epicurean circle, school or group.
31 See [Jean-Marie Guyau], *Morale Anglaise Contemporaine*, second part.
32 T.N. The French here is '*elle y court*', which could also be translated as 'she runs there'. I could not locate the reference for this quote.
33 Diogenes Laertius, *Lives of Eminent Philosophers*, X, 138, 140: *Achōriston tēs hēdonēs tēn aretēn monēn, ta d' alla chōrizesthai, oion brota ... Ouk estin hēdeōs zēn aneu tou phronimōs kai kalōs kai dikaiōs, oude phronimōs kai kalōs kai dikaiōs aneu tou hēdeōs* (translated above). [T.N. Compare with Hicks' translation: 'Epicurus describes virtue as the *sine qua non* of pleasure, *i.e. the one thing without which pleasure cannot be, everything else, food, for instance, being separable, i.e.* not indispensable to pleasure' (138); 'It is impossible to live a pleasant life without living wisely and well and justly, and it is impossible to live wisely and well and justly without living pleasantly' (140).]

3

Progress in Humanity

I. On the antagonism between the fundamental idea of every religion and the idea of progress. That the idea of progress is inherent in every naturalist and sensualist doctrine, and that it was virtually contained in the systems of Epicurus and Democritus.
II. Epicurus' and Lucretius' texts indicate the extent to which the idea of progress reached self-consciousness in Epicureanism. The method of modern sociology employed for the first time by Lucretius. Three main causes of progress. Prehistorical humanity. The state of nature and the state of war. First discoveries of human beings. Constitution of the family and then of the first societies. – The idea of a social pact expressed by Epicurus and Lucretius. – The respect of the social pact as a condition of existence for peoples. – Epicurean theory of language. – Discovery of copper and iron. – The loom and the first clothing. – Industrial and fine arts. – Lucretius' conclusions: overview on the progress of humanity. – Lucretius' ideas expressed again by Virgil and Horace. – The same ideas as developed by Seneca. How they are transformed and passed on to modern times.
III. Reasons that hindered the [full] development of an idea of progress in antiquity. Ascetic prejudices that, intertwined with Epicureanism, prevented Lucretius from appreciating the real value of the progress of industry and arts.

I. – One generally agrees with the idea that the notion of progress was absent from ancient thought. One can find it neither in Socrates and Plato, nor in the Stoics until Seneca. In fact, this idea made a late appearance [in antiquity], and it remained a vague idea for a long time. In the Middle Ages, one also fails to find it in the scholastics, except for Roger Bacon. It is only in the Renaissance that the idea of progress is reawakened.

It is indeed interesting to ask oneself why it took so long for man to become aware of the movement that propels him forwards, and which makes him incessantly search and discover what is best.

It is possible to say that the idea of progress is in a relation of antagonism with religious ideas, and that, if the former has been stifled for such a long time, it is because the latter were dominant for the longest time. However, with the development of naturalistic systems the notion of progress would sooner or later have to develop as well.

Believing in progress is to believe in the inferiority of the past in relation to the present and the future. Now, for thought, this inferiority corresponds to a primitive imperfection or a primitive powerlessness. Most religions, on the other hand, place in the origin of things a great power fashioning the world and man according to its own image. In this case it is difficult to understand how a world since its origins and coming out of the creator's hands would be imperfect and evil. It seems that in order to find the good, it is necessary to direct one's attention to the beginnings of things, towards an epoch in which the world was somehow more divine, being at the same time younger. To go back to past ages would be to get closer to God. Every religion is thus constrained to explain the evil that one finds in the world in terms of a decadence, instead of explaining the good that one finds in the world through progress.

Let us add to the cult of gods the cult of ancestors and of heroes, which is significantly connected to it. During the first period of life, the parents appear to the children more as a kind of superior beings than as equals, and they never completely lose this character in their children's eyes. In addition to this, the parents themselves are led to diminish the significance of the present time and to declare the epoch in which they enjoyed their youth and vigour as a superior one. Because of this double illusion produced by filial respect and by a natural association of ideas, one imagines the decay of men and of the world. Our ancestors, whom we have not met and whose high deeds are embellished by tradition, seem to us even wiser and stronger than our parents. One can always measure oneself in relation to the living, judging whether they are superior; however, one cannot measure oneself in relation to the dead, whose grandeur tends to be increased in the memory of human beings, in the same way that one could see the grandeur of Homer's gods. Memory[1] enhances things as much as imagination does, especially when one has the help of a religious [form of] reverence. The first humans were, then, a strong race; divine blood flowed in their veins, they were the sons of the gods. Gradually, the gods, the ancestors and the past fuse into one and the same cult. Every religion tends to become adoration of the past.

Consequently, if one day one seeks to realize and place somewhere the ideal of a happy life, that is to say a golden age conceived in opposition to the present, he will naturally place it in the past and not in the future. Religion and tradition seem to tell us: – in order to contemplate the ideal, you must seek and not look forwards but backwards; turn back like Orpheus did according to the ancient legend. However, this ideal, thus placed behind us, escapes us; when turning back to it, we suddenly lose it and see it disappearing into the vanishing depths of the past. There is nothing more incompatible with the spirit of primitive religions – still foreign to the metaphysical refinements of modern philosophies – than the conception of a progress realizing itself every day in humanity, of a better state which we could reach for ourselves, with our own strength and without divine help or intervention. Man, on his own, can only fail and fall; but to rise again and to give a step forwards, he needs divine help. It is the doctrine of the Fall as opposed to that of progress.

By contrast, once one leaves religion aside, one cannot conceive of a theory of the world that would not have as its principle or as its consequence the belief in some sort of evolution, a slow progress in time. In effect, with Democritus and Epicurus, one is constrained to resort to the hypothesis of a primitive chaos gradually organizing itself under the laws of mechanics[2] or through spontaneous action. Aristotle himself is not that far from [adopting] this hypothesis. He presupposed an immobile ideal inspiring and dominating the work of things, which is perhaps not necessary. This gradual organization of the world already constitutes an evolution, a progress, even if only formal [in character]. Then, when placing the human being in the *kosmos* thus constituted, it is impossible to suppose that humanity arrived at the world at once and in the same civilizational point that we know it has reached. Since human beings do not receive civilization already made from a divine creator, it is then in their hands to build it up in the course of time. They must invent language, which is their first tool, and then other more exterior tools, which we see today in our hands.

Human intelligence must gradually develop, and human customs need to purify themselves. Finally, society must be born and begin to evolve by itself throughout the centuries. And thus every non-religious theory of the world has as its corollary and as its confirmation a history of human progress.[3] One cannot exclude the marvellous[4] from the world without at the same time excluding it from humanity. Now, the only hypothesis that completely excludes the marvellous [of the world] is that of a slow and continuous transformation throughout time, of a march forwards, step by step – *pedentim*, as Lucretius puts it. Thus, the abruptness of miracle is made useless, and the idea of progress comes to oppose that of creation.

If to this sort of *independent* metaphysics[5] one adds a sensualist psychology like that of Democritus and Epicurus, or that of Locke or Condorcet, then there will be the opportunity for the appearance of an idea of progress in such a system.[6] In effect, sensualist theories conceive intelligence as a product of sensation, instead of making it the faculty capable of apprehending truth and the good immediately by intuition. All human knowledge is then conceived as clusters of accumulated sensations. According to Condorcet's remark, this cluster is assembled incessantly throughout time. Time becomes the essential factor in all our knowledge,[7] and the human mind is a sort of great *sensorium* that offers, century after century, an extended surface to all possible impressions. For a sentient being,[8] or for a succession of sentient beings, the mere fact of duration constitutes a form of progress, because in each new instant, new sensations come to engraft the background of previously acquired sensations. In this way, the idea of progress seems to have first appeared in the doctrines that have preferred to consider the human being as a sentient being.[9] Bacon, one of the promoters of this idea, was a sensualist. Sensualism dominated the eighteenth century, when the ideas of indefinite perfectibility were formulated and disseminated everywhere. Finally, in our days, the naturalist and sensualist schools insist upon the insight that there is progress in nature as there is in man, relating it to a universal evolution.[10]

In short, the idea of progress or evolution seems inherent in every naturalist or sensualist doctrine; it was virtually contained in the systems of Democritus and Epicurus, like in every other analogous system. It remains to be seen whether this idea reached any form of explicit self-consciousness in these philosophers, and whether Epicurus was one of the rare ancient thinkers who believed man was susceptible of progress. This is what we will now look for in the texts of Epicurus and Lucretius.

II. – In a passage from his letter to Herodotus, Epicurus says that the different beings, including man, have their origin in the world in which they dwell and not outside of it. After having brought the human being's existence back to a fully earthy or natural origin, he dedicates the following words to humanity: 'We must suppose that experience and necessity came to help nature and taught humankind. Later, reasoning perfected what was received from nature and added new discoveries to it, more rapidly in some cases than in others and with greater progress in some periods than in others.'[11] In these few lines we can already see the three main causes of progress in humanity briefly indicated: the experience that teaches us (*didachthēnai*), the necessity that drives us forwards (*anankasthēnai*), and finally reasoning (*logismos*) that develops every notion we receive from nature, and that ultimately engenders science. Additionally, one finds the essential role of time, which multiplies experiences indefinitely and makes it possible to solve more or less difficult problems throughout more or less long periods. Epicurus gives the example of language, which according to him, the human being acquired spontaneously, and gradually improved by means of a slow and continuous work.

But it is with Lucretius that we find a veritable and more complete analysis of the successive stages of humanity's progress. Up to the present, one has rarely seen in the fifth book of *De rerum natura* anything other than an effort to destroy the fables about a golden age, as well as a desire to refute the reveries of poets and theologians. What has perhaps not been sufficiently understood is that it was not possible to suppress the theological conception of the golden age without replacing it with the modern idea of progress; and that it is this wholly new idea that Lucretius opposed to the ancient fables. In the works of scholars such as Ritter, Zeller or Lange, as well as in the work of the main historians of philosophy, we do not find Lucretius cited among the first defenders of the idea of progress. Undoubtedly, one has already found in Lucretius a good number of modern ideas, such as that of evolution and natural selection. However, the idea of human progress, [that is to say] moral, intellectual and industrial progress, which is neatly expressed in his work, has been barely noticed until now. Yet Lucretius' insights in the fifth book [of *De rerum natura*] are remarkably analogous to insights we find in Condorcet's *Esquisse des progrès de l'esprit humain*. When Lucretius introduced the idea of progress and evolution in [his understanding of] humanity, he anticipated modern sociology, which bases itself on history and the sciences, and proceeds not *a priori* but *a posteriori*, limiting itself to an interpretation of facts in order to deduce the tendencies that characterize the movement of humanity, and thus to deduce its moral or social laws.

For Lucretius, as for Epicurus, progress has three main causes: [i] need (*usus*), which makes us search and grope[12] in every direction; [ii] experience (*experientia*), which accumulates the results of our successive research and groping throughout time; finally, [iii] reason (*ratio*), the 'tireless reason', which works continuously on sense data, extracting everything that is contained in it. Lucretius carefully distinguishes these different causes, placing them against the background of *time* (*aetas*), which 'slowly brings each discovery to light', and *reason*, 'which sheds light on them'. With the help of time, reason 'gradually taught men to progress step by step'.[13]

In his analysis of human progress Lucretius begins in a scientific manner by making *tabula rasa* of everything we owe to a more or less advanced civilization. He supposes primitive man to be deprived of every kind of tool, not knowing how to cover himself with the skin of animals, still yelling out inarticulate cries. Moreover, this man of the dawn of times had a much stronger physical constitution than ours today. He had powerful bones and strong musculature, his skin hardened by cold and heat. Lucretius' hypotheses here perhaps correspond to the conclusions reached by anthropology today.[14] He adds that human beings would, like the wild beast, wander in packs; they lived mainly off fruits and vegetables, placating their thirst in streams and rivers. An ancient belief says that sunset very much frightened the first humans; for when the sun disappeared from the sky in the end of the day, they would have cried for it to come back in loud laments until dawn. In a remarkable scientific attitude, Lucretius rejects this belief.[15] Humans, he says, were habituated since childhood, like other animals, to the succession of days and nights;[16] they did not see anything astonishing in that fact, and did not fear that an eternal night would come to reign upon earth.[17] Such a conception would have been too learned and complex for their minds.

Although the first men were unclothed and unarmed, they had robust hands and agile feet. According to Lucretius, these features enabled them to better equip themselves in the struggle for life. They would flee when confronted with large animals, but they would attack the less dangerous ones, throwing stones at them from afar, and when close, beating them with heavy clubs. When night would fall upon the earth, they would shelter in the bush, just like wild boars, or retreat into caves.[18]

According to Lucretius, back in those times human beings 'were not capable of occupying themselves in the search for the common good. They did not know, then, laws or moral rules in their relationships with others, and each one immediately seized the plunder offered by chance; out of the spontaneity of his nature, each one knew how to preserve and watch out for himself, and to thrive'.[19] Such was the natural state, which Hobbes would later depict in the same colours: it is the state of egoism, it is life for oneself alone; it is also the state of war, in which the right of the strongest reigns.

Three great discoveries mark the first progressive developments of humanity, and were responsible for taking human beings out of an almost bestial condition: [i] man learned how to dress himself with the skin of animals; [ii] he conceived the construction of huts; and finally, [iii] he mastered fire. 'Through the use of fire and through these new inventions, those who had a more ingenious mind and a more powerful intellect, day after day introduced change in forms of nourishment[20] and in the old ways of living'.[21] One could ask, however – how was the art of fire first discovered? It is possible[22] that it was lightning that first brought fire to earth, setting forests ablaze; or it is possible that it was caused by the violent friction of tree branches rubbing together, agitated by strong winds.[23]

Either way, when fire was discovered, when the first huts were built, then there emerged the family. Man and woman, until then united by chance in the woods, now gather around the hearth,[24] and under the same roof. Lucretius stresses that with the advent of the family a new period in the history of humanity begins. On the one hand, bodies are softened by this more comfortable existence; on the other hand, the fierce souls of the parents become milder because of the caresses of their children.[25] Following Lucretius' insightful observation, the child would have played a very important role in civilization, and reacting [upon man], the child ended up shaping the adult man after its own image, in the same way that the child was shaped after man's image.

Once the family is constituted, then we witness the birth of society, which is no different than an association of families. However, in order to subsist, society requires the existence of a certain form of justice among the individuals that compose it. How could justice be established among people who, according to Lucretius and Epicurus, are moved only by personal interest and who do not recognize any other rule than that of force? In order to solve this difficulty, Lucretius, following Epicurus, appeals to the idea of the contract: at the origin of society he posits a more or less encompassing pact, consensual among all individuals. When this pact does not exist, then there is no more society or justice among human beings than among animals. It is this pact that, accomplishing a new progress in humanity and in the world, creates justice. 'Then neighbours began to form bonds, agreeing to abstain from injustice and violence and to reciprocally protect women and children, expressing through their gestures and inarticulate sounds that it is fair for everyone to show mercy for the weak.'[26] One notes that for Lucretius the primitive agreement that is at the origin of social justice did not need articulated language in order to be established. Human beings understood each other initially through signs, like animals do; it is still in this manner that travellers communicate their peaceful intentions to savage tribes. In this way, Lucretius and Epicurus avoid the utopia of Hobbes and his successors, who seem to suppose a contract in its proper and due form, sealed by the first human beings.

Once the pact is sealed not everyone sticks by it, and here and there the concord that had been achieved was broken more than once; but, as Lucretius says, 'the majority and the best of people will loyally observe the pact'. The most striking proof that justice, once established, has had numbers and force on its side is to be found, according to Lucretius, in the very survival of humankind: without the pact, 'humanity would already have been wholly destroyed and the human race would not have been able to propagate itself for generations'.[27] Thus, by an application of the law of natural selection, which he had already formulated, Lucretius shows us that a key condition for the existence of peoples lies in justice and in the observance of the social contract. Our own life today is testimony to the triumph of justice in the past, and in order for our own descendants to live it will be necessary that justice triumphs again in the present and in the future.

Human association preceded the existence of articulated language, but it did not take long for the former to lead [us] to the appearance of the latter through natural progress. According to Lucretius, and to Epicurus before him, language originally was the utterance of certain sounds in harmony with the sensations and ideas of each human being.[28] Even among animals we see that this or that emotion, this or that feeling, is expressed through particular sounds that are very different from one another, and whose spectrum already constitutes a certain form of rudimentary language. 'If different sensations give animals no choice but to utter different sounds, dumb as they may be, how much more likely it was for man with his wide range of sound to indicate and distinguish different objects by particular sounds.'[29] Therefore, in every being each feeling tends to be translated externally by means of a sign that represents it. These signs will necessarily be more perfect and will be constantly perfected in the case of human beings, since they are the most gifted of animals. Lucretius claims that children prefigure language when they point their fingers at the things that interest them, and so seek to share their emotions with others. Furthermore, language originated in the expression of individual ideas and will vary according to different individuals and places. It is only later that convention intervenes among people of a single nation, giving each word a specific and uniform meaning.[30] Gradually, a term that originally expressed an absolutely individual emotion or thought came to express thoughts and feelings of a whole people. In what concerns words designating nonsensible things, people of higher intelligence introduced them later; they are not at all primitive.[31]

The problem of the formation of language is unquestionably one of the most difficult issues that the adversaries [of the notion] of divine creation and miracles have to solve. We must highlight here the solution given by Epicurus, which would later be recovered by Lucretius: it could be easily assimilated into the modern theories of Darwin and Spencer. It also confirms the hypothesis, developed by the Epicureans, of a gradual and continual progress in humanity.

We have seen that, according to Lucretius, 'man's first tools were his hands, fingernails and teeth, then stones and branches, and finally fire and flame'.[32] Let us note here that this progression is accurate and scientific. It was much later that humans discovered metals and the way to forge them. The first metal they used was copper. As Lucretius says: 'The use of copper[33] precedes the use of iron because it was easier to work and more common.'[34] One knows today how modern science confirms this hypothesis. After another period of time, men came to know iron, and this harder metal would progressively replace copper.

With the development of the knowledge of metals, especially that of iron, human industry begins. 'The plaited garments came before woven cloth; the weaver's craft came after the discovery of iron: only with iron one was able to make delicate instruments such as the loom's tackle, the treadles, spindles, shuttles, clacking heddles.'[35] Additionally, Lucretius claims that men and not women were the ones to discover and first employ these instruments, 'for they are more industrious and excel women in every art'.[36] Later, men would delegate to women these labours that did not require great physical strength and so that they could dedicate themselves to heavier labour. In his *History of Materialism*, Lange thinks that this thought displays remarkable finesse, and adds: 'Nowadays, when one introduces female labour gradually, or sometimes suddenly, into the careers opened and long explored by men only, this thought seems to us much more natural than it could have seemed in the time of Epicurus and Lucretius, when this kind of revolution in entire fields of industrial labour had not yet been produced.'[37] In reality, Lucretius' hypothesis is more contestable than what Lange believed; for the inferiority of women in relation to men in industrial labours, especially in those which require skill, is no more proven today than in antiquity.

Simultaneous with the art of weaving, human beings learned, through a series of trials and errors, the art of cultivating the land, of sowing and grafting. Little by little, people began to despise the wild fruits and acorns of yore, as well as beds made of leaf litter and grass, and animal-pelt garments. However, writes Lucretius, 'I imagine that the inventor of such rough garments was once the object of general envy, and that other men could have ambushed and killed him, sharing the spoil without nevertheless being able to enjoy it themselves. However, new discoveries devalue the old ones and completely changes our taste.'[38]

To the merely industrial arts the fine arts were later added. They began as a simple amusement, a joyful expansion that followed meals, especially in the beautiful season.[39] Later on, the fine arts became one of the most important domains of human activity.

We know how Lucretius explains the birth of music through the imitation of birdsongs. Poetry, this music of words, is, according to him, related to this same origin. 'Thus, time gradually reveals each discovery, and human reason puts them in full light.'[40]

Finally, incrementally civilizing themselves, human beings learnt to build cities and fortresses; land would be parcelled into plots and divided among their dwellers; the sails of ships covered the seas. Nations developed links through pacts analogous to those which once linked individuals. Poets, through their songs, bequeathed events and deeds to posterity. Subsequently, writing was invented in order to fix men's memory. In what regards the primitive times preceding this epoch of relative civilization, we have gradually lost every trace of it. It is only through the work of reason that we can reconstruct the history of these forgotten ages.[41]

Following on from this sketch of human history the conclusion Lucretius reaches is truly masterful. He extracts the notion of progress from the facts he exposes and it is with the affirmation of progress that he ends book V.[42] 'Navigation and agriculture, architecture, jurisprudence, weaponry, roads, clothing and all innovations of this sort; the arts that make life pleasant, such as poetry, painting, sculpture are seen to emerge both from experience and the activity of the mind: needs and experience have gradually taught men these skills, step by step. So, time incrementally brings to light all the discoveries, and reason sheds light upon them.[43] We have seen genius shining in the arts one after the other, up to those who have reached the very summit.'[44]

One notes that Lucretius clearly expressed the law of progress, and not only was he the first to express it, but he has also demonstrated his claim through science, deducing it from the history of humankind. However, let us remark that this doctrine of human intellectual and moral progress in Lucretius, as well as in his master, coexists without contradiction with another doctrine, which is rationally deduced from the principles of Epicureanism: that of the final dissolution of the world and its gradual decline and ultimate perishing. Our earth, for the Epicureans, is one vast organism, and as such it is subjected to ageing and death. It has once produced plants and other beings which were far more vigorous than what they are now; the first men themselves had a stature and muscles much more developed than ours. However, this muscular degeneration is not in opposition to the progress of intelligence. Modern scholars concur with Lucretius that just as our old earth loses its heat and its fecundity, so our organism becomes weaker and seems to become impoverished. However, do these scholars think that it follows from this that our intelligence was not, in fact, enriched and cannot be further enriched? In what regards the final dissolution and the downfall of the world, chanted for the first time by Lucretius, there is no doubt that it could abruptly halt the march of human progress. This is still too distant and uncertain, however, to be taken as the object of an exaggerated concern. It is one thing to know whether progress, as Condorcet will audaciously maintain, is absolutely indefinite and unlimited; it is another thing to ascertain the actual existence of progress. Epicureanism affirmed the existence of progress and demonstrated it as well it could have done in its time.

The ideas expressed in the fifth book of *The Nature of Things* were evidently new in Lucretius' time, if we judge by the impression they produced in his contemporaries. In effect, we find in Virgil and Horace a summary of this book. Virgil engaged with Epicurean cosmogony. Horace, who, as Martha notes, is more of a *moraliste*,[45] focuses on the human aspects of the book.[46] 'When human animals crawled forth upon primeval earth, as a dumb and hideous herd, they fought for their acorns and shelters with nails and fists, then with clubs, and so on progressively with the weapons which need had later forged, until they found words and language with which to express their feelings and designate objects. Thenceforth war (of each man against the other) began to cease; human beings began to build towns, surrounded by ramparts, and to establish laws to prevent thievery, banditry and adultery ... It is the fear of injustice that led us to devise law;[47] when one looks back at the origins and turns over the annals and records of the world, one must admit that justice was born of the fear of injustice.'[48] We find once more in these verses of Horace the doctrine of progress associated to that of conventional law[49] and of justice founded on a pact of utility. Moral ideas are, like all the rest, an invention, a discovery; justice is born at a specific time in human history, like the arts and sciences. Justice is born from [the combination of] need[50] and intelligence, which are two major factors of progress.

Later Seneca, this Stoic nourished by Epicurean ideas, will place himself at the point of view where Lucretius arrived before him in the conclusion of the fifth book. He then reminds us of the time when men were still coarse and young and still erred blindly in their groping around for the truth; a time when everything was new to them. Nevertheless, by repeated effort, the same things [that they looked for in their blind trials] become easier and more known. And Seneca adds, in a natural induction, taking us from past to future: 'There will come a time when that which is hidden today will be revealed to future generations ... The future will know what we now ignore, and it will be astonished by the fact that we ignored what it knows ... Some mysteries do not lift all their veils in a day. Eleusis keeps its revelations only for those who come to interrogate it. Nature does not reveal all its secrets all at once. Truth does not come to offer itself and lavish all eyes; it hides and withdraws into the deepest sanctuary: our century has discovered only an aspect of it; the centuries that will follow will know how to contemplate the others.'[51]

The triumph of Christianity came to suffocate the idea of progress for a certain time.[52] It was under Seneca's inspiration that it reappeared in the Middle Ages with Roger Bacon. One can also find it in Pico della Mirandola and in Montaigne, who was an avid reader of Seneca and Pascal's master. But it is especially with Francis Bacon, Descartes and Pascal that this idea truly comes to the fore in opposition to the idea of authority. It is with Turgot and Condorcet that the notion of progress is reflectively affirmed, and they develop it in all its consequences. Nowadays, the idea of progress has finally merged with the idea of evolution, with which it was already intertwined since the Epicureans.

III. – As we have shown, the idea of progress was born in antiquity. It is from antiquity and its naturalist systems that it emerges from. One might ask what hindered the development of this idea for other ancient thinkers. There are several reasons for that. First, the ancients lacked a peremptory demonstration of progress. Humankind was not yet sufficiently advanced in its route in order to be able to look behind, gazing at the whole road it had travelled until then. What was missing in ancient times was a positive history, different from the legend that amplifies its characters and elevates them above us.

Lucretius has rendered a great service to the idea of progress by attempting for the first time to oppose to the legends [of his time] a sort of historical sketch based on a series of deductions. From this moment, when a bit of light is shed onto past ages, we find a first acknowledgement of progress. Later, as times went by and history was made, and as centuries of history followed the centuries of legends, the idea of progress developed, and gradually penetrated deeper into human minds. Nevertheless, in the Middle Ages, the idea of progress would find a new obstacle in the notion of authority, which is at the bottom of every religion. However, moral ideas and intellectual conceptions, since they are invincible, can only grow in their struggle against other ideas; they even need to encounter resistance in order to acquire their full strength. It was by reaction against authority and revelation that the idea of progress reappeared, clearer and stronger, in the thirteenth and seventeenth centuries. The religious principle, against which it was in a relation of opposition since its beginnings and which tends to destroy it, would on the contrary force the idea of progress to revive and affirm itself in all its plenitude.

Let us finally add a third cause that delayed the development of the idea of progress. It is not enough to ascertain [the existence of] progress, one must also understand its moral value. If one leaves aside the moral point of view and adopts only the scientific perspective, progress would then only appear as variation, multiplication of effects: it diversifies laws and customs increases ad infinitum the knowledge of nature, produces and perfects the arts. One can surely admit progress in this form, as certain contemporary pessimists do, without, however, believing that it constitutes any real and profound improvement. It is under this form that the ancients, and particularly the Epicureans, were led to positively conceive the notion of progress. The Epicureans, being utilitarians, sought to estimate the sensible utility that human beings extracted from intellectual progress. Now, from the perspective of sensibility, progress produces two effects: on the one hand, the multiplication of needs, on the other, the diversification and refinement of pleasures. However, according to Lucretius, as according to Epicurus, the multiplication of needs is not a good thing. If one has only need of an animal skin to protect oneself from the cold, one is more perfect, less exposed to anxiety and trouble of every sort, than if one requires luxurious garments. Furthermore, for the austere doctrine of Epicureanism, the refinement of pleasures is not a good thing either. Epicurus said that to vary pleasure is not to increase it. Civilization, making sensibility more exquisite, makes it more vulnerable to every sort of suffering, something that did not affect primitive men. From this perspective, Lucretius seems to condemn the progress of industry and even of the arts, like the good old Romans did, and as do all religions. Lucretius, like Rousseau, shows a certain weak spot for the humans of the earliest times. He admires their easy enjoyments – vivacious although somehow coarse. He resents our civilization. Asceticism is the enemy of progress, and there is as much asceticism in the apparently so languid Epicurean philosophy as there is in Stoicism and the majority of ancient philosophies and religions. Epicureanism was too closed in itself as a system for being able to understand the full extension of the idea of progress. We have seen, though, how it contributed to it the emergence of this idea. It remained a task for modern doctrines to develop further this yet imperfect idea and to communicate to humankind a full awareness of the labour which is constantly accomplished within it.

Notes

1. T.N. The French expression here is *le souvenir*.
2. T.N. Guyau's use of the phrase 'laws of mechanics' here is evidently anachronistic.
3. T.N. Guyau uses the plural 'progresses'.
4. T.N. I have tried to stay as close as possible to the original (*merveilleux*), but one could also think of other valid alternatives in the same semantic filed: 'miraculous' or even 'supernatural' could be good options here.
5. T.N. It is not fully clear what Guyau means here; perhaps 'independent of religion'?
6. T.N. the notion of 'sensualism' here refers to a philosophical position in the theory of knowledge: the senses and sensations as fundamental instances and as the origin of knowledge. It is semantically related to empiricism, by emphasizing the role of experience. From the epistemological perspective, the sensualist position argues that perception and sensation are the primary and most important form of cognition.
7. T.N. *connaissances*.
8. T.N. *être sentant*.
9. T.N. That is to say, a being primarily defined by the sensation.
10. T.N. Guyau's reference here is clearly to Herbert Spencer.
11. Diogenes Laertius, *Lives of Eminent Philosophers*, X, 75: *Alla mēn hupolēpteon kai tēn tōn anthropōn phusin polla kai pantoia hupo tōn autēn periestōtōn pragmatōn didachthēnai te kai anankasthēnai; ton de logismon ta hupo tautēs parenguēthenta, kai husteron epakriboun; kai prosexeuriskein o men tisi, thatton; en de tisi, braduteron; kai en men tisi, kata periodous kai chronous meizous apo tōn tou apeirou; en de tisi, kat' elattous* (translated above).
12. T.N. *tâtonner*.
13. Lucretius, *On the Nature of Things*, V, 1386; 1445.
14. Lucretius, *On the Nature of Things*, V, 923.
15. Lucretius, *On the Nature of Things*, V, 970.
16. T.N. Even though Guyau uses the pair day/night, the Latin original uses *cernere semper alterno tenebras et lucem*, literally they perceived the succession or alternance of darkness [or shadow] and light.
17. T.N. Lucretius, *On the Nature of Things*, V, 970.
18. Lucretius, *On the Nature of Things*, V, 969.
19. Lucretius, *On the Nature of Things*, V, 955: '*Nec commune bonum poterant spectare, nec ullis / Moribus inter se scibant, nec legibus uti. / Quod cuique obtulerat praedae fortuna, ferebat, / Sponte sua sibi quisque valere et vivere doctus*' (translated in the text; [T.N. I have translated from Guyau's translation, consulting the Latin; I have also used some of A. E. Stallings' phrases. It is important to note that Guyau seems to intentionally neglect the stylistic and poetic aspect of Lucretius' text, focusing strictly on the ideas he expresses. His translations are more or less literal paraphrases of Lucretius' thought, rather than a poetic version of it. I have tried to preserve that aspect in the translation].
20. T.N. This is absent from both Rouse's and Stallings' translations; Guyau is probably translating the word *victum* in the Latin original. *Victum* (from *victus*) means both a way of life, with reference to the necessities of life and that upon which one lives: sustenance, nourishment, provisions or victuals.
21. Lucretius, *On the Nature of Things*, V, 1105: '*Inque dies magis hi victim vitamque priorem / Commutare novis monstrabant rebus, et igni, / Ingenio qui praestabant, et corde vigebant*' (translated above).

22 T.N. Possibilistic explanations, as well as explanations by analogy and hypotheses, play a key role in Epicurean physics: it is often the case that Epicureans provide multiple and equally possible or plausible natural causal explanations; see, for example, *Letter to Pythocles*, 99–115. See also George K. Strodach, 'Introduction', in Epicurus, *The Art of Happiness* [*The Philosophy of Epicurus: Letters, Doctrines, and Parallel Passages from Lucretius*], translated by George K. Strodach, London & New York: Penguin, 2012, 34–6.
23 Lucretius, *On the Nature of Things*, V, 1090.
24 The French here is *foyer*. The foyer, or the Roman *lar*, was an essential figure in ancient culture. See Fustel de Coulanges, *The Ancient City: A Study on the Religion, Laws and Institutions of Greece and Rome*, translated by Willard Small, Boston: Lee & Shepard, 1877.
25 Lucretius, *On the Nature of Things*, V, 1010.
26 Lucretius, *On the Nature of Things*, V, 1019: '*Tunc et amicitiam coeperunt jungere, habentes / Finitima inter se, nec laedere, nec violare; / Et pueros commendarunt, muliebreque saeclum, / Vocibus, et gestu, cum balbe significarent / Imbecillorum esse aequum misererier omnium*' (translated above). The plural form of *vocibus* in this passage could only be non-articulate (or not-yet-articulate) sounds: the formation of language is later described by Lucretius, and he follows a historical order in his exposition.

The conception of the social pact has not been sufficiently highlighted in readings of Epicurus and Lucretius; nevertheless, it has capital importance in Epicureanism, an importance reflected in Diogenes Laertius' texts (*Lives of Eminent Philosophers*, X, 150). Lucretius, faithful to the doctrine of his master in every detail, reproduces this idea. *Jungere amicitiam . . . nec laedere nec violare* ['began to form bonds of friendship . . . abstaining from injustice and violence'] is evidently the Latin translation of the Greek *sunthēkas poieisthai tas huper tou mē blaptein allēlous mēde blaptesthai* ['to make contracts with an aim at not harming each other, and not let oneself be harmed' (Diogenes Laertius, *Lives of Eminent Philosophers*, X, 150)]. Later, and on several occasions, Lucretius will employ in the same sense *foedus* [pact, contract] or *foedera* [pacts, contracts] to translate the Greek *sumbolon tou sumpherontos* ['pact of utility']. – One has not sufficiently remarked that the idea of contract – which Hobbes and Rousseau will later employ – is a more or less unconscious reminiscence of Epicureanism.
27 Lucretius, *On the Nature of Things*, V, 1023: '*Non tamen omnimodis poterat concordia gigni; / Sed bona magnaque pars servabant foedera casti: / Aut genus humanum jam tum foret omne peremptum, / Nec potuisset adhuc perducere saecla propago*' ['Concord would not be able to emerge in all circumstances, / But a good part among them [people], the virtuous ones, respect pacts: / Without that, humankind would have already been destroyed, / And the lineage would not have been able to prolong itself from generation to generation until today'].
28 Lucretius, *On the Nature of Things*, V, 1027. Cf. Diogenes Laertius, *Lives of Eminent Philosophers*, X, 75.
29 Lucretius, *On the Nature of Things*, V, 1075 [the passage seems to be rather 1089. I have based my translation upon Stallings'].
30 T.N. Would this lead to the hypothesis of a primal common human language? Or to a plurality of languages corresponding to the plurality of individuals?
31 Diogenes Laertius, *Lives of Eminent Philosophers*, X, 76.
32 Lucretius, *On the Nature of Things*, V, 1280.

33 The English for the Latin *aes* (*aereus, aeris*) is both something made of copper or bronze. I used copper respecting Guyau's choice, *cuivre*. *Aerifice* refers to the art of working with bronze.
34 T.N. Lucretius, *On the Nature of Things*, V, 1270.
35 Lucretius, *On the Nature of Things*, V, 1348. [In Rouse's translation, 1350: 'Woven cloth comes after iron, because iron is needed for equipping the loom, nor without it can such smoothness be given to the treadles and spindles, shuttles and noisy leash-rods'].
36 Lucretius, *On the Nature of Things*, V, 1332.
37 Lange, *Histoire du matérialisme et critique de son importance à notre époque* [*Geschichte des Materialismus und Kritik seiner Bedeutung in der Gegenwart*, 1866], translated by B. Pommerol, Paris : Reinwald, 1877, 146 [my translation].
38 T.N. Guyau provides no reference for this quote; it is Lucretius, *On the Nature of Things*, V, 1420–5.
39 T.N. No reference; it is Lucretius, *On the Nature of Things*, V, 1390.
40 Lucretius repeats this thought for the third time [V, 1388].
41 T.N. Here Guyau paraphrases Lucretius, V, 1445–7.
42 Lucretius, *On the Nature of Things*, V, 1455: '*Navigia, atque agri culturas, moenia, leges, / Arma, vias, vestes, et caetera de genere horum / Praemia, delicias quoque vitae funditus omnes, / Carmina, picturas, et daedala signa polire, / Usus et impigrae simul experientia mentis / Paulatim docuit pedetentim progredientes. / Sic unum quidquid paulatim protrahit aetas / In medium, ratioque in lumini eruit oras. / Namque alid ex alio clarescere corde videmus / Artibus, ad summum donec venere cacumen*' (translated above).
43 T.N. This is the fourth repetition of these verses in the poem (book V).
44 T.N. Lucretius, *On the Nature of Things*, V, 1455.
45 T.N. I have decided to preserve the French term *moraliste* given its connotation in the original; the *moralistes* were not only 'ethicists' in the strict sense of the term, but also 'psychologists' in the broad sense of the term, interested in human nature and passions. 'Moralist', however, should not be understood here as the English negative adjective.
46 Martha, *Le poème de Lucrèce* [*morale, religion et science*, Paris: Librairie Hachette, 1869], 299.
47 T.N. The French here is *droit*. Although my preference has been to use the English term 'right' for *droit* and 'law' for *loi* (a law), it is important to stress that *le droit* can also be translated as Law. I am grateful to Ann Thomson for this remark.
48 T.N. Horace, *Satires*, I, iii, 99. In H. Rushton Fairclough's translation [Cambridge MA: Harvard University Press, 1942, 41], the clause 'It is the fear of injustice that led us to devise law', which Guyau renders as an interpolation, ends the passage: 'When living creatures [Guyau: 'human animals'] crawled forth upon primeval earth, dumb, shapeless beasts, they fought for their acorns and lairs with nails and fists, then with clubs, and so on step by step [Guyau: 'progress by progress'; 'progressively'] with the weapons which need had later forged, until they found words and names [Guyau: 'language'] wherewith to give meaning to their cries and feelings. Thenceforth they began to cease from war [Guyau adds: (of each man against the other)], to build towns, and to frame laws that none should thieve or rob or commit adultery. [...] If you will but turn over the annals and records of the world, you must confess that justice was born of the fear of injustice.'
49 T.N. Again, *droit*. Here Guyau means the body of laws, Law or Right (as in the German *Recht*). See note 47 above.

50 T.N. *besoin*.
51 Seneca, *Natural Questions*, VII.
52 One has wished to assimilate to the idea of a progress towards the better a Jewish and Christian conception of the 'kingdom of God', opposed to secular life [*vie du siècle*]. However, this conception of a kingdom of God suddenly realized by the coming of a Messiah is totally different from the idea of a human and natural progress, of a gradual evolution, in which all terms are linked to one another and follow from each other without miraculous or supernatural intervention. There is, between these two doctrines, the same distance that separates science from religion and, in some regards, from superstition.

4

Epicurean Piety. The Struggle against Divinity understood as Efficient Cause

I. That the world has neither a first cause nor a final one. The argument drawn from the existence of evil, boldly employed by the Epicureans.
II. How, according to Epicurus, the absence of every cause[1] acting upon the world does not lead to atheism as a conclusion. On the universal fact that one should take into account: the belief in immortal and blissful gods. That this belief must have its basis in certain facts of experience. On our representations of the gods. – That these representations are partially true; that one should purify them of foreign elements. – That the idea of a deity creating or assuring the order of the world does not have logical priority;[2] that it is instead derivative and inexact. – Epicurus' attempt to return to the *primitive* notion.[3] – That the gods are blissful, and consequently inactive, because action presupposes effort and trouble;[4] that they are invisible to our eyes; that they are infinite in number, etc. On the logic of Epicurus' doctrine, which deduces consequences all the way through from inexact principles.
III. The cult of the gods according to Epicurus. – Epicurus at the temple of Jupiter. – Why the Epicureans revered their gods. Remarkable consequence to which the Epicurean system leads: that, among all virtues, piety is the only disinterested one.
IV. Is Epicurean theology sincere? – A contemporary historian's opinion about Epicurus' doctrine. Did Epicurus honour divinity as a simple ideal or as a reality? Should one assimilate his doctrine to that of Vacherot and Renan? – That the Epicurean gods were, for him, very real beings. – Identity of subjective and objective, of ideal and reality, on which relies Epicurus' doctrine.

Epicurus' ethics, as we have seen, is absolutely independent of any religious idea. Similarly, Epicurean cosmology does not invoke any divine intervention. Epicurus' system, taken as a whole, rejects every idea of a first and a final cause.

In order to show that the world indeed exists without any help from divinity, Epicurus invoked one of the first arguments that modern thinkers would largely exploit, namely the existence of evil. This argument is, in fact, the only one he mobilizes, for it seems sufficient to him. According to Lucretius, the existence of evil is an indisputable fact, insofar as our world[5] is not what it could be: covered by forests, mountains, swamps and seas, the earth confronts human beings with obstacles that are often insurmountable. The human being, who is the most perfect animal on earth, is also the most miserably divided.[6] In nature, nothing is distinctively an end to be pursued without failure, nothing bears the sign of a God. Admittedly, if the world were divine, it would be the best [possible world].[7]

Based on the existence of evil, which he easily demonstrated, Epicurus puts forward an argument to which neither the ancients nor the moderns were able to respond. We find this argument cited by Lactantius. He says, 'Either God wants to suppress evil and is not able to do it; or he is able to do it and does not want to; or he does not want to do it and is also not able to do it; or, finally, he wants to suppress evil and is able to do it. If he wants to suppress evil, but cannot do it, then he is impotent, which is unsuitable to God; if he is able to suppress evil and does not do it, then he is envious, which, as a matter of principle, cannot suit God. If he neither wants it nor is able to do it, he is simultaneously envious and impotent, and thus he is not God. However, if he wants and is able to suppress evil, which is the only option suitable to God, then where does evil come from? Why does God not suppress it?'[8] Thus, for those who admit a first cause, the only way to explain the existence of evil is to refer it to this cause, which is impossible.

II. – Now, if there is no divine creator, is one necessarily led to atheism? According to Epicurus, this [conclusion] would be too hasty. We recognize here a universal fact: the belief in the gods. Therefore, a philosophy founded on facts must take *this* fact into consideration and endeavour to explain it.

We know that, following Epicurus, every general idea (*prolēpsis*) is formed by the accumulation of sensations and that, furthermore, every sensation is true [in itself]; what follows from this is that every general idea has some ground in reality. And the same must be valid for the idea and the belief in the gods. According to Cicero, Epicurus was the first philosopher to invoke man's universal belief in favour of divine existence; and he was also the first to extract some objective certitude from this completely subjective foundation.[9] Epicurus attempted to show that the idea of the gods does not come to us from the outside, [that is to say,] that we cannot simply attribute it either to education or custom, or to any human law. The belief in the divine is solid and unanimous among human beings, something that seems to be imprinted in our soul by nature itself.[10] Independently of every idea, of every philosophical system, we feel, we experience, that there are gods. And not only does nature arouse in us this tenacious belief, but it also adds to it a sort of representation of the gods under this or that particular aspect. It is, for example, a [received] idea among all peoples that the gods not only exist, but also that they are immortal and happy.[11] Existence, beatitude and immortality: these are the most important and incontestable attributes under which we conceive of the gods.

Now, if one seeks to penetrate more deeply into this idea that humanity produces about the gods, if one asks about its origin and tries to explain it, then, according to Epicurus, one must consider the [following] empirical fact[12] which engenders this idea. When we are awake or asleep, more or less distinct phantoms[13] frequently present themselves to us, sometimes very vividly. These phantoms walk, they talk to us, then suddenly disappear, and their aspect remains imprinted in our mind. In antiquity, religion assumed more sensible forms, more accessible to the imagination than in our days, and these fantastic visions must have been even more frequent then. The ancients lived among their gods; statues and images were found everywhere as a reminder of their form, making them present to sight and to the mind. It is not surprising, then, that all these images and forms embellished by sculpture would come to haunt people's imagination [when] in the solitude of sleep. In our days, the supposed vision of God supposes two things: [i] it is necessary that the sick mind,[14] and by a double effort, attributes a sensible form to the divinity, and then [ii] makes this form to appear before its eyes. In antiquity the first of these two tasks was accomplished in advance: every god had its form, and an idea that was associated with its image. A small effort was enough to recall simultaneously the idea and the image, and this sort of hallucination thus understood was less exceptional and less abnormal than it is for us today.

Let us add, in order to ably explain the theory of Epicurus, that the phenomena of hallucination were still unexplained in antiquity. One could rarely distinguish between hallucination and true sensation then. At the bottom of Epicurean canonic[15] we find a confusion between these two things[16] and the belief that every sensation is true. By that Epicurus did not mean that we are never mistaken; he only maintained that our senses are never mistaken. Everything they reveal to us, he maintains, does indeed exist. Error comes from what intelligence adds to sensation when interpreting it. Pure sensation[17] is always true: there is always outside, in reality, something that explains it or produces it. Thus, when images present themselves to us under a persistent form, regardless of how strange they are, we must then admit that these phantoms are not only mere phantoms, and that behind these visions we find realities. Given that the gods appear to us, they *are*.[18] But their bodies are not as coarse as ours. And because we internally represent them [to ourselves] as beautiful, blissful and immortal, they must be so, and so they are indeed. In this way, the Epicurean theory of the gods is founded upon a fact and a sensation.

Now, how can we reconcile the existence of the divinity with the existence of evil in the world? It seems that in attempting to do this we are thus led to contradiction: on the one hand, human intelligence affirms the existence of the divinity; on the other, it has to admit[19] that the existence of a divine creator or an ordering deity is incompatible with the existence of our imperfect world.

In order to solve this difficulty, we must, according to Epicurus, simply make the effort to purify in ourselves the natural notion of divinity. We must separate it from the elements that are strange to it and which have, nevertheless, been associated with it for a long time.[20] The primitive idea of the gods is true; but this idea does not presuppose a divine creator. It is because of this powerlessness to penetrate the causes of natural phenomena (*aitiologein*) with a still insufficient science that human beings imagined a divine intervention in the tumult of the world. The great events of nature, like lightning and the storms, seemed divine to men because they appeared to them as something dreadful.[21] Similarly, without being able to explain the regular course of the stars by natural laws, human beings found a way to explain it by divine will. Their god became, as for the tragic poets, a *deus ex machina*.[22] They depicted the world as being crafted in the same way as the objects which man makes use of, and that is through hammer blows,[23] 'with bellows and anvils'.[24] However, the world is, in reality, a more delicate machine; and making gods labourers is only to abase them.

The idea of creation is far from being inseparable from that of divinity; according to Epicurus, it cannot really be attached to it. Divinity has supreme happiness as its main attribute. Now, supreme happiness presupposes the absence of every worry, trouble or effort. But to create a world, and to to create it imperfectly, having to constantly watch over it and adjust it, that is a heavy task, incompatible with sovereign felicity. The gods are not involved in the affairs of this world, and it is necessary to correct the popular idea of the divine on this point. Epicurus' gods live entirely detached from things, having no trouble or suffering, no anguish, harming no one; they do not punish or reward anyone, nor do they nourish anger or affection, because 'this sort of feeling comes only from weakness'.[25]

If we further investigate the nature of these eternally happy and tranquil gods, Epicurus shows us that they cannot have a nature as coarse as ours. Nevertheless, they have a sort of body (because nothing exists apart from atoms and the void); however, the atoms that compose them are of a subtlety that cannot be compared to anything down here [in our world].[26] Thus, the gods are invisible to our eyes; it is only internally within ourselves, as if by a kind of profound vision, that we can have an apperception of the images that flow from them. These subtle bodies would be dissolved if we placed them in our universe, among the atoms that clash against each other; they must, therefore, live outside of it. Indeed, they float in the void, in the gaps [*intervalles*] separating the different worlds.[27] They are infinite in number,[28] like the worlds themselves. Fertile nature has sown countless gods and spheres[29] in the space. These gods have human form, for it is the most beautiful and most perfect.[30] The Epicureans maintain that the gods must even eat since no [material] body can subsist without repairing its losses.[31] They also assign them different sexes.[32]

One notes how the Epicurean theory arrives at bizarre conclusions. Nevertheless, as we have said before, these follow logically from the principles. In this series of deductions there is something that resembles the dreams of hallucinating people; still, all this theory is an attempt to rationally interpret the superstitious beliefs that can ultimately be reduced to a form of hallucination.

III. – When, from the knowledge of the gods, we move to the examination of the cult people dedicate to them, and the nature of religious sentiment, our investigation will arrive at this point, which is rather curious for a utilitarian system: religious sentiment and the cult of divinity become entirely disinterested. Epicurus does not expect anything from the gods, and his piety rests on the belief that they are indifferent and impotent. Prayer becomes, then, useless and absurd; pure worship replaces it, but a form of worship detached from every personal feeling. Vulgar piety is always mixed with feelings of fear and hope. People pray to the gods in order to obtain the goods they desire, or to eliminate the evils they fear. The Epicurean, on the other hand, does not fear anything coming from the gods, nor does he expect anything from them, and nevertheless, he worships them. Why? Because they are [the expression of] an ideal form of happiness and serenity; because they represent that which the Epicurean ought to be; because they are beautiful to contemplate, and they enchant our own thoughts, just like the marbles of Phidias please our sight.

As we know, Epicurus assiduously attended temples. The first time Diocles saw him, he wrote: 'What a spectacle! I have never understood the grandeur of Jupiter so well than after seeing Epicurus on his knees.' Antiquity was astonished, like Diocles, at the piety of Epicurus and his disciples. Seneca correctly remarks that disinterestedness, banished from Epicurean ethics, finds a place in its cult of the gods, and he sees in this an objection to [the teaching of] Epicurus.[33] Why do the Epicureans fulfil duties towards their gods of whom they do not expect any advantage? Why do they not act towards the gods in the same way as they do towards men? All their virtues are mercenary, except piety. – However, the piety of the Epicureans is indeed less astonishing than it seems, especially if one realizes that it does not cost a great deal of effort [to them], [or] if one realizes that effort and trouble would be much greater if one were to succumb to vulgar beliefs. Their piety also seems less astonishing if one realizes that these beliefs themselves have a natural ground and are quite rational in their principles. The gods really exist according to Epicurus; they are beautiful and happy. They are like an embellished image of ourselves: why wouldn't we, then, bow before them?

IV. – Epicurus' doctrine on the gods has always seemed strange to historians of philosophy. A number of philosophers, including Posidonius (quoted by Cicero), believed that the idle gods of Epicurus were a last resort, and that the hypothesis did not express the core of his thought, and that he was, in fact, a disguised atheist and, what is more, a hypocrite. Modern criticism has shown this not to be the case: in the time of Epicurus, one could deny the gods without danger, and in any case one was free not to worship them.[34] The time when Socrates drank the hemlock was long gone. Socrates himself, as we know, had been persecuted more for his political opinions than for his religious innovations. If Epicurus clearly affirmed the existence of the gods, if he consecrated a full work to piety,[35] and if he offered his life as an example of the piety he praised in his writings, this is because he really believed in the existence of the gods, which he worshipped as genuinely real beings. Nevertheless, one recent historian of materialism, Lange, formulated a new hypothesis about Epicurus' theology in his great work. Following Lange, Epicurus' gods did not have real existence: they were simply ideals.[36] 'Undoubtedly, Epicurus honoured the belief in the gods as an element of [the] human ideal, but he did not see in the gods themselves exterior beings. Epicurus' system would reveal itself as fully contradictory were we not to look at it from the perspective of this subjective respect for the gods, which creates a harmonious agreement within our soul.' According to Lange, while the many worshipped the gods because they believed in their existence, Epicurus did the opposite: he did not believe in them, but nevertheless worshipped them. When Epicurus revered the gods for their perfection, 'it mattered little to him whether this perfection showed itself in exterior acts, or if it was employed only as an ideal within our thought'.[37]

Lange's thesis is surely original and ingenious. It tends to make of Epicurus a predecessor of Vacherot and Renan. However, this thesis does not rely on any text. Lange only invokes an alleged contradiction that would exist in Epicurus' doctrine, one that could not be resolved unless we admit his hypothesis. We have seen that, on the contrary, Epicurus' doctrine does not contain any contradiction but only a certain number of unsound deductions. For Epicurus, the gods certainly represent an ideal, but it is a realized ideal, as well as a living ideal. With Epicurus we are far from Hume and Kant. His system rests precisely on the identity of the subjective and the objective, for he claims that every sensation necessarily corresponds to a reality. Additionally, according to him, given that every idea has its roots in sensation, the human mind cannot have any ideal superior to reality itself. It is from reality that our mind borrows the ideal it conceives.

Epicurus' gods were not mere ideals and, as we have seen, they even nourished themselves with very real food, like simple mortals. Philodemus even asks himself whether or not the gods sleep. Ideals do not eat or sleep. We should not attribute modern doctrines to Epicurus, doctrines that are born from the progress of the sciences and of thought. Epicurus' system, with its strong and weak points, simply accords with its own time.

Ultimately, the gods of Epicurus were the gods of Greece, to whose existence he attributed a philosophical education, and in whom he instilled his own principles. He thought it was not useful to renounce the multiplicity of gods. In effect, if one admits the existence of one god, there is no decisive reason why not to admit the existence of an infinity. In this regard, the doctrine of Epicurus is consistent. Admitting this point,[38] Epicurus found the already-made gods of his country, who had inspired the Greek genius, and whose form ancient art had already fixed. He took them up as his own, and for him it was enough to exclude the possibility of their intervention in our world. These gods, who represented an accomplished Epicureanism, existed for the Epicurean as living proofs of his doctrines. Their presence worked for him as a sort of encouragement. The Greeks kept on living with their gods, who were the personification of their past and future. Olympus remained standing, and the Jupiter from the Parthenon remained shining eternally at the front of the great temple, immobile and harmless.

Notes

1   T.N. Guyau seems to refer to transcendent causes here.
2   T.N. Guyau's French here reads *primitive*. By this he designates not only 'first in time', but also 'logically first' and 'simple'; we could say also 'primordial' or 'immediate'; he means that the idea of a deity creating the world is not simple, primitive and 'first'; but that it is rather a complex or derivative idea.
3   T.N. See previous note.
4   T.N. The French here is *peine*.
5   T.N. *Terre*, or quite literally 'earth'.
6   T.N. The idea is that men are separated from each other by these obstacles.
7   Lucretius, *On the Nature of Things*, V, 196.
8   [T.N. In the 2002 French edition of *La morale d'Épicure*, Jean-Baptiste Gourinat writes the following note: Guyau only translates Epicurus' quote but not Lactantius' commentary accompanying it, which Guyau reproduces in Latin in a footnote. Lactantius' text reads as follows:] '*Quodsi haec ratio vera est, dissoluvitur etiam argumentum illud Epicuri:*' ['If this reasoning is true, then the following argument by Epicurus is also shattered:'] '*Deus, inquit, aut vult tollere mala, et non potest; aut potest, et non vult; aut neque vult, neque potest; aut et vult et potest. Si vult, et non potest, imbecillis est, quod in Deum non cadit: si potest et non vult, invidus, quod aeque alienum*

a Deo : si neque vult neque potest, et individus et imbecillis est, ideo nec Deus ; si vult et potest. Quod solum Deo convenit, unde ergo sunt mala? aut cur illa non tollit?' (translated above). [Following Gourinat, after this quote by Epicurus, Lactantius adds:] *'Scio plerosque philosophorum, qui providentiam defendant, hoc argumento perturbari solere, et invitos paene adigi, ut Deum nihil curare fateantur; quod maxime quaerit Epicurus'* ['I know many philosophers who defend providence, usually troubled by this argument, who are almost obliged to say, despite themselves, that the gods are not concerned with anything: this is what Epicurus has examined'].

9 Cicero, *De natura deorum*, I, 16, 43; Diogenes Laertius, *Lives of Eminent Philosophers*, X, 123.
10 Cicero, *De natura deorum*, I, 16, 43.
11 Diogenes Laertius, *Lives of Eminent Philosophers*, X, 123; Cicero, *De natura deorum*, I, 17, 45, 19, 51; Lucretius, *On the Nature of Things*, II, 646; V, 165.
12 T.N. The word here is *sensible*, that which refers to the senses.
13 T.N. *fantômes*. I have chosen to preserve the ambiguity of the French original; the English 'phantom' works well with the description Guyau gives of this phenomenon, but a more 'sober' translation could be 'image', since he seems to be referring to the Epicurean *phantasmata*.
14 T.N. *l'esprit malade*.
15 T.N. *canonique*. This term designates the theory of knowledge of an ancient system, sometimes subsumed under the discipline of logic.
16 T.N. Namely hallucination and sensation.
17 T.N. *la sensation brute*.
18 T.N. *Ils sont*, or, literally, 'they exist'.
19 The French here means, literally, to confess: *avouer*.
20 Epicurus *apud* Diogenes Laertius, *Lives of Eminent Philosophers*, X (*Letter to Menoeceus*, beginning).
21 Lucretius, *On the Nature of Things*, V, 1217; V I, 35.
22 Cicero, *De natura deorum*, I.
23 T.N. *à coups de marteaux*.
24 Ibid. [Cicero, *De natura deorum*, I].
25 Ibid. [Cicero, *De natura deorum*, I].
26 Cicero, *De natura deorum*; *De divinatione* [*On Divination*], II, 17; Lucretius, *On the Nature of Things*, V, 148; Metrodorus, *Peri aisthētōn* [*On the sensible*], col. 7 (Plut.) – One has rightly brought together this point of Epicurus' doctrine and the confused ideas of the first Christians, who accepted the notion that God had a body. If our senses were more refined, Tertullian says, we would be able to see this body (Tertullian, *De anima*, 22).
27 *Ta metakosmia, ta metaxu kosmōn diastēmata* ['The interworlds [*metakosmia*; *intermundia*], which are the intervals between worlds']. Cicero uses the expression *intermundia* [interworlds] (*De finibus*, II, xxiii).
28 Cicero, *De finibus*, I, xix, 50.
29 T.N. The author seems to be referring to other worlds and heavenly bodies.
30 *Epikouros anthrōpōideis men tous theous, logō de pantas theōrētous, dia tēn leptomereian tēs tōn eidōlōn phuseōs*. Stobaeus, *Eclogues*, I, 66. – Cicero, *De finibus*, I, 18, 46; *De divinatione*, II, 17, 40; Sextus Empiricus, *Outlines of Pyrrhonism* [*Pyrrhōneioi hupotypōseis*, or *Outlines of Scepticism*], III, 218; [Pseudo-]Plutarch, *Placita philosophorum*, I, 7,18. – See also Phaedr., *Fragm.*, col. 7 [T.N. The editors could not identify this reference].

31 Philodemus, *Volum. hercul.* [*Papyrus Herculanensis*], *Peri tēs tōn theōn eustochoumenēs diagōgēs, kata Zēnōna* [*On the Way of Life of the Gods*, or *On the life properly lived by the gods, against Zeno*], col. 12.
32 Ibid., I, 34, 95 [T.N. It is not clear which reference Guyau repeats here]. – According to Philodemus, the gods speak Greek or, at least, a language that would be very close to Greek (*Volum. herculan.* [*Papyrus Herculanensis*], col. 14).
33 Seneca, *De Beneficiis* [*On Benefits*], IV, 19.
34 See Zeller, *Die Philosophie der Griechen*.
35 Diogenes Laertius, *Lives of Eminent Philosophers*, X, 12.
36 T.N. Guyau uses the plural here.
37 Lange, *Histoire du matérialisme et critique de son importance à notre*, volume 1, 93.
38 T.N. Namely the existence of god and of a plurality of gods.

Conclusion

Epicureanism and its Analogies with Modern Positivism. The Success of Epicureanism in Antiquity

I. – After working on the same subject and looking in the same direction for a long time, the human mind gets tired and exhausts itself. After having been passionate about a problem without being able to solve it, in a natural reaction the human mind suddenly abandons it and turns towards a completely different set of ideas. Throughout history – for instance, in Epicurus' own century – this kind of intellectual weariness was often produced. Humanity as a whole can be considered as a single individual who cannot accomplish a great number of works except by fulfilling the condition of varying these works uninterruptedly, passing without rest from one to the other.

Moreover, it does not follow from the fact that at a given epoch the human mind seems to abandon a certain problem that it will renounce that issue forever. On the contrary, the research undertaken with a different sort of idea can sooner or later be useful in the process of solving the same difficulty that could not be resolved when attacked frontally by the human mind. Epicurus, for example, has not blocked the way of our modern metaphysicians and moralists. As we will see, he has rather provoked the rise and development of their thinking. Within the intellectual domain, every step we take in a certain direction allows us to subsequently advance more easily in a completely different direction; with time, problems change their form, the same questions then appear under a new point of view, and this simple change of aspect already constitutes a considerable progress. In the history of human thought one could only solve a great number of problems by constantly modifying the terms under which these problems had been posed. Similarly, we recognize innovative spirits less by the fact that they are able to solve a great number of particular questions and more by the fact that they all of a sudden change the general viewpoint from which one had until then regarded things.

In Epicurus' time, after long centuries of metaphysical speculation, Greek thought was as tired of vain research regarding the absolute, just as it is in France today. In the same way that, in our century, Auguste Comte endeavoured to change the direction of human thought, and wanted to turn it towards a different set of problems, so did Epicurus in antiquity. Bringing the era of metaphysics to a close, Epicurus created a sort of positivism in many ways analogous to that of Auguste Comte.

The role of those who limit human thought in this way is to give it more vigour and concentrate it, especially when it is dispersed among too many different objects. This was the task of Epicurus in antiquity. He reacted more than any of his predecessors, and more powerfully than Democritus himself, against the *a priori* speculations where the thought of Socrates, Plato and even Aristotle wandered and went astray. Until then, the metaphysical idea of final cause dominated natural, human and social sciences.[1] Epicurus had dispelled this idea, and he thus introduced in these sciences a completely new spirit. It is enough to read one page of Aristotle and one page of Lucretius in order to see the profound difference that separates the ancient doctrine from the new. Aristotle constantly mixes experimental considerations with metaphysical ones; he only observes the facts that are enclosed in a network of relatively contestable *a priori* deductions. In Lucretius, the almost complete suppression of any idea of final cause gives a more modern and scientific character to his observations. In effect, there is nothing more opposed to the general disposition of the modern spirit than the consideration of the final cause. Not only is such a consideration 'sterile', following the now self-evident expression of Bacon, but it easily leads to absurdity. In effect, the majority of phenomena exist in correlation with one another in such a way that, given two coexisting things, we cannot identify *a priori* which one is primary and which one is derived, which one was made *by* the other and *for* the other. For example, it would be too hard for a pure mind foreign to our world to know *a priori* whether it was my outfit that was made for me, or whether it was me who was made for my outfit; in certain cases, couldn't this mind maintain that it was the man who was made for the outfit? Aristotle, like the Scholastics after him, committed a whole series of mistakes of this sort. This is because, within the great Whole, each single thing ended up adapting itself to every other thing. The world is a chain whose rings are held together and unroll throughout time. However, if we do not take time into account, considering instead the series of facts only from a metaphysical point of view, then the last fact, the last ring of the chain, which is by nature the less important, appears to us as the dominant and primary fact. Indeed, all the other facts contributed to produce it, and therefore it is in a certain way adapted to every other [of the facts that produced it]. Consequently, all the others seem to be made for it and it seems to be the final cause of all the rest. Let us take language as an example. According to Epicurus, Lucretius and many contemporary scholars, language is a fact derived from the social state;[2] it is a consequence, one of the most remarkable and complex consequences of that state. Aristotle, however, observes that language and society currently coexist. Then, placing himself as usual in the metaphysical perspective, he concludes that language was made for society, and that man was born sociable because he possesses the faculty of speaking. Society becomes, then, the derived fact and language the primary fact. It is thus that the metaphysician is led to give [logical] priority precisely to facts that have less objective importance and that took place last in the order of time. One can say that in the natural sciences, in sociology and even in ethics, Epicurus had opened the path to modern thought. Utilizing his still rudimentary experimental method, in place of the metaphysical trends that dominated [the intellectual world] since Socrates, he introduced the idea of time and succession in the sciences, so replacing the idea of final cause. Epicurus showed that the order of things is precisely the inverse[3] of the order of thought.

Through this sort of revolution Epicurean positivism has probably exercised greater influence upon the human mind than modern positivism will ever do. Nevertheless, it is interesting to note the analogies that exist between the two systems. Both wish to forbid man from conducting inquiries that are too lofty and speculations that go too far. The difference is that, in order to do this, Epicurus relies on a positive principle, namely human happiness and intellectual serenity, beyond which one should pursue nothing else; whereas Auguste Comte relies on a principle of doubt and negation, namely the impotence of the human mind to grasp the idea of causation, and even its inability to perceive the further rings of the chain of phenomena. Nonetheless, the practical outcomes of the two systems are analogous, and both made the same mistakes. Epicurus, for example, in the name of his utilitarian positivism, claimed that we could never explain celestial phenomena in a systematic and univocal way. He rejected as impotent and useless sciences such as pure mathematics. Similarly, Auguste Comte in his *Cours de philosophie positive* displays the same intolerance towards certain forms of scientific research. For example, it is curious to note how he claims that sidereal astronomy is doomed to remain forever uncertain precisely at the dawn of the day in which spectroscopy would reveal the composition of the stars. In the same way, just before the discoveries of the school of Alexandria, when Archimedes and Hipparchus wouldn't take long to measure the volume of the earth and its approximate distance in relation to the moon, Epicurus repeated the same old mistakes of ancient philosophers regarding the celestial bodies. Auguste Comte finds that in chemistry the question of knowing whether defined proportions are the rules of combinations is not as important as one believed; and this in the very moment when this hypothesis would be verified everywhere and would lead to a whole series of discoveries. In ancient positivism, as in modern positivism, we see the same errors reproduce themselves with the difference of time.

Both Auguste Comte and Epicurus have the same narrowmindedness, for they have not understood the vastness of human thought, which needs to have a great open horizon before itself. Nonetheless, they find their place in the development of the systems [of thought]. They represent, as we have already said, that moment when thought, turning entirely towards particular points, sheds more light upon them, and gains in power what it loses in extension.

II. – Epicureanism had great success arousing among its disciples an enthusiasm that cannot be compared to any modern doctrine. Only religion was ever able to produce such a fervour among its followers. This is because this attractive system had then an aesthetic and moral colour that it has lost over the centuries. For Epicurus, the doctrine of utility was not as cold and dry as modern utilitarianism with its harshness of calculation. Epicurus' philosophy had the gracefulness of antiquity, and a *laisser-aller* [attitude] that did not impede its logic. Epicurus in Athens had the charm of a Plato or a Socrates, together with the practical sense of a modern [thinker]. He loved nature, even more than the ancients usually did. He recommends life in the country to the sage. He himself was the first, as Pliny says, to transport the country into the city, establishing a garden in the middle of a district of Athens.[4] There he lived with people who surrounded him with affection and admiration. It is said that on his door one could read the following inscription: 'Stranger, here you will find yourself well, [for] here dwells pleasure, the supreme good.' Antiquity was tempted by Epicureanism, and a great crowd of disciples rushed up to hear the word of he who announced a novel truth.

There was in early Epicureanism a pervasive poetry which is lacking entirely in modern Epicureanism. How different it is to go, for example, from Epicurus to Hobbes, to pass from this philosopher who has all the seductions of a sophist (and we take this word here in its true meaning) to the English thinker, so arid and dry and whose system conceals a certain tone of misanthropy! Ancient Epicureanism knew how to present itself in the ways of the ancient Greek statues, in a majestic and inimitable elegance. The ancients have always spoken and lived a little bit for show, for the 'crown'[5] as one would say then. As for ourselves, we live primarily for ourselves and for logic. Epicureanism seduced even more to the extent that it was out of the ordinary and poetic:[6] it took its strength from its ability to make human beings happy, always and anywhere. It claimed to give man an invincible force in every possible circumstance of life. Ancient utilitarianism thus reaches heroism, which transforms it. Epicurus, as Seneca said, is 'a hero disguised as a woman'.

Happiness, the real aim of life, is [now] placed within everyone's reach; the gods of paganism are overthrown; spontaneity is introduced into nature and replaces necessity; the sage is completely independent in the face of every accident of life. These are the most attractive ideas that Epicureanism put forward. We should not be surprised by the repercussions these ideas generated in antiquity. Epicurus appeared to all, and considered himself to be, a liberator of minds in the same way some heroes had been liberators of the body and limbs chained by servitude; – [Epicurus was] a sort of saviour who came to knock down the gods and the idols, whereas others came just to replace them. Thus, the title of sage will be given to him and he will accept it, a title that for a long time no one had dared to give to those even who modestly called themselves the friends of wisdom. But this title of sage was not enough. Colotes threw himself on his knees, so as to adore Epicurus. 'It is a god,' writes Lucretius, 'yes, a god, he who first discovered this disposition of life called wisdom, whose *genius*, removing human life from great torments and such deep shadow, and placed it in a tranquil and blazing light.'[7] The Epicureans would assemble at fixed dates in solemn gatherings to celebrate his memory among themselves, just like Epicurus himself had prescribed, certain as he was about his own immortality.[8] Finally, and so that this memory would never abandon them, they constantly took with them, carved on their cups, or even on their rings, the image of their master, so that its contours remained clear in their souls. According to Diogenes Laertius, Epicurus' school was never abandoned. When every other school had been killed by the blows of public misfortune, and every other sect had been dispersed, the Epicurean school alone continued to flourish and where one crowd of disciples came after another. The harmony that existed among the Epicureans, as an ancient [author] said, resembled that which must reign in a well-organized republic.[9] This was so, because, among the Epicureans there wasn't only respect for what they believed to be the truth discovered [by their master], but rather enthusiasm for the good that was discovered, [that is] for the happiness that was brought to human beings, and for the tranquillity that was brought to their souls. They even regarded Epicurus' doctrine as a sort of divine dogma that they faithfully transmitted to each other without daring to change it from their own initiative. It would be difficult to find another ancient philosopher with a more ardent faith than that of Lucretius towards the principles of his master. In Epicurus there is something of the sacred prophets, he seemed to be moved by the condition of people, and desiring to soften their misery, he sincerely wished to teach them the real means to happiness. It seems that it was with a sort of charity that he reveals to his fellow human beings the doctrine of egoism properly understood.

After having been the most popular doctrine of antiquity, the role and importance of Epicureanism does not come to an end with the end of antiquity. We must now follow its traces in the Middle Ages and, especially, examine the modern thinkers that reconstituted and gave it new vitality.

Notes

1 T.N. Guyau somehow anachronistically uses the phrase *les sciences de la nature, de l'homme et de la société*.
2 T.N. *état social*.
3 T.N. *renversement* could also be translated as 'reversal' or 'overthrowing'.
4 '*Primus hoc instituit Epicurus otii magister. Usque ad eum moris non fuerat in oppidis habitari rura*' ['Epicurus was the first leader of a school to institute that [i.e. a garden]. Up to Epicurus, to dwell in the country instead of the city was not part of customs [*moeurs*]'], Pliny, *Natural History*, XXIX.
5 T.N. Guyau's French here is *vivre pour la galerie, pour la "couronne"*. The expression is of difficult translation, it expresses the fact that the ancients lived under the gaze of others, they aimed to be seen. It also denotes a concern with appearances as opposed to introspection and a withdrawn attitude; specifically, the phrase denotes that the ancients acted elegantly and dramatically, perhaps ostentatiously, 'for the crowd'. In a way, they 'played for the gallery'. Additionally, Melissa Pawelski drew my attention to the fact that the word *couronne* here could be a reference to the Roman *couronne triomphale*, the laurel wreath, which was a public sign of distinction, honor and merit. In this sense, Guyau also seems to mean that the ancients lived for achieving distinction and public recognition.
6 T.N. The adjective is of difficult translation: *romanesque*.
7 Lucretius, *On the Nature of Things*, V, 6.
8 Laertius, *Lives of Eminent Philosophers*, X, 18; Cicero, *De finibus*, II, 31; Seneca, *Epistles*, 21. – See also Gassendi, [*Animadversiones in decimum librum Diogenis Laertii, qui est*] *de vita, moribus, placitisque Epicuri*, II – One could note an analogy between these Epicurean gatherings and the meetings of modern disciples of Comte on the festive days of the positivistic calendar.
9 Numenius *apud* Eusebius, *Praeparatio evangelica* [*Preparation for the Gospel*], book XIV, ch. V.

Book Four

The Modern Successors of Epicurus

1

The Epoch of Transition Between Ancient Epicureanism and Modern Epicureanism – Gassendi and Hobbes

I. That Epicureanism was the only ancient philosophy to be essentially incredulous.[1] – How Epicurus was designated as the model of incredulity. – The Epicureans of the Middle Ages and of the Renaissance. – Gassendi opposed Epicurus to Aristotle and wished to make him the leader of the moral, intellectual and religious revolution that was then just beginning. – The influence of Gassendi. – The *"libertinage"* in the seventeenth century. – Pascal reproduced the antithesis between Epicureanism and Stoicism, which he attempts in vain to reconcile in Christianity. – Why incredulity, already widespread in the seventeenth century, was still semi-impotent; that which made its real power in the following century.

II. Hobbes. 1. *Man according to Hobbes*. – Peace as the condition for every good; force as the condition for peace. – Mechanism and fatalism. – Identification of the good with the object of desire. – Relativity of all good. – The good and the beautiful reduced to the useful. – The moral sentiments reduced to diverse transformations of egoistic sentiments. – Definition of the supreme good. – 2. *Man in his relations with others*. – Man is not a naturally sociable being. – Natural *right*[2] of everyone to everything. – The war of all against all. – There is no justice before the existence of the contract. – Natural *law*[3] founded on the calculus of interest properly understood, and opposed to natural *right*,[4] which relies on blind desire.[5] – Prescriptions of the natural law: first of all, to enter into contractual relations, or to effect the exchange of rights, aiming at peace; second, to maintain these contracts. – That force is required in order to sustain natural morality.[6] – The *number* and the agreement of the contractors; their *union* and their *personification*. – The establishment of government. – 3. *Hobbes' city*. – The weak point of Hobbes' system. – Is the strongest government the same as despotic government? – Middle ground between *anarchy*[7] and the *empire: freedom*. – Hobbes' place and role in the history of Epicurean and utilitarian doctrines.

I. – Epicureanism was the only philosophical system to briefly survive Christianity. It prolonged its existence for four hundred years after Jesus Christ. At that point, completely suffocated, it seemed to have completely disappeared. However, despite

Christianity's triumph, certain traits of the Epicurean spirit had always remained alive, intertwining itself with the spirit of incredulity.

Epicureanism was, indeed, the only ancient sect to be essentially incredulous, denying all miracles, and never giving any space to religious and mystical feelings in the explanation of things. By contrast, in the background of the Stoic system there was a vague religiosity, a pantheism that admitted within the world constant divine action, a perpetual providence or, to put it differently, a perpetual and eternal miracle. The Stoic, who believed in fate and predestination, believed in oracles, he consulted and feared them, nourishing [in himself] a great part of the superstitions of the vulgar.[8] The same is valid for the Platonists. Platonism, which had found new life with the school of Alexandria, found itself combined with doctrines of theurgy and magic; in effect, it was unable to resist a religion founded on miracles, since it sought to produce them in its own accounts. Epicureanism alone was the absolute enemy of any religion whatsoever, because every religion relies to a certain extent on the idea of creation, on notions of providence and miracle, and on the idea of a solidarity existing between God and world. It is thus not without reason that the designation of 'Epicurean' has quickly become synonymous with being 'incredulous' and 'irreligious'.

A few centuries after Jesus Christ we can already see the [Early] Fathers of the Church encompassing within the same refutations and the same maledictions the Epicureans together with all sorts of free thinkers. Similarly, the Talmud designates under the name of Epicureans the Sadducees[9] and free thinkers in general. Under the eyes of Jews and Christians, every incredulous man found himself in the party of Epicurus, and it is Epicurus who, among all ancient philosophers, appeared as the real adversary of Christ and the Bible.

In the same way, at the beginning of the twelfth century, when a wave of incredulity began to be produced in Europe, and especially in Italy, and when secret societies were formed aiming at the destruction of Christianity,[10] the most logical individuals among these partisans of a new spirit did not hesitate to invoke Epicurus' name. In Florence, in 1115, a party[11] of Epicureans was formed, strong enough to become the object of sanguinary disturbances.[12] The heresy of the Epicureans, as Benvenuto d'Imola remarks, was, among all others, the one which had the greatest number of partisans.[13] 'Farinata,' claims Benvenuto, 'was the leader of the Ghibellines and believed, as Epicurus before him, that paradise should be sought in this world only. Cavalcante had as his principle: *Unus est interitus hominum et jumentorum* (men and beasts have the same death).'[14] Dante places all these Epicureans together with 'thousands of others' in a special circle of hell, inside tombs of fire.[15] And yet Dante's friend, the poet Guido Cavalcanti, was considered to be an atheist and an Epicurean.

Epicurus' name, then, could be found implicated in the dissensions of the Middle Ages. It is even possible to find it quoted with praise by the orthodox John of Salisbury.[16] However, it is especially with [the advent of] the Renaissance and its sprit of freedom and research that the Epicurean ideas regain all their strength. Erasmus strives in vain to reconcile Epicureanism and Christianity by showing that the Christian is, indeed, the best disciple of Epicurus.[17] The Epicureans, those who are so by reasoning or by instinct, feel that they are the enemy for Christianity. They hide or disguise themselves. Montaigne, this double- or triple-layered author,[18] as Saint-Beuve would refer to him, is only partially Pyrrhonean; he is also an Epicurean, and summons faith in his help to mask the whole of his position.[19] But, in the end, what comes out of his book, its 'marrow',[20] as Rabelais would say, is Epicureanism. Evidently, we are referring neither to Epicurean cosmology nor to its atomism; Montaigne ridicules the atoms, he does not want to hear about all these reveries. Nevertheless, when it comes to the very principle of Epicurean ethics, Montaigne's language changes: 'All the opinions of the world agree in this, that pleasure is our end ... Let the philosophers say what they will, the thing at which we all aim, even in virtue is pleasure. It amuses me to rattle in ears this word, which is reluctantly so strong to them.'[21] It is not without reason that Pascal will oppose Montaigne to Epictetus, in the same way some have opposed Epicurus to Zeno [the Stoic]. Undoubtedly, Montaigne does not have a defined system, or, if he has one, he only rarely allows himself to articulate it, leaving it to his readers to formulate it, which is the same.[22]

A few years after Montaigne's death Epicureanism found its martyr in Vanini. Indeed, Vanini had his tongue cut off and was burnt in Toulouse, much more because of his moral and religious ideas, which were inspired by Epicurus and Lucretius, than by his metaphysical ideas, borrowed from the Peripatetics.

Finally, around the same epoch, the erudition of Gassendi would completely reconstruct Epicurus' doctrine without mixture. Gassendi, versed in history and philology, sought an ancient doctrine that was strong enough to oppose the doctrine of Aristotle, which was still the dominant teaching among the different schools, and Epicurus' doctrine appears to him as the most akin to his own spirit and, simultaneously, to the modern spirit. Thus, as early as 1624, that is to say five years after Vanini's death, Gassendi wrote a book entitled *Exercitationes paradoxicae adversus Aristoteleos* (*Exercises in the form of paradoxes against the Aristotelians*), in which he already articulated the ethics of Epicurus. In the preface, Gassendi explains Epicurus' position on pleasure: '"He shows us, indeed, how supreme good is found in pleasure[23] and how the merit of human action and virtues is measured according to this principle."[24] The *Exercitationes paradoxicae* were so audacious that Gassendi, after printing and handing them to his friends, finally decided on their advice to burn the five books. This work, even when abridged, will remain influential. Long before Descartes' *Discourse on the Method* Gassendi had already dared to frontally attack the old authority of Aristotle, and this in the name of ideas inspired by Epicureanism and opposed to many of the ideas that Descartes would later formulate.

We know how, on the one hand, Gassendi dedicated important works to the recovery of the Epicurean doctrine and, on the other, to a skilfully executed controversy with Descartes, in which he shows himself to be simultaneously a disciple of Epicurus and a predecessor of Hobbes and Locke. Indeed, most of his life was dedicated to taking up [the philosophy of] Epicurus and opposing it to Scholastics and Cartesians. Gassendi had a unique admiration for Epicurus, bordering on a real cult, and we find in this modern author the same respect for the master that it is possible find in his ancient disciples. He had in his possession two effigies of Epicurus: one had been sent to him by his friend Naudé; the other, a cameo, had been given to him by Henri Dupuy, philologist from Louvain. Gassendi himself quotes the praising inscription with which Dupuy accompanied his gift: 'Contemplate, my dear friend, the soul of the great man which still breathes through these traits. It is Epicurus, with his face and his glance. Contemplate this image, which deserves to attract everyone's gaze.'[25]

Although younger than Hobbes, Gassendi was in a way his master on account of the quicker development of his spirit. He was also an influential author for Descartes. In effect, he came to form a genuine school, opposed to the Cartesian school, which divided the Sorbonne into two camps.

While reconstructing Epicureanism in order to make it the foundation for a new system, Gassendi had understood well the trends of his own century. One must not forget that the eighteenth century is already present in the seventeenth in a germinal state. We are accustomed to considering these two epochs of history as separate from each other, and so we miss the ties that bind them together. From the seventeenth century onwards, faith is weakened, and everywhere incredulity begins to burst forth. This is clear if we consider Pascal who articulated more neatly than any other thinker [at the time] the dilemma between Epicureanism and faith. The society in which Pascal lived was for years 'libertine', and by this word in the seventeenth century one would not understand the *libertinage* of customs,[26] but rather that of independent thought. 'He intended to make speeches to the libertines,' says Madame Périer. One began to pose questions and began to search for solutions. Later, an ill Pascal, converted and fanatical, would receive visitors asking him for advice in religious and moral issues. It is only then that he would nudge his iron belt; the thorns that lacerated his flesh were but the image of those which, following M. de Saci's expression, 'lacerated his soul'.[27] And this inner illness of which Pascal suffered was also the illness that his own century felt with more or less intensity.

The whole of this epoch oscillates between a rejuvenated Epicureanism and a decaying Christianity. One can recall the famous Epicurean Des Barreaux and the Epicurean society he presided over, of which Chapelle and Théophile Viau were members. The youth of the age was also inclined towards Epicurus. Nevertheless, this movement that stirred minds lacked an idea, an idea that the eighteenth century would bring to light and would somehow seek to reconcile with the principles of Epicureanism. To the faith that was gradually fading away, one did not oppose anything [concrete] just yet. Incredulity, when too complete, becomes impotent. If incredulity prevailed in the eighteenth century, it is because to religious faith it opposed a different kind of faith, to the love of Christ it opposed a different kind of love; to divinity it opposed humanity. The eighteenth century as a whole had faith in humanity, and even the utilitarians devote themselves to this active and disinterested cult. It is in this new conception [of humanity] that they would find the power capable of deeply stirring minds. In spite of the efforts of Pascal, Epicureanism, to some extent allying itself with Stoicism, completed the moral and intellectual revolution that was underway.

II. – At the same time when Epicureanism was being revived in France, it was also in the process of being reconstituted in England under an original form by Hobbes, a friend and almost disciple of Gassendi. Hobbes' system, albeit well known, merits a brief analysis.

One of the characteristic tendencies in Epicurean doctrine is its attraction towards *peace*. In order to enjoy something, one must first possess it; in order to possess it, one must *acquire* and *conserve* it. Now, one can only *acquire* something and even more *conserve* it in a state of peace and security. In this way, we will see Epicurus and Hobbes consistently talking about peace as the greatest good because it is the first and fundamental condition of all the other goods.

There is, however, between Epicurus and Hobbes a serious disagreement, which will result in an even more serious divergence in the development of their until now convergent systems. Epicurus understands *peace*, above all, as serenity of the soul, and he conceives this inner peace as absolute independence and involving an absolutely indifferent freedom. Since this security in freedom is above all spiritual, if we wish to obtain it, the means we must employ can only be spiritual. It is enough to detach oneself from exterior things through an indifferent will and to retire into oneself. – Hobbes, on the contrary, understands the idea of *peace* in a very material and exterior sense. For him, to be in peace means having nothing to fear regarding other men, to acquire without rivals and to conserve what is acquired without envious opponents: all happiness resides here. Now, the means required for attaining this material peace must themselves be material. What could be the use of Epicurus' inner freedom when it comes to establishing an equilibrium between inimical physical forces? This alleged freedom must itself become a force, it must become flesh, and it needs to enter the domain of physical struggles. It can only achieve the peace it aspires to by taking up arms and conquering it. The only means to end war to the benefit of [the aspired] peace, and to prevent this war from starting over again, in short, the only weapon and the only guarantee of he who wishes to obtain well-being[28] is, therefore, *material power*.[29] *Power* as a means for *peace*; peace as a means for *enjoyment*:[30] this is the whole of Hobbes' ethics. Hobbes admits a necessity that is as determined as Epicurean freedom is undetermined. Within and around us, Hobbes places a mechanism whose regular functioning alone assures our security, and a mechanism according to which the intensity of our enjoyment can be exactly calculated according to the intensity of our force.[31] To be independent, that is to be happy, said Epicurus. To be strong, that is to be happy, said Hobbes.

One must note that in Hobbes' system, everything is arranged on the same plane, both man and city. Hobbes is pleased with the viewpoint of a crude mechanism, that of a force that operates by bending everything to itself. He places a master everywhere: in the State, it is the sovereign; within the human being, it is appetite.[32] Wouldn't it be necessary, after all, to explain every phenomenon by referring it to a single cause and the same reason? Wouldn't this cause and this reason be the force of nature, which is itself the same as the force of logic?

Once one accepts fatalism, one simultaneously suppresses every absolute good, every absolute evil, and every end which would be really final. Hobbes appreciated this consequence with perfect clarity. The good is that which we desire; the evil, that which we run away from. Everything that is good is so only in relation to someone or something: nothing is absolutely good. Something is *a good* only to the extent that it is desired, and, to the extent that it is *pleasing* when possessed. This is the only difference between the good and [that which is] pleasing. Let us add that beauty is simply the joining together of exterior signs which promise a good to come. Finally, utility is discovered when, instead of considering something in itself, one considers it from the perspective of the chain of goods and evils that it brings with itself. As he develops Epicurean ideas Hobbes comes to appreciate that things are not isolated in nature; rather, they often form series whose terms are mutually implicated. A good is never a good on its own; rather, it is followed by goods that increase its value, or by evils that cancel it. The consideration of the useful must then rule over that of the good, the beautiful and that of the pleasing.[33] The [category of the] useful encompasses all other things.

Can the sovereign good, that is happiness, be achieved in this life as Epicurus and Zeno believed? Not at all; because if one could achieve the final end one would not lack anything, and thus one would not desire anything else. Therefore, the good would no longer exist for us. We would no longer feel anything; nor would we be alive anymore. It follows from this, and this is a remarkable consequence, that 'the greatest good is to advance, finding only a few obstacles, towards ulterior ends';[34] and that 'the enjoyment of the thing desired is, at the very moment in which we enjoy it, a desire, that is to say a movement of the soul through the parts of the thing which it enjoys. Because life is a perpetual movement, when it cannot advance in a straight line, it becomes a circular movement.'[35] – This is a sharp analysis of enjoyment, but also a discouraging one, especially when applied to the desired end. In the scenario Hobbes depicts, this end will be desirable only to the extent to which we cannot possess it. Epicurus would have rejected this definition of pleasure, which he would have considered inferior and even vile. For Epicurus, as we have seen, true pleasure resides in rest; Hobbes, by contrast, returns to the Cyrenaic doctrine: pleasure is [to be found] in movement, it is movement itself. Generally speaking, to be active is a good, to be in motion is a good. The fact of advancing and making progress towards a goal is equally a good, because the whole of life itself is movement, activity, the unfolding of forces and progress. All pains and pleasures, as well as every desire and, in a word, every 'affection' of the soul have their origin in the conscience of an inner and solitary power,[36] whose expression without obstacles or limitation is enough to produce an infinite variety of sentiments.

After considering *the human being* in general, we must consider him in his relations with his fellowmen, that is to say, [we must consider man] as *citizen*.

Let us bring together several of the mechanisms that Hobbes has assembled with [the notion of] sensation and that he sets in motion through [the idea of] interest. What are the general relations that will be established between them? For Hobbes, human beings are no different from 'feeling machines';[37] man is a force which takes itself as its sole end, a force that, in any direction in which it seems to project itself, returns after relatively long detours to this same point: 'the self'. Is it the case that placing this human being in the company of one or more fellow human beings would be enough to produce slight deviations in the direction he follows, or any change regarding the end he pursues? Not at all. Even when in society with others, man will never cease to desire his own advantage [above all else], like the stone does not cease to fall in a straight line, even when we throw it into space together with other stones. One should not speak of the inherently sociable nature of man when it comes to Hobbes. For him, man is egoistic by nature, and so Aristotle's definition of man as *zōon politikon* (*political animal*) is false; man is not born apt or immediately suitable for society. Epicurus and Metrodorus have already reacted against the Aristotelian definition, by showing that human beings in the savage state[38] were 'animals ready to devour one another'. If human beings, Hobbes adds, naturally loved one another they would do so irrespectively of the advantages or honours that they could obtain [from this love]; they would naturally love everyone equally, which is not the case. We do not seek society naturally, but we do so because of the advantages it can bring to us. What we love in a companion is, first of all, his [or her] utility, and only secondarily his [or her] person. If human beings loved one another irrespectively of interest, how could envy and slander be explained? Why do we enter society if not because of the pleasure of hearing something bad said about our neighbour, of demeaning others, and elevating ourselves at their expense? No, man is not born sociable. His nature presses him to seek domination and not the equality required by society. From this, however, it does not follow that the human being does not have the *desire* for society; it does not follow that fortuitous gatherings are impossible. Nonetheless, there is a difference between *desire* and *capacity*, between fortuitous unions and civil societies.[39]

Given that society, from which results the state of peace, is not natural, and since there is nothing in human beings to bring them together, except their interest, it is evident that the natural state, the primitive[40] state of man, is, par excellence, war. There is no middle ground between society and war, between harmony and struggle. In effect, all human mechanisms tend towards a single aim, [that is] enjoyment. There will be, among men, many who will simultaneously desire the same object of enjoyment. Now, if hypothetically they cannot enjoy this same object at the same time, nor can they share it, then war is triggered, and when force is at work, it is the stronger force that will prevail.[41]

For Hobbes, one should not condemn this victory of force, for on what basis could we condemn it? Isn't it the case that everyone is fatally and necessarily moved by desire or repulsion? Now, that which is necessary is reasonable, and that which is reasonable is just; it is a *right*.[42] This word, *right*, means the freedom or power[43] that everyone possesses to use their faculties according to the right reason,[44] that is to say [the freedom or power] to pursue one's natural end. This natural end is the preservation of one's life and of one's person.[45] However, from the right to this end it follows we also have the right to the means to be employed in order to pursue and achieve it. The final formula of natural right will then be the following: everyone has the right to employ all means necessary and to realize all actions necessary to one's self-preservation.[46] Now, there is nothing that could not appear as necessary to one's preservation; therefore, there isn't anything to which one hasn't a right to. Thus, according to natural right, everything is for everyone.[47] The only measure of this right is utility, its only sanction is force; its consequence, war. War of all against all, this is the primary fact, as well as the first right of nature.[48]

Let us not object by saying that Hobbes condemns human nature: in this clash of forces produced by the clash of interests there is no sin. There is no injustice, since the laws do not yet exist. Justice and injustice do not concern man *qua* man, but only to man as citizen. In nature, force and cunning are virtues. Don't we find it completely natural to travel accompanied and to bring arms? Don't we find it natural to lock our doors because we fear thieves? Dogs bite who they do not know, and at night they bark at everyone, so do men in the state of nature. Is war not the only law of savage peoples?[49]

Is it not the same among us, subject to the law of princes and peoples, and among whom the state of nature still subsists? When plunged into general disagreement, mistrust and weakness, a man, shaking and breaking every constraint, rises above others, the means he employs does not matter, even if this man was Cain and his victim Abel. Before this representative of force and cunning Hobbes would be ready to yell after Callicles: it is in him that shines the justice of nature in all its brightness![50]

The conception of war as the primordial state of humankind is key for Hobbes. We will later find this doctrine of a state of universal war, fertilized and transformed by science in the naturalist theory of 'the struggle for life', a struggle declared not only by every man against every other, but by all beings against all beings. Extended in this way to the whole of nature, and thus enlarged and applied beyond the limited horizon in which it was originally thought, this law seems to become a good rather than an evil: it is, indeed, the only means for this selection, which for inferior beings, and even for humankind in its early stages, was the sole cause of any possible progress.

Once the state of war is deduced from human nature and firmly established, how does Hobbes think we could then exit it?

The first and fundamental law of nature is, as we know, that we must seek peace, because peace is the greatest of all goods. Now, the immediate consequence of this law is that, in order to obtain the peace that we desire we must abandon the right that nature gave us to everything, which produces war. We must transfer it to others, on the condition that they transfer theirs to us. For example, I must say to my fellow men: cede to me the right [you have] to [eating the] fruits I pick with my own hands, and I will cede to you the right you have over the fruits you pick with your own hands. This reciprocal transfer,[51] this exchange of rights that are naturally absolute, and which, through the wonderful phenomenon of exchange, limit one another – that is the *contract*, the origin of society. Hobbes' contract is not that different from the *sumbolon tou sumpherontos* (*pact of utility*) which Epicurus already spoke about, except that it is developed in a more complex form.

The first precept of natural law, by taking us from the state of war to the contract, has led us to take important steps. But it is not enough, for the existence of society requires not only the existence of conventions, but [equally] of conditions that endure.

In order for natural laws to become the law or effective links, the force of reason is not enough. In order for them to be effective they need to be supported by fear and a certain physical force. In other words, the threat of *sanction* must precede and accompany the guidance of the *law*.

The first means to put force on the side of law is number. The greater the number of loyal contractors, the more those who break the contract will be exposing themselves to risk. Each one, thus perceiving behind each other person the force of all, will feel held at bay: *Satius sibi esse uterque putet manus cohibere quam conserere* (*both parties will think it better to stay their hand than to start fighting*).[52] However, the ethicist will not be fooled by this hypocritical handshake, he will see in the number and the *agreement*[53] of the contracting parties (*multorum concordia*) the only cause of peace.

However, [this] agreement is not enough to produce lasting peace. The agreement of all relies on the will of each one, and the will that Hobbes places within the human being, which is to say the dominance of the strongest desire, or of the most intense movement, is essentially variable. We need something more constant and necessary, and, consequently, something stronger [than our changing desires]. Not only is it necessary that all wills agree with each other on certain points, but also that they pose certain general rules, and what is more, that they give a body to these rules, bringing them to life and making them powerful. It is necessary to appoint a great physical force to guard them, that is, a person. In unanimous agreement, diverse wills can be considered as *one single will*. However, this unity is an abstraction, which can be made to disappear with only the least change in the diverse wills that compose it. On the contrary, if one realizes this abstraction in a person that embodies it, that is, if one gives a representative and a protector to this abstraction, it will survive anything that happens to it, ready to restore order and to bring back to its living unity anyone that seeks to subtract himself [from it]. This personification of the will of all, be it in a single man, be it in an assembly, is what Hobbes calls the *union*, which he carefully distinguishes from mere *agreement*.[54]

This is a fragile point in Hobbes' doctrine. Up to this point, from the premises he has established for his system, namely that man is considered as non-sociable animal and deprived of freedom, Hobbes extracted rigorous conclusions, and one can hardly reproach his logic. However, from a certain point onwards, he will no longer be this careful and impartial philosopher, but rather the champion of absolute monarchy, friend and master of Charles II. Thus, his deduction will cease to be exact: the logic of the partisan is not as valid as that of the thinker.

In the same way that the political part of Hobbes' writings will have less scientific value and will contain less truth, it will also have less historical value and less influence on the formation of the [philosophical] systems to come. The despotism of which Hobbes became the advocate was overthrown by William of Orange and was refuted by Locke. From this moment onwards this despotism is definitively driven out of utilitarian and Epicurean systems: Helvétius is a liberal, as are d'Holbach and Diderot, and so is Saint-Lambert and Volney. The English utilitarian school, largely influenced by Hobbes' doctrine, knew how to skilfully compensate Hobbes with Locke, jettisoning Hobbes' political conclusion, and following the principles of his adversary [Locke], who in many points is nothing but Hobbes' consequent disciple.

One can concede to Hobbes that the will of all, especially in order to exit the state of war in which he places us, needs indeed to be personified in someone; in addition, it needs to be fixed and to be *unified*, so to say. But there are two ways to produce this *union*, namely [i] *delegating* a limited power for a limited time to an assembly; [ii] *alienating* to the advantage of an assembly or of just one man a limitless power, for an unlimited time. Hobbes, as we will see, only examines the second hypothesis, and he all too easily triumphs over the partisans of freedom. Between a sovereign man and a sovereign assembly, on the one hand, and a mandatary[55] assembly, on the other, there is indeed little difference. Hobbes divides the great treatise *On the Citizen* into two main parts,[56] in which he successively depicts man in two different states, namely in the state of nature where division and chaos[57] rule, that is, the state which he designates with the more or less exact name of *Freedom*; then, in a later state of peace, [resulting from an] overcoming of the state of war, under absolute despotism. This is Hobbes' ideal, the state which he opposes to primitive chaos and which he calls *Empire*.[58] For Hobbes, the whole of human history can be summarized by these two words: *chaos* and *empire*.

The former designates the point of departure, the latter the end point.[59] – Between these two states, Hobbes does not seem to admit the existence of any other. However, is it not the case that between despotism and chaos[60] there is space for that freedom whose meaning Hobbes does not seem to understand? Here, we are not making a critique of Hobbes' utilitarian system. We are simply drawing attention to a forgetting on his part, as well as a flaw in his reasoning. From the perspective of the logician this flaw jeopardizes truth, and from the historian's perspective his political doctrine. In any case, let us examine Hobbes' idea of *Empire*, which is for him the only means to universal peace, and which Epicurus would hardly have accepted, inimical as he was to any invincible force, to any *factum*.

According to Hobbes, in order to move from simple *agreement*[61] to *union* properly understood all [individual] wills must be *subjected* to the will of *just one*. This alienation of all in favour of *one* will not be different from a new contract, whose aim is to secure the first one. Here is its formula: 'I transfer my right to this sovereign, on condition that you also transfer yours to him.'[62] Moreover, this all-powerful sovereign does not necessarily have to be just one individual: it can also be a collection, an aristocracy, a democratic assembly, as long as it is a body, a unity, and as long as its power is unlimited. Hobbes' preferences for monarchy, however, are clearly indicated;[63] for him the situation is all or nothing, despotism or [chaos and] anarchy, unbreakable fasces or the struggle between all forces. Hobbes is the enemy of those tempered forms of government, of the 'three powers astonished by the tie that joins them together'; he is the enemy of those governments whose divisions, while creating the conditions of future war, also produce actual impotence in the present. Force, this is the last word of Hobbes' politics, as well as of his ethics and psychology. Once everyone subjects their will and transfers their rights to just one, he [the sovereign] will acquire such great force that, 'through the fear it inspires, he will be able to make all wills conform to unity and peace'.[64]

Through this contract and this alienation of all rights the city is formed.[65] The city, a wonderful thing, is an artificial harmony between naturally discordant forces. The highly diverse parts of the city, this admirable monster, are ready to escape [each other] and disperse in every possible way, and they only remain united because of the appeal of interest and by the links established by power.[66] Once Hobbes, with all the resources of his genius, has constructed this strange entity, he was amazed by his creation and sought a symbolical name for it. After having created it, and watched it grow, elevating to maximal power[67] this sovereign *king*, this civil person to whom he gives breath, and makes walk and rule the State, what is left for Hobbes but to adore and to deify his creation? This wondrous being is more divine than human; it is the mortal god, Leviathan. In the same way, our ancestors surrounded themselves with giant idols of stone, which they erected with their own hands, and which shook without ever collapsing, eternally threatening the worshippers who kneeled before them in religious horror. Hobbes' god, just like the god of the first peoples, is a god of force; and perhaps it is precisely because of this that it is a mortal god.

In sum, the political part of Hobbes' system, which we will not examine here in detail, does not lack vigour or logic. Since one admits a *sovereign*, and not only a *mandatary*, all consequences Hobbes puts forth must then be accepted in advance. His politics fails above all because of the principle from which it is deduced, and it will [in time] perish with it. What Hobbes' successors retain, and at the same time transform, is the vast naturalist and sensualist system of which he was the great renovator in modern times, and which was originally created by Epicurus and Democritus in antiquity. In effect, Hobbes exercised a great influence on the development of Epicurean ideas both in France and England. We will find all his principles in Helvétius and in Hobbes' translator d'Holbach. Finally, many of his ideas were even passed on to his adversaries, for these ideas were not less useful to the cause they fought against than to the cause they sought to promote. Hobbes was, indeed, the first who attempted to treat ethics and politics as deductive sciences, to bind them together with all the rigour of logic. Until then, in politics one had sought to observe, as for Hobbes he wanted to demonstrate. He was outraged by those who claimed that the principles of the State could not be treated philosophically. – If these principles, they said, could be so readily demonstrated they would have been demonstrated already. – However, replies Hobbes, hasn't there been a time in which men did not know how to build [houses]? Well, they have learned how to do so. Similarly, one will be able to learn to build, through the sole effort of reasoning this political edifice, which [now] seems a work of chance. Politics and ethics are sciences and can thus be demonstrated *a priori*.[68]

Now, if we consider Hobbes only as a continuator of Epicurus, and if we ask what Epicureanism has gained from his contribution, we then find Hobbes' system to be more profound, but also narrower in some respects. We are far removed from what was attractive about Epicureanism: the idea Epicurus had of interest was wide and synthetic, and the role that physical force played in his system remained completely modest. By contrast, Hobbes only grasps the most mechanical aspect of interest and, by deepening the narrow idea that he has of it, he aims to place the greatest interest in force. Thus, Hobbes made himself the apostle of force, in the same way others made themselves apostles of kindness or benevolence.

Hobbes' system is, above all, remarkable for its scientific rigour. It is concatenated with a logical force as irresistible as the material force that links together his city and his citizen. However, we never find in his system any impetus[69] towards sensibility,[70] nor any precepts of philanthropy, benevolence, charity, as we will find in d'Holbach, Diderot and the eighteenth-century Epicureans. We find instead the most fatal and tightest of deductions. Hobbes is a sort of misanthropic logician; he believes in the natural depravation of the human being: *pravitas generis humani*. His moral system, assuming the principles of sensualism,[71] is only weak in one point, the same point in which his political system also reveals its weakness: I refer to the conception, so fundamental for him, of a physical and despotic power[72] as the condition of well-being and peace for the individual. 'What a peace!' Montesquieu would say. 'The silence of a city that the enemy has just occupied.'[73]

Notes

1 T.N. The French word here is *incrédule*.
2 T.N. *droit*.
3 T.N. *loi*.

4   T.N. *droit*.
5   T.N. Note Guyau's opposition between right and law. This distinction, under the form of opposition, appears in his choice of words: *droit* and *loi*; the former designates the right to everything (based on desire), the latter rests upon on the calculus of interest properly understood. The English terms 'right' (*droit*) and 'law' (*loi*) clearly preserve the opposition proposed by Guyau.
6   T.N. *morale naturelle*. Although Guyau uses the term *morale* here, I have chosen the English word 'morality', since Guyau seems to be referring to moral life: in this case, the result of the prescriptions of natural law and the social sphere of morality.
7   T.N. Guyau's term here is *l'anarchie*; I have translated the term differently in its next occurrences in order to avoid ambiguity.
8   T.N. Literally, the superstitions of *le vulgaire*, of those who are vulgar, ordinary, ignorant or uneducated.
9   T.N. *Sadducéens*.
10 Frédéric Ozanam, *Dante et la philosophie catholique au XIIIème siècle* [*Dante and Catholic philosophy in the 13th century*], Paris: V. Lecoffre [1839] 1845 [Guyau quotes the second edition], 47; 345.
11 T.N. The French here is *parti*.
12 Ozanam, *Dante et la philosophie catholique au XIIIème siècle*, 48.
13 'E chussi poteano dire pluy de centomilla migliara.' See Ernest Renan, *Averroës [et l'Averroïsme*, Paris: Durand, 1852], 285.
14 T.N. *Iumentum* is a beast of burden, most likely a donkey.
15 Dante, *The Divine Comedy*, 'Inferno', IX & X.
16 John of Salisbury, *Policraticus, sive de nugis curialium et de vestigiis philosophorum*, Leiden [Lugduni Batavorum]: ex officina Ioannis Maire, 1639 [English edition: *Policraticus: Of the frivolities of courtiers and the footprints of philosophers*, translated by Cary J. Nederman, Cambridge: Cambridge University Press, 1990], book VII, ch. 15.
17 Erasmus, *Colloquia familiaria* [1518, Guyau quotes p. 543].
18 T.N. *à double ou triple fond* is an unusual qualification; Guyau seems to be quoting Saint-Beuve here. This image could be read in metaphorical terms: in the same way a drawer can have a fake bottom where something is hidden, so does Montaigne have secrets under or beneath appearances. In a word, Montaigne's thought has many layers.
19 T.N. Guyau's image is much more powerful and subtle in the original: like a Janus, Montaigne is Pyrrhonian on one side, but on the other side he is Epicurean; he resorts to faith as a way to cover this heretic duality.
20 T.N. The French here is *la 'moëlle'*.
21 Michel de Montaigne, *Essais*, I, 19 [See Montaigne, *The Complete Essays*, translated by Michael A. Screech, London & New York: Penguin, 1993; I have also used and modified Charles Cotton's translation].
22 One of Montaigne's contemporaries, Cardan [Girolamo Cardano], professed a sort of Epicureanism turned upside down: his doctrine did not conduce to asceticism by a refinement of the will; he maintained that since pleasure emerges only in contrast with pain, one should search for and maximize pain and suffering in order to obtain the highest sum of pleasure by their cessation. He has lived, or at least he claimed to have lived his life in accordance with this principle. Girolamo Cardano, *De Subtilitate rerum*, Johann Petreius, Nuremberg, 1550 [*The De subtilitate of Girolamo Cardano*, translated by John M. Forrester, Tempe AZ: Arizona Center for Medieval and Renaissance Studies, 2013] 1, XIII; [See also] *De Vita propria* [1576], Paris: Iacobus

Villery, 1653 [*The Book of my Life*, translated by Jean Stoner, New York: New York Review of Books, 2002].

23 T.N. *volupté*.
24 T.N. I have followed Guyau's translations of Gassendi's quotes.
25 Pierre Gassendi, *De vita et moribus Epicuri* [*Animadversiones in Librum X Diogenis Laërtii, qui est de vita, moribus, placitisque Epicuri*, Lugduni: Barbier, 1649], preface.
26 T.N. *libertinage des moeurs*.
27 T.N. The translator could not find the reference for this quote.
28 T.N. *bien-être*.
29 T.N. *puissance matérielle*.
30 T.N. I have preserved Guyau's telegraphic style in this passage.
31 T.N. *force*.
32 T.N. *l'appétit*.
33 T.N. *l'agréable*.
34 '*Bonorum maximum ad fines semper ulteriores minimè impedita progressio*' (translated above), [Thomas Hobbes], *De homine*, XI, 15 [English edition: *Man and Citizen* (De Homine *and* De Cive), translated by Charles T. Wood, Bernard Gert and Thomas S. K. Scott-Craig, Indianapolis & Cambridge: Hackett, 1991; Guyau probably uses D'Holbach's 1772 French translation: *De la nature humaine*, Paris: Vrin, 1991].
35 T.N. Hobbes, *De homine*, XI, 15.
36 T.N. *puissance*.
37 T.N. *machine à sentir*.
38 T.N. *état sauvage*.
39 Hobbes, *De cive* [*On the Citizen*], Preface, 'Liberty [*Libertas*]', I, 1.
40 T.N. Primitive here should also be understood as primary and original. This is a descriptive rather than normative term in this context.
41 Hobbes, *De cive*, 'Liberty', I, 6; Cf. Lucretius, *On the Nature of Things*, I, V.
42 T.N. *droit*.
43 T.N. *puissance*.
44 T.N. *droite raison*. In Hobbes' Latin original, the term is *rectam rationem* (*De Cive*, edited by Howard Warrender, Oxford: Oxford University Press, 1983, 94; I – 'Libertas', 7). I have followed Richard Tuck and Michael Silverthorne in their use of the English phrase 'right reason' (*On the Citizen*, Cambridge: Cambridge University Press, 1998, 27).
45 T.N. Literally *conservation de sa vie et sa personne*.
46 T.N. *conservation*.
47 Hobbes, *De cive*, 'Liberty', I, 7–8, 10.
48 Hobbes, *De cive*, 'Liberty', I, 12.
49 T.N. Here one should take a step back and note Guyau's ethnocentrism.
50 Hobbes, *De cive*, 'Liberty', [Guyau quotes p. 6 of the edition he is using]; see also *Leviathan*, *De homine* [Part I: Of Man], XIII.
51 T.N. *translation*.
52 Hobbes, *De cive*, 'Government [*Imperium*]', V, 3. [T.N. I have used Tuck and Silverthorne's translation here].
53 T.N. *accord*; Hobbes' original Latin here is *consensio*; Tuck and Silverthorne have chosen the English term 'accord'.
54 Hobbes, *De cive*, 'Government', V, 6, 7.
55 T.N. *mandataire*.

56 The third part [of *De cive*], *Religio*, was probably secondary for Hobbes, who was incredulous [or irreligious] like most Epicureans.
57 T.N. The French here is *anarchie*.
58 T.N. Guyau is here referring to the section entitled *Imperium* in the Latin original, which Tuck and Silverthorne translated as 'Government'.
59 T.N. *la fin*.
60 T.N. *anarchie*.
61 T.N. *accord*.
62 Hobbes, *De cive*, 'Government', VI, 20; *Levitahan*, 'Part II: Of Commonwealth', XVII.
63 Hobbes, *De cive*, 'Government', X; *Levaithan*, 'Of Commonwealth', XIX.
64 [Hobbes, *De cive*, 'Government', V, 8.
65 Hobbes, *De cive*, 'Government', V, 9: '*Civitas est persona una, cujus voluntas, ex pactis plurium hominum, pro voluntate habenda est ipsorum omnium; ut singolorum viribus et facultatibus uti possit, ad pacem et defensionem communem*' ['The city [*cité*, or, in Latin, *civitas* – which Hobbes calls in 'commonwealth' in the *Leviathan*] is also a [civil] person whose will, resulting from a pact among several men, should be considered as the will of them all, in such a way that it can make recourse to the forces and faculties of singular individuals in order to assure common peace and defence'].
66 T.N. *puissance*.
67 T.N. *puissance*.
68 Hobbes, *Leviathan*, 'Of Commonwealth', XXX; Cf. *De homine*, X, 5.
69 T.N. *élan*.
70 T.N. *sensibilité* is here understood in the moral sense, for instance, someone who is sensitive to a certain moral issue.
71 T.N. As mentioned above, in French this is a way to designate empiricism, or a theory of knowledge entirely based on the senses.
72 T.N. *puissance*.
73 T.N. *Quelle paix!* The reference here is Montesquieu, *The Spirit of the Laws*, book 5, chapter 14: 'While the principle of despotic government is fear, its end is tranquillity; but this is not a peace, it is the silence of the towns that the enemy is ready to occupy.'

2

La Rochefoucauld – The Psychology of Epicureanism

On La Rochefoucauld's moral system. – I. – Individual virtues. The principle which dominates them all: interest. Interest in courage, temperance, humility, pride [*fierté*].¹

II. Social virtues. Interest in the feelings of admiration and trust. Interest in probity,² justice, goodness, pity, love and hate. Interest as the explanation of remorse and repentance. Interest as a spring of human society.
III. Sensualist and fatalist doctrine of La Rochefoucauld, [as] deduced from his utilitarian doctrine.
IV. Ultimate unity to which human passions can be referred, including the pride [*orgueil*] that dominates and produces them all: – self-love,³ that is the love of oneself.⁴ – La Rochefoucauld's misanthropy. – Influence of the book of *Maxims* on the development of Epicurean ethics.

Utility must always and everywhere be the end goal of man – this is the principle of every Epicurean and utilitarian system. However, before showing that it ought to be the end, it is necessary to show that utility can be this end, and that, as a matter of fact, it is so already. Is it possible to refer all human action, without exception, to this single end, [that is, to] interest? Is the entire soul implied in this simple word, in this sole idea?

From practical considerations about the aim of our actions, Epicureanism should naturally pass to a psychological examination of ourselves; it should try referring back to itself everything that seemed to escape it. Epicurus had already attempted [to elaborate] curious psychological analyses: one recalls his theory of friendship and of the main virtues; one also knows the efforts of the Epicureans, such as Manlius Torquatus, in the sense of reducing the search of an alleged heroism to self-interest.⁵ Hobbes, in his turn, interpreted important sentiments, such as pity or benefaction, from the perspective of interest.

La Rochefoucauld, a contemporary of the English philosopher, will give continuity to his efforts concerning this point. He will penetrate deeper into the human soul, reaching into both interest and egoism. Few psychologists could be compared to La Rochefoucauld in terms of *finesse* of analysis; no psychologist ever grasped with as much insight that hidden part of all human feeling, where egoistical thoughts, sometimes invisible to the eye, come to find refuge. This thought from 'the recesses of the mind' is one that La Rochefoucauld perceives and brings to light. Nothing escapes his gaze; he distinguishes between the slenderest sentiments; he untangles the most complex ones; he follows their path of the most sinuous; he explains the most spontaneous ones in terms of necessary consequences. He finds delight in every circumvolution of the human heart. Has he seen, to quote Voltaire, the great route[6] in it?

Every pleasure, Hobbes claimed, can be reduced to two key pleasures: for the body, enjoyment; for the soul, vanity. Hobbes, however, had insisted above all on the former, and had mistaken it for its cause or its immediate means, namely force. In La Rochefoulcauld, the second pleasure[7] predominates and effaces all the others; to the physical power, to Hobbes' crude *being* he substitutes *seeming*.[8] A nobleman among noblemen, he had lived with them, taken part in intrigues and flattered the master. When, finally, leaving the life at the court, he begins his life as a thinker. He then retired into himself, observed and scrutinized himself, and especially observed and scrutinized those proudly hypocritical people among whom he once lived. Wherever he turns his gaze, all he perceives is hypocrisy; behind this hypocrisy he sees vanity, and yet behind all of this, both as a consequence and as a principle, he sees baseness and interest. In the face of such display of feelings and emptiness, he is ready to cry out with the Bible or Bossuet: All is [nothing] but *vanity* – and he understands this word in its strict sense. And, then, he reconsiders: underneath the void of vanity, the only thing that is not vain conceals itself, namely interest and egoism. All is but interest. The more this interest presents itself as small and the more it shies away, the bigger and indeed more alive it is, because greater is the vanity involved. Thus, for La Rochefoucauld, the measure of vanity lies in the sorrow he experiences in discovering it; the more hidden vanity is, the worse it is. He would perhaps go as far as to say that where one cannot sense vanity, that is where it is most alive.

We can see that La Rochefoucauld is, above all, a psychologist, even if he has not exercised his psychological analysis outside of a narrow circle of human beings. His point of departure is diametrically opposite to that of Hobbes, and still he arrives at the same conclusion. Hobbes built up his system almost *a priori*, by employing the geometrical method; La Rochefoucauld, on the other hand, begins by observing the facts, gradually penetrating the human soul, and then he classifies his observations and builds up a system. One should not believe that La Rochefoucauld did not go as far as Hobbes [in the task of formulating a system];[9] one should be misguided by the apparent disorder of the *Maximes*; if they seem scattered and disjointed they are, in fact, internally connected to one another by the firmest, most obstinate and reasoned belief in universal egoism. La Rochefoucauld's religious faith could only moderate or dissimulate this belief with respect to some particular points. Furthermore, this is where we find the value of the *Maximes*, and this is what made them so influential; La Rochefoucauld is not only an author of *thoughts*, but he is a true thinker, and a systematic thinker: if he were not, he would not have been so influential in the development of the Epicurean ideas.

'All our virtues,' he says, 'are often not different from an art of seeming [or appearing] honest.'[10] 'Virtue would not go far if vanity did not keep her company.'[11] 'That which the world calls virtue is generally nothing but a phantom formed by our passions, and which one generally deems honest in order to do what one wants with impunity.'[12] 'No matter how hard one strives to conceal one's passions with the appearance of piety and honour, they *always* appear through these veils.'[13] 'What we term virtue is often but a mass of various and diverse interests, which fortune, or our own industry, manage to arrange.'[14] '*Vices* enter into the composition of *virtues* as poison into that of medicines. Prudence collects and blends the two and renders them useful against the ills of life.'[15] All these thoughts and images are synthesized in this image which clearly affirms the principle of Epicureanism: 'Virtues lose themselves in interest as rivers are lost in the sea.'[16] – However, one can say that in the same way certain rivers, long after having left the shore, still flow in the middle of the Ocean, changing from afar the colour of its waters, so perhaps these virtues will be found and will show themselves, in faded and pale colours, within the interest with which one wants to envelop them. To make them fade and to efface them, to destroy every trace of them, or, in a word, to make them disappear forever in what La Rochefoucauld will call the 'abyss of interest' – this is the goal of the book of *Maximes* as a whole.

If every action has interest as its principle those which seem to come from a virtuous and disinterested intention are untruthful and dubious: the thinker will have as his task to interpret these actions in their true sense, revealing their hypocrisy: 'Our actions are like rhymes[17] which someone can refer to whatever he likes.'[18]

If we examine the different actions, under the appearance of virtue, then we will [be able to] distinguish the reality of egoism. All of you who believe to be accomplishing a good action and, according to the Greek phrase, to be doing a good and beautiful thing, a work perfect in its genre, a sort of accomplished and lasting poem; well, you have not done anything different from a rhymed end,[19] and to this sole rhyme you have produced anyone can add the verses they wish, to fill the gap you have left however he pleases, with beauty or ugliness, interest or disinterestedness, duty or egoism. Your action has a thousand meanings, according to the perspective from which one looks at it; or, rather, it does not have more than one meaning, it cannot mean more than one thing, it cannot repeat more than a word: interest.

For example, what is courage? 'Apart from a great vanity, heroes are made like every other man.'[20] 'Vanity, shame and, especially, temperament make the valour of men, and the virtue of women.'[21] From military courage, let us look at moral courage, at the strength of the soul: still and always, we find interest. 'Magnanimity is the good sense of pride [*orgueuil*] . . .;[22] it despises everything for having everything . . .;[23] it makes man master of himself by making him master of everything else.'[24] 'Generosity is but a disguised ambition . . . an industrious use of disinterestedness to achieve a greater interest.'[25] 'Philosophy triumphs over the past evils and the evils to come; but the present evils triumph over philosophy.'[26] 'We often believe to have constancy when facing misfortune, when all we have is weariness or weakness; and we suffer [misfortune] without being able to confront it, like cowards who let themselves be killed because of the fear of defending themselves.'[27]

If interest is the only end, the only good is sensible good; therefore, death, as the absence of all sensible good, will be the greatest evil for La Rochefoucauld as it is for Hobbes. Both differ from Epicurus on this point. In the face of death even the most confident courage dies away. 'Neither the sun nor death can be looked at directly.'[28]

'Those who are condemned to death affect sometimes a constancy and contempt for death which is only the fear of facing it; so that one may say that this constancy and contempt are to their mind what the bandage is to their eyes.'[29] 'The wisest and bravest are those who take the best means to avoid reflecting on death, as every man who sees it in its real light regards it as dreadful.'[30]

Temperance, like courage, is but transformed interest. 'Sobriety is the love of health, or an incapacity to eat much.'[31] 'We could eat more but we fear to make ourselves ill.'[32] After temperance properly said comes the moderation of the soul, the contempt for wealth and honours. 'Moderation is the languor and sloth of the soul, Ambition its activity and heat.'[33] 'Moderation cannot claim the merit of opposing and overcoming ambition: they are never found together ...;[34] the one is debasement of the soul, the other is its elevation.'[35] 'The moderation of those who are happy arises from the calm produced be the possession of the good ...;[36] it is a fear of the envy and contempt which haunt those who are inebriated with their happiness; it is an ostentatious display of mental strength.'[37] 'The philosophers' contempt of riches was only a hidden desire to avenge their merit for the injustice of fortune, by despising the very goods of which fortune had deprived them; it was a secret to guard themselves against the degradation of poverty, it was a back way by which to arrive at that distinction which they could not gain by riches.'[38] As for ambition, which certain men seem to ignore, it is perhaps foreign to them to the extent it is impossible [for them]. The hatred of those favoured [by fortune] is no different from the love of favour [and advantages the favoured enjoy]. Moderation in fortune, just like the moderation in eating and drinking, is nothing but an effect of interest, of course, and especially an effect of vanity.

As we have already analysed the temperance regarding sensible goods, let us now turn our attention to what we can call moral temperance, modesty and humility. La Rochefoucauld, when facing such 'Christian' virtues, apparently opposed to all [self-] interest, seems to experience a certain form of religious respect. Don't we know, in effect, that supreme interest is the interest of vanity? If there is, then, a virtue that one could really call disinterested, that will be the one that more openly contradicts pride, namely humility. This virtue alone could halt the self-love and egoism that penetrate the deep regions of our souls; this virtue alone could resist, inexplicably, to all [analytic] efforts of the utilitarian psychologist. La Rochefoucauld says, as if to reassure himself: 'Humility is the true proof of Christian virtues; without it we retain all our faults, and they are only covered by pride to hide them from other people, and often from ourselves.'[39]

Yet would not humility, which seems so far away from pride [*orgueil*], touch it at its root? Would not these sentiments refer to one another? Supreme virtue is, perhaps, not different from a transformation of the first of [all] interests. When so deeply analysing humility, La Rochefoucauld still sees, almost in spite of himself, the shadow of the virtue he thought he had seized hold of now eluding his grasp. The thought about humility, which he had intentionally made more concise in the second edition of the *Maximes*, is indeed one of the most remarkable thoughts in the book: 'Humility is often just fake submission, which one uses in order to subject everyone else. It is an artifice of pride [*orgueil*], which bows before men in order to rise above them. Humility is pride's disguise and its first stratagem; but even if its changes are almost infinite, and even if it is admirable under every sort of appearance, one must confess that it is never as rare or extraordinary than when it hides itself under the cloak of humility: then, we can see it, eyes lowered, in a modest and reposed composure; all its words are pleasant and respectful, full of esteem for others and disdain for itself. It is pride that plays all these characters who we take for humility.'[40]

Modesty itself, a sentiment deriving from moral humility, is even more mistreated: 'The refusal of praise is only the wish to be praised twice.'[41] 'A man would rather speak ill of himself than say nothing.'[42] 'The modesty which pretends to refuse praise is but in truth a desire for more sophisticated courteous praises.'[43]

True modesty does not exclude a certain sentiment of pride [*fierté*] of character and personal dignity but must rather be accompanied by it. What is this sentiment of pride [*fierté*] for La Rochefoucauld? 'Pride [*orgueil*], as if weary of its artifices and its different metamorphoses, exhibits itself with its natural face, and is discovered in its pride [*fierté*]; so much so that we may truly say that pride [*fierté*] is but the declaration and open display of pride [*orgueil*].'[44]

This examination of individual and private virtues is already enough for us to dispel the 'phantoms to which one gives the name of honesty'.[45] After leading us directly into the inner self of man, La Rochefoucauld then introduces the notion of interest into this self. Let us now analyse the relations between self and others. Once man's feelings and affections are extended, we then need to widen his feeling of pride [*orgueil*] until we have encompassed all secret passions in the increasing and impassable circle of interest.[46]

Admiration is one of the feelings that seem to link us to others in the purest and most disinterested way. This is not at all the case. 'It is more a matter of giving oneself a share in the good action [of others] than a matter of praising them wholeheartedly.'[47] 'It is oftener by the estimation of our own feelings that we exaggerate the good qualities of others than by their merit, and when we praise them we wish to attract their praise.'[48] 'Usually we only praise to be praised.'[49] 'We do not like to praise, and we never praise without interest. Praise is flattery, artful, hidden, delicate, which gratifies differently him who praises and him who is praised. The one takes it as the reward of merit; the other bestows it to show his impartiality and knowledge.'[50]

The same applies to other sentiments such as trust and sincerity: 'what we usually see is only an artful dissimulation to win the trust[51] of others.'[52] 'The aversion to lying is often a hidden ambition to render our testimony credible, and to attach to our words a religious respect.'[53] 'The confidence we have in ourselves arises in a great measure from that that we have in others.'[54] 'Most frequently we make confidants out of vanity, a love of talking, a wish to win the confidence of others, and make an exchange of secrets.'[55] 'Confidence is a distension of the soul caused by the number and weight of things of which it is full.'[56]

The same applies to more strict virtues that would seem to categorically govern our will: 'it is hard to distinguish integrity from skill.'[57] 'Fidelity is an invention of self-love, by which, while elevating himself to the position of a depositary of precious things, man makes himself infinitely precious.[58] Of all the commerce of self-love, it is the one in which the latter makes the greatest profit with the least initiative. It is a refinement of its policy, through which it engages men by their goods, by their honour, by their freedom and their life, which they are obliged to entrust sometimes, to elevate a loyal man above everyone else.'[59]

Justice is [presented as] even more openly interested: 'Justice is merely an intense fear that our belongings will be taken away from us. That is what leads us to be considerate and respectful for all our neighbour's interests, and scrupulously diligent never to harm him ... without such fear, one would be constantly making raids on other people.'[60] 'We complain of injustice, not because of an aversion to it, but because of the damage it does to us.'[61] 'In judges justice is merely love of their own eminence.'[62]

All other affective and social virtues, in general, are not more disinterested than generous goodness or observant justice: 'He who superficially considers the effects of goodness, which makes us look beyond ourselves and by which we sacrifice ourselves continuously for the well-being of all, [he] will be tempted to believe that, when he acts out of goodness, he then forgets his self-love.[63] A belief according to which, by generously letting go of himself, he allows himself to be impoverished without realizing it, in such a way that it would seem that self-love is deceived by goodness. Nevertheless, goodness is the most useful means for self-love to achieve its own goals. It is a hidden path through which self-interest makes its way back to itself, richer and more abundant. The disinterestedness of goodness is actually usury, it is a refined resource by which self-love assembles, disposes, putting every man at its favour.'[64] When goodness is not calculated it is not, however, more meritorious: 'No one should be praised for his goodness if he has not strength enough to be wicked. All other goodness is but too often idleness or powerlessness of will.'[65]

The virtue of goodness is closely linked to the feeling of sympathy or to that of pity. On the one hand, La Rochefoucauld, like Hobbes, refers it to a sort of fatal and pathological affection. On the other hand, he refers it to a refined calculus of interest: 'Pity is often a feeling of our own ills, prompted by the ills of other people. It is a clever way of anticipating the misfortunes that could possibly befall us. We help other people so that they will be obliged to help us when comparable circumstances arise; and the services we render them are, strictly speaking, good deeds that we do for ourselves in advance.'[66]

As for gratitude:[67] it 'is as the good faith of merchants: it holds commerce together; and we do not pay because it is just to pay debts, but because we shall thereby more easily find people who will lend.'[68]

With mutual goodness, sympathy and gratitude[69] we can engender friendship. There will not be, in friendship, nothing more than the elements which compose it. 'Even the [apparently] most disinterested friendship is but trade, in which self-love always expects to gain something.'[70] '*We cannot love anything except when considered in relation to ourselves*, and do nothing else than following our own taste and our pleasure when we prefer our friends to ourselves.'[71] And this is how interest explains devotion.

As for love, strictly speaking, it is nothing but a 'fever of the senses'. 'There is no passion so powerfully ruled by self-love as love.'[72] 'If you think you love your beloved for her own sake, you are very much deceived.'[73] 'The reason why lovers are never bored with each other's company is because they are always talking about themselves.'[74] 'The severity of women is a kind of adornment and make-up that they add to their beauty.'[75] It is a fine and delicate appeal, a disguised sweetness.'[76] Or yet, 'it is because of their aversion that they act with severity.'[77] 'There are few virtuous women who are not weary of their metier.' Elsewhere, one finds a refined analysis of the constancy in love. The spirit of the system[78] bursts with all its subtlety: '[Constancy in love] is a perpetual inconstancy, which makes our hearts successively attached to all the qualities of the person we love, preferring now one, now another – so that such constancy is merely inconstancy contained in and confined to a single subject.'[79]

Since we do not truthfully love anyone, the misfortunes which happen to those we appear to love will leave us cold: 'We all have the strength to withstand the misfortunes of others.'[80] 'We are easily consoled for our friends' misfortunes when such things give us a chance to display our affection for them.'[81] And, what is more, 'In the adversity of our best friends we always find something that does not displease us.'[82] If, instead of a temporary misfortune, our loved ones are taken from us by death, will our affliction, then, be true? No. Just like pride [*orgueil*] can humble and disguise itself as humility, just like interest masks itself as devotion [and dedication to the other], in the same way does egoism know how to mourn and counterfeit love's despair: 'In mourning there are different kinds of hypocrisy. In one, under the pretext of mourning the loss of someone who is dear to us, we mourn for ourselves; [we regret the loss of his good opinion;][83] we mourn for the reduction in our well-being, our pleasure, our prestige. Thus, the dead are honoured with tears shed only for the living. I say it is a kind of hypocrisy, because in sorrows of this sort we are deceiving ourselves. There is another form of hypocrisy which is not so innocent, since it strives to impress everyone else. This is the sorrow of certain people who aspire to the glory of a beautiful and endless pain. [. . .][84] There is yet another kind of tears, which come only from little springs, flowing easily and drying up easily: people weep to be regarded as loving; they weep to be pitied; they weep to be wept over; and finally, they weep to escape the shame of not weeping.'[85]

In the same way we have found vanity and interest under the mask of friendship and love, we will also find it underneath that of enmity and hate. The principle of enmity is, indeed, envy; and is not envy wounded vanity? [As La Rochefoucauld writes,] 'Our evil deeds do not bring on us as much persecution and hatred as our good qualities.'[86] One of the main occasions for envy, and similarly one of the most frequent causes of hatred, is the excess of good deeds. – As Tacitus wrote, good deeds are only pleasant to the extent that it seems possible for us to repay them. – As Pascal explains, an excess of services irritates [he who receives them]: we usually wish to have the means to outpay the debt they generate. – According to La Rochefoucauld, 'It is less dangerous to do evil to most men than to do them too much good.'[87] 'Not only are men apt to forget favours and insults; they even hate those to whom they are obliged, and stop hating those who have wronged them.'[88] In the same way envy – which is ultimately pride [*orgueil*] – suffices to produce enmity, so laziness, this 'remora that is strong enough to stop the greatest ships', suffices to appease it: one hates due to the interest of one's own vanity, one makes peace because of the interest in one's own rest: 'Reconciliation with our enemies is merely desire to improve our position, weariness of conflict, or fear that something bad will happen.'[89]

If, on the one hand, La Rochefoucauld identified the deepest and most secret springs of the individual's conduct, on the other, he dedicated far less attention to society and to the springs by means of which the legislator could order them and distribute their movements in society. He is a psychologist in his *Pensées*, and a politician in his

Mémoires; he is not, however, a political philosopher in the way Hobbes is. Nonetheless, it is conceivable that he could readily have said of the social body what he has said of military bodies: 'Victory is produced by an infinity of actions, which, instead of having victory itself as their goal, regard only the particular interests of those who act, because every single individual who makes up an army, seeking their own glory and their own elevation, produce a good which is greater and more general [than the good of each individual soldier].'[90]

Furthermore, one finds *en germe*[91] in La Rochefoucauld an idea that will later play an important role in the social systems of Helvétius and Owen, namely that of the happy influence exercised upon man by the desire to be praised. Indeed, without the more or less conventional praise given to virtue, what would become of virtue left to itself? If, on the one hand, praise becomes pernicious when it degenerates into flattery, then, on the other hand, and looked at from a different perspective, it can be considered to be the supreme utility and the [first] condition for other virtues. As La Rochefoucauld says: 'At least the praise that is bestowed on us *helps to keep us practising virtue*.'[92] In this sense, would not praise operate the miracle of putting vanity – that is to say, man's fixed and dominant passion – at the service of virtue? Without praise, dragged from one interest to the other, we would take up or reject virtue according to the needs of the moment, as a useful or inconvenient instrument according to the circumstances. However, 'the desire of being worthy of the praises one gives us strengthens our virtue; and the praises one gives to one's spirit, worth or beauty tend to augment them.'[93]

Since interest is everywhere, in society as well as in the individual, how then to explain this very complex feeling which follows from the accomplishment of actions which are contrary to virtue, this sentiment that is always given as a proof of our essential morality, repentance? La Rochefoucauld has no difficulty to refer primarily to interest that which we could call exterior repentance or the confession of one's faults: 'We confess our faults so that our sincerity may repair the damage they do us in other people's eyes.'[94] As for interior repentance, 'Our repentance is not so much a regret for the ill that we have done, as a fear of the ill that could happen to us as a result.'[95]

In short, La Rochefoucauld has a very firm and reasoned doctrine focused on the interested character of every human action. He is in agreement with Epicurus, he anticipates Helvétius and La Mettrie, and he is as penetrating as Hobbes. It is intriguing that these two thinkers [Hobbes and La Rochefoucauld], employing very different methods, arrive at the same point: Hobbes employs predominantly the method of deduction and reasoning, whereas La Rochefoucauld employs especially induction and observation. Both follow the same path, but in opposite directions, and both are successful in following it to the end. Like Hobbes, who deduces his utilitarianism from his physiological and psychological system, La Rochefoucauld will [analogously] extract physiological and psychological consequences from the utilitarianism he posited as a principle.

If our actions are produced only by interest, then they are produced by the desire for pleasure, that is to say by passion, which also means that they are produced by an affection which comes from the outside and which is independent of our will. There are few ideas to which La Rochefoucauld loves returning to more than that of the determinism of our actions. We are slaves to our passions. All that is left for us is to surrender, to let ourselves be conducted and dragged along by our passions. The will is nothing; fortune is everything. 'Nature creates merit, and fortune puts it to work.'[96] 'Though men pride themselves on their great deeds, these are not often the result of great plans, but rather the result of chance.'[97] '*All* our qualities, good as well as bad, are doubtful and indeterminate; and almost all of them are at the mercy of circumstances.'[98] 'Our wisdom is no less at the mercy of fortune than our possessions are.'[99] 'One would have to be able to predict one's fortune in order to be able to know what to do with it.'[100] 'We make various virtues out of various different deeds that fortune orders as it pleases.'[101] 'It seems that our deeds have lucky or unlucky stars, to which they owe a large part of the praise or blame that is bestowed on them.'[102]

Moreover, La Rochefoucauld is not deceived by these expressions he employs, *chance* and *fortune*. In reality, fortune is related to necessity, and chance brings us back to the idea of fate. The secret of our decisions resides simply in the stable or unstable balance of our passions. It is a matter of mechanics: 'If we resist our passions, it is due more to their weakness than to our own strength.'[103] 'Men's merits have their season, as fruits do.'[104] 'Man often thinks he is the leader when he is being led; and while his mind is pointing him in one direction, his heart is imperceptibly drawing him in another.'[105]

Since we cannot act freely and independently, it depends even less on us to persevere in the action we initiate. It is impossible for us to be accountable for our actions in the present, and even less in the future: 'Perseverance deserves neither blame nor praise, because it is merely the persistence of tastes and feelings that we can neither discard nor acquire by any means.'[106] 'We have no more control over the duration of our passions than over the duration of our lives.'[107]

However, one could ask: don't we have the power to reject certain passions, pushing them away from ourselves? If we are in a state of servitude, are we not able to achieve our liberation? The most famous representative of English utilitarianism, John Stuart Mill, will himself admit, although being a determinist, that we have the power to 'modify our character', to free ourselves from certain passions. To do that, he says, all we have to do is desire it. – However, La Rochefoucauld denies all power of this sort. We can only *desire* to modify ourselves if this desire comes to us; and it can only come to us through the diminishing or replacement of another desire.[108] Whenever a passion is defeated, in fact it is not we ourselves who triumph over it, but rather a contrary passion. 'In the human heart,' says La Rochefoucauld, 'passions are perpetually being generated – so that the downfall of one is almost always the rise of another.'[109] 'We only perceive outbursts and extraordinary movements of our humours and temperament; but almost no one realizes that the body's humours follow a normal, regular course, which imperceptibly and gently bends our will, impelling it towards different courses of action. They progress together and successively exercise secret dominion[110] over us, so that they play a considerable part in all our actions, though we are not able to recognize it.'[111]

Thus, we cannot boast about *quitting* our vices. It is the opposite that happens: 'our vices quit us.'[112] 'It may be said that, during the course of our lives, the vices await us like hosts at whose inns we must successively lodge.'[113]

We are at the mercy of desires and passions; now, the passions contradict themselves, we consequently contradict ourselves: 'Nothing must reduce our self-satisfaction as much as the observation that we disapprove at one time what we approved at another.'[114]

Now, if there is nothing other than passions within us, to what can these passions be reduced? What is the ultimate reality that constitutes us? It is sensations, and the sensations lead us to the body: 'All passions are merely differing degrees of heat or cold in the blood.'[115] 'Strength and weakness of mind are ill-named: in reality they are only good or bad conditions of the body's organs.'[116]

Thus, in the same way that Hobbes found utilitarianism at the bottom of Epicurean sensualism, La Rochefoucauld re-encounters sensualism at the bottom of utilitarianism. One should not state, as most of his critics do, that his doctrine is unconscious, implicit, free-floating. On the contrary, no doctrine is clearer or more profound. Epicureans and utilitarians, especially the modern ones, frequently attach themselves to general and vague phrases. They posit *pleasure, well-being, happiness*, and many other motives as the aim of our conduct, without, however, telling us exactly what they are. Is it a matter of my pleasure only? Or is it a matter of yours? Would we be talking about my well-being and happiness, or also of yours? La Rochefoucauld, in turn, does not leave any space for vagueness. His role in the history of Epicureanism has been, so to say, to *particularize* every term, clearly distinguish interests, and draw the clear contours of egoism. Finally, his role was that of discovering, as he puts it, the unknown lands of self-love. From the start, he seeks to dispel all the attractiveness from the words *sympathy* and *benevolence* (words which will later reappear with the English school), and he does this by dispelling their ambiguities. No one has better explored the doctrine of interest than La Rochefoucauld. He has seen into the very core of interest.

What is then, to summarize, the fundamental unity to which amount all these passions which seem to stir and trouble human beings in diverse and contradictory ways and that, nevertheless, have all the same origin and the same end? Indeed, there is a general passion, which, as we have seen, dominates and encompasses almost all the others, which is vanity, [or] pride [*orgueil*]. We already know the importance that La Rochefoucauld attributes to this passion: 'The most violent passions sometimes give us some respite, but vanity is continually stirring us.'[117] '*All men* are equal in pride [*orgueil*]; *the only difference* is in the ways (honesty or crime) and means (virtues or vices) by which it is brought to light.'[118] It is hard to find a more explicit statement.

Now, pride [*orgueil*] itself, as well as all the passions it encompasses, is situated under and can be reduced to another passion, which is even more general: self-love. Self-love is the centre around which take place all the other movements of the soul that we have described. What is more, self-love is the soul itself, it is life. This is why we sometimes fall inert and lose consciousness, so to say, and this is also why we suddenly recover ourselves, 'according to how our interest gets closer to us or distances itself from us.'[119] 'Self-love is the love for oneself, and [love] of all things through and for the sake of oneself ... Just like bees rest on flowers, self-love only dwells in foreign things in order to take from them what suits it ... Its suppleness cannot be represented; its transformations are beyond metamorphoses, and its refinements surpass those of chemistry. One cannot fathom the depths of its abysses nor see through its shadows. In these deep regions self-love is invisible even to itself. But this thick barrier of obscurity that hides it cannot prevent it from seeing perfectly what is outside of itself; in this regard, it is analogous to our eyes ...'[120]

Because of the way he scrutinizes the heart of man, finding everywhere within it the eternal interest, La Rochefoucauld is seized by a sort of vertigo and a sort of dread: the psychologist, who is most of the times so cold and indifferent, is [suddenly] moved. 'That,' he writes, 'is the portrait of self-love, whose entire life is merely one big long flurry of agitation. The sea is a tangible image of it; and in the perpetual ebb and flow of the waves, it finds a faithful picture of its own eternal restlessness and the turbulent succession of its thoughts.'[121]

Many have contradicted La Rochefoucauld's *Maximes*, denying the exactitude of his psychology, and accusing him of partiality. Here, where it is enough for us to expose his doctrine in its relations to the development of Epicureanism, we have not attempted to formulate any particular judgement, neither about this doctrine nor about its author. We would only like to highlight that fact that, according to La Rochefoucauld, interest is not always conscious or reflected. It is often *invisible to itself*, it merges with our very nature and directs us, in spite of us. When understood in this way, La Rochefoucauld's doctrine is deeper than one usually considers it, and it is not quite different from the doctrines of contemporary English psychologists.

What gives to La Rochefoucauld's doctrine and personality their *sui generis* character in the development of Epicureanism is that he was not satisfied with the [mere] principle of interest. Instead of finding consolation, like Helvétius, in the thought that every human action is linked to an innocent egoism; and instead of finding in it a 'light', like Bentham, rather, La Rochefoucauld sees in interest only a source desperation and misanthropy. He is afflicted and troubled by his discovery. While not being able to go beyond his own system by means of the intellect, he does so at least in his heart, by lamenting its conclusions. Seneca said that Epicurus' doctrine was sad and austere; and La Rochefoucauld's becomes equally sad and austere. He feels gloomy before this 'human comedy in which self-love and pride [*orgueil*], which are intertwined and merge with each other, play alone the role of all characters'.[122] 'In every profession and every art,' he adds, 'each person puts on a pretended look and outward appearance to make him seem to have the merit for what he wants to; so that we may say that the world is made only of appearances. Our effort in seeking the real is useless.'[123]

As a matter of fact, underneath all these appearances there is always a reality, namely interest and pride [*orgueil*]. Although La Rochefoucauld wished he could find something different, not even all the *finesse* of his mind could find anything else. Thus, his naturally melancholic character became embittered. 'I think my melancholy would be fairly tolerable and fairly gentle if it came only from my temperament; but so much of it comes from other sources, and it fills my imagination and busies my mind to such an extent, that most of the time I am either daydreaming without uttering a word or else giving very little attention to what I am saying.'[124]

Although in his time La Rochefoucauld was very much admired and commented on, he was poorly understood. It is only a century later that there appears a book that is both the continuation and the social application of the *Maximes*, namely *De l'esprit*. If this work found an immense success, and if it solidly founded utilitarianism in France, this is due to the fact that the widespread reading of La Rochefoucauld prepared everyone for the reading of Helvétius. In order to represent accurately the influence that La Rochefoucauld exercised both in the development of Epicurean and utilitarian ideas and in their success, we could recall Voltaire's words: 'His *Mémoires* are read [still], and we know his *Pensées* by heart.' Helvétius recognized in La Rochefoucauld his predecessor and his master. This is his appreciation of the *Pensées*, especially concerning a common misunderstanding which mixes up the meaning of *self-love* and *vanity*: 'When the renowned La Rochefoucauld says that self-love is the principle of all our actions, how many people turned against this illustrious author on account of their ignorance about the meaning of this phrase *self-love*! ... It should have been easy, however, to realize that self-love, or the love of oneself, was but a sentiment engraved within us by nature, and that this sentiment could become, in each man, virtue or vice ... The knowledge of these ideas would have saved La Rochefoucauld from the much-repeated reproach according to which he saw only the darkest side of humankind; [on the contrary] he *knew it as it really is*.'[125] And La Rochefoucauld has not only known it for what it really is – or believed to know it: indeed, he also presented it to the whole eighteenth century, and his doctrine, passing through Helvétius, d'Holbach, Saint-Lambert, Volney, will leave France with them: it will extend its influence to Bentham's country[126] and his many disciples.

Notes

1. T.N. The term *fierté* here also indicates self-love, close to a sense of personal dignity, confidence, self-respect and self-esteem. Even if the term is relatively ambiguous, it does not have, in this context, the negative connotations of the word *orgueil*, which is closer to a vain and self-entitled form of pride, or vainglory. It is important, then, to distinguish two forms of pride in Guyau's reading of La Rochefoucauld: *fierté* and *orgueil*. Moreover, La Rochefoucauld's analysis of passions and sentiments can sometimes reveal more nuanced meanings in both forms of pride, which further complicates this schematic distinction. E. H. and A. M. Blackmore and Francine Giguère (La Rochefoucauld, *Collected maxims and other reflections*, Oxford: Oxford University Press, 2007), have used both 'pride' and 'arrogance' to translate the original *fierté*; however, they have also used the English 'pride' for the French *orgueil*, not indicating the difference existing in the French original, which sometimes introduce further ambiguity. Willis Bund and Hain Friswell (La Rochefoucauld, *Reflections; or Sentences and Moral Maxims*, London: Simpson Low, Son, and Marston, 1871), by contrast, translated *orgueil* as 'pride' and *fierté* as 'haughtiness', which I believe also do not capture the positive tones *fierté* can have. In any case, the ambiguity persists; therefore, I have decided to keep the original French in square brackets in the text, so that the reader is aware of the complexity of the notions of 'pride' in question.
2. T.N. E. H. and A. M. Blackmore and Francine Giguère have used 'integrity' for the original *probité*. I have chosen to stay closer to the French original, by choosing the English term 'probity'.
3. T.N. The French here is *amour propre*.
4. T.N. *amour de soi*.
5. T.N. Up to this point I have used 'interest' for the French *intérêt*. However, in this chapter, the use of this term is perhaps close to English self-interest, which I will occasionally employ when the context requires it.

6   T.N. *la grande route.*
7   T.N. That is to say, the pleasure of the soul, vanity.
8   T.N. The contrast in the French original here is between *être* and *paraître.*
9   'It would be severe,' says Jouffroy (*Cours de droit naturel*, volume 1 [Paris: Librairie de L. Hachette, 1843]) 'to attribute the whole system of Hobbes to the author of the *Maximes*.' Being severe here would mean only being capable of following a certain thought to its last consequences; one is never severe enough when it comes to the great thinkers. Moreover, it is enough to introduce a little bit of logical order into the *Maxims* – which La Rochefoucauld has laid down randomly, according to the time when he conceived each of them – in order to reveal the close link between them, and to extract from them a moral or ethical system even more profound than Hobbes'.
10 T.N. Guyau provides the references for the *Maxims* in a series of five or more in a same footnote; this procedure renders the references difficult to locate. In order to simplify the reader's access to the references, I will provide the references for each individual quote, following the French text of the 2007 Oxford bilingual edition: La Rochefoucauld, *Collected maxims and other reflections*, edited and translated by E. H. & A. M. Blackmore & Francine Giguère, Oxford: Oxford University Press, 2007; sometimes, there are some discrepancies in the references, since Guyau seems to refer to the 1664–5 edition of La Rochefoucauld's *Maxims*. When Guyau's references coincide with Blackmore & Giguère's French text (which presents versions from six editions of the *Maxims*), I will not add any further comment; when Guyau's quote diverges, I will indicate the corresponding maxim in Blackmore & Giguère's edition of the French text, highlighting this procedure through the use of square brackets. Here, Guyau references La Rochefoucauld, *Maxims*, 206. In J. W. Willis Bund & M. & J. Hain Friswell's translation (*Reflections; or Sentences and Moral Maxims*, London: Simpson Low, Son, and Marston, 1871) this appears as 'First Supplement, XXXIV'. I have translated the quoted maxims myself, indicating how each particular quote appears in one of the existing English translations I have consulted; when I use the existing translation in the text, these exceptions are indicated in the footnotes.
11 T.N. Guyau references *Maxims*, 54. In Blackmore & Giguère's bilingual edition this appears as V: 200 (*Collected maxims and other reflections*, Oxford: Oxford University Press, 2007, 57).
12 T.N. Guyau references *Maxims*, 55. In Blackmore & Giguère's edition this maxim is I: 179.
13 T.N. La Rochefoucauld, *Maxims*, 12.
14 T.N. La Rochefoucauld, *Maxims*, 1, I have here used Willis Bund & M. & J. Hain Friswell's translation.
15 T.N. La Rochefoucauld, *Maxims*, 182.
16 T.N. LA Rochefoucauld, *Maxims*, 171.
17 T.N. The French here is *bouts-rimés*. According to Willis Bund & Hain Friswell, the *Bouts-Rimés* was a literary game popular in the seventeenth and eighteenth centuries, 'the rhymed words at the end of a line being given for others to fill up' (see comment on maxim 382).
18 T.N. Guyau references *Maxims*, 104. In Blackmore & Giguère's edition this is V: 382.
19 T.N. *bouts-rimés.*
20 T.N. La Rochefoucauld, *Maxims*, 24.
21 T.N. Guyau references maxim 225. In Blackmore & Giguère's edition, this is maxim 220.
22 T.N. Guyau here references maxim 218, when it seems to be 285 in Blackmore & Giguère's edition.

23 T.N. La Rochefoucauld, *Maxims* [Blackmore & Giguère], 248.
24 T.N. La Rochefoucauld, *Maxims* [Willis Bund & Hain Friswell], LIII (1665, No. 271).
25 T.N. La Rochefoucauld, *Maxims* [Blackmore & Giguère], 246.
26 T.N. La Rochefoucauld, *Maxims* [Blackmore & Giguère], 22.
27 T.N. La Rochefoucauld, *Maxims* [Blackmore & Giguère], 420.
28 T.N. La Rochefoucauld, *Maxims* [Blackmore & Giguère], 26.
29 T.N. La Rochefoucauld, *Maxims* [Blackmore & Giguère], 21.
30 T.N. La Rochefoucauld, *Maxims* [Blackmore & Giguère], 504.
31 T.N. La Rochefoucauld, *Maxims* [Willis Bund & Hain Friswell], First Supplement, XXV.
32 T.N. La Rochefoucauld, *Maxims* [Blackmore & Giguère], IV.
33 T.N. La Rochefoucauld, *Maxims* [Blackmore & Giguère], 293.
34 T.N. Idem.
35 T.N. The editors could not locate this second sentence in the *Maxims*.
36 T.N. La Rochefoucauld, *Maxims* [Blackmore & Giguère], 17.
37 T.N. La Rochefoucauld, *Maxims* [Blackmore & Giguère], 18.
38 T.N. La Rochefoucauld, *Maxims* [Blackmore & Giguère], 54.
39 T.N. La Rochefoucauld, *Maxims* [Blackmore & Giguère], 358.
40 T.N. La Rochefoucauld, *Maxims* [Blackmore & Giguère], 254. I believe only the abridged version of this passage was translated by Blackmore & Giguère.
41 T.N. La Rochefoucauld, *Maxims* [Blackmore & Giguère], 149.
42 T.N. La Rochefoucauld, *Maxims* [Blackmore & Giguère], 138.
43 T.N. La Rochefoucauld, *Maxims* [Blackmore & Giguère], 149 (1665 edition).
44 T.N. La Rochefoucauld, *Maxims* [Willis Bund & Hain Friswell], First Supplement, VI (1665, No. 37).
45 T.N. Guyau's quote is inexact and non-literal. The original would be closer to the following: 'this phantom whom one call honest'; he also does not provide the reference. The same quote is found in Nietzsche's *Human All too Human* §36.
46 T.N. This is an obscure paragraph. There are two predominant meanings here: (i) The reach and scope of man's feelings becomes broader, and now we must widen the pride, and thus the circle of interest in order to encompass all secret passions; (ii) man's feelings appear bigger under our gaze, let us now also magnify or amplify interest and pride, so as to encompass all passions (in this case, the metaphor here could be more visual, e.g. the magnifying glass).
47 T.N. La Rochefoucauld, *Maxims* [Blackmore & Giguère], V: 432.
48 T.N. La Rochefoucauld, *Maxims* [Blackmore & Giguère], 143.
49 T.N. La Rochefoucauld, *Maxims* [Blackmore & Giguère], 146.
50 T.N. La Rochefoucauld, *Maxims* [Blackmore & Giguère], 144.
51 T.N. Bund and Friswell used 'confidence' here, which I think can be ambiguous.
52 T.N. La Rochefoucauld, *Maxims* [Blackmore & Giguère], 62.
53 T.N. La Rochefoucauld, *Maxims* [Blackmore & Giguère], 63.
54 T.N. La Rochefoucauld, *Maxims* [Willis Bund & Hain Friswell], First Supplement, XLIX (1665, No. 258).
55 T.N. La Rochefoucauld, *Maxims* [Willis Bund & Hain Friswell], 'Reflections on Various Subjects,' I. On Confidence.
56 T.N. This quote appears in the French edition as a footnote to maxim 239.
57 T.N. La Rochefoucauld, *Maxims* [Blackmore & Giguère], 170.
58 T.N. La Rochefoucauld, *Maxims* [Blackmore & Giguère], 247.
59 T.N. Guyau refers *Premières pensées*, 89. The editors could only find a translation for this quote in the secondary literature. Henry Clark (*La Rochefoucauld and the*

language of unmasking in Seventeenth-century France, Geneva: Droz, 1994, 152) translates it as follows: 'Fidelity is a rare invention of self-love, by which man, making himself a depository of precious things, renders himself infinitely precious; of all the commerce of self-love, it is the one in which the latter makes the greatest profit with the least initiative; it is a refinement of its policy with which it engages men by their goods, their honour, their liberty and their life (which they are compelled to risk on certain occasions), to raise the *fidèle* above everyone else.'

60 T.N. La Rochefoucauld, *Maxims* [Blackmore & Giguère], I: 88. Guyau refers *Premières pensées*, 22.

61 T.N. La Rochefoucauld, *Maxims* [Blackmore & Giguère], I: 90. Guyau refers *Premières pensées*, 24.

62 T.N. La Rochefoucauld, *Maxims* [Blackmore & Giguère], I: 89. Guyau refers *Premières pensées*, 23.

63 T.N. *amour-propre*.

64 T.N. La Rochefoucauld, *Maxims* [Blackmore & Giguère], V: 236. Guyau refers *Premières pensées*, 77. Guyau's version seems to come from the 1665 edition (where it is §250). The second edition (1666) of the *Réflexions morales* brings a different version of the text ('more precise and correct'), much more concise, in §236. For concision and clarity, the translator has used the 1666 version of this quote. Guyau's original quote, however, uses the 1665 version (§250).

65 T.N. La Rochefoucauld, *Maxims*, 237, I have used Willis Bund & Hain Friswell's translation here.

66 La Rochefoucauld, *Maxims* [Blackmore & Giguère], V: 264, I have used and modified Blackmore & Giguère's translation here.

67 T.N. The French here is *reconnaissance*; both Blackmore & Giguère's and Willis Bund & Hain Friswell's English translations employ the term 'gratitude', which I have followed. However, one should also think of a broader semantic field encompassing the notions of 'acknowledgement' and 'recognition'.

68 La Rochefoucauld, *Maxims*, 223 [T.N. Here I used Willis Bund & Hain Friswell's translation].

69 T.N. Here, again, the French is *reconnaissance*.

70 T.N. Here Guyau references *Maxims*, 178, paraphrasing the passage. I have translated Guyau's version. In Willis Bund & Hain Friswell's translation this appears as maxim 83 instead. Blackmore & Giguère's translation introduces the idea of social contract, which is in the original French *société* (instead of Guyau's *commerce*), which makes it more coherent with Guyau's discussion of friendship in Epicurus.

71 T.N. Guyau here refers: *Maxims*, 179. In both Blackmore & Giguère's French text and Willis Bund & Hain Friswell's translation, the maxim in question is 81.

72 T.N. Guyau refers *Maxims*, 267. In Blackmore & Giguère's French text, this is 262.

73 T.N. Guyau refers *Maxims*, 396 [Blackmore & Giguère, 374].

74 T.N. Guyau refers *Maxims*, 319 [Blackmore & Giguère, 312].

75 La Rochefoucauld, *Maxims*, 204.

76 T.N. Guyau added this clause to the maxim as if it were part of the quote.

77 T.N. Guyau paraphrases the maxim as if it were a direct quote. [Blackmore & Giguère, 333: 'Women never behave with total austerity where they feel no aversion.']

78 T.N. Guyau's phrase is *l'esprit de système*, which could also be rendered as 'systematic spirit'.

79 La Rochefoucauld, *Maxims*, 175.

80 T.N. Guyau provides no reference.

81 T.N. La Rochefoucauld, *Maxims*, 235; I have used Blackmore & Giguère's translation here.
82 T.N. La Rochefoucauld, *Maxims* [Blackmore & Giguère], I:99.
83 T.N. Guyau omits this part in his quote.
84 T.N. Guyau omits the rest of the passage without indicating it.
85 T.N. La Rochefoucauld, *Maxims* [Blackmore & Giguère], V:233. Guyau shortens the maxim.
86 T.N. La Rochefoucauld, *Maxims* [Blackmore & Giguère], V:29.
87 T.N. La Rochefoucauld, *Maxims* [Blackmore & Giguère], V:238.
88 T.N. La Rochefoucauld, *Maxims* [Blackmore & Giguère], V:14.
89 T.N. La Rochefoucauld, *Maxims* [Blackmore & Giguère], V:82.
90 T.N. La Rochefoucauld, *Maxims* [Blackmore & Giguère], I: 232. Guyau does not provide the reference.
91 T.N. I have proposed to use the French expression, since it seems to synthesize different meanings: (i) in germ, in an embryonic state; (ii) the seed of, the principle; something in potential or virtual state.
92 T.N. La Rochefoucauld, *Maxims* [Blackmore & Giguère], I: 155.
93 T.N. Guyau here quotes *Premières pensées*, 43, 44. The quotes appear as §§149–50 in the 1780 French edition of the *Maxims* (La Rochefoucauld, *Maximes et refléxions morales du duc de La Rochefoucauld*, Amsterdam, 1780).
94 T.N. La Rochefoucauld, *Maxims* [Blackmore & Giguère], V:184. Guyau refers *Maxims*, 189.
95 T.N. La Rochefoucauld, *Maxims* [Blackmore & Giguère], V:180. Guyau refers *Maxims*, 184.
96 T.N. La Rochefoucauld, *Maxims* [Blackmore & Giguère], V:153.
97 T.N. La Rochefoucauld, *Maxims* [Blackmore & Giguère], V:57.
98 T.N. La Rochefoucauld, *Maxims* [Blackmore & Giguère], V:470.
99 T.N. La Rochefoucauld, *Maxims* [Blackmore & Giguère], V:323.
100 T.N. Blackmore & Giguère propose a slightly different and less literal translation of this passage: 'If you cannot predict your future fortunes, you cannot predict what you will do with them.' (I:70).
101 T.N. La Rochefoucauld, *Maxims* [Blackmore & Giguère], I: 293.
102 T.N. La Rochefoucauld, *Maxims* [Blackmore & Giguère], V: 58.
103 T.N. La Rochefoucauld, *Maxims* [Blackmore & Giguère], V: 122.
104 T.N. La Rochefoucauld, *Maxims* [Blackmore & Giguère], V: 291. Guyau refers *Maxims*, 299.
105 One can relate this last thought to the following: 'The mind [*esprit*] is always the dupe [*dupe*] of the heart.' When reflecting on this topic Madame de Schomberg wrote:
    I don't know if you hear it as I do, but what I hear [and understand] is this, nicely said: the mind, though its resourcefulness and reasoning, seems to believe it can make the heart do what it [i.e. the mind] wants; but the mind is wrong, for it is the mind that is the real fool [*dupe*]; it is always the heart that makes the mind act; one follows all the movements of the heart, and that in spite of oneself and even when one believes not to follow them. This is clearly seen, above all, in actions of gallantry [*galanterie*], and I remember a few verses on this topic, which is appropriate to reproduce: *La raison sans cesse raisonne / Et jamais n'a guéri personne, / Et le dépit le plus souvant / Rend plus amoureux que devant.*' La Rochefoucauld unfortunately does not see things as Madame de Schomberg; the heart is for him the fatal ensemble of passions that always dominate and govern reason, even when reason believes itself to

be a sovereign master: the will is, within us, always the fool [*dupe*] of passion, and freedom is a dupe of servitude. [T.N. The passage quoted in the text is La Rochefoucauld, *Maxims* [Blackmore & Giguère], V: 43.]

106 T.N. La Rochefoucauld, *Maxims* [Blackmore & Giguère], V: 177. Guyau refers *Maxims*, 181.
107 T.N. La Rochefoucauld, *Maxims* [Blackmore & Giguère], V: 5.
108 T.N. Guyau's La Rochefoucauld sees desire more as something that happens to us than an active decision.
109 T.N. La Rochefoucauld, *Maxims* [Blackmore & Giguère], V:10.
110 T.N. *empire secret*.
111 T.N. La Rochefoucauld, *Maxims* [Blackmore & Giguère], V:297. Guyau provides a slightly different and longer version, quoting *Premières pensées*, 13.
112 La Rochefoucauld, *Maxims*, 197 [T.N. This also appears as §197 in the French 1780 edition of the *Maxims*.]
113 T.N. La Rochefoucauld, *Maxims* [Blackmore & Giguère], V:191. I have modified the translation. Guyau quotes *Maxims*, 196.
114 La Rochefoucauld, *Maxims*, 51 [Blackmore & Giguère, V: 51].
115 T.N. La Rochefoucauld, *Maxims* [Blackmore & Giguère], I: 13. Guyau quotes this passage as *Premières pensées*, 2.
116 La Rochefoucauld, *Maxims*, 44 [Blackmore & Giguère, V: 44].
117 T.N. La Rochefoucauld, *Maxims* [Blackmore & Giguère], V: 443.
118 T.N. La Rochefoucauld, *Maxims* [Blackmore & Giguère], V:35, modified. Italics by Guyau; the items in parentheses were also added by Guyau.
119 *Lettre à la marquess de Sablé* [T.N. La Rochefoucauld, *Maxims* [Willis Bund & Hain Friswell], Second Supplement, LXVI, Letter do Madame de Sablé (Fol. 211)].
120 T.N. I translated Guyau's version of this passage; he is probably quoting from *Premières pensées*. La Rochefoucauld's version in the *Maxims* is slightly different and can be found in Blackmore & Giguère's translation (I: 1): 'Self-love is the love of oneself, and of all things for the sake of oneself. It makes men idolize themselves, and it would make them tyrannize other people, if fortune gave them the means to do so. It never finds any rest beyond the self; and it settles on alien things only as bees do on flowers – to draw from them what suits itself. Nothing is as impetuous as its desires, nothing is as secret as its plans, nothing is as clever as its conduct. Its convolutions are beyond imagining; its transformations surpass those of any metamorphosis, and its subtleties those of chemistry. No one can fathom the depth of its chasms, or penetrate their darkness. There it is hidden from the most perceptive eyes; there it twists and turns in a thousand imperceptible ways. There it is often invisible even to itself; there, unknowingly, it breeds, nurtures, and raises a vast number of affections and hatreds. Some of them are so monstrous that, when it has given birth to them, it either fails to recognize them or cannot bring itself to acknowledge them. Its absurd opinions about itself are born from the night that envelops it. From that source come its errors, its ignorances, its uncouth and silly ideas about itself. From that source come its belief that its feelings are dead when they are merely dormant, its fancy that it no longer wishes to progress merely because it has come to a halt, and its idea that it has lost all the tastes that it has merely satiated. But the thick darkness that hides it from itself does not prevent it from seeing clearly what is outside itself. In that respect it is like our eyes, which discover everything and are blind only to themselves. Indeed where its greatest interests and most important affairs are concerned, when the violence of its desires summons up its full attention, it sees, feels, hears, imagines,

suspects, perceives, and deduces everything. As a result, we are tempted to believe that each of its passions has a kind of magic that is distinctively its own.'

121　T.N. Guyau does not reference this quote. It is found in La Rochefoucauld, *Maxims* [Blackmore & Giguère], I: 1.

122　T.N. Guyau paraphrases, see *Maxims* [Blackmore & Giguère], I:37: 'After pride has played every part in the human comedy all by itself, finally, as if weary of its artifices and its various transformations, it shows its natural face and reveals itself as arrogance – so that, properly speaking, arrogance is the affirmation and spontaneous display of pride.'

123　On this maxim, Madame de Schomberg writes: 'What do you say about [La Rochefoucauld's thought according to which] each one puts a mere exterior appearance of what he wants to look like, rather than what he really is? I have meditated upon this and a long time ago I said that everyone was wearing a costume [*mascarade*], and was more disguised than one would be at [the *mascarades* of] the Louvre.' [T.N. My translation of Guyau's version, which he quotes from *Premières pensées*, 92. In Blackmore & Giguère's edition a version of this maxim appears in V:256: 'In any profession each person puts on a pretended look and outward appearance to make him seem what he wants people to think him. So we may say that the world is composed only of appearances.']

124　T.N. Guyau does not provide the source; in Blackmore & Giguère's edition we find it in the section 'Portrait of Monsieur R – – d, by Himself', in the '*Addenda* to the Miscellaneous Reflections' (p. 277).

125　T.N. My translation; I could not find the reference for Helvétius' appreciation of La Rochefoucauld.

126　T.N. The addition of this word is an interpretive choice and not at all a literal translation. Guyau says that La Rochefoucauld extended his influence until '*chez* Bentham'; this *chez* could designate a place, Bentham's place or home. He is referring to England and the development of utilitarianism.

3

Spinoza – Synthesis of Epicureanism and Stoicism

I. Spinoza, metaphysician of utilitarianism. – Relativity of perfection and imperfection; relativity of good and evil. The good is the useful; the useful is that which produces joy when satisfying a desire; desire is the tendency of being to persevere in being. Virtue is the *power*[1] to persevere in being; happiness is *succeeding* [to do so]. Identity of virtue and happiness.

II. Individual ethics. – For the individual, virtue is to obtain the greatest happiness by satisfying the best as possible its own nature. – However, the nature or essence of man is reason. – Understanding[2] is, therefore, virtue par excellence. – Synthesis attempted by Spinoza of Epicureanism and Stoicism, [and] of mysticism and naturalism in the idea of reason understanding eternal necessity, which is Nature or God, and finding in this knowledge perfect happiness.

III. Social ethics. – Geometry of customs.[3] – Love, hate, sympathy, emulation[4] reduced to theorems. – Importance of the theorem in which Spinoza demonstrates that one loves above all a being that one believes to be free. – Opposition between human passions; fear as a means to smother this opposition; reason [as a means] to reconcile it.[5] – Epicurus and Zeno, personal interest and general interest reconciled in the interest of reason.

IV. Politics. – Utilitarian liberalism. – The need [or necessity] of thinking is identical to the freedom to think. – That government should have simultaneously the physical power[6] and the power of reason;[7] that the strongest physical power is democracy; that the greatest rational power is general reason.[8] – Spinoza's synthesis of utilitarian ethics and rationalist ethics.

Spinoza's vast system, which absorbs the systems of Epicurus and Hobbes, contains the fundamental theories of the French and English schools. At the same time, however, it seeks to surpass them by recasting the ethics of happiness in terms of an ethics of intelligence and placing the highest pleasure in supreme knowledge.[9] Spinoza exercised direct influence on d'Holbach, and a more or less indirect influence on all the other thinkers that we will discuss later on, such as Helvétius.

I. – An absolute negation of all that we understand by morality and a reduction of everything, including the will, to the necessary laws of nature, which are also the necessary laws of intelligence: this is, in concise terms, what Spinozism is. There is no other absolute than eternal necessity, which is the cause of existence of everything that exists. Everything else is relative. The absolute is that which is; and when we speak of what *could* or *should* be, we are simply uttering judgements on perfection and imperfection, on good and evil. Through a strange illusion we take these judgements for what is most absolute, when in fact there is nothing more relative than them. For what are, in effect, perfection and imperfection, which the Platonists wished to posit as [the] absolute archetypes of our intellect? Perfection and imperfection are simply relations between things and our thinking. 'If someone has decided to make something, and has finished it, then he will call it perfect – and so will anyone who rightly knows, or thinks he knows the mind and the intention[10] of the author of the work.'[11] You see an unfinished house; if the builder wanted to finish it but did not succeed, the house is imperfect, if, on the other hand, he wanted to take it only to the point in which we find it, then it is perfect. All perfection is relative to the thought of the agent. Accordingly, would we have the right to say that the works of nature are perfect or imperfect, as if nature had ideas and intentions, as if it were guided by ideal types[12] imagined by Plato? 'As the vulgar[13] commonly say – that Nature sometimes fails or sins and produces imperfect things – I count among the chimeras[14] [...][15] Perfection and imperfection, therefore, are only modes of thinking, that is, notions we are accustomed to feign because we compare individuals of the same species or genus to one another.'[16]

In the same way in which perfection and imperfection are relative to our thought, so good and evil are relative to our desires, as Epicurus and Hobbes have shown. 'For one and the same thing can, at the same time, be good or bad, and even indifferent. For example, music is good for one who is melancholic, [bad for one who is mourning,][17] and neither good nor bad to one who is deaf... Good and evil do not indicate anything positive in things considered in themselves.'[18]

Thus, when we say that something is imperfect, it is because we compare it to what it *could be* according to us; but this possibility indicates only a way of thinking, since in fact everything is necessary. Similarly, when we say that something is evil, we are actually comparing it to how we think it *should* be, that is to say, we compare it to that which we desire it to be. We make our desires – and our thoughts – the measure of things, and thus we create the chimera[19] of an absolute moral order, which would surpass the relative orders of physics and logic. On the contrary, it is morality that is relative, while nature is absolute. This is the implied principle of every Epicurean and utilitarian system, expressed in all its rigour: Spinoza brings it to light with his unshakeable logic.

Since there is no absolute good, what is, then, the relative good? – Spinoza answers the same as Hobbes and Epicurus: 'By *good* I shall understand what we certainly know to be useful for us.'[20] The useful, in turn, is that which produces joy, and joy is caused by the satisfaction of desire: it is still the Epicurean definition, except that Spinoza adds a metaphysical complement to it: desire is the tendency of our being to persevere in being. This desire is the base of self-love, just as Hobbes and La Rochefoucauld described it. 'No one strives to preserve his being for the sake of anything other than himself.'[21]

For any being the good is to succeed in this effort to conserve and satisfy its nature. The good, therefore, is nothing other than this *success* and it amounts to *power*;[22] and it is this power that we call virtue: 'By virtue and power I understand the same thing.'[23]

Now, he who is *able to* satisfy the fundamental desire of conservation is he who *knows* what is the best means to achieve it. *Power*,[24] for a rational being such as man,[25] is *knowledge*. Therefore, true power[26] resides in reason, without which we would not be able to calculate utility with certainty. From this follows the theorem: 'Acting absolutely from virtue is nothing else for us but acting, living and preserving our being (these three signify the same thing) by the guidance of reason, and all this according to the rule of interest that is particular to each one.'[27] This is the fundamental theorem of the utilitarian system. 'The essence of virtue is the very effort to preserve one's own being, and happiness consists in [one] being able to effectively preserve it.' This power[28] merges with virtue itself. Striving[29] would be but its ground and success its achievement. In this way, there is an identity between happiness and virtue. 'Blessedness[30] is not the reward of virtue, but virtue itself.'[31] To really be able to preserve oneself is the same as being successful in doing so; additionally, to act in this way is to enjoy,[32] and to enjoy is to be happy. On the other hand, to act in this way is also to be virtuous. Virtue, then, is not different from happiness itself, as all Epicureans and utilitarians maintain.[33]

II. – The human being can be considered both as an individual and as a member of society. From this fact, it follows that there are two relative points of view in this equally relative science that one calls ethics, or the science of virtue and happiness.

If we [first] consider the individual, leaving aside society, then virtue for him consists in obtaining the greatest possible happiness. In order to do this, he must satisfy his true nature in the best possible way. Now, this true nature is reason, since reason is the essence of the human being. The activity which is proper to reason is that of understanding, and understanding is to perceive the necessity of things. This necessity is Nature or, if you wish, God. Thus, Spinoza refers the ethics of happiness to the ethics of intelligence, that is to say, Epicureanism to Stoicism. 'What we strive for from reason is nothing but understanding; nor does the soul, *insofar as it uses reason*, judge anything else useful to itself except what leads to understanding.'[34] We know nothing that is *certainly good* or *bad* except that which leads us to really understanding things, or that which can prevent us from understanding them.[35] The soul[36] only acts when it understands; and it is only in this case that we can say that the soul acts virtuously in an absolute sense. Understanding is, then, the absolute virtue of the soul. Now, the supreme object of our intellect is God. Therefore, the supreme virtue of the soul is understanding or knowing God.[37]

To understand the absolute necessity of eternal nature amounts to understanding that which, while being subject only to its own law, is free. Therefore, understanding this necessity means understanding eternal freedom. It is through understanding that one participates in this freedom and identifies with it. The science of necessity and the science of freedom are one and the same thing. Again, Spinoza adds a Stoic principle to Epicureanism. The point where these two doctrines come together is the intellectual intuition which crowned Aristotelian ethics, namely the identity of human and divine thought, or the consciousness of eternity. 'We feel and know by experience that we are eternal.'[38] This awareness, which produces supreme joy, is the real love of oneself, and it is simultaneously the love of God. The mystical ideal of the Hebrews and the Christians seems here to merge with the moral theories of antiquity and in the broad synthesis proposed by Spinoza. His conception of nature is all-encompassing: the utility of the greatest possible happiness is nature enjoying itself; and the intellectual freedom of the Stoics, which is the very knowledge of necessity, is nature possessing itself. Finally, the mystical ecstasy, through which individuality is absorbed in universal being, is nature penetrating itself and finding its eternal existence underneath its ephemeral modes.

III. – Spinoza has shown the nature of the good for the individual: the individual's relative good is that which satisfies his desires. His absolute good is that which is no longer individual, it is not merely in relation him but is universal and necessary: it is nature or God. For, again, there is no other absolute than being itself in its eternal necessity.

Now, the human being cannot exist alone. In fact, man is but a mode of existence which is inseparable from all other modes. Thus, in order to understand [and, therefore, to satisfy his nature], it is not enough for man to know himself: he must know other beings and, especially, those that most resemble him. Finally, if he is to be happy, the human being needs to know that he is not self-sufficient: he needs the help of fellow humans and other beings. His existence, his thought and his desire are equally linked to the existence, thought and desire of humankind and, indeed, of the world as a whole. Hence the recognition of the movement from egoism that will engender society. Social passions and the love of others are, ultimately, transformations of self-love. This physics of customs[39] that the French Epicureans would later erect, and that psychology of custom under the law of association that the English utilitarians would later establish, Spinoza conceived them first – and he did something even more remarkable: he constituted a geometry of custom. 'I shall consider human actions and appetites just as if it were a question of lines, planes and bodies.'[40] Spinoza proceeds *a priori*, by deduction, and he contemptuously opposed his method to that '*historiette* of the soul', *haec historiola animae*, which was still satisfying to Bacon and his school.[41] The effort to persevere in being, insofar as it is conscious of itself, is [called] desire.[42] From desire both joy and sadness arise, and here we find the principle of all passions. 'Love is nothing but joy with the accompanying idea of an external cause, and hate is nothing but sadness with the accompanying idea of an external cause.'[43] The mechanism of the ideas, or of the 'images of things',[44] which links one representation to other, explains the mechanism of the passions.[45] Spinoza does not limit himself, as the English utilitarians do, to positing the law of association of ideas empirically. Rather, he deduces this law and draws its consequences. It is this law that explains, for instance, the sentiment of sympathy, which will play a major role in the English school. 'I know, of course, that the authors who first introduced the words sympathy and antipathy intended to signify by them certain occult qualities of things. Nevertheless, I believe we may be permitted to understand by them also qualities that are known or manifest.'[46] Sympathy is thus reduced to a theorem: 'If we perceive or represent an object that is similar to us (for instance, another man), and towards which we previously had no affect, to be affected with some passion, we are thereby affected with a similar passion.'[47] From this fact derive both *pity* and *emulation*. 'This communication of the affects,'[48] when it is related to sadness is called *pity*; but related to desire it is called *emulation*, which, therefore, is nothing but the *desire for a thing which is generated in us from the fact that we imagine others like us to have the same desire*. [Guyau adds the following:] If the thing desired cannot belong to the two at the same time, then emulation turns into envy.'[49] This proves that the same mechanism, according to the different outcome, is at the basis of virtue or vice.

Among these theorems, there is one of capital importance, namely the one regarding the love of others. 'When I say the lover's will to join himself to the thing loved is a property of love, I do not understand by *will* a consent, a deliberation of the mind,[50] or a *free decision*; for we have demonstrated that this is a fiction.'[51] This is the fundamental issue, not only for psychology, but also for ethics itself. If we are not morally free, then there is nothing else within us than desires and interests; therefore, [both] the exclusive love for others and full disinterestedness are but appearances. Self-love is what is real, and the Epicureans win the quarrel. Spinoza, while rejecting freedom, acknowledges that it is for us the condition that sets the value of love. He writes the following theorem, which Fouillée highlighted in his *Histoire de la philosophie*: 'Given an equal cause of love, love towards a thing will be greater if we imagine the [loved] thing to be free than if we imagine it to be necessary. And, similarly, for hate.[52] If we imagine as necessary the thing that is the cause of this affect, then we shall imagine it to be the cause of the affect, not alone, but with many others. Consequently, our love or hate towards it is less.[53] From this it follows that because human beings consider themselves to be free, they have greater love or hate towards one another than towards other things.'[54] Ultimately, love is reduced to an illusion, and this is also the last word of the Epicurean system.

Nevertheless, it must be possible to establish among human beings, if not love, at least the appearance and the equivalent of love. The social problem consists precisely in this. And there is only one way to solve it: making the interests of one [agent] coincide with the interests of another. This is what[55] all Epicureans have sought, from Epicurus himself to Helvétius.

Now, from where does the opposition between human beings come? From the opposition that exists between their passions. 'Men, insofar as they are torn by the conflict of passive affects, are contrary to one another.'[56] The interest of the passions is what divides men, and that which is also often used as an objection to the ethics of interest. However, according to Spinoza, there are two remedies for this [state of] division [among human beings]. One can subject men's passions, bringing them to unity [and making them converge] either by means of the power[57] of a stronger passion, namely fear, or through the power of reason.[58] These are the two main sources of the social order: the law of fear and the law of reason. 'And surely we do derive, from the society of our fellow men, many more advantages than disadvantages ... Men still find from experience that through mutual help[59] they can provide themselves much more easily with the things they require and that, by joining forces, they can avoid the dangers which threaten on all sides.'[60] From this interest derive society and the social pact, as well as the sovereign power instated to protect this pact by force. For 'no pact has any value except because of its utility; if utility disappears, the pact fades with it and loses its authority. It is folly to pretend to chain anyone to their word forever, except that one would do so in such a way that breaking the pact brings more damage than profit to the violator of his oaths.'[61] These are Epicurus' and Hobbes' principles.

The first means to maintain society, then, is physical power,[62] along with the fear it inspires. Insofar as human beings are slaves to their passions, force is the only means to govern them. Reason, however, joins its logic to the physical power [*puissance*] of force in order to maintain the social contract, and to condemn all perfidy. 'Suppose someone now asks: What if a man could save himself from the present danger of death by treachery? Would not the principle of preserving his own being recommend, without qualification, that he be treacherous? To this I reply that if reason should recommend that, it would recommend it to all men' – it is Kant's criterion – 'from which follows that reason would recommend, without qualification, that men should make agreements to join forces and to have common laws only by deception – that is, that they really should have no common laws, which is absurd.'[63] In other words, if [on the one hand] treachery can be the effect of passion, and a fatal and necessary effect, [on the other] it is not logical from the point of view of reason, which has brought human beings together by the need of forming a society.

If passion divides men it is reason unites them. Indeed, the object of reason is the understanding of truth. Now, truth is the same for all, and everyone can know it at the same time. As we have seen, reason is the true good of each man. It transpires that the real good of each one is also the true good of all the others. Thus, we possess the principle which will be able to produce peace and concord among men. The conciliation of interests finds its place in the common interest of reason. 'A man acts entirely from the laws of his own nature when he lives according to the guidance of reason; and only to that extent must he always agree with the nature of other men.'[64] In this way, the more each man seeks that which is useful to him, the more he is useful, precisely because of that, to other men. 'For the more one seeks what is useful to oneself,[65] and strives to preserve himself, the more he is endowed with virtue, or what is the same, the greater is his power of acting according to the laws of his own nature, that is, of living according to the guidance of reason. But men most agree in nature when they live according to the guidance of reason. Therefore, men will be most useful to one another, when each one most seeks what is useful to him.' Here one finds Epicurus and Zeno finally reconciled: to live according to nature, or to live according to reason, is to live according to one's particular interest, and to the interest of all; which amounts to being happy and virtuous. Therefrom we can turn to this other theorem, which Socrates as well as Aristotle would have admitted: 'The greatest good of those who seek virtue is common to all and can be enjoyed by all equally.'[66] This good is, in effect, the knowledge[67] of the eternal truth, or of God. Here we return to the final absorption of all in God, which is the sovereign good of the mystics: 'The good which everyone who seeks virtue wants for himself, he also desires for other men; and this desire is greater as his knowledge of God is greater.'[68] 'This love towards God cannot be tainted by an affect of envy or jealousy: instead, the more men we imagine to be joined to God by the same bond of love, the more it is encouraged.'[69] This love, however, is by no means free; it is rather a necessity of reason, [for] it is still an interest. However, insofar as it is rational, this interest is also universal. There is, therefore, a coincidence between interest and disinterestedness, between self-love and love towards others. For Spinoza's God is ultimately ourselves, in our eternal substance. Hence, to love God is to love oneself and all others, it is one and the same love. The ethics of particular utility strives to identify itself to a universal ethics.

IV – In what concerns politics, we find the same [theoretical] movement in Spinoza and Hobbes. The latter wanted a complete abdication of the individual in favour of the sovereign; but, as a matter of fact, this abdication is [ultimately] impossible.[70] Indeed, there is a power and a right which we can never abdicate: the power of thinking. Why? Because this power expresses the very necessity of our nature, that is to say, our reason. We cannot be deprived of our reason, which will be the refuge of freedom in Spinoza's politics. It dwells within man as an inalienable power[71] and as an inalienable right: it is the necessity of thinking which is identical to the freedom of thought. The true goal of politics is to organize[72] the strongest possible physical power to prevent passion from tearing man apart; and, at the same time, it is to make this physical power increasingly useless, replacing it with the power[73] of reason. Now, the strongest physical power is not that of the absolute monarch, as Hobbes believed, but it is rather the general force of the whole people,[74] or the force of democracy. On the other hand, the greatest rational power[75] is that of general reason;[76] the more this reason develops in the individuals, the more these individuals are united among themselves. Therefore, in Spinoza, we find a relatively liberal politics which aims to place the greatest interest within the greatest freedom of thought; that is to say, within the greatest necessity of reason, or in the greatest possible unity of all [particular] interests by the universal interest of reason. This liberal[77] revolution in utilitarian doctrine will be henceforth an accomplished fact: Hobbes will remain as the sole partisan of despotism.

In this way, the great system of the rationalist Spinoza effected a synthesis between Epicurean or utilitarian ethics and Stoic ethics. The only element that seems to be absent from Spinozism is the ideal of a real progress of nature, or the idea of *evolution*, an idea which the German metaphysicians (especially Hegel) and the English ethicists[78] (especially Spencer) will stress. To this metaphysics of universal evolution, they will add an ethics of universal evolution. Nevertheless, and in the end, the principles remain the same: a relative good takes the place of the absolute good; this relative good is ultimately reduced to a progressive knowledge[79] of a progressive utility, by means of which the interest of each individual is more and more identified with a universal interest.

Notes

1 T.N. The French here is *pouvoir*; here to be understood quite literally as 'being able to'.
2 T.N. *comprendre*.
3 T.N. *moeurs*.
4 T.N. Here one reads *émulation*, which could also be rendered as 'imitation'.
5 T.N. *la ramener à l'unité*, a more literal alternative here would be to bring or reconduct these passions (currently in opposition) to unity.
6 T.N. *la puissance physique*.
7 T.N. *la puissance de la raison*.
8 T.N. *raison générale*.
9 T.N. *savoir*.
10 T.N. Curley's choice was to translate this word as *purpose* (see Benedict de Spinoza, *Ethics*, London & New York: Penguin, 1996). As I have explained above, my choice was to include and prioritize Guyau's variations, translating the French quotations used by Guyau or translated by him into French. Guyau occasionally changes and adapts or emphasizes certain aspects of the translations for the sake of his argument.

11 Spinoza, *Ethics*, Part IV, Preface.
12 T.N. *types idéaux*. Guyau's reference here is the Platonic idea or form, which, being perfect, would serve as the model in relation to which one asserts the imperfection of material things. In this context, the French word *type* is used by Guyau as a synonym of 'model' or 'archetype'.
13 T.N. Although it does not appear in Curley's translation, the French original here reads *le vulgaire*, explained in other footnotes above. This is a figure that reappears in Spinoza's work, with a negative connotation or in contrast to the sage. It could also have the pejorative sense of 'populace'.
14 T.N. In Curley's translation one reads 'fictions'; Guyau's original French reads *chimères*.
15 T.N. 'I treated in the Appendix of Part I.' Guyau omits this part of the passage.
16 T.N. *Ethics*, Part IV, Preface. Guyau does not provide the reference for this quote.
17 T.N. Guyau omits this part of the quote.
18 T.N. Guyau finished the quote with the opening sentence of the same paragraph, which he displaced. I preserved Guyau's choice.
19 T.N. Both Curley and Shirley (see Spinoza, *Complete Works*, translated by Samuel Shirley, edited by Michael L. Morgan, Indianapolis & Cambridge: Hackett, 2002) use 'fiction', my choice was to preserve Guyau's original.
20 Spinoza, *Ethics*, Part IV, Definition 1.
21 Spinoza, *Ethics*, Part IV, Proposition 25. Curley translates it as follows: 'No one strives to preserve his being for the sake of anything else.'
22 T.N. *puissance*.
23 Spinoza, *Ethics*, Part IV, Definition 8. [T.N. Guyau's reference is Definition 7].
24 T.N. Guyau uses the French *pouvoir* which also means 'being able to'. The noun 'power' [*le pouvoir*] preserves that meaning, while at the same time indicates the particular power of the human being, which in this case is *reason*. In Guyau's explanation reason is an expression of our *conatus* and of our desire, and it is the condition for being successful in our effort for conservation and 'satisfaction' of our nature. Additionally, in the original Guyau's use of *pouvoir* and *savoir* can be seen as two infinitives: to be able to [*pouvoir*] is to *know*.
25 T.N. I have preserved Guyau's literal phrasing, common in French, *l'homme*. A less gendered option would be 'human being', which is the idea here. For this reason, in some of the occurrences of the term *homme*, I have decided to use 'human being'. In quotes from Spinoza's text, I have usually followed Guyau, Curley and Shirley.
26 T.N. *puissance*.
27 Spinoza, *Ethics*, Part IV, Proposition 24. I have preserved Guyau's version of the text. Curley and Shirley translate it differently: 'Acting absolutely from virtue is nothing else in us but acting ... by the guidance of reason, *from the foundation of seeking one's own advantage*.'
28 T.N. Guyau's term is *pouvoir*. Here, it means the condition of being able to preserve one's being.
29 T.N. *effort*.
30 T.N. *beatitude*.
31 T.N. Guyau does not provide the reference. The passage is found in *Ethics*, Part IV, Proposition 42.
32 T.N. *jouir*.
33 Way before Bentham, Spinoza protests the principles of asceticism; he laments the fact that the virtuous life is usually presented to men as a sad and grim life, a life of privation, in which all pain is grace and all enjoyment [*jouissance*] a crime: 'To use

things, therefore, and take pleasure in them as far as possible – not, of course, to the point where we are disgusted with them, for there is no pleasure in that – this is the part of a wise man. It is the part of a wise man, I say, to refresh and restore himself in moderation with pleasant food and drink, with scents, with the beauty of green plants, with decoration, music, sports, the theatre, and other things of this kind, which anyone can use without injury to another.' Spinoza, *Ethics*, Part IV, Propostion 45, Scholium. [T.N. Guyau's reference 'Ibid., Part II' is mistaken].

34 Spinoza, *Ethics*, Part IV, Proposition 26.
35 Spinoza, *Ethics*, Part IV, Proposition 27.
36 T.N. *âme*.
37 Spinoza, *Ethics*, Part IV, Proposition 28.
38 T.N. Guyau does not provide the reference: Spinoza, *Ethics*, Part V, Proposition 23, Scholium. In the original French, Guyau's phrasing would be closer to the following sentence: 'We experience our eternity,' or 'that we are eternal'.
39 T.N. *moeurs*.
40 Spinoza, *Ethics*, Part III, Preface.
41 T.N. This reference comes from Fouillée's *Histoire de la philosophie*, Paris: C. Delagrave, 1893, 293.
42 T.N. See Spinoza, *Ethics*, Part III, Proposition 9, Scholium.
43 Spinoza, *Ethics*, Part III, Proposition 13, Scholium.
44 Spinoza, *Ethics*, Part III, Propositions 19, 20, and the following.
45 T.N. *Ep* [*Letters*]. II, 393.
46 T.N. Spinoza, *Ethics*, Part III, Proposition 15.
47 Spinoza, *Ethics*, Part III, Proposition 15 [as referenced by Guyau. This passage actually seems to be EIII P27, in which Spinoza formulates the important notion of 'affective imitation'].
48 T.N. Curley's translation is slightly different: 'This imitation of the affects'.
49 T.N. Spinoza, *Ethics*, Part III, Proposition 27, Scholium.
50 T.N. I have exceptionally rendered *âme* as 'mind' here.
51 Spinoza, *Ethics*, Part III, Definitions of the Affects, 6.
52 T.N. Guyau omits this part and adds part of the demonstration of the EIII P49 to the 'theorem'.
53 T.N. These two sentences are originally part of the demonstration of EIII P49. The following clauses are part of the scholium of the same proposition.
54 Spinoza, *Ethics*, Part III, Proposition 49.
55 T.N. A more literal translation would be: 'This means [to solve the social problem] is that which all Epicureans have looked for.'
56 T.N. The full sentence, in Curley's translation is: 'Insofar as men are torn by affects which are passions, they can be different in nature (by P33), and contrary to one another (by P34).' Curley's and Shirley's translations coincide here.
57 T.N. *puissance*.
58 T.N. *puissance de la raison*.
59 T.N. *secours mutuels*.
60 Spinoza, *Ethics*, Part IV, Proposition 35, Scholium.
61 Spinoza, *Theological-Political Treatise*, XVI.
62 T.N. *puissance physique*.
63 Spinoza, *Ethics*, Part IV, Proposition 72, Scholium. [T.N. I have corrected Guyau's reference: he quotes the TTP as well as EIV P62.]
64 T.N. Spinoza, *Ethics*, Part IV, Proposition 35, Corollary.

65 T.N. In Curley's translation we read: 'The more one seeks his own advantage.'
66 Spinoza, *Ethics*, Part IV, Proposition 36.
67 T.N. *connaissance*.
68 T.N. Spinoza, *Ethics*, Part IV, Proposition 37.
69 T.N. Spinoza, *Ethics*, Part V, Proposition 20.
70 T.N. See Spinoza's *Ep.* [*Letters*] L, to Jarig Jelles, where he explains to his friend and correspondent the difference between his political philosophy and that of Hobbes, especially in what concerns natural right and transfer.
71 T.N. *puissance*.
72 T.N. In his 1902 text comparing Nietzsche and Guyau ('The Ethics of Nietzsche and Guyau', *International Journal of Ethics*, 13, 1), Fouillée claims that whereas Nietzsche was the philosopher of *power*, Guyau was the philosopher of the *organization of power*. As Fouillée explains: 'Quantity [Fouillée refers to the idea of 'intensity of life', central both for Nietzsche and Guyau] in the rough meant to him only 'power' to which 'order' should be added, that is an *organisation of power* in view of some end to be attained' (p. 23). Fouillée argues that if, for Nietzsche, the end to be achieved was power and intensity as such, for Guyau, 'The end always remains to be determined' (23). Additionally, this idea of *organization* points to the fundamentally social – or societal – and political aspect of Guyau's philosophy: as he highlights in the *Esquise d'une morale sans obligation ni sanction*, the expansion of life in its fecundity is always social, extensive to others and ultimately collective. As Fouillée explains, 'Guyau sees the genuinely intense life in the generous and fruitful life, which "lives for many others"' (24).
73 T.N. *puissance*.
74 T.N. A literal translation of *people* after Guyau's text would be 'the whole nation'. This argument is close to Spinoza's description of the *multitudo* in the *Political Treatise* (TP), although Guyau makes no reference to it and seems to prioritize the TTP (and EIV) in his reconstruction of Spinozist politics.
75 T.N. *puissance*.
76 T.N. *raison générale*. We could read this notion of *raison générale* as a sort of collective reason.
77 T.N. 'Liberal', here, refers to freedom and liberty. One should avoid reading the phrase in terms of its contemporary (and contextual) meaning in English. Guyau's idea is that of a revolution of freedom: it is the freedom of thought, on the one hand, and the freedom of the people organized in a democracy, on the other, which is the opposite to Hobbes' 'despotism'. Freedom, here, refers to both collectively organized power and collective reason.
78 T.N. Although Guyau often refers to the tradition of the French *moralistes*, my choice for ethicists aims at highlighting the difference between this tradition and that of positivistic and scientific attempts to found morality and a science of ethics, which is here represented by Spencer. In Guyau's perspective, positivism, utilitarianism and evolutionism are linked in what he calls *morale anglaise*. This term loosely designates what Guyau sees as the 'school' of thought which represents modern Epicureanism in England.
79 T.N. *connaissance*.

4

Helvétius

Bentham's assessment of Helvétius. – Introduction of the notions of [the social] ideal and progress in utilitarian politics and ethics.

I. Ethics understood as an experimental science; the *physics of customs*[1] succeeds the *geometry of customs*. – First principle: universal necessity. – Desire and interest remove the moral universe from inertia. – [That] man is ultimately incapable of love, merit and demerit. – Benefaction[2] and devotion founded on the absence of real benevolence[3] and on mutual egoism.

II. That interest is the only driving force of human actions and that it should be their only judge. – Analysis of probity or justice for an individual, groups of individuals and for the State. – Several inconsistencies in Helvétius' thought: are they essential to the Epicurean doctrine? – Justice in different centuries and peoples. – The explanation of the variation of customs in terms of the variation of interests. – The struggle of interests, opposition between three forms of *probity* and three forms of *justice*.

III. The legislator in charge of bringing order amidst the struggle of interests. – Harmony of interests as a condition to virtue. – That one must necessitate [or constrain][4] men to the exercise of virtue. – First, by penal sanction. – Second, by the sanction of opinion. – Third, by means of education. – The legislator must willingly produce virtue, genius and heroism. – The legislator oversees customs. – What Helvétius understands by good customs. – Further inconsistencies of Helvétius; are they inherent in [any] utilitarian system? – Doctrine of public safety[5] – State religion: divinized interest.

IV. Fundamental identification of ethics and legislation, or *ethocracy* in Helvétius. – The ingenious critique of the method of codification. – That the codes should form a well-connected system, linked to one principle only. – According to Helvétius, the ethicist[6] and the legislator join efforts and transform human nature.

V. Are there still probity and justice where there is no law? That there will only be justice concerning humankind by establishing international sanctions, regulating the relations between peoples. – Universal philanthropy rejected. Helvétius as Bentham's immediate predecessor. – The progress that Epicurean ethics achieves with Helvétius.

La Rochefoucauld's work, combined with that of Locke,[7] Hobbes and Spinoza will inspire Helvétius, exerting an influence upon his great two works, *De l'esprit* and *De l'homme*. One knows the extraordinary popularity that his books met not only in France, but also in England, in Germany and [everywhere] in Europe.

This is how Bentham, the great English utilitarian, appreciated Helvétius, the French utilitarian: 'Important is the service for which the science of ethics and legislation stand indebted to this work [*De l'esprit*],' says Bentham, 'it is difficult to give an exact idea in a few pages of all that this work has done and left undone.[8] The light it spreads, on the field of this branch of art and science, is to that steady light which would be diffused over it by a regular institute or say didactic treatise, like what the meridian sun sheds over a place when bursting forth one moment from behind a cloud it hides itself the next moment behind another, is to that comparatively pale but regular and steady system of illumination afforded to a street by two constantly lighted rows of lamps.'[9]

Intentionally neglecting certain aspects of Helvétius' books that would make criticism rather too easy,[10] let us try to understand this author at his best, let us try to penetrate his thought, and to approach it with more benevolence than he did when treating his adversaries, those 'egoists' as he calls them. Is not Helvétius the representative of a new and important idea in the development of Epicureanism?

Hobbes had already regarded the legislator as establishing good and evil at his discretion, assigning to each action, with no reserve or resistance, the just and unjust character which he judges appropriate to it. However, thinking that the legislator was a being superior to the legislated [subjects],[11] and [thinking] that one could neither ask him to be accountable nor give him advice, Hobbes gave him the role of [the] absolute and arbitrary master of the law. He attributed to every law the same value and utility, provided that it was the work of a despotic and irresponsible will. Helvétius, on the other hand, challenges the order that Hobbes has given to any loyal subject not to desire anything different from the laws of his State.[12] Helvétius believes in the possible improvement of these laws. While remaining a son of his time, he also aspires to the progress of social institutions; and for him the rule of this progress is not the arbitrary will and pleasure of the sovereign, but the general interest of the subjects. Thus, introducing the idea of progress in ethics and legislation, an idea that was neglected by Spinoza, he places at the end of this progress a social ideal that the legislator and the ethicist should seek to realize. Legislation is not merely a caprice, it is, rather, a 'science' and Helvétius identifies this science with ethics. He will confer on it a social strength and legitimacy that is not different from the recognition of its utility. The legislator, says Hobbes, is all-powerful, and thus everything he decrees is good; [by contrast] the legislator, says Helvétius, is all-powerful, but this omnipotence[13] is but a means to an end, which is the greatest interest.

For Hobbes, the supreme good, after several transformations, ultimately became [identified with] the interest of the sovereign; for Helvétius, the aim to be pursued is the interest of all, identified with that of each single individual through the law, and with the help of two means: punishment and instruction. – This is an important idea, which will henceforth be part of all utilitarian systems. Let us see how this idea is developed in the books *De l'esprit* and *De l'homme*.

I. – Like Hobbes, Helvétius begins by announcing that he has attempted to treat ethics scientifically. He wishes to give it a precision as scrupulous as that of geometry. In this regard, rationalists and utilitarians can only applaud his initiative. However, whereas Hobbes and, especially, Spinoza intended to establish ethics, like geometry, [i.e.] through deduction, Helvétius wants to ground it upon this 'pyramid of facts' of which Bacon spoke about, and to build 'ethics as an experimental physics', referring it to a single principle: sensation. It is with Helvétius that we find for the first time in France, if not in words, at least in fact, the opposition later articulated by the English utilitarians between *inductive* and *intuitive* ethics.[14] Helvétius' effort will be that of constructing what Kant will call a 'physics of custom', without introducing any metaphysical or even moral element: his goal is the substitution of morals by physics.

The first postulate upon which rely the physical and mathematical sciences is the hypothesis of universal necessity, which is the condition of the regularity of phenomena. This is, so to say, the first postulate of every experimental ethics: 'Our thoughts and will follow necessarily from the impressions we have received ... A philosophical treatise on moral freedom would not be different from a treatise on effects without cause.'[15]

The absence of inner freedom corresponds, in us as in all the material world, to inertia: 'Idleness is natural to man, [...][16] he constantly gravitates towards rest, as bodies towards a centre.'[17]

In order to remove a body from inertia a shock is required, that is a movement coming from the outside. This impact, which will waken us from our rest, is sensation, and the movement that will propel us is interest, that is, the pursuit 'of everything which can bring us pleasure or remove pain'.[18] 'If the physical universe is subject to the laws of motion, the moral universe is equally so to those of interest.'[19]

One cannot summon any motive to explain action other than interest. I cannot wish the absolute good with a disinterested will; I only desire it in relation to myself. In order to demonstrate it, Helvétius employs an original argument: he thinks of the love of the good by analogy, comparing it to the love of evil for the sake of evil, which is impossible: 'It is as impossible for man to love good for the sake of good as it is for him to love evil for the sake of evil.'[20] 'The sentiment of self-love,'[21] he adds, 'is the only basis upon which one could lay the grounds of a useful ethics.'[22] 'Men are not at all evil, but rather subject to their own interests. The cries of the moralists will surely not change this spring of the moral universe.'[23] Helvétius could have added that if men are not *wicked*, they are nevertheless not *good*, and he understood quite well this consequence [of his argument].

Where the fatality of passion reigns there cannot be merit or culpability. Now, non-culpability invites [us] to indulgence. Helvétius often insists on this practical consequence of utilitarian fatalism, which was already deduced by Spinoza in [his] pantheistic fatalism. Helvétius recommends kindness and patience towards everyone, even when they are wicked. In order to defend his system, he appeals to the sentiments of charity and piety, understood, however, in his own way. Helvétius clearly perceived this consequence of the Epicurean system: man's actual incapacity to love others. Nevertheless, Helvétius believed mutual benefaction was possible even in a society of egoists. What is more, he founds this benefaction precisely upon that which would seem to destroy it, namely the belief in universal egoism. Here we can see one of the most important outcomes of egoistic morality: the hope of establishing the benefaction of actions without presupposing the benevolence of wills, and the hope of the mutuality of external services without inner recognition [or gratitude].

Because of the very fact that everyone is a self-interested egoist, each one should be inclined towards indulgence, mercy, benefaction. First, he thinks, one should suppress anger: 'One must consider men as they are: to be upset at the effects of their self-love is like complaining of rain in springtime.'[24] Second comes the suppression of contempt: 'Instead of despising the vicious ones, we should rather pity them, and we should happily thank the heavens for not giving us the taste and passions which would force us to search for our happiness in the misfortune of others. Because one always follows one's own interest.'[25] Thus, for the same reason one suppresses love, one also suppresses hate: Helvétius, without asking if he earns the equivalent of what he loses, is pleased with this result. '*Men are, thus, that which they should be; all hatred against them is unfair*; a fool bears follies just as a wild bush bears bitter fruits … Indulgence will always be the effect of enlightenment,[26] as long as passions do not intercept its action.'[27]

It seems, then, that according to this ideal of utilitarian society it would be enough for us to understand that we do not love one another in order for us to act immediately towards others *as if* we loved them. In this way, one of the most curious conceptions of human thought is revealed: to base the destruction of hatred among men exactly upon the destruction of love. Instead of telling men: 'In order to end war between you, love one another,' the utilitarian says rather: 'In order to end war, convince yourselves that you do not love one another.'

Helvétius made the effort to practise himself this indulgence and this benevolence without love: one can recall the numerous anecdotes about his equanimity towards his friends, [the anecdotes] about his generosity and kindness towards his vassals. These virtues came rather from a system than from the heart, and Helvétius had a reserved attitude towards them rather than an effusive one, [he had more] patience than real benevolence. And what really is this patience? If the utilitarian fatalist suffers patiently the injuries and the hatred of other men, it is not because he feels superior to them, at least concerning the following point: whereas others let themselves be dragged into the unknown by [their] passion, he knows that passion drags him along and he also knows exactly how it drags him. He observes this phenomenon as if watching the 'showers of spring', with the same scientific indifference, with the same superiority of intelligence. Indeed, this patience is ultimately nothing but the feeling of [a certain] superiority, and La Rochefoucauld was right to trace it back to egoism. When we get angry at someone's anger, when we are outraged by someone's wrath, their passions and their faults, are we not giving them more credit than we would if we were to respond to them with the well-grounded coldness of reason? This coldness[28] is intellectual disdain, and even moral contempt. Thus, the good qualities through which Helvétius put his system into practice often had little success with his vassals and his friends. According to Diderot, Helvétius' neighbours in the countryside had aversion towards him despite his benevolence. The peasants broke the windows of his castle, cut his trees and tore down his walls. It is related that, one day, Helvétius complained to d'Holbach about the fact that he kept little intimacy with his old friends: 'You have obliged[29] many of them, replied d'Holbach, and myself, who have done nothing for any of mine [my friends], I have been living constantly with them for twenty years.' This is because the benevolence in action is nothing without the benevolence of the heart.

To the happy consequences of egoism that we have highlighted above, Helvétius adds devotion. According to him, devotion is a form of benevolence that has a deeper source, but not any less fatal.[30] It does not stem only from a reasoned belief: one is charitable when one is benevolent not only by means of reason, but also by nature. In this sense, there are people who are born with the quality of devotion or naturally develop a propensity to it: 'The humane man is he for whom the sight of someone else's misfortune is *unbearable,* and who, to escape this horrible spectacle, is *forced,* so to say, to help the misfortunate. For the inhuman person, by contrast, other people's misery is a *pleasant* spectacle: it is in order to prolong his pleasures that he refuses to help the misfortunate. Now, these two men, although very different, tend to their pleasures and are, nevertheless, *moved by the same spring.*'[31] Helvétius concludes, employing terms very similar to La Rochefoucauld's, stating that 'virtues and vices are the result of the different modifications of personal interest'.[32]

However, Helvétius poses this objection to himself: 'If one does everything for the sake of oneself, then [would it be the case that] one owes no gratitude[33] to one's benefactors?'[34] He escapes this difficulty, however, with a specious answer. 'The benefactor, at least, is not in his right to demand it [recognition or gratitude]; otherwise that which he has done would be [part of] a contract instead of a gift.'[35] However, this does not answer the question. What is to be known is not whether the benefactor should demand gratitude and to practise the good deed with a view to receiving something in return; for, in that case, his action, being an interested one, would not have the right to this very reward. The real question is the following: Don't we owe gratitude to someone who has not sought it precisely because he has not sought it? – Helvétius' original insight is that gratitude is fundamentally an optical illusion: ideally, it should be supressed. However, in the current state of society, gratitude is useful, and it is the interest of the miserable that erects it as a law until the day when it will have become useless. 'It is in favour of the unfortunate and miserable ones,' says Helvétius, 'and in order to multiply the number of benefactors, that *the public* rightly *imposes* the duty of gratitude on the obliged.'[36] Reasoning in this way, Helvétius could not find it but absolutely mean when his friend Palissot, who still owed him money, chose to write a comedy against him instead.

This is, then, the second social consequence of egoistic morality: human beings would help one another without the need of mutual gratitude [and recognition].

This theory as a whole has as its first principle the original proposition that Helvétius expresses: 'It is as impossible to love the good for the sake of good as it is to love evil for the sake of evil.'[37] A singular and intriguing analogy, and yet a consequent one.[38]

II. – If interest is the driving force of all human actions, it will also be their evaluator and judge; in the same way it incites action, it will judge it; in the same way that it is the source of movement in the moral world, will it also be its end and, consequently, its rule?

Since Epicurus one had ceased to conceive interest as a rule that would be imperative, if not in an absolute sense, at least in a relative one. Hobbes, it is true, admitted a *natural law,* a series of wholly logical prescriptions, with a view to properly understanding the nature of interest. However, as soon as he made the individual enter the State, he seemed to believe that the law of interest as a whole was from that point on completely abrogated or, at least, encompassed by civil law. On the other hand, La Rochefoucauld, in his profound analyses, sought to show that the pursuit of interest is a fact without ever thinking to posit it as a rule or a duty. He merely observed human beings without prescribing anything to them. Finally, Spinoza's ethics, viewed as utilitarian from one side and rationalist when viewed from the other, elevated itself above practical and down-to-earth utility. Since Epicurus there has not been a purely and entirely utilitarian ethics. The moral philosophy articulated by Hobbes at the beginning of his system corresponded to the usage of savage peoples, not yet united under a master by means of mutual contracts, and this morality did not matter much to us, for we [already] have civil law, as the expression of sovereign power.[39] Helvétius will lay the foundations of a utilitarian morality appropriate to all civilized peoples.

Helvétius methodically proceeds to the analysis of virtue, which he designates by the word *probity*, understood in a very broad sense. He first considers probity relative to an individual, then relative to a group of individuals, then to the public or the State, to different centuries and, finally, to the whole world. There is clearly an effort, which we should acknowledge, of applying the rigorous methodologies of mathematical sciences to ethics.

This is the *criterium* of probity relative to a particular [individual]: 'Each person calls (and ought to call) *probity* (that is, *justice*) in others nothing but the habit of actions that are useful to him.'[40]

In order to experimentally verify this rule of action, let us consider two examples: 'Almost all men, attentive only to their own interests, have never taken general interest into account. Focused on their well-being, these men only call "honest" actions that are personally useful to them. A judge absolves a culprit, a minister honours an unworthy individual; both the judge and the minister will be *just* from the perspective of the criminal and the unworthy person.'[41]

Therefore, probity in relation to any particular individual varies endlessly according to the individuals considered. The tiger would be the kindest of animals for the grass and insects; the sheep will be, for them, the most ferocious beast, for the sheep devours the grass and its insects. 'Interest is, on this earth, a powerful enchanter who changes in the eyes of all creatures the form of all objects.'[42]

Nevertheless, there are some exceptions to this general rule. For some, personal interest, which is the criterion of probity, is not in opposition to public interest. 'There are men for whom a *natural happy disposition*,[43] and a lively *desire* for *glory* and *esteem*, inspire a love for justice and virtue, which is the same love men generally have for grandeur and wealth. Actions that are *personally useful* to these virtuous men are just actions, which correspond to *general interest*, or, at least, *which are not contrary to it.*'[44] Some have seen in these words a contradiction with that which precedes them [in Helvétius' work].[45] This is by no means the case. Helvétius' doctrine of interest is too positive and determined to allow for this kind of contradiction. The men we are referring to here do have a natural happy disposition, and they have also this *desire for glory*, which Helvétius himself possessed. How astounding is the fact that these men, while being simultaneously driven by these two forces of nature and desire, accomplish acts that are convergent with general interest? Helvétius even stresses that these acts do not have general interest as their end strictly speaking, but they are simply *not contrary to it*. Thus, it is still their own *personal utility* that these [virtuous] men obey, and their love for virtue is but love for themselves. The parallelism between particular and general interest is, for those men, a simple physical parallelism of movements. Those who seemed to be an exception to the general rule of egoism in fact confirm this very rule. In this sense, Helvétius could, if we follow only the logical development of his thought, 'believe himself entitled to conclude that personal interest [i.e. self-interest] is the only interest that can serve as a criterion of appreciation when judging the merit of men's actions'.[46] 'We necessarily esteem only ourselves in others.'[47]

This is the case for private morality, which has many analogies with Hobbes' natural right:[48] considered as individuals each one cannot, and should not, reasonably pursue anything but his own greatest interest, be it in conformity or in conflict with the interest of others. Now, let us consider, instead of a single individual, a small collection of individuals who have made their interests common.[49] 'From this viewpoint, probity is the habit of performing actions that are particularly useful to this small society.'[50] Incidentally, certain smaller societies which subsist within the larger one often seem, like certain individuals, to abandon their own interests in favour or public interest; however, by doing so, these societies 'only satisfy the passion that an *enlightened pride*[51] gives them as virtue'.[52] La Rochefoucauld could not think of it differently.

Moreover, an absolute opposition between a particular group and the general society is physically impossible, given the necessary relations that exist between each thing and its milieu. Helvétius states: 'the interest of each citizen is always attached by some kind of link to public interest; and that, similar to the stars, which according to some of the ancient philosophical systems, are moved by two fundamental forms of motion. The first, slower and common to the whole of [the] universe, and the second one, faster, is particular to each star. Each society is differently moved by two different forms of interest. The first, *which is weaker*, is common to general society, that is to say, to that of the nation; the second, *more powerful*, is absolutely *peculiar* to it [the individual or the small society in question].'[53]

Probity or justice relative to an individual or to a small group of individuals is not what we usually understand by justice or probity, and Helvétius is careful to warn us about it. Real probity is that which concerns the large number, yet enlarged by all the smaller collectives and by all the isolated individuals, that is, the State. The criterion of this extended probity, or national probity, will not be the same as the criterion of other forms of probity: 'A man is just when all his actions tend towards public good ... The public only ascribes words such as "honest", "great" or "heroic" to actions that are useful to it.'[54] Curtius and Sappho, for instance, have both thrown themselves in the abyss: Curtius did it in order to save Rome, whereas Sappho did it for despair and love. The former's action was extremely useful; whereas the latter's deed was useless; therefore, Sappho is [simply] mad, while Curtius is a hero. 'The public will never name fools those who are beneficial to it.'[55] Ultimately, according to Helvétius, these are neither more nor less mad than the others.

From the standpoint of the Epicurean doctrine Helvétius is up to this point perfectly right. Given the principles which constitute his starting point, his logic is correct.

However, his love of paradox will lead him too far astray: 'The public,' he adds, 'does not grant its esteem for this or that action based on the amount of strength, courage or generosity which is needed to accomplish it, but rather its esteem is based on the importance of this action [to the public], and the benefit it gets from it.'[56] This is an entirely sophistic induction; the Epicureans themselves easily exposed its vicious character.[57] We will neglect this particular inconsistency.

We have [already] considered probity in relation to the nation. Now, in what concerns different centuries and countries, one cannot speak of a general or eternal probity, although one could speak of a temporal and particular probity for each nation considered individually. This probity has interest as its rule, and because interest varies it also varies. When viewed in these terms, it is possible to explain this diversity or contradiction of customs and habits invoked by Montaigne and the sceptics, which Epicurus had already understood and known how to use to the advantage of his utilitarian system. There are many different forms of probity and justice because there are multiple types of interests.

There is, however, a point that we have had to leave aside until now, which we should now more carefully examine. All these different notions of *probity*, all these different ideas of *justice*, which follow and become different from one another – probity concerning the particulars, probity as related to small societies, probity concerning nations – all these notions will retain the logical order in which we have placed them; and since they contradict each other theoretically, won't they contradict each other [also] practically? Will they not fight with each other? I am not only a social and collective being; even if I belong to certain societies, even if I belong to a State, I first belong to myself, and as such I ought only to obey my own interest; I am thus armed with Hobbes' natural right. I have before me three different forms of probity, three forms of justice, three moralities, that is to say I find myself confronted with three interests; how, then, should I act? Among these interests, morality prescribes that I choose my own interest, even if I were to be called guilty or unjust; morality, in a sense, prescribes immorality.

It is at this point of the system to which we have now arrived that the contradiction that the physics of customs implies seems to become clear. It is the war of which Hobbes talked about. But Helvétius offers us an escape route, by providing us with an entirely physical means. In order to end this war a force is required, one that, with the aid of an exterior action, would be capable of making the interest of each individual coincide with the interest of all: this will be legislation.

To this force of material constraint that Hobbes had already employed, but which he had conceived as arbitrary, Helvétius assigns a specific end: utility, happiness. Ethics, that is to say, the physics of custom, will not be entirely created by civil law, by the physics of law; it will only be protected by it. Here, the principal idea of Helvétius' system begins to show its contours.

III. – We have seen, at the beginning of Helvetius' system, the moral world in a state of immobility, inertia, almost in a state of death. The passions then came onto the scene, bringing with them the agitation of life, and in this way all parts of this moral world, heated by desire, have become animated and have been put in motion, like the spheres of the visible universe. However, this force that puts our minds in motion is twofold or threefold, it contradicts itself, and these minds, like the 'celestial vault of the ancients',[58] are pulled in multiple directions at the same time, both from the side of collective interests and the side of individual interests. Harmony tends to be destroyed and discord soon erupts. Where could one find an intelligent, regulative power,[59] like the one that seems to have organized the physical world? Who will be the demiurge towards whom humankind should lift its eyes and reach out to?

In order to establish order, one must posit necessity. Now, we know that there is no necessity [that could possibly be] more certain than interest. The legislator will seek to place interest alongside all other social duties: 'All the art of the legislator consists in *forcing* men, by *the sentiment of self-love*, to be always just to each other . . .'[60] Therefore, one ought not to complain of the wickedness of humankind, but of the ignorance of the legislators, who have always placed private interest in opposition to general interest . . .'[61] Men, sensitive only with regard to themselves, and therefore indifferent with respect to others, are neither good nor bad, but ready to be either, according to the common interest that unites or divides them . . .'[62] It is by meditating on these preliminary ideas that one learns why the passions, of which the forbidden tree is [. . .][63] only an ingenious image, bear equally on it branches of good and evil fruit. By meditating on these ideas, one also understands the *mechanism* by means of which the passions *produce* our vices and our virtues. Finally, it is thus that the legislator discovers the *means* to *constrain human beings to probity*, by *conditioning* and directing the passions in such a way as to bear only the fruits of virtue and wisdom.'[64]

This valuable device to constrain and lay men under necessity is, first and foremost, sanction: 'The whole study of ethicists[65] consists in determining the use that one should make of rewards and punishments, and the assistance that may be drawn from them, in order to *connect the personal with the general interest*. This union is the masterpiece that ethics should aim to achieve. If citizens were not capable of achieving their own private happiness without promoting public good, then only the vicious among them would be the fools; every man would be *constrained* towards virtue, and the happiness of nations would then be an achievement of ethics.'[66] Furthermore, sanction is a component of the law: 'In effect, if it is true that force resides in the greater number, and if justice consists in the practice of actions that are useful to the many, then it is evident that justice is, by its nature, always armed with sufficient power to repress vice and place human beings under the necessity of being virtuous.'[67] It is possible to note the rigour of this reasoning: if one concedes to Helvétius that a physical force, some fatal power, could be able to produce this moral force that would constitute the virtuous man, he will then demonstrate that the law is capable of doing that, because it is the strongest of all forces. When the laws are not put into action, that is a proof of the legislator's ignorance. If he had known how to organize the social mechanism in such a way that to every violation there would always be a respective sanction, then all violation would cease. If punishment were to be always inevitable the law would be fully observed, and human beings, linked by their interests, would be linked by the most immutable necessity, while at the same time they would enjoy together the most stable happiness.

There are two forms of sanctions. One that rules in the name of the interest of the body, and another in the name of the interest of the soul; one that acts through the fear of pain, the other through the fear of shame. 'Reward and punishment, glory and infamy, [when] subjected to the legislator's will, are four deities, with which he can always bring about public good.'[68]

By means of the second form of sanction, that of opinion, the legislator acts directly on customs. He will act even more directly through education. No one has understood better than Helvétius the importance and the great power of education. Plato had already ascribed these expressive words to Callicles: 'We are the ones who make the law; [by] moulding the best and the strongest among us; we capture them young like lions and, by chanting spells and incantations over them, we enslave them.'[69] In this subjection of the interest of each one to the interest of all, Helvétius sees the happiness of the State. Not only should one identify personal interest and public interest through sanction, but one should also persuade everyone that these two forms of interest converge through education: 'Similarly to the sculptor, who from a tree trunk crafts a bench or the image of a god, so does the legislator when he shapes virtuous people', and, what is more, he forms 'heroes and geniuses'.[70]

Where do the exaltation in virtue which we call heroism and the elevation of spirit that we call genius come from? As we know, man is exclusively the product of the impressions he receives: there is nothing else in ourselves but impressions and the faculty that perceives them. This faculty has no reason not to be equal in everyone: we are born equal, and inequalities[71] [only] stem from the impressions experienced by each one of us, from the milieu in which we find ourselves, and above all, by the education that is given to us. Therefore, we depend on these silent masters which are exterior objects, but especially on these human masters that surround us. We are all equal by nature and unequal by chance. We are a pawn in the game of unknown causes: 'The genius is common (Helvétius could have said, according to his theory, that the genius is universal), but the circumstances which favour its development are rare.'[72] In the genius, he adds, 'chance plays the role of those winds which, dispersed around the four corners of the earth, are loaded with those inflammable materials that compose meteors. These materials, if loosely dispersed in the air, do not produce any effect, until the moment when, blown one against the other by contrary winds, they collide at a certain place; it is then that lightning flashes and shines, and the horizon is illuminated in a blaze.'[73]

Because chance simultaneously makes both the genius and the hero, the legislator must have only one goal: namely to know which means chance employs, so as to seize these means; to uncover, as much as possible, the hidden causes that act upon and transform ourselves, in order to put them at work [at his will] after having discovered them. In short, the legislator, who is himself a product of chance like all others, must diminish in all others the role of chance, replacing it with necessity.[74] He will force human beings towards genius in the same way in which he will force them towards virtue. – Education is, therefore, strictly linked to legislation, and the art of governing men is identified to the art of forming them.[75] One can hardly achieve any great change in public education without before having accomplished change in the State's constitution.[76] However, when one improves the laws, fusing all interests together through sanction,[77] then the great role of the educator will begin to take place. As for interest, [i.e.] the motor that propels everyone without their knowledge, the educator will not fear making it known to everyone, because he will, at the same time, show them how this [self-]interest is not different from public interest and justice: 'One could compose a catechism of probity, whose simple and truthful maxims, accessible to all minds, would teach the people that virtue is invariable in what concerns its aim (public happiness),[78] but it is not invariable in what concerns the appropriate means employed to achieve this aim; [this catechism would teach] that one should regard all actions as indifferent in themselves; [to] understand that it is the State's affair to determine which among them are worthy of esteem and of contempt ... Once these principles are accepted, how easy would it be for the legislator to extinguish superstition, to suppress abuse, to reform barbaric customs!'[79] Helvétius is not afraid of light; on the contrary, he calls for enlightenment. He does not see any inconvenience in the fact of revealing to all the human machines the spring that moves them. And he adds, not without an element of truth: 'Happy is the nation whose citizens would only allow crimes of interest! How ignorance multiplies them! ... Ignorance, hiding from every nation their true interests, prevents action and the union of [the nation's] forces, and thus shields the guilty one from the sword.'[80] Therefore, first of all one should destroy prejudice, and show where is the only possible salvation,[81] namely in the identification of ethics and legislation.

However, in this war against prejudice one must act prudently. 'One must send, like the doves of the ark,[82] some truths off to the world, to see if the flood of prejudice still covers the whole face of the earth,[83] if the errors have begun to subside, and if one perceives here and there certain islands emerging, where virtue and truth could find rest for their feet, and communicate themselves to humankind.'[84]

By concealing the sentiment of self-love[85] one will never prevent human beings from obeying it; one will never be *useful* for them, but rather *harmful*, since societies owe most of their advantages to the fact of possessing at least a vague knowledge of the principle of self-love. It is this vague knowledge that made legislators *confusedly* appreciate the need for sanction and the 'necessity of founding the principles of probity on the basis of personal interest'.[86] Instead of veiling self-love it is better to expose it to broad daylight. However, one will not abandon it to itself; rather, one will excite it by one of the most efficient among sanctions, that of opinion.[87] Helvétius, undoubtedly because of his own experience, ascribes great importance to the desire for reputation. It is there that he finds this intimate place, at the very centre of the soul, where the contrary interests of the individual and of the collective are joined together with no artificial soldering.

To instruct, punish and reward, these are, in a nutshell, the great means which will be used by the legislator to bring about justice in humankind. Through instruction, he will turn the souls of human beings towards the desirable end; through the fear of punishment[88] and the desire for reward, he will turn them away from inferior ends. Everything will be in his hands; he will sculpt society according to his own thinking, through the unbreakable decrees of his almighty power.

Not only will the legislator regulate the exterior relations between human beings; not only will he constrain them to justice and probity; his mission is not restricted to this. He will also constrain them to virtue in every sense of the word. He will watch over customs, usages and opinions: 'One can only take pride in effecting change in the ideas of a people after having effected change in legislation; it is by the reform of the laws that one should begin the reform of customs.'[89] However, in order to appreciate good customs, good practices and the just opinions, the legislator will evidently make use of the criterion of interest: for example, why would one condemn *libertinage*?⁹⁰ The 'courtesan women',⁹¹ instead of distributing money to anonymous charities and perpetuating beggary and idleness, pull a mass of workers out of indigence. If it were not for them, who would go to the ribbon-weaver, the fabric or fashion merchant? These women make of their wealth a 'much more advantageous use' than other women; and because they are useful, they are praiseworthy. The legislator, by allowing and encouraging *libertinage*, will thus contribute to the true good customs as well as the utility of the many.⁹² In addition, he will also at the same time suppress the falsity of women.⁹³ Moreover, he will be able to make the vice of adultery disappear by employing an excellent means, namely by effacing the law that defends it, instituting the community of women and declaring all children to be children of the State. In this way he will additionally ban a social danger: 'he will prevent the people from splitting into an infinity of families and small societies, whose interests are always opposed to public interest and extinguish all sorts of patriotic love in people's souls.'⁹⁴ One concludes that for Helvétius the 'reform of customs' is accomplished in the name of interest. However, let us remark that when considering this utility Helvétius committed serious mistakes.

There is, however, a consequence of the principle of utility applied to legislation, which is more logical than the preceding ones. The doctrine of public safety⁹⁵ articulated in Helvétius' work was soon after put into practice, and it caused there to be several victims. If public interest is the end to be achieved, then every particular interest which, in a specific circumstance (even if only rarely),⁹⁶ finds itself in open opposition to this supreme end must therefore be sacrificed. It will even be good and praiseworthy to sacrifice it, since all means become good and praiseworthy when they contribute to achieving the supreme end. 'Public utility,' says Helvétius, 'is the principle of all human virtues and the foundation of every legislation. Public utility should force peoples to subject themselves to its laws. It is, finally, to this principle that one ought to *sacrifice all of one's sentiments*, even the very sentiment of *humanity*'. It is, however, this sentiment that Helvétius calls elsewhere 'the only true sublime virtue.'⁹⁷ It is true that he distinguishes two sorts of humanity, namely *private* humanity and *public* humanity; now, 'public humanity is sometimes merciless towards the particulars.'⁹⁸ When a vessel is surprised by famine, one randomly chooses a victim by sortition and one 'cuts his throat without remorse' so as to nourish oneself [and all the others]. 'The vessel is the emblem of every nation; *everything* becomes legitimate and even virtuous when it comes to public safety.'⁹⁹ In the face of this statement Rousseau, the great eighteenth-century representative of the doctrine of imprescriptible rights, would write the following words: 'Public safety amounts to nothing if all the particulars are not safe.'

In the same way that there is a virtue of the State, as well a justice of the State, there will also be a religion of the State, which will neither sustain any mystery nor torment with vain fears, but rather divinize public interest, granting a sacred and respectable aspect to utilitarian ethics: this sublime religion will one day embrace the whole world.¹⁰⁰ Helvétius' god makes one think of the equally harmless gods of Epicurus.

IV. – To sum up, [with Helvétius] we have found in legislation a true science, in the legislator we have found a true power,¹⁰¹ and in positive law we found a true duty. We have no reason to fear that interests and passions, after introducing life in the moral world, would [also] bring disorder, turmoil and death to it. The legislator is there, ready to make every cog enter the social mechanism, including those which would derange themselves and thus disturb the harmony of the whole. He has only two weapons in his hands, but they are two invincible ones: sanction and education. His almighty power comes from the fact that he has identified law and ethics in that which d'Holbach will call *ethocracy*.[102]

Law without morality [and ethics], that is to say, law without rules of utility, amounts to nothing. On the one hand, a law owes everything good that it contains to an indistinct vision of utility. On the other hand, morality without law, that is to say the abstract whole of rules of utility, also amounts to nothing. Every vice is connected to the legislation, and willing to destroy a particular vice without changing the legislation is to 'wish for the impossible'. An apophthegm does not make a hero; declamations do not change facts: Helvétius believes that a moral theory is absolutely unable to enter the practical domain without the assistance of the law, that is to say, without shame or fear.

The task, then, is to unite law and ethics: in other words, [to make] the rules of morality (which is to say the rules of utility) guide the prescriptions of the law and to make the latter command and realize the former. According to how one unites or separates these two sciences (which are made to help and sustain each other), ethics and legislation, one produces misery or happiness among peoples.

By contrast, in our present time legislators make a serious mistake of perpetuating the dangerous habit of accepting customs as they are, without assuming the task of organizing them and making them dependent on a single and ultimate end. Helvétius says – and his words should be approved by both the partisans of the law and those of utility – 'the laws, when incoherent among themselves, seem to be the work of pure chance: guided by different views and different interests, the legislators who made them did not pay enough attention to the *relationship between them*. The formation of this body [of laws] happens analogously to the formation of certain isles: peasants, wishing to clear their fields of woods, stones and useless herbs and silt, throw them in the river; then, I see these materials carried by the currents, accumulating *near* some reed, consolidating, and finally forming firm land.'[103]

We should replace this empiricism by a method: how could the laws produce the compulsion of virtue in men if they were not in themselves the product of a necessary logic, if they were not connected to one another by constant and invariable relations, and if they didn't somehow respond to one another? 'The laws owe their excellence to their interdependence and to the uniformity of the legislator's views. In order to establish this interdependence one must refer all these laws to a single simple principle.'[104] Here, Helvétius seems already to announce and prefigure those systematic legislators who would compose, years later, the Declaration of the Rights of Man. There we find true legislation, in which all components refer to each other and depend on one another, because they all refer to the same end and depend on the same principle. Instead of calling *right*[105] this principle of legislation, which is also its end, Helvétius calls it *utility*. 'This simple principle is that of public utility, that is to say the greatest number of men subjected to the same form of government.'[106] And he adds, with the confidence in new ideas that was typical of his century: 'No one has ever understood the full extension or the fruitfulness of this principle; it encompasses all morality and legislation; many people, however, repeat it without understanding it, and legislators still have only a superficial idea [of its meaning].'[107]

Just as the legislator must apply himself to ethical researches, so must the ethicist strive to include his theories in the law: let them rely on one another, and [let] their efforts converge as should their objects! 'The vices of a people are always hidden in its legislation; it is there that one should excavate so as to extract the roots of these vices. He who is not gifted either with the enlightenment or with the courage to do this is of almost no use to the universe...'[108] In order to make themselves useful to the universe, philosophers must consider their objects from the legislator's point of view. Without exercising the same power, they must be guided by the same spirit. It is up to the ethicist to recommend certain laws to the legislator, [laws] which the latter should enforce, affixing the seal of his power [to them].'[109]

To help in the accomplishment of this great work – [i.e.] the happiness of States through the transformation of their laws – not only is there required a great mind, but also a 'great soul'. Helvétius, who barely seems to understand the love of individuals, elevates himself to [the place of] a higher intelligence of national philanthropy: it seems that his idea of love is purified as the object of this love grows bigger. He reproaches certain ethicists whose 'spirit has gradually enclosed itself within the circle of their own [individual] interest, having lost the strength required in order to elevate itself to the point of greater ideas ... In the domain of the moral sciences, in order to grasp the truths that are really useful for human beings, one must be stirred by the passion of the general good; [and] unfortunately, in ethics as in religion, there are too many hypocrites.'[110] Even coming from Helvétius these are beautiful and true words. Elsewhere he declares that he loves human beings and 'desires their happiness, without hating or despising any of them in particular'.[111] One could reply that, if he was to be consistent with his own system, then he could not claim to exactly love human beings in themselves, but only the praise and glory that he thinks he can receive from them. In this case, while aiming for the contrary, is he not also a little guilty of the sin of hypocrisy?

In any case, one cannot deny that in the whole of this last part of Helvétius' doctrine, [that is], in this pursuit of happiness by means of the identification of legislation and ethics, there is a certain warmth of heart and at the same time an evident originality. While neglecting the dangerous aspects of his system in order to shed light [only] upon those aspects which are attractive and philanthropic, Helvétius allows himself to be carried away by enthusiasm: 'who would doubt that the ethicists,' if they knew that the science of ethics is not different from that of legislation, 'could still take their science to a higher degree of perfection, which good minds cannot yet but only glimpse, and to a degree that they have never perhaps imagined possible.'[112]

Which obstacles could be capable of opposing the legislator's will and halting the indefinite progress of the laws? Indeed, no one can resist the legislator because it is upon facts that he founds the laws. He will be able to calculate the effect of education and sanction upon human beings like one is able to calculate the effect of weight upon bodies, and his physics of customs will obtain results as precise as those of the physics of material phenomena. The same order will reign in both the material and the moral world. These human beings whom the legislator has received from nature weighed down by inertia and divided by their passions, in absolute rest or in irremediable war, he in a certain way reshapes them, he creates them for a second time, he completes and transforms nature through habit: he is stronger than nature, and he is far 'stronger than the gods'.[113]

As we can see, Helvétius' moral system does not lack either grandeur or beauty; it evidently holds an element of truth. This tendency to scientifically and methodically approach morals and legislation will reappear, as we have already remarked, in the theorists of the French Revolution: what will change is the object and the goal of this scientific enquiry, and for the authors of the Declaration of the Rights of Men, utility will give way to justice. But not completely: in theory the Constituent [Assembly] and the Convention will seem only to consider the imprescriptible rights of man and only to keep sight of this ideal, whereas in practice they often invoke contrary principles. The Constituent and the Convention will speak of social utility, of public interest, of public safety: apparently generous ideas, [but] behind which one has sometimes hidden regrettable acts. Now, if Helvétius had only lived a few years more, he would have seen what human legislators – whom he compared to gods, as long as they acted in the name of public utility, welfare and safety – are capable of; he would have seen his principles inspiring almost every harmful thing done in the French Revolution. He would have witnessed in the facts the development of all the consequences that his thought could not perceive. The sentiment of *right*[114] presided all the great actions of the Revolution; but, in the same way, the ideas of public utility and safety have also shed much of the blood and are alone responsible for the crimes committed. One called Saint-Just a false Platonist; [similarly,] one could be right to call him a false utilitarian, and a false disciple of Epicurus, Hobbes and Helvétius.

V. – We still have to extract a curious consequence from Helvétius' system, one which will be very important for the development of utilitarian and Epicurean doctrines. Up to this point, we have only considered the nation and the State; from that perspective, the principle of laws and actions is, according to Helvétius, the greatest [possible] utility for the greatest number of men that are *subjected to the same form of government*.

Let us now see beyond the limits of the State. Let us attempt to grasp eternal and universal utility, the utility that concerns not only particular people in this or that group, but rather the totality of human beings, those who presently exist and those who are still to come. Is there, then, a universal morality, universal justice and probity, or a series of rules to which our conduct should always conform?

First of all, let us define this new type of probity to which we are referring here: 'If there was a probity concerning the universe, it would not be different from the habit of actions that are useful to every nation.'[115]

Now, is this probity possible in practice? Helvétius' answer is negative, for 'there is no action that would be able to immediately exercise influence upon the happiness or unhappiness of all peoples. Even the most generous action, by the benevolence of example, cannot produce in the moral world a more discernible effect than the effect that a stone thrown in in the ocean produces on the seas, whose level it necessarily increases.'[116] The truth is that Helvétius exaggerates the practical impotence of justice and charity; a great action, a generous idea, is not always simply like a stone that one loses as soon as it is thrown: they are sometimes like a new world; one which no ocean in nature could restrain, and one which would be enough to raise the level of the human ocean, more than it has been raising for a century.

If Helvétius seems to be mistaken in what concerns *practical* probity, that is, in what concerns the effective power of just actions, he is not mistaken with regards to what he calls probity of *intention*. For instance, given that we always and everywhere obey our own interest, we can seek the interest of the totality of human beings only as long as, by a series of legal prescriptions and sanctions, it becomes one with our own interest. A utilitarian will easily become a good patriot: penal sanctions and the sanctions of opinion, as well as habit and education, have linked his interests to those of his fellow citizens in an indissoluble connection; but this does not mean that this link concerns the whole of humankind. In this sense, [i] either ethics is not the same thing as legislation, being thus independent of and superior to it; [ii] or, on the contrary, it falls into the domain of legislation forming one and the same thing. In the first case [i], Helvétius would have to abandon his system in its totality lest he becomes inconsistent; if the second is the case [ii], he must not extend probity of intention beyond the limits of the State. Helvétius choses the latter path. 'In what concerns probity of intention, which could be reduced to the constant and habitual desire for the happiness of mankind, and consequently the wish for universal bliss, [well, I maintain that] this sort of probity is still only a Platonic chimera.'[117] Indeed, patriotic love, 'so desirable, virtuous and praiseworthy in a citizen',[118] in fact *excludes* universal love. 'In order to bring this kind of probity into existence, it will be necessary for nations to unite among themselves through reciprocal *laws* and *conventions*, just like families come together to constitute the State; [in other words], it is necessary to unite the particular interests of nations, subjecting them to a more general interest. Finally, patriotic love will be extinguished in people's hearts, while the flame of universal love continues to grow.'[119] Because this supposition will not become a fact for a long time, Helvétius concludes that 'there cannot be practical probity, not even probity of intention with respect to all humankind'.[120]

One cannot deny that Helvétius' doctrine is here perfectly logical and perhaps irrefutable if one considers only the principles of utility. In our days Darwin, following a [completely] different path, arrived at consequences which are analogous to those admitted by Helvétius.[121] Nations are, relative to one another, like large individuals; for as long as individuals are not ruled and united by laws there will be no justice among them. Why wouldn't it be the same when it comes to nations? Don't we know that only legality constitutes legitimacy? Therefore, one must find laws which are able to regulate international relations in a precise way, and one must be ready to punish anyone who transgresses them. Alongside the other thinkers of the eighteenth century, Helvétius tends to [subscribe to] universal philanthropy. However, without being able to extract it from his own moral system, he will end up renouncing it, and will be satisfied with national philanthropy. He prefers to be less philanthropic and more logically consistent. We do not find the same resignation in all utilitarian thinkers, and we surely do not find it in Dalembert or d'Holbach, for instance.

In the preface to his book *De l'esprit*, Helvéitus requests his readers to first understand him 'before condemning him, and to follow the chain [of reasons] which binds together the whole of his ideas'.[122] It is this concatenation, in effect, that we sought to follow and reproduce here. If we have realized certain arguments and intermediary rings were missing in this chain, we have tried to briefly note it *en passant*. Nevertheless, Helvétius' moral system is overall well linked together, and it does not merit the disdain that it often meets with.

In short, the main progress that Helvétius accomplished for the utilitarian doctrine was removing it from the realm of mere speculation, by positing interest as a practical end of action and, especially, [as the aim] of the laws that direct these actions. Viewed from this perspective, Helvétius is Bentham's immediate predecessor. This is what Bentham himself acknowledges. 'Helvétius,' he says, 'was the first' (Bentham forgets about Epicurus) 'to apply the principle of utility to a practical use, [that is to say,] to the direction of conduct in the affairs of life.'[123]

When Helvétius' book *De l'esprit* first appeared, Madame du Deffant characterized its author with a phrase often repeated thereafter: 'He has stated everyone's secret.'[124] If he did reveal this secret, he did so only after La Rochefoucauld. Therefore, one could thus correct Madame du Deffant's words: everyone has two secrets; the first is that all actions are interested in one way or another; the second is that all actions, viewed from another perspective, tend towards disinterestedness. Helvétius, writing in the wake of La Rochefoucauld, revealed only the first of these secrets; he did not penetrate the second secret, one which is really important, for it may be the secret of the future.

Notes

1 T.N. The French here is *moeurs*.
2 T.N. *bienfaisance*.
3 T.N. *bienveillance*.
4 T.N. The sense of *nécessiter* here is to make compulsory, to create conditions in which men *have to* be virtuous.
5 T.N. The French here is *salut publique*, it could be translated as 'public welfare' or 'public safety'. The term reappears in the French Revolution with the Committee of Public Safety [*Comité de salut public*], created in 1793. Its role was to protect the republic against external and internal attacks. I have chosen the term 'safety' in order to preserve this historical reference, which Guyau emphasizes when he mentions the practical outcomes of the doctrine (see, in this chapter, §III).
6 T.N. *moraliste*.
7 Locke has had no considerable influence as an ethicist [*moraliste*] in the strict sense of the term. His influence was considerably stronger as a psychologist and a political theorist: we will not dedicate a special study to his thought. When encouraged by his friends to write a moral treatise, Locke declined to take up the task. In a letter to Molyneux he wrote: 'But the Gospel contains so perfect a Body of Ethicks, that reason may be excused from that Enquiry...' [T.N. Letter from Locke to Molyneux, 30 March 1696, in John Locke, *Some Familiar Letters Between Mr. Locke and Several of His Friends*, *The Works of John Locke*, volume 3, London: Arthur Bettesworth, John Pemberton & Edward Symon, 1727, 546]. The principles of ethics that can be extracted from his *Essay concerning Human Understanding*, as well as the two notes on the topic in his *Common-place Book* – namely *Virtue and vice*, and *An Utilitarian Scheme of Life* (Lord King, 292, 304 [T.N. Guyau's reference is probably Peter Lord King, *The Life of*

John Locke, with Extracts from his Correspondence, Journals, and Common-Place Books, Two Volumes, London: Henry Colburn & Richard Bentley, 1830]) – are the same as Hobbes' principles and consist of an amalgamation of Epicureanism and Christianity, which is still the background of moral beliefs of the British people. According to Locke, the *matter* of virtue is interest; as for the *obligation* that is attached to it, it comes from the will of God, and this will of God only acts upon us by the pains that it reserves to us (*An Essay Concerning Human Understanding*, 1. II, chapter XXVIII, §8). Locke's successors, Helvétius included, will abandon the mystical dimension of this ethics in embryonic state, in order to develop its practical dimension, that is, the utilitarian ideas that converge with the ethics of Epicurus, Hobbes and even Spinoza: 'I will therefore make it my business to seek satisfaction and delight, and avoid uneasiness, and disquiet; to have as much of the one, and as little of the other, as may be. But here I must have a care I mistake not; for if I prefer a short pleasure to a lasting one, it is plain I cross my own happiness [...]. I will carefully watch and examine, that I may not be deceived by the flattery of a present pleasure to lose a greater' ([T.N. Here Guyau's reference is:] Lord King, p. 304; Fox-Bourne, I, 164 [the latter probably corresponds to Henry Richard Fox Bourne's *The Life of John Locke*, volume 1, New York: Harper & Brothers, 1876; the text quoted appears in Peter Lord King, *The Life of John Locke, with Extracts from his Correspondence, Journals, and Common-Place Books, Volume II*, London: Henry Colburn & Richard Bentley, 1830, 'Miscellaneous Papers', 121–2]). One recognizes here Epicurus' *summetrēsis (measure by comparison)*, which will later become, with Bentham, the arithmetic calculus of pleasure. These are the most durable or lasting pleasures of this life according to Locke: 1) *health*, without which no pleasure of the senses can take place; 2) *reputation*, 'for I think it makes everyone rejoice'; 3) *knowledge [savoir]*, 'for the little of it I possess, I feel I would not sell it for any price and would not *exchange it for any other pleasure*'; 4) *benevolence*, for one quickly forgets 'the succulent dishes one has tasted' or 'the parfums one has inhaled', whereas one indefinitely remembers the pleasure one has had in doing good (surely, a superficial analysis); 5) *the expectation of an eternal and incomprehensible happiness in another world*, for this 'expectation procures a constant pleasure'. The majority of Epicureans (both Greek and French), whose logic leads to stress the intellectual dimension of things, mercilessly rejected this [fifth and] last form of pleasure, which partially rests upon the incomprehensible; the English utilitarians, like Mill and Spencer, are more tolerant with regards to this very innocent form of enjoyment, which plays an important role in life. [T.N. I have translated the quoted phrases; Guyau does not provide the reference.]

8 T.N. The second clause in the English original is 'but to give in any small number of words any correct and complete conception of the virtues of that service is scarcely possible'. I have chosen to preserve Guyau's version of the quote.

9 T.N. This quote is from the 'Article on Utilitarianism – Short version' (in Bentham, *Deontology, Together with A Table of the Springs of Action and the Article on Utilitarianism*, edited by Amnon Goldworth, Oxford: Oxford University Press, 1983, 325); Guyau's version is slightly different, in this case, since the author quoted in English, I have chosen to privilege the original, instead of Guyau's version (translated by Benjamin Laroche, Paris: Charpentier, 1834). In the French translation of the book, one finds a section titled '*Coup d'oeil sur le principe de la maximisation du bonheur, son origine et ses développements*', where one finds Guyau's quote. Ann Thomson quotes this passage in her book, *Bodies of Thought. Science, Religion and the Soul in the Early Enlightenment*, Oxford: Oxford University Press, 2008, 235–6.

10 Helvétius seems to have had an obsession throughout his whole life: he wanted to make a name for himself, he sought reputation and glory and, if possible, immortality. He first tried to excel in fencing and dance; some of his panegyrists say that he even danced in the opera wearing a mask, and that he was enthusiastically applauded. From dancer he became a poet; but 'poet was no longer fashionable' (Charles Collé, *Journal historique* [*ou Mémoires critiques et littéraires*, volume 2, Paris: Imprimerie Bibliographique, 1807]); and so, he soon abandoned this endeavour. He then turned his attention to mathematics for some time, until he finally chose philosophy, which he said was the sole thing to give one 'great celebrity'. In order to gather the material for his work, he used to 'hunt ideas', cross-examining everyone, speaking himself every now and then, but always listening carefully. As Morellet writes, Helvétius would 'toil for writing a single chapter, redrafting it twenty times'. – Towards the end of his life, discouraged and disappointed with philosophy, but still guided by the desire for glory, he returned to poetry. 'The only thing missing for Helvétius was *génie* this tormenting demon; one cannot write for immorality when one is not possessed by it' (Friedrich Melchior Grimm, *Correspondance littéraire, philosophique, et critique* [volume 2, Paris: Furne, 1829]; [T.N. Guyau refers here to a letter from January 1772; the reference is imprecise, since Grimm's appreciation of Helvétius appears in letters from August 1758 and February 1959; a similar passage to the one Guyau quotes appears in the 1758 letter, where Grimm writes that even those who appreciated the quality of *De l'esprit* denied attributing *génie* to its author. As in other cases, Guyau's quote here is indirect: the sentence quoted ('*Il ne manque à Helvétius que le génie, de démon qui tourmente*') is not Grimm's, but comes from Jules Barni's *Les moralistes français au dix-huitième siècle* (Paris : Germer Baillière, 1873, 130–1], which Guyau probably consulted when writing or correcting the fourth part of the *Ethics of Epicurus*]). Helvétius' taste for philosophy was itself a utilitarian taste.

By the time when Helvétius began to write, Montesquieu was publishing his *Esprit des lois*; Helvétius' ambition was to conquer a place if not above at least at the side of this great man. He wished to rewrite the *Esprit des lois* in order to outweigh it, by giving it more general reach and scope. Rather than considering the spirit [*esprit*] of the laws [*des lois*], he undertook the task of considering the *spirit* itself. Aiming for a vague generality, instead of achieving generality by the wide reach of his thinking, he was satisfied with the title *De l'esprit*. – 'A questionable title,' Voltaire would say; and he added: 'A work without a method, filled with many ordinary or superficial things, and its novelty false or problematic . . . Still, many excellent passages.'

Indeed, *De l'esprit* is a singularly composed work: its most important part, that which is responsible for the book's success, at least among serious readers, is its moral part, where the utilitarian doctrine is explained; – and this part, precisely, is a *hors-d'oeuvre* in a work of psychology. In this way, the value of *De l'esprit* comes from a defect in composition [*faute de composition*]. Without this digression, the book would barely have the necessary; it would not be more than a collection of paradoxical banalities and commonplaces, in which philosophy sometimes becomes the pretext for telling stories and anecdotes, and 'sweeping salons' ['*balayures de salons*'].

11 T.N. A non-literal option could go along these lines: 'regarding the legislator as superior to those [upon whom] he legislates . . .'
12 T.N. Guyau ignores, here, Hobbes' formulation of a right of resistance to unfair and unjust laws.
13 T.N. *toute-puissance*.
14 Helvétius, *De l'esprit; De l'homme*, II, 19.

15 Helvétius, *De l'esprit*, I, 4. [*De l'esprit, or Essays on the Mind and its Several Faculties, Translated from the French to which is now prefixed A Life of the Authors*, translated by n/a, London: J. M. Richardson, Sherwood, Nelly and Jones, 1809, 32, T.N. For the next quotes, I will provide the page number of the English edition in square brackets].
16 T.N. Guyau omits a part of the quote, without signalling it.
17 Helvétius, *De l'esprit*, III, 5; *De l'homme*, IV, 24.
18 Helvétius, *De l'esprit*, II, 1, footnote. [37].
19 Helvétius, *De l'esprit*, II, 2; *De l'homme*, recap.
20 T.N. In the 1809 English translation, one reads: 'What other motive can determine men to generous actions? It is as impossible to love virtue for the sake of virtue as to love vice for the sake of vice' (57).
21 T.N. *amour de soi*.
22 Helvétius, *De l'esprit*, II, 5 [179]; *De l'homme* [Ibid.?], note 2, 24.
23 Helvétius, *De l'esprit*, II, 5 [first footnote], [57]; *De l'homme* [Guyau references as '*Ibid*'], note 2, 24.
24 T.N. Helvétius, *De l'esprit*, I, 4 [29].
25 T.N. Helvétius, *De l'esprit*, II, 2 [42].
26 T.N. *lumière*. Here, the 1809 English translation proposes: 'Indulgence then is always the effect of superior light, when it is not intercepted by passions' (Helvétius, *De l'esprit*, II, 10 [89]).
27 Helvétius, *De l'esprit*, I, 4; II, 2; II, 10. – One knows that the Sorbonne condemned the following words: 'Like a wild bush [*sauvageon*] of bitter fruits.' – 'Ah! Savages [*sauvageons*] of the school,' Voltaire writes, 'you persecute a man because he does not hate you.' [T.N. Voltaire plays here with the ambiguity of the term *sauvageon*].
28 T.N. *froideur*; in the sense of cold or cool indifference.
29 T.N. This word in the old French of the quote seems to refer to help rather than constraint, even though one is bound by retribution when receiving someone else's services.
30 T.N. *fatale*. The sense here is 'necessary' and 'inexorable'.
31 T.N. Helvétius, *De l'esprit*, II, 2 [41].
32 Helvétius, *De l'esprit*, II, 2, footnote. [T.N. Here, I have used the 1809 English translation. Guyau refers to the note, but only part of the quote is found in the footnote of Chapter 2 of the second Essay, the rest is in the text].
33 T.N. As explained above, I have chosen to render *reconnaissance* as gratitude, but its semantic field is wider and includes the idea of recognition. Since these are two different terms in English, I add them to the text in square brackets to remind the reader of the complexity of *reconnaissance*.
34 T.N. Helvétius, *De l'esprit*, II, 2, footnote.
35 T.N. Helvétius, *De l'esprit*, II, 2.
36 Helvétius, *De l'esprit*, II, 2, footnote.
37 T.N. Helvétius, *De l'esprit*, II, 5.
38 The ideal of a society without love or hate, without esteem or contempt, without benevolence or malevolence, without gratitude or ingratitude, without anger or pity, was already sketched by Spinoza (see the preceding chapter [book IV, chapter 3]).
39 T.N. *puissance*.
40 T.N. Helvétius, *De l'esprit*, II, 2.
41 Helvétius, *De l'esprit*, II, 2. – La Harpe correctly notes: One knows that in the hall [*antichambre*] of a corrupt [*dissipateur*] minister, all those that he makes rich at the expense of the people will sing his praises; but will these praises be sincere? And, what

is more, is it not rare to see those who profit from a man's corruption and injustices being the first to accuse and condemn him, not in public, but in intimate confidence?

42 Helvétius, *De l'esprit*, II, 2.
43 T.N. One could understand this *heureux naturel* as a 'fortunate nature' or a 'happy disposition'.
44 T.N. Helvétius, *De l'esprit*, II, 2.
45 See [Jean-Philibert] Damiron, *Mémoire sur le dix-huitième siècle*, I, 413 [*Mémoire pour servir à l'histoire de la philosophie au dix-huitième siècle*, volume 1. Paris: Librairie Philosophique de Ladrange, 1858].
46 Helvétius, *De l'esprit*, II, 2.
47 Helvétius, *De l'esprit*, II, 4.
48 T.N. *droit*.
49 T.N. The French here is *mettre en commun*, literally to put their interests in common.
50 T.N. No reference in the original.
51 T.N. *orgueil éclairé*.
52 Helvétius, *De l'esprit*, II, 7 [T.N. As quoted by Guyau; the passage is actually part of the opening paragraph of II, 5.]
53 Helvétius, *De l'esprit*, II, 8.
54 T.N. Helvétius, *De l'esprit*, II, 11. I have preserved Guyau's phrasing (using the word 'interest').
55 Helvétius, *De l'esprit*, II, 6; II, 2.
56 T.N. Guyau does not provide the reference for this passage. It is found in Helvétius, *De l'esprit*, II, 11.
57 Let us consider an example given by Helvétius. An ignorant general (a Soubise no doubt) wins three battles against another general even more ignorant than him: will the public, if it ever knows that these victories result only from ignorance and chance, admire these victories in the same way it admires those of a skilful general? Evidently not. Helvétius seems to consider actions detached from the power that executes or realizes them; but no one considers actions in this way: in order for a man to be worthy of admiration and public approval, it is not enough for him to have acted well only by chance, for in this case his action would not depend on him, but on the conjunction of fortuitous circumstances; a mere conjunction that happened to be useful. In order for the general himself to be useful, he must act with skill [*capacité*], and one must find in him – and not in exterior circumstances – the cause that has produced the action in question, and which will allow to be able to produce actions of the same kind in the future. Hence, one will be looking not only at a present utility, but also at a future one. The general who has won three battles by chance was no doubt useful at a particular moment in time; however, he will not be able to be useful all of the time. Furthermore, all the battles that he could still win by chance would not give him this attribute of utility. Even if a bad and incapable general was to be successful in battle throughout his whole life, and a capable and skilful general were to be defeated through his, the latter would still be personally more useful than the former, and therefore more worthy of esteem than the former. Indeed, as soon as fate ceases to work against him, he would obtain victory. As for his rival, as soon as fate ceases to win his battles in his place, he would be defeated. One is a solid arm in the defence of the nation that no blow can break or bend; the other is like the bee sting, which can only hurt once. The skilful general is of lasting utility [for the nation], whereas the other is of fortuitous and necessarily ephemeral utility.

Therefore, for every agent, beyond the action itself, one must consider a *physical* and *intellectual* power [*puissance*]: it is according to this power – a real or presumed power – that the public should judge his actions. Moreover, even from a utilitarian or deterministic point of view, there is a certain moral power [*puissance morale*] that we cannot neglect in our judgement of human actions. Why, for example, when appreciating certain actions, do we attempt to know the *intention* which has governed them? The answer is simple: he who acts with good intention has more inner *capacity* [*capacité*] than the person who acts in the same way but following a self-interested intention: the former has more chance to reproduce his action, and he is more useful than the latter. *Intention* is, therefore, the measure [corresponding to] one's most intimate *capacity*, which one could call moral capacity. In this sense, intention cannot and should not be neglected – not even by Helvétius and the fatalists; in the same way, one can say that the *difficulty* and *rareness* of an action are the measure [or the measuring criteria] of the *physical* and *intellectual capacity of the agent*. Now, it is evident that the more capable a being is, the more useful it is. Helvétius was thus wrong when he wrote that the public does not grant its esteem to 'strength, courage and generosity'; in saying so, he was stating something false, even according to his own system. One has tried to refute Epicurean utilitarianism by refuting the illogical and paradoxical conclusions that Helvétius extracts from it; however, as one can see, the true Epicurean doctrine is much harder to refute.

58 Helvétius, *De l'esprit*, II, 8.
59 T.N. *puissance*.
60 T.N. Guyau refers here the *De l'esprit*, II, 13. However, the quote comes from essay II, 24 (p. 185 in the English translation, which I have used and modified). Guyau adds to this passage a quote from another part of the book (namely essay II, 5, footnote), which in the 1809 English translation reads as follows: 'They ought not therefore to complain of the wickedness of mankind, but of the ignorance of the legislators, who have always placed private interest in opposition to general interest' (57). He then links it to the passage quoted from II, 24 (185). I will describe this procedure in the following notes.
61 T.N. Here, Guyau interpolates a different quote from another part of the *De l'esprit*, namely II, 5, footnote.
62 T.N. Guyau now returns to II, 24. I have modified the English translation.
63 T.N. Guyau omits the expression 'according to certain Rabbis'.
64 Helvétius, *De l'esprit*, II, 13; II, 5, footnote. [T.N. I have used and modified the 1809 English translation. Guyau omits the passages in square brackets without signalling it.]
65 T.N. *moralistes*.
66 Helvétius, *De l'esprit*, II, 22. [171; I have used and modified the English translation here].
67 Helvétius, *De l'esprit*, II, 24.
68 Helvétius, *De l'esprit*, II, ch. 22.
69 T.N. Guyau does not provide the reference to this quote. He is actually paraphrasing Plato's *Gorgias*, 484a: 'What do we do with the best and strongest among us? We capture them young, like lions, mould them, and turn them into slaves by chanting spells and incantations over them which insist that they have to be equals to others and that equality is admirable and right' (Plato, *Gorgias*, translated by Robin Waterfield, Oxford: Oxford University Press, 1994, 66).
70 Helvétius, *De l'esprit*, II, 22.
71 T.N. Guyau seems to be conflating *inegalité* and *différence*; being different does not presuppose inequality.

72 T.N. Helvétius, *De l'esprit*, III, 30.
73 Helvétius, *De l'esprit*, III; *De l'homme*, I, 8, footnote; ibid., III, 3 [T.N. Not clear if the last reference is; the passage quoted comes from *De l'esprit*, IV, 1].
74 Helvétius, *De l'homme*, I, 8.
75 Regarding the question of education, Helvétius will propose a certain number of reforms, from which many are still to be put into practice today. He demands one to replace to the insipid study of words the study of ethics [*morale*] . . . physics, history and mathematics. He writes: 'What could be more absurd than wasting eight or ten years in studying a dead language, which one soon forgets? [. . .] What could be more ridiculous than dedicating many years to memorize facts and ideas that one could, with the help of translations, know by heart in two or three months?' In effect, he supports a professional [form of] instruction.
76 Helvétius, *De l'esprit*, IV, 17; *De l'homme*, X, 10, 11.
77 T.N. Note the importance of sanction and the contrast with Guyau's *Esquisse*.
78 T.N. *bonheur public*.
79 Helvétius, *De l'esprit*, I, 17. [T.N. Guyau refers I, 17. The quote actually comes from II, 17. In the 1809 English translation it reads as follows: 'we might (. . .) compose a catechism of probity, the maxims of which being simple, true and level to all understandings, would teach the people that virtue, though invariable in the object it proposes, is not so in the means it makes use of; that, consequently, we ought to consider actions as indifferent in themselves; to be sensible, that it is the business of the state to determine those that are worthy of esteem or contempt (. . .). These principles being once received, with what facility would the legislator extinguish *the torches of fanaticism* [phrase in italics absent in Guyau's quote] and superstition, suppress abuses, reform barbarous customs.']
80 T.N. Guyau does not provide the reference for this quote. It is found in *De l'esprit*, I, 24.
81 T.N. *salut*. As mentioned above, it could also to be understood here in the sense of public safety or public welfare.
82 T.N. Helvétius here uses a biblical metaphor: the reference is to the doves Noah sent from the ark, after the flood, and which will bring back to him branches of trees. See Genesis 8:8.
83 T.N. Helvétius, *De l'esprit*, II, 24. I have chosen this phrase for translating the French because it is closer to the original, as well as to the original Hebrew word used in the Bible: פני (meaning 'the face of').
84 T.N. Guyau does not provide the reference here.
85 T.N. *amour de soi*.
86 Helvétius, *De l'esprit*, II, 24.
87 Helvétius, *De l'esprit*, III, 4 ; IV, 22.
88 T.N. *peines*.
89 T.N. Helvétius, *De l'esprit*, II, 15.
90 T.N. The term is of difficult translation in this context; an English translation for *libertinage* could be 'debauchery'. In this context it rather seems to signify a form of relationship with money characterizing consumerism.
91 T.N. *femmes galantes*.
92 We have insisted, in what concerns the consequences that Helvétius thought he could deduce from his system, that they prove the very falsity of the system itself. Unfortunately, as we have already seen, these consequences are often illogical even from the point of view of Epicureanism. Here, for example, *libertinage* cannot be useful, not even from the viewpoint that Helvétius proposes us to look at it: his words,

indeed, presuppose a fallacy, a sophism refuted by Bastiat and which can be found in the well-known argument of the broken window [*vitre cassée*]. Jacques Bonhomme [also rendered in English as James Goodfellow] has broken a window; he gets the window glass replaced by a glazier, paying him a sum of money, and he images, as the parable goes, to be helping industry to advance; – the glazier's industry no doubt; but not at all industry in general –; and, indeed, Jacques Bonhomme has found a useful purpose for employing his money; he employed it in commerce; instead of giving work to a glazier he could have done so with a mason or a carpenter, there would be, then, if the glass was not broken, an equal sum of good and work in society, and yet an extra glass. The cost [or expense, *dépense*] of that glass is called *unproductive* [*improductive*] in political economy, and it is this sort of unproductive expense that could characterize the sort of expense practised in *libertinage*.
93 T.N. Note Guyau's prejudiced view on women in this passage.
94 Helvétius, *De l'esprit*, II, 14–15, 5.
95 T.N. Here, again, *salut public*.
96 T.N. I added the brackets to preserve Guyau's long sentence while at the same time making it readable in English.
97 Helvétius, *De l'homme*, I, 14.
98 T.N. Guyau provides no reference for this quote.
99 T.N. Again, *salut public*.
100 Helvétius, *De l'homme*, I, 10, 13–14.
101 T.N. *puissance*.
102 T.N. *éthocratie*.
103 T.N. Helvétius, *De l'esprit*, II, 17 [135].
104 Helvétius, *De l'esprit*, II, 17.
105 T.N. *le droit*.
106 T.N. Helvétius, *De l'esprit*, II, 17.
107 Helvétius, *De l'esprit*, II, 17.
108 Helvétius, *De l'esprit*, II, 15.
109 Helvétius, *De l'esprit*, II, 15 [125]
110 Helvétius, *De l'esprit*, II, 15 [125]
111 Helvétius, *De l'esprit*, Preface [xxi].
112 Helvétius, De l'esprit II, 17 [135].
113 Helvétius, *De l'esprit*, III, 15; *De l'homme*, VII, 14, footnote.
114 T.N. *droit*.
115 Helvétius, *De l'esprit*, II, 25 [187].
116 Helvétius, *De l'esprit*, II, 25 [187].
117 Helvétius, *De l'esprit*, II, 25 [187].
118 Helvétius, *De l'esprit*, II, 25 [188].
119 Helvétius, *De l'esprit*, II, 25 [188].
120 Helvétius, *De l'esprit*, II, 25.
121 See our *Morale anglaise contemporaine*, first part.
122 T.N. Helvétius, *De l'esprit*, Preface.
123 T.N. Guyau's quote is probably Bentham's 'Article on Utilitarianism: Long Version' (*Deontology*, 290): 'In this work [*De l'esprit*], a *commencement* was made of the application of the principle of utility to practical uses.'
124 T.N. Guyau does not provide the reference. He probably refers to Marie Anne de Vichy-Chamrond, marquise du Deffand (1696-1780); note that Guyau's spelling is 'Deffant'.

5

The Spirit of Epicureanism in Eighteenth-Century France

I. La Mettrie, Helvétius' predecessor – The *Anti-Seneca* – Critique of disinterestedness; critique of remorse. – Is there an animal ethics? – That happiness can be compatible with injustice.
II. The movement leading the Epicurean system towards humanitarian ideas. – Dalembert – D'Holbach – Virtue, its own reward. – Saint-Lambert.
III. Utilitarian politics – D'Holbach, Dalembert – Utilitarian liberty, equality and fraternity.
IV. Humanitarian utilitarianism brought back to egoism by Volney. – That Epicurean ethics in France, from the beginning to the end of its development, employs the most rigorous logic.
V. Why the eighteenth-century French mind was fundamentally utilitarian and why it embraced Epicurean ideas with fervour.

I. – Helvétius is the most famous representative of Epicurean doctrines in eighteenth-century France, and his influential ideas rapidly spread everywhere in Europe.[1] And yet he was not alone: we must place a whole constellation of writers around him. In England, a multitude of utilitarian thinkers came after Hobbes almost without interruption up to Mill and Bain. In France, this wave of thinkers seems to have simultaneously appeared all at once in a single epoch of our history.

Helvétius' doctrine of interest strikes us with its rigorous and logical attributes. In it, there is no confusion between personal and social interest: I can and should act in conformity with social utility only when the latter conforms with my own personal utility.[2] This doctrine is logically deducted in Helvétius, and we can [already] find it even more pronounced in La Mettrie. This convinced Epicurean took pleasure in rekindling the ancient fight against the Stoics in his *The Anti-Seneca*, which appeared ten years before Helvétius' book *De l'esprit*. 'Truth and virtue,' La Mettrie said, are 'the sort of entities which have no value except for those who possess them ... But for lack of such and such a virtue and such a truth, will science and society suffer? Probably, but if I do not deprive society of these advantages, then it is I who will suffer! Now, is it for the sake of other people or for my own sake that reason commands me to be happy?'[3] It is a commentary on Fontenelle's saying: 'If I had my hand full of truth, I would be very careful not to open it.' On this point La Mettrie is more open and frank than Helvétius. Moreover, like Helvétius, he equally denies the allegedly elevated instincts that lead human beings towards an apparently disinterested conduct. According to La Mettrie, however, men are differently constituted, and they ought to conform to their nature. 'If nature has made you a swine, do not hesitate to wallow in the mud, as swine do; you would be unable to enjoy any higher happiness.'[4]

Morality, like intelligence, depends on the state of the brain and [the condition] of the rest of the organism. "A trifle, a tiny fibre, something that the most subtle anatomical study cannot discover, would have made fools of both Erasmus and Fontenelle."[5] In the same way, what would have been necessary to change the courage of Caius Julius, Seneca or Petronius into pusillanimity? A simple obstruction of the spleen, of the liver or of the portal vein [would do]. All conduct that agrees with an individual's nature is rational; now, that which is rational is also just and good. La Mettrie relies on this principle to sustain his critique of remorse. Remorse is an absurdity because it comes after action instead of preceding it and preventing it from happening. Hence there are two possibilities, either action has inauspicious consequences, and in this case remorse would only add new sorrow to the existing ones; or it could be the case that an action has a positive outcome, which would mean that remorse no longer has a reason to be and should therefore be banished. Additionally, remorse, just like moral obligation, the belief in a specific moral law, and many other phenomena of this sort, which fall under a scientific domain, are not exclusive to humankind. The 'celestial' voice of conscience is nothing other than a voice with a very earthly and brutal origin, who knows how to make itself understood even by animals. La Mettrie prefigures here, with remarkable perspicacity, the modern doctrines of Darwin, which rely on the hypothesis of natural selection. Such a passage from the *Machine Man* [*l'Homme-machine*] and from the *Man as Plant* [*l'Homme-plante*] can justly be compared to those of the great naturalist. According to La Mettrie, there is no specific character that establishes a clear-cut division between the human being and other animals. Is it not the case that both man and animal pursue the same goal, enjoyment? If we could make an ape speak, then we would no longer be able to distinguish ourselves from it. The purported moral law exists in animals in the same way that it exists in the human being. The dog knows remorse; does it not repent after having bitten his master? Even the lion seems to show gratitude to its benefactor.

The conclusion aimed at by La Mettrie is very curious and characteristic: 'If you manage to suppress remorse, I claim, you – even if [you are a] parricide, incestuous, etc. – will be happy nevertheless; but, if you do want to live, be careful! Politics is not as accommodating as is my philosophy; for justice is its [politics'] child, and the gallows and executioners are under its command; you should fear them more than [you fear] your conscience and the gods.'[6] – Here one finds the logical consequence of Epicureanism: given the fact that, for the Epicureans, sanction is what constitutes moral obligation, once we remove remorse, which is interior sanction, and the laws, which are an exterior sanction, then obligation will also disappear. Nevertheless, as we have said, Epicurus and Philodemus held that there is in pure justice and in virtue, independently of their consequences, something beautiful and harmonious, which makes them preferable for the sage: La Mettrie has not elevated himself as high as [to accept] this conception.

II. – As one can see in La Mettrie and Helvétius, Epicureanism does not retreat in face of any obstacle except inconsistency. Their Epicureanism is narrow and closed, but logical to the point of excess. Both La Mettrie and Helvétius think unambiguously and speak unceremoniously, neither do they hide anything from themselves nor do they fall silent before others. The first form of the utilitarian doctrine thus attains perfect clarity. La Rochefoucauld's influence dominates the whole of the doctrine that he, in part, gave rise to. But it will not take long for this influence to disappear. We have already seen how the ancient Epicureans were in a difficult position with regards to friendship and devotion; they did not want to renounce them, and they sought to elevate their system until reaching these two high virtues. A similar evolution will take place in modern Epicureanism.

Shortly after the publication of *De l'esprit*, Dalembert, who will also come to be associated with the utilitarian school, stressed the importance of the sentiment of humanity. According to him, for the human being virtue consists in the greatest possible enlargement of one's affections. If the objects of our affections are particular, then the affections themselves will be exclusive and, therefore, contrary to virtue. This is why one should give them an object which is so broad and general that it embraces all others, without excluding any. One should, as a philosopher used to say, prefer one's family to oneself, one's country to one's family, and humankind to one's country. [One could perhaps claim that u]niversal love of humanity is the 'spirit of virtue'.[7]

The eighteenth century, weary of religion and no longer persuaded by metaphysics, had placed its faith entirely on humanity: every system, in order to be successful, should in some way reflect this great sentiment. In this sense the utilitarian doctrine, by means of one of its many admirable metamorphoses referred to by La Rochefoucauld, should also become a humanitarian doctrine. Upholding as the starting point, Helvétius halted before charity and justice as if in face of an unattainable ideal. On this basis only he resisted the current which dragged his whole century towards the ideas of humanity and philanthropy. However, this current was stronger than him, and also dragged his system along with it.

One can clearly follow this transformation in d'Holbach, whose claims on virtue are far from Helvétius' affected indifference. On the one hand, according to d'Holbach, we always and only obey our interest, that is to say to 'one's gravitation upon oneself',[8] and that which we call moral obligation is not different from the need of being useful to oneself both through oneself or others.[9] On the other hand, virtue is essentially sympathetic. Borrowing Leibniz's terms, d'Holbach defines it as 'the art of making oneself happy about the happiness of others'. In virtue, which is not different from sympathy, d'Holbach seeks to find a middle ground between the interests of the individual and those of the collective, a middle ground that Helvétius sought only in legal sanction. D'Holbach goes even farther. In his view, not only is virtue sympathy, but it is also, to a certain extent, something independent of the object with which one sympathizes. Through virtuous action we join our happiness with that of others, and in this very act it seems that we find a [form of] satisfaction that is *sui generis* and proper to ourselves. On the one hand, we thrive on the happiness of our fellow human beings, we enjoy their affection and their esteem. On the other hand, we create happiness for ourselves, we merit our own esteem. In effect, we love humanity, and this sublime sentiment is simultaneously within ourselves and in others, because humanity is genuinely worthy of love in and by itself. 'Virtue is its own reward... When the whole universe is unjust to the good man, what is left for him is above all to love and respect himself, to dive with pleasure into his own heart'.[10]

Nothing can be more surprising than this leap from Epicureanism into Stoicism. We have already seen, in many regards, how Epicurus' philosophy converges with that of Zeno [the Stoic]. However, ancient Epicureanism, more coherent than its modern offspring, never attempted such a complete rapprochement. And this is indeed a remarkable evolution. Spinoza, in whose work the systems of Epicurus and Zeno are almost finally reconciled, thought of both self-esteem[11] and remorse, demerit and merit, as inner illusions.

Saint-Lambert, author of the *Catéchisme universel*, starting from the same principles as Dalembert and d'Holbach, also aims at the love of humanity. 'Nature prevents you from serving your country in ways that are harmful to humankind... You must develop the habit of doing and saying that which can bring men together... If you cannot love someone as an individual, respect the man in him.'

III. – In the same way that Epicureanism became humanitarian in France, it was also not possible for it not to become liberal and reformist. Helvétius is still vague in terms of politics; he speaks against despotism, without, however, prescribing any remedy to it. D'Holbach, on the other hand, was one of Hobbes' translators and accepted his principles; however, he deduced from these principles very different consequences. His theory of government, inspired by Locke and Spinoza, is diametrically opposed to Hobbes'.[12]

Epicureanism in France would easily ascend to a conception of political *freedom* and *equality*: interest, here, seems to converge with what one usually understands by law.[13] But utilitarian doctrine rises even higher. Sometimes by an unconscious contradiction, sometimes by appealing to the sentiments of sympathy, benevolence, philanthropy, natural sociability, it was able to embrace the sentiment of universal *fraternity*, or at least getting very close to it. In this way, the utilitarians joined [the group of] the *a priori* moralists in their approval of the motto of the French Revolution: liberty, equality, fraternity. Helvétius himself would have given total assent to this motto; however, since he did not give that much importance to sympathetic sentiments as did his successors, he would have remarked that one can only be a brother to all human beings as human beings to the extent that one receives advantages from them. He would have declared universal fraternity to be an excellent thing, but nevertheless impossible to practically realize until further notice.

IV. – At the same time when the utilitarian doctrine came, as if by a natural deviation, to forget its own principles in the works of Dalembert, d'Holbach and Saint-Lambert, it was also suddenly brought back to its point of departure by Volney. His work, *La loi naturelle*, is the most complete and logical summary of Epicureanism: the whole work of the eighteenth century on ethics is condensed in this book. Volney's was one of the most remarkable attempts to found, to use Helvétius' phrase, a 'physics of customs'. The *Loi naturelle*, or *Principes physiques de la morale, déduits de l'organisation de l'homme et de l'univers* – this is the characteristic title that Volney choses for his work – recalls Spinoza's system and prefigures Herbert Spencer's.

The conservation of beings – this is, according to Volney, the formula of natural law. It is the same force that makes waters flow downwards and that governs human actions. [For Volney, t]here is no distinction between physical and moral good. Moral good is in fact physical good continued and preserved. There are five individual virtues, that is to say, five main means to the preservation of being, namely science, temperance, courage, activity and, finally, *propriety*,[14] which is not the least important of these virtues.[15] Volney seems to have forgotten the gymnastic exercises; the Cyrenaics, on the other hand, have never forgotten them, especially because they placed the strength of the body among the virtues. [For Volney, a]fter individual virtues, there are the virtues of the family, followed by the social virtues. They all equally rely on physical principles. How could the love for one's neighbour, for instance, be a precept? It could be such 'by means of equality and reciprocity; in threatening the life of another we risk harming our own, also by an effect reciprocity. In contrast, by doing another person good, we have the right to expect something in return, the equivalent retribution, and this is the nature of social virtues, namely that of being *useful* to the man who practises them because of the *right of reciprocity* that they give [in relation] to those whom they have benefited.'[16] Furthermore, to this right of reciprocity one must add sympathy in order to found society: sympathy is not different from the 'reflexion' of the sensations of others in ourselves. 'From this [reflexion] are born the simultaneous sensations of pleasure and pain which charm us and form an indissoluble link of society.'

An important principle, if admitted by Volney, could have engendered a true revolution in his all too down-to-earth ethics. According to Volney, the conservation of being, the law upon which morality is grounded, implies the perfecting of being and perpetual *progress*. On the other hand, *degradation* is a diminishing of being, [or] the beginning of its destruction. By deepening this conception Volney would have been able to place the moral ideal in the highest state of being, in a sort of nobility superior to petty interests and capable of viewing life from above.

In short, Epicureanism, in the beginning and in the end of its development in France, took on precise and methodical forms. It rejected all other principles beyond interest properly understood; it also rejects all other rules or imperatives which are not the force of the law or the force of things. It stands alone, with all its consequences and nothing more; it hopes to achieve self-sufficiency.

V. – We have briefly reviewed the majority of the important writers who, in eighteenth-century France, have shown themselves to be partisans of utilitarian and Epicurean doctrines.[17] However, these men dragged by the flow of the same current of ideas, this group of thinkers who became the apostles of utility, were not an exception; the whole of the eighteenth century – except Rousseau and Montesquieu – shows an unavoidable preference towards this new principle in ethics [i.e. utility]. It is curious to note that there was an almost universal agreement of minds: these men of the eighteenth century, in the very moment in which they want to *declare* their rights, often speak of their interests. Helvétius' doctrine represented a progress in relation to that of Hobbes, both in theory and in practice: for too long the kings of France, like Hobbes' ideal sovereign, have recognized nothing but their own pleasure as their rule of action. Subjecting their actions to the rule of utility was a significant step. This is how one developed the habitude of linking by an unbreakable link the ideas of [political] liberalism and that of utility.

Let us add that the French mind, predisposed to systematizing, classifying, deducing and universalizing, has found its [natural] satisfaction in the Epicurean ideas.

First of all, utilitarian ethics is completely *independent*; it does not rely on anything foreign, it has its basis and its ground in itself alone. It seems to be able to form a self-contained whole, [or] a system. In this way, it was able to seduce the whole of the eighteenth century, which was ardently yearning for new ideas, especially by ideas which could give it, in the sphere of thought, the same freedom it would soon conquer in the practical sphere. Through Epicureanism, philosophy felt itself free from hindrances; it no longer had the need to invoke the dogmas of revealed religion; philosophy was then able to cut the thread still binding faithful souls to virtue – [namely] the 'fear of the devil' – diving fearlessly into the realm of speculation, now certain of not losing anything by letting go of religious beliefs. Thus, utilitarian ethics, fully independent, has become a guarantee of freedom of thought; a freedom which one has long wished for and preferred. To liberate man's thought in order to soon deliver man himself: wasn't this the greatest idea of eighteenth-century France?

Additionally, utilitarian ethics had an aspect of universality. It took up the task of responding to the fierce interrogations presented by Pascal in the preceding century, by showing that this or that river and this or that meridian are in no way decisive in what concerns truth or justice; it has also shown that climate has a secondary importance [in what concerns human action];[18] and, finally, that under the apparent diversity of mores one finds the unity of interest.

In this way, by a singular inversion of roles, the utilitarians defended the universality of moral principles against the theologians. They represented science confronting revelation. In an academic report on Saint-Lambert's *Catéchisme*, Suard says that 'there is an all too human ethics that is founded solely on man's nature and the inalterable relations between men, which is therefore always valid in every climate, under any political system, the truth and utility of which are equally recognized from Peking to Philadelphia, Paris or London.' Thus, Epicurean naturalism was, for the French *esprit*, a means to elevate itself to universal considerations, [that is, it was] a way to ascend from the particular to the most general, overcoming every limit or boundary. Acquiring this new point of view, this system [i.e. Epicurean naturalism] gave thought more freedom, liberating it from the hindrances that space, time and chance seemed to put in its way blocking the unfolding of its impetus. Interest, hand in hand with justice, helped it breaking through these geometrical and geographical lines, these meridians and rivers, which Montaigne and Pascal opposed to it.[19]

Undoubtedly, the eighteenth century, by wanting to make of ethics a *science* in the full sense of the word, accomplished a great *oeuvre*. Nevertheless, in order to make it a science, it based itself on a calculus of interests, often grounding the latter on a still crude form of egoism.

In order to assess the philosophical conceptions of the eighteenth century it is often better to examine the end to which they aim, instead the principle upon which they are grounded. The end, the goal towards which are oriented all its thoughts, and towards which all its efforts are made, was the emancipation of humanity. As for its principles, they were subject to variation and change. The eighteenth century is a century of movement. If, on the one hand, a body at rest needs a solid base and a cornerstone; on the other, a projectile crossing the space does not need anything else in order to achieve its goal than the attraction this goal exercises upon it. The eighteenth century put itself in motion owing to its great energy: and it [also] had a great end to direct this motion; however, in terms of grounds, cornerstones and principles, and in terms of exterior and logical means, it remained deficient for a long time.

Notes

1. Helvétius' book *De l'esprit* had more than fifty editions in France and abroad.
2. T.N. The idea here is, quite simply, that social utility should be constructed in conformity with individual utility.
3. T.N. Julien Offray de La Mettrie, *Discours sur le bonheur* ou *L'Anti-Sénèque* (in *De la volupté: anti-Sénèque ou le souverain bien; l'École de la volupté; système d'Épicure*, edited by Ann Thomson, Paris: Desjonquères, 1996, 45; I will provide the corresponding page numbers from Ann Thomson's English translation in brackets [La Mettrie, *Anti-Seneca or the Sovereign Good*, in *Machine Man and Other Writings*, Cambridge: Cambridge University Press, 1996]. I have based my translation of this passage on Thomson's. I have stayed closer to the passage as Guyau quotes it. Note the slight difference: 'And have nature and reason invited me to enjoy well-being for the sake of other people or for my own sake?' (130).
4. T.N. Guyau does not provide the reference. Moreover, the quote is inexact; Guyau is probably quoting from Pommerol's French translation of Lange's *History of Materialism* [*Histoire du matérialisme, et critique de son importance à notre époque*, volume 1, Paris: Reinwald, 1877, 523], where the passage appears exactly as Guyau quotes it. The original passage in La Mettrie reads: '*si non content d'exceller dans le grand art de voluptés, la crapule et la débauche n'ont rien de trop fort pour toi, l'ordure et l'infamie restent pour ton glorieux partage ; vautres-y toi, comme font les porcs, et tu seras heureux à leur manière*' (La Mettrie, *Discours sur le bonheur ou L'Anti-Sénèque* [*De la volupté*, 92].
5. T.N. I have followed Thomson's translation of this passage (La Mettrie, *Machine Man and Other Writings*, 10).
6. La Mettrie, *Discours sur le bonheur ou L'Anti-Sénèque* [*De la volupté*, 91].
7. Dalembert [in Guyau's spelling; or Jean Rond d'Alembert], *Essai sur des éléments de philosophie (1759)* [edited by Richard N. Schwab, Hildescheim: Georg Olms, 1965], III, 1. – Dalembert is clearly utilitarian. When reading the following passage on disinterestedness one believes one could be reading a passage from a modern British utilitarian, such as Bentham or Mill: 'If one calls well-being [*bien-être*] that which is beyond absolute need [*besoin*], it follows from this that to sacrifice one's well-being to the need of others is the principle of all social virtues and the remedy to all passions. However, is this sacrifice *found in nature*? In what does it consist? *No natural or political law can oblige us to love others more than ourselves*; this heroism, if we can use this word to qualify such an absurd feeling, would not be found in the human heart. *But the enlightened* [*éclairé*] *love of our own happiness* [*bonheur*] shows us that

peace among ourselves and the affection of our fellows [*semblables*] are a kind of good that is preferable to every other; and most certain means to procure this peace and this affection is to dispute with others as little as possible the enjoyment of conventional goods, which arouse the avidity of men; thus, the enlightened love of ourselves is the *principle of all sacrifices*.' Considered from this perspective, morality becomes a sort of 'tariff' [i.e. something we 'pay' in order to assure peace and concord].

8   T.N. *gravitation de soi sur soi*.
9   [Paul-Henri Thiry, Baron] d'Holbach, *Système de la nature* [*ou des loix du monde physique et du monde moral*], I, 10 [Guyau references p. 183, without specifying the edition]; *Système Social* [*ou Principes naturels de la morale et de la Politique, avec un examen de l'influence du gouvernement sur les mœurs*, London: N/A., 1773], [Guyau references p. 71]. – D'Holbach is one the first [thinkers] to have attempted to found ethics upon physiology or, as he says, *medicine*: 'If one consulted experience instead of prejudice, medicine would then provide ethics with the key to the human heart ... If we knew, with the help of experience, the elements that form the foundation of a man's temperament, or the [temperament of that] greater number of individuals that forms a people, we would know what is convenient for them to do, the laws that are necessary for them, and the institutions that are useful to them ... Ethics and politics could greatly benefit from materialism, in a way that they will never benefit from the dogma of spirituality, which prevent them from even contemplating such goods' [this quote appears in d'Holbach, *Système de la nature (nouvelle edition avec des notes et des corrections, par Diderot)*, volume 1, Paris: Étienne Ledoux, 1821, 148].
10 D'Holbach, *Système de la nature*, I, XV, [Guyau references p. 342; the quote appears on p. 386 in the 1821 edition of the *Système de la nature* (Paris: Étienne Ledoux)]. In the *Nouvelle Héloïse*, Rousseau says of D'Holbach that he is represented by Wolmar's character: 'he does good without any hope for reward; he is more virtuous and more disinterested than all of us' [see Jean-Jacques Rousseau, *Julie, ou la nouvelle Héloïse* (originally entitled *Lettres de Deux Amants, Habitants d'une petite ville au pied des Alpes*), Amsterdam: Marc-Michel Rey, 1761; in English: *Julie, or The New Heloise. Letters of Two Lovers Who Live in a Small Town at the Foot of the Alps*, translated by Philip Stewart and Jean Vaché (The Collected Writings of Rousseau, volume 6), Lebanon NH: Dartmouth College Press & University Press of New England, 1997].
11 T.N. *estime de soi*.
12 Government, according to D'Holbach, is the sum of social forces placed in the hands of those who one judges to be those more appropriate to conduce men towards happiness (*Système Social*, II, p. 6). However, they can only derive their authority from a contract, and not only from a contract that links the governed [subjects] among themselves, as Hobbes wished, but also a contract that would link the rulers [those who govern; *les gouvernants*] to those whom they govern [*les gouvernés*]: 'there is no legitimate sovereign but by the avowal of his nation' (*Système Social*, II, p. 11 [T.N. The page number provided by Guyau coincides with the 1773 edition. However, Guyau's quote in French is inexact; he seems to be paraphrasing the original, which reads '*Un Souverain légitime ne regne que de l'aveu de sa Nation*']. The origin of government is, thus, the will of the people; but what would its form be? To solve this problem, one must ask oneself what is the aim [*but*] of government. We know that this aim is happiness; now, the immediate condition of happiness is freedom, which is not different from the power to employ [to put at work; *mettre en oeuvre*] the means necessary to achieve happiness. The best form of government, therefore, is the one that

would be as close as possible to its goal, and consequently will assure for the governed society the greatest possible sum of freedom (*Système Social*, II, 35). The *freer* one is, the more one can act [*plus on peut*]; the more one can [act], the more *means for* [achieving] *happiness* one has. The more *means* one has, the more one can deploy them in order to be *happy*. What is, then, the form of government that will give maximum freedom to all? It is the government by representatives (*Système Social*, II, 503). 'A government exists for a nation, not the nation for a government; and a nation is entitled to revoke, suspend, restrict or explain the power it has given to a government' (*Système Social*, II, 55 [T.N. Guyau seems to provide an incorrect reference: the passage actually appears on p. 57 of the 1773 edition]). Since government must secure freedom for all, it must also secure civil *equality* [*égalité civile*]: because someone's superiority always constitutes the inferiority of others, and all inferiority is a lack of freedom. Civil equality is, therefore, the condition for freedom; now, we have just noted that freedom is the condition for happiness: the government must, therefore, *equally* assure to all the governed [subjects] the free possession [or property, *possession*] of themselves and of their goods, that is to say, the possession of all the means for achieving happiness. – D'Hobalch has not, in fact, arrived at this conclusion; but Dalembert easily reaches it in his *Éléments de philosophie*.

13 T.N. Although our choice has been to preserve the distinction between Right [the system of right] and law, rendering *le droit* as *right* here could create ambiguity.
14 T.N. *properté*.
15 Constantin-François Volney, *La loi naturelle* [*Les ruines. La loi naturelle*, Paris: Librairie de la Bibliothèque nationale, 1879], chapter V [On individual virtues]. [T.N. *La loi naturelle* was originally published in 1793, with the subtitle *Catéchisme du Citoyen français*].
16 Volney, *La loi naturelle*, chapter XII [Development of social virtues].
17 We will not focus on Diderot who, with his enthusiast and changing nature, is more idealist than utilitarian, and more Stoic than Epicurean; both atheist and religious in Spinoza's way; and an advocate of Seneca: he proposes sometimes paradoxes and sometimes great ideas, but he has no unified and coherent ethical system.
18 According to D'Holbach, *nature* forms the body; *climate* gives a body its temperament; nature and climate shape the physical dimension of human beings, but leave their moral dimension to personal initiative, guided by laws. D'Holbach reacts here against Montesquieu, who attributed a sometimes exaggerate influence of *climate* upon customs. D'Holbach writes: 'It is not climate that shapes men, but opinion, which is the ensemble of ideas transmitted and perpetuated through education, religion, legislation and, finally, the government' (*Système Social*, III, p. 20 [T.N. Guyau's quote is inexact, or a paraphrase; in volume 3 of the 1773 edition, the passage appears on p. 3).
19 T.N. That is to say: interest gave justice a universal aspect, overcoming the limitations of particularities of time and place, climate and culture; it took justice beyond the critical limits set by thinkers such as Montaigne and Pascal.

Conclusion

Contemporary Epicureanism

No doctrine has been more targeted, attacked and criticized than ancient and modern Epicureanism. No other doctrine, on the other hand, has so fiercely clashed with received opinions about the two things that are dearest to the human heart, namely morality and religion.

As we know, ancient Epicureans had the Stoics as their main adversaries. And the Stoics were violent adversaries who disfigured the Epicurean doctrine, against which they organized a resistance. The ancients, and especially the Romans, ignored frank and courteous discussion, as well as the common and unbiased research for truth. In this way, Epicureanism comes to us either distorted by Stoicism or through Cicero's grandiloquence. Despite the defenders of Epicureanism, such as Gassendi, most historians have only seen Epicurus through Cicero's eyes, and they were therefore unable to justly appreciate his doctrine in its true value. Even one of the most respected historians of ancient philosophy, Ritter, continues to endorse this unjust judgement of Epicurus: 'We cannot see in the whole of Epicurus' doctrines a totality in which the parts fit together. It is evident that his canonics and his physics are just a clumsy appendix to his ethics. But who would be able to praise Epicurus' ethics? Who could praise it because of the truths it contains? Who would be able to praise it for its originality, or for the logical concatenation of ideas to be found within it? We do not find it original in the first place ... We cannot say that it is well linked together either ... This doctrine seems to us of little scientific value.'[1] We hope to have justified Epicurus in what concerns part of these reproaches. Mr Zeller himself, the most accomplished historian of ancient philosophy, remains quite severe in his judgement on Epicurus. Zeller provides an exact summary of Epicurus' doctrine, but one that is still incomplete. Nevertheless, he is still too hostile to the fundamental ideas of Epicureanism to be able to understand its true value and the place it occupies in the historical series of [philosophical] systems. Kant, whose authority cannot be ignored, even in [the field of] the history of philosophy, nevertheless said that if, on the one hand, Plato is the greatest philosopher of intelligible things, Epicurus, on the other, is par excellence the philosopher of the sensible things.

All modern Epicureans have met with the same fate as their master. First, [there is] Hobbes, whose pitiless logic and frankness exasperated his century. 'One could hardly cite a writer,' says Lange, 'who was as insulted as Hobbes, simultaneously attacked by men of all schools [of thought] at the very moment in which, by his extraordinary clarity, he compelled all of them to think with more precision and clarity.' Later on, La

Mettrie equally provoked a reaction of all the writers of his century against him. His doctrine, as we have remarked, was less immoral than [many] others like that of Mandeville, for example; nevertheless, it was even more attacked than any other. This was even more the case because La Mettrie had the huge fault of dying of indigestion. Helvétius was condemned by the parliament and by the Sorbonne for his book *De l'esprit,* and he had to make a public retraction. D'Holbach's *Le Système de la nature* provoked a thunderstorm. Everywhere, the affirmation of Epicurean ideas had excited against its authors the most violent reactions, and the Epicureans have had until now more adversaries than [true] judges.

Nevertheless, after some years, especially abroad, a movement in favour of Epicurus has taken place in philosophical opinion. Whereas in France we remain too attached to the old traditions of classical philosophy, in Germany, Lange recovered the materialist doctrines, showing the important role they played in the development of our modern ideas, and placing Epicurus among the most influent materialist thinkers.

The moment to truly appreciate Epicurean doctrine and to seek the truth it encloses seems to have arrived. In truth, it is impossible to fully appreciate a [philosophical] system before it definitively completes its development. There is a sort of internal criticism, which works within every system and which forces it to continuously perfect itself, as well as to reappear under new forms at the very moment when it was thought to be defeated. Such has been the case with the Epicurean system throughout history, and even in our time its development is not yet completed. It still lives and continues its development, now under a new form with the contemporary English school. One cannot assess Epicureanism without also considering the contemporary English doctrines; this is why we proposed to study specifically these doctrines elsewhere.[2] For now, rather than attempting a still premature appreciation, we will limit ourselves to highlighting some of the key points of Epicurus' thought that were developed by his modern successors. The history of a doctrine's progress is no different from a sort of living critique, which is often more interesting and more useful [for understanding a doctrine] than a judgement that will never be definitive.

All the Epicureans agree, and this is the fundamental idea of their doctrine, that pleasure and pain are the only forces that set a being in motion, the sole levers with whose aid we can produce any action.

Once this principle is posited Epicurus and his successors conclude that if pleasure is the only end of beings [then] ethics is the art of obtaining the greatest sum of personal pleasures. Ethics thus understood is, as a utilitarian once said, nothing but the regularization of egoism. Before Spinoza, Hobbes attempted to erect a *geometry of customs*, Helvétius, then, constructed a *physics of customs*; finally, d'Holbach founds a *physiology of customs*. However, under all these different names, Epicurean morality is nothing but the search of personal interest; it rests upon the courageous merging of *fact* and *duty. De facto*, it believes that the individual only pursues its own pleasure. *De jure*, it is therefore his own pleasure that he ought to pursue, either when this pleasure is by chance in opposition with the pleasure of others, or when this pleasure finds itself in harmony with the pleasure of others. Nevertheless, all Epicureans, including La Mettrie, agree about the need to commit the individual to not entrenching himself in foolish egoism, through the cultivation of friendship, sociability and benevolence. It is a fact, according to them, that there usually is harmony between the pleasure of the individual and the pleasure of others. However, let us be clearly understood: this is not a primitive and fundamental harmony. The egoisms of individuals function together like pendulums, without merging into one another, and without becoming deeply united. Ethics does not have as its goal to produce this union, since that would be impossible. Regarding this point, Epicureanism in France has advanced very little; Dalembert, d'Holbach, Volney sometimes seem to prefigure the contemporary English school, but they never fail to [always] return to personal interest as the clear principle of all morality. Here we can note a difference between the Epicureans and the contemporary English school. This difference gradually grows from Bentham to Mill and, especially, to Mr Spencer, with whose principles one is able to build up, for the first time, an almost complete physics or physiology of customs. The English ethicists still preserve personal pleasure as the only lever capable of setting being in motion. However, instead of positing this pleasure as a legitimate goal for the moral being, their effort is that of having the moral being pursue the pleasure of others. Expressed in this way, their utilitarianism seems, at first glance, to be manifestly inconsistent; and elsewhere we will examine whether it implies inconsistency.[3] Nevertheless, there is in this doctrine something profound which we now wish to bring to light.

What would a purely egoistic and personal pleasure be? Is there any pleasure of this kind? What role could pleasures of this sort play in life? When, in thought, we descend in the ladder of beings, we note that the sphere in which each of them moves is narrow and almost self-enclosed. When, on the contrary, we ascend towards [the sphere of] superior beings, we can see their sphere of action opening up, expanding, and increasingly combining with the spheres of action of other beings. The *self* is less and less distinguishable from other *selves*; and, in fact, it has more and more need of others to constitute itself and to subsist. This ladder of being along which our thought thus travels is one that the human species has already partially travelled across in the course its evolution. Its starting point was, indeed, egoism; but egoism, by virtue of the fecundity of life,[4] was led to grow, to create new centres for its own action outside of itself. At the same time, sentiments that are correlative to this centrifugal tendency, slowly emerged, and have somehow enveloped the egoistical sentiments that served as their principle. We are now on our way to an epoch when egoism will turn back and retreat further and further into ourselves, becoming less and less recognizable. In this ideal epoch [human] beings will no longer be able to enjoy [pleasure][5] in solitude: their pleasure will be as if part of a *concert* in which the pleasure of others will take part as a necessary element. Moreover, is it not already like this in most cases? If we compare the part left to pure egoism to that of 'altruism' in everyday life, we will note how small the former is. Even the most egoistic pleasures, because they are purely physical, like eating or drinking, only acquire their full charm when we share them with others. This predominant part played by sociable sentiments must be acknowledged by every doctrine, and in whatever way they may conceive the principles of ethics. In effect, no doctrine can shut down the human heart. We cannot mutilate ourselves, and pure egoism would be pure nonsense, a true impossibility. In the same way that the *self* is considered by contemporary psychology to be an illusion, that there is no personality and [that] we are composed of a multitude of beings and tiny consciousnesses, so in the same way we could say that egoistic pleasure shows itself to be an illusion. My pleasure does not exist without the pleasure of others; to a certain degree, all society must collaborate in it, from the small society that surrounds me, from my family, to the greater society in which I live. In order not to lose anything in intensity, my pleasure must preserve all its extension.[6]

Evolutionist ethics, which in a way could be considered as a development of Epicureanism, is also its best criticism. It clearly shows the insufficiency of the principle of pure egoism, an insufficiency which already appeared in Epicurus himself and the Roman Epicureans. With respect to other points, the Epicurean system has been considerably improved throughout history. Thus, when deepening the reflection on the nature of the pleasure that gives life a goal, Epicurus defined it as a state of rest of body and soul, a state of mental equilibrium and of intellectual 'ataraxy'. Given such a conception of pleasure, Epicurus deduces from it that the ideal for every being is to fold itself upon itself,[7] searching for rest and peace within itself and with no exterior aid. This doctrine, which at first glance does not lack grandeur, in practice leads to the most deplorable consequences. In this regard, Hobbes brings a positive change to the Epicurean system, by returning to the ideas of Aristippus and claiming that pleasure is essentially motion, action, energy and, consequently, progress. To enjoy is to act; and to act is to advance. Doubtlessly, we could maintain with Epicurus that pleasure is accompanied by an inner balance, of a harmony between all faculties. However, all this is but the condition for pleasure, and if we examine it more deeply and in itself, we will recognize that this inner balance is precisely that which allows us an action which is more and more expansive in all directions. In our days, the English school goes even further: it will show that sensibility accompanies our activity in its progressive development. Pleasure is not something immobile as Epicurus believed it to be, it rather varies ceaselessly. Habit and heredity attach it to new [forms] of action; so placing it under the domain of the universal law of evolution: it is in itself evolution and a development of being.

In what concerns the problem of freedom, we find ancient and modern Epicureans in open disagreement. As we know, Epicurus admitted the notion of free will, and placed a kind of spontaneity, which took from itself its own principle of action, not only in the human being, but also in nature and the atoms. Hobbes, Helvétius, d'Holbach and all modern Epicureans, on the contrary, reject freedom and are openly deterministic in their thinking, and in some cases, like that of Hobbes and La Mettrie, even excessively fatalistic. Our intention here is not to examine or assert the absolute truth of these opposing doctrines. Nevertheless, we can ask which one is more faithful to Epicurean principles. Now, one must recognize that the belief in freedom is an anomaly in the Epicurean system. Epicurus, after having posited happiness as the end goal, recognizes that tranquillity of soul is the necessary condition of happiness, and he believes that the idea of a universal necessity governing nature would be incompatible with the tranquillity of soul. As we know, according to Epicurus, there is something sombre and troubling in the sentiment of fatalism; and this is why he rejects it. Once he begins to reject it, then he banishes it from everything, with remarkable logical spirit, and places everywhere spontaneity. However, what he has not proven is that spontaneity itself can exist; he does not even try to prove it. For him spontaneity, like moral freedom, is an evident fact of consciousness. Now, having posited man's freedom, he energetically deduces the spontaneity of nature. However, he does not realize that only one of these two things can be true: either moral freedom is doubtful, and this incertitude would then encompass his whole system; or this freedom is certain, and therefore constitutes a new [and unique] principle that one must acknowledge. If I have freedom, then I can establish an ethics upon it, and entirely dispense with the principle of interest. From the very idea of freedom one can deduce duty without there being any need of appealing to pleasure. That a determinist could also be a utilitarian is understandable. It is, however, a contradiction for a partisan of free will, who believes to feel within himself something of the absolute and experience himself as a living cause acting by itself and possessing intrinsic value and dignity, to submit [himself] to an external rule of action, turning it towards a foreign end and making it a mere instrument of pleasure. One has rightly subtracted the modern Epicureans from this contradiction. On this point, the Epicurean system has acquired in our days new strength and homogeneity. Epicurus lamented the fact that the idea of universal determinism weighed upon the human soul, for the human being suffers from having to sacrifice his full and complete independence to nature. He forgot that ethics, as much as any other science, cannot consider the question of individual preferences. Every science seeks not that which pleases our intelligence or sensibility, but rather that which is. It does not pursue absolute happiness, this utopia of ancient Epicureanism, but rather relative happiness, that which is compatible with reality, and which does not retreat in the face of any truth, not even the harshest ones.

It is for the same reason that modern Epicureanism has renounced the consolations that the ancient Epicurean theory of death claimed to offer. Generally, the modern utilitarians, these practical men, were more concerned with life than death. According to them, ethics has governing our conduct in life as its goal; it is not concerned with modifying our ideas regarding death: that is rather the task of metaphysics and the different religions.

The relationship between ancient and modern Epicureanism is much stronger in what concerns social theory. First of all, we find in Hobbes, and later in the eighteenth century, this ingenious theory of Epicurus, which founds society upon [a] contract. The Epicureans, clearly seeing human beings as fundamentally selfish, and consequently enemies, have searched for an artificial means for bringing them together and uniting them. The idea of contract presented itself to their minds as the most capable of linking human beings among themselves. Epicurus, however, conceived of this contract as a sort of primitive agreement between men, more spontaneous than reflected. In his theory, human animals would have gathered together and, even before knowing how to speak, would have agreed[8] through signs to live in peace and friendship. This will no longer be the conception of the contract in Hobbes and his successors. For them, the primitive agreement among human beings appears as a contract in fine shape, celebrated before witnesses, and with perfectly defined and precise causes. Such an imagination, partly scholastic and partly fantastic, loses all its historical value. By contrast, the original character of Epicurean sociology, as it was formulated by Lucretius, is that it claimed to rest upon facts and to be deduced from history. It is also upon history that the most faithful continuators of the Epicurean tradition found their theories. For them, human societies were not born all at once by a sudden act of individual wills: rather, they were built gradually, through the accumulation of habits and customs, and by the gradual accommodation of individuals to one another: the ideas of justice, right, charity and philanthropy, far from being the product of society, rather ensue from society. Far from explaining it they are rather explained by it.

That is precisely why Epicurean ethics is essentially historical, presupposing an idea of evolution and progress. It is in Lucretius that we found the idea of progress expressed for the first time. Helvétius reproduced the same idea, by applying it to law[9] and legislation; it is still this same idea that we find in d'Holbach and most eighteenth-century thinkers, Epicurean or not. The idea of progress is the cornerstone of liberalism, and this is why it had to be affirmed with such great energy in the eighteenth century on the eve of its great demand for freedom. We have seen the great role played by the representatives of Epicureanism in the movement that then carried away people's minds. In politics and in social ethics the eighteenth-century Epicureans reasoned much better than they did in the case of pure ethics. Helvétius is openly liberal, whereas d'Holbach is a radical who virulently attacks royalty and its inevitable disadvantages.

The Epicureans are not less innovative and audacious with regards to religion. It is curious to note, in the history of the Epicurean doctrine, how its representatives were in direct or indirect hostility with regards to received religion. Hobbes' system is essentially irreligious; if it weren't for the will of the prince, which came to forcefully sustain it, religion would have been at great risk. Hobbes attacks miracles, and ascribes to religion no other natural seed (*semen naturale*) than fear, ignorance and, in a word, 'man's innate tendency for hasty conclusions'.[10] The venerable Gassendi himself, who has never completely abandoned his great respect for the religion of which he was a priest, when speaking of his master Epicurus, claimed: 'If Epicurus attended some of the religious ceremonies of his country while at the same time disapproving of them deep in his heart, his conduct was to a certain point excusable. In fact, he attended them because civil order demanded that of him: [but] he disapproved of them because nothing can force the soul of the sage to think in the same way as does the ordinary man ... The role of philosophy was then to think like the few but to speak and act like the multitude.'[11] One cannot avoid thinking that by writing these lines Gassendi was reflecting upon himself and thinking of his century no less than Epicurus'.

As for the eighteenth-century Epicureans they lift the veil once and for all. La Mettrie, Helvétius and d'Holbach openly attack religion. In fourteen long chapters of the *Système de la nature*, d'Holbach strives to overthrow the idea of God under all its forms with an audacity that few philosophers have had until then. It is largely upon Epicureanism that the eighteenth century grounds its incredulity. As one can see, the disciples went farther than their master, maybe even too far, for they have not seen that religious sentiment existed in fact, and one should count on it and acknowledge it as a tendency, legitimate or not, of human nature, and that philosophy should seek to satisfy it to a certain extent.

In short, Epicurean doctrines have unquestionably exercised an influence upon the development of human thought. In the natural sciences, the cosmological system of Democritus and Epicurus seems to be triumphant today. In the moral and social sciences, the doctrines that derive from Epicureanism have never been so powerful. In this very moment, the English school is proposing, in face of the Stoicism restored by Kant, an Epicureanism renewed by the findings of modern science. From how many old ideas and rooted prejudices has Epicureanism helped to free the moral domain! In the same way, as we have seen, in the religious sphere, Epicurus has worked harder than any other ancient philosopher to free human thought from the belief in the marvellous, the miraculous and the providential. Long before the advent of Christianity, Epicurus had already attacked pagan religion and reduced it to powerlessness. In our days still, it is the spirit of Epicurus that, combined with new doctrines, works against and undermines Christianity. How many, among the free thinkers of today, deserve the sobriquet of 'Epicurean' under which the [Early] Fathers of the Church and the Jewish thinkers placed the free thinkers of yesterday!

Notes

1. Ritter, *Histoire de la philosophie ancienne*, III, 412. – We have shown in Epicurus' ethics a rigorous chain of ideas and a true scientific system, which already displayed the main features of modern utilitarianism. We have also demonstrated the link that exists between his ethics and his canonics and physics.
2. See our *Morale anglaise contemporaine. Morale de l'utilité et de l'évolution* [second edition], Paris: Félix Alcan, 1885.
3. See the second part of *La morale anglaise contemporaine*.
4. T.N. *la fecondité même de toute vie*.
5. T.N. 'To enjoy' is a transitive verb; the correct English form would here be 'enjoy themselves in solitude' or 'to enjoy pleasures in solitude'. I have chosen, however, to preserve the French structure here [*jouir en solitude*] given the philosophical dimension of this term in Guyau's original.
6. See our *Esquisse d'une morale sans obligation ni sanction* [first edition, Paris: Félix Alcan, 1885], 24.
7. T.N. *se replier sur soi-même*.
8. T.N. The French here (*convenir*) also evokes the conventional aspect of the pact.
9. T. N. Here one reads *droit*, which in this context could also be rendered as 'right' understood as the body or system of laws.
10. Hobbes, *Leviathan*, ch. VI, 45; ch. XII, etc.
11. Gassendi, *De vita et moribus Epicuri*, IV, 4.

Bibliography

Ancient texts & modern editions

Claudius Aelianus [or Aelian], *Varia Historia* [*Historical Miscellany*], translated by N. G. Wilson, Cambridge MA & London: Harvard University Press, 1997.

Alexander of Aphrodisias, *De anima* [*On the Soul. Part I: Soul as Form of the Body, Parts of the Soul, Nourishment, and Perception*], translated by Victor Caston, London & New York: Bloomsbury, 2014; *Supplement on the Soul*, translated by R. W. Sharples, London & New York: Bloomsbury, 2014.

Athenaeus, *Deipnosophistae*, [*The Learned Banqueters*], translated by S. Douglas Olson, Cambridge MA & London: Harvard University Press, 2006.

Aristotle's *Metaphysics*, volume 1, translated by W. D. Ross, Oxford: Oxford University Press, 2020.

Aristotle, *De caelo (On the Heavens)*, translated by C. D. C. Reeve, Indianapolis: Hackett, 2020.

Augustine of Hippo, *Confessions*, translated by Henry Chadwick, Oxford: Oxford University Press, 2008.

Marcus Tullius Cicero, *Tusculanae Disputationes*, [*Tusculan Disputations*], translated by J. E. King, Cambridge MA & London: Harvard University Press, 1945 [1927].

Marcus Tullius Cicero, *Epistulae ad Familiares* [*Letters to Friends*], volume 1, edited and translated by D. R. Shackleton Bailey, Cambridge MA & London: Harvard University Press, 2001.

Marcus Tullius Cicero, *De natura deorum* [*On the Nature of the Gods*]; *Academica*, translated by H. Rackham, Cambridge MA & London: Harvard University Press, 1951.

Marcus Tullius Cicero, *De finibus bonorum et malorum* [*On Ends*], translated by H. Rackham, Cambridge MA & London: Harvard University Press, 1931 [1914]; Cicero, *Des suprêmes biens et des suprêmes maux* (followed by *Éclaircissements relatifs à l'histoire de l'épicurisme*, by Jean-Marie Guyau), translated by Regnier Desmarais, edited by Jean-Marie Guyau, Paris: Librairie Charles Delagrave, 1875.

Marcus Tullius Cicero, *De fato*, in *On the Orator: Book 3. On Fate. Stoic Paradoxes. Divisions of Oratory*, translated by H. Rackham, Cambridge MA & London: Harvard University Press, 1989.

Marcus Tullius Cicero, *De divinatione*, in *On Old Age, On Friendship, On Divination*, translated by William A. Falconer, Cambridge MA & London: Harvard University Press, 1923.

Clement of Alexandria, *Stromata*, in *The Writings of Clement of Alexandria*, two volumes, translated by William Wilson, Edinburgh: T. & T. Clark, 1869.

Diogenes Laertius, *Lives of Eminent Philosophers*, translated by R. D. Hicks, Cambridge MA & London: Harvard University Press, 1931.

Epictetus, *Discourses and Selected Writings*, translated by Robert Dobbin, London: Penguin, 2008; *The Discourses as Reported by Arrian*, translated by W. A. Oldfather, Cambridge MA & London: Harvard University Press, 1998 [1925].

Epicurus, *The Epicurus Reader. Selected Writings and Testimonia*, edited and translated by Brad Inwood & L. P. Gerson, Indianapolis: Hackett, 1994.

Epicurus, *The Art of Happiness* [*The Philosophy of Epicurus: Letters, Doctrines, and Parallel Passages from Lucretius*], translated by George K. Strodach, London & New York: Penguin, 2012.

Eusebius, *Praeparatio evangelica* [*Preparation for the Gospel*], translated by Edwin Hamilton Gifford, Eugene: Wipf & Stock, 2002.

Horace, *Satires*, translated by H. Rushton Fairclough, Cambridge MA & London: Harvard University Press, 1942.

Jerome of Stridon [St. Jerome], *Against Jovinianus*, in *St. Jerome: Letters and Select Works*, translated by William H. Fremantle, New York: Christian Literature Company, 1893.

Lucian of Samosata, *Alexander the False Prophet*, in *Works*, Volume IV, Cambridge MA & London: Harvard University Press & William Heinemann, 1925.

Titus Lucretius Carus, *De rerum natura*, translated by W. H. D. Rouse, Cambridge MA & London: Harvard University Press, 1992 [1924]; *The Nature of Things*, translated by A. E. Stallings, London: Penguin, 2007.

Metrodorus, *Peri aisthētōn* [*On the sensible*]; *Metrodori De sensionibus commentaries, Herculanensium voluminum quae supersunt*, t. 6, Naples: Ex regia typographia, 1839; no English translation found.

Philodemus, *Peri rhētorikēs*, Volumina Herculan. [*Papyrus Herculanensis*], v. a. col. 25; *On Rhetoric, Books 1 & 2, Translation and Exegetical Essays*, edited & translated by Clive Chandler, London: Routledge: 2006.

Philodemus, Volum. hercul. [*Papyrus Herculanensis*], *Peri tēs tōn theōn eustochoumenēs diagōgēs, kata Zēnōna* [*On the Way of Life of the Gods*, or *On the life properly lived by the gods, against Zeno*]; listed in Vuola Tsouna, *The Ethics of Philodemus*, Oxford: Oxford University Press, 2011; no English translation found.

Philodemus, *De vitiis*; listed in Vuola Tsouna, *The Ethics of Philodemus*, Oxford: Oxford University Press, 2011; no English translation found.

Plato, *Euthyphro*, in *Five Dialogues*, translated by G. M. A. Gruber, Indianapolis: Hackett, 2002.

Plato, *Apology*, in *Five Dialogues*, translated by G. M. A. Gruber, Indianapolis: Hackett, 2002.

Plato, *Phaedo*, in *Five Dialogues*, translated by G. M. A. Gruber, Indianapolis: Hackett, 2002.

Plautus, *Captivi* [*The Captives*], in *Amphytrion, The Comedy of Asses, The Pot of Gold, The Two Bacchises, The Captives*, translated by Wolfgang de Melo, Cambridge MA & London: Harvard University Press, 2011.

Pliny the Elder, *Naturalis Historia* [*Natural History*], translated by John Bostock & H. T. Riley, London: Taylor & Francis, 1855; also published in ten volumes (Loeb Classics), translation by H. Rackham, W. H. S. Jones, A. C. Andrews, & others, Cambridge MA & London: Harvard University Press, 1949–83.

Plutarch, *Against Colotes; or Reply to Colotes in Defence of the Other Philosophers*, in *Moralia*, volume XIV, translated by Benedict Einarson & Phillip De Lacy, Cambridge MA & London: Harvard University Press, 1967.

Plutarch, *Non posse suaviter vivi secundum Epicurum* [*That Epicurus Actually Makes a Pleasant life Impossible*], in *Moralia*, volume XIV, translated by Benedict Einarson & Phillip De Lacy, Cambridge MA & London: Harvard University Press, 1967.

Plutarch, *On Superstition*, in *Moralia*, volume II, translated by Frank Cole Babbitt, Cambridge MA & London: Harvard University Press, 1928.

Plutarch, *De sollertia animalium* [*Whether Land or Sear Animals are Cleverer*], in *Moralia*, volume XII, translated by Harold Cherniss & William C. Hembold, Cambridge MA & London: Harvard University Press, 1957.
Plutarch, *De fraterno amore* [*On Brotherly Love*], *in Moralia*, volume VI, translated by William C. Hembold, Cambridge MA & London: Harvard University Press, 1939.
Plutarch, *Lives*, nine volumes, translated by Bernadotte Perrin, Cambridge MA & London: Harvard University Press, 1914–20.
Pseudo-Plutarch, *De placitis philosophorum*, in *Plutarch's Morals*, edited by William W. Goodwin, Cambridge MA: Little, Brown, and Co., 1874.
Lucius Annaeus Seneca, *Epistles*, translated by Richard M. Gummere, three volumes, Cambridge MA & London: Harvard University Press, 1996 [1917]; *Letters on Ethics: To Lucilius*, translated by A. A. Long & Maragaret Graver, Chicago & London: University of Chicago Press, 2017.
Lucius Annaeus Seneca, *De consolatione ad Marciam* [*Consolation to Marcia*], translated by Harry M. Hine, in Seneca, *On Hardship & Happiness*, Chicago & London: University of Chicago Press, 2014.
Lucius Annaeus Seneca, *De Beneficiis* [*On Benefits*], translated by Miriam Griffin & Brad Inwood, Chicago & London: University of Chicago Press, 2014.
Sextus Empiricus, *Adversus Mathematicos* [*Against the Professors*], translated by R. G. Bury, Cambridge MA & London: Harvard University Press, 1946.
Sextus Empiricus, *Outlines of Pyrrhonism* [*Pyrrhōneioi hupotypōseis*, or *Outlines of Scepticism*], translated by Benson Mates, New York & Oxford: Oxford University Press, 1996.
Simplicius, *On Aristotle's Physics, 1.3–4*, translated by Pamela Huby & C. C. W. Taylor, London & New York: Bloomsbury, 2011; *On Aristotle Physics 1.5–9*, translated by Han Baltussen, Michael Atkinson, Michael Share & Ian Mueller, London & New York: Bloomsbury, 2014; *On Aristotle's Physics, 2*, translated by Barrie Fleet, London & New York: Bloomsbury, 2014; *On Aristotle's Physics, 3*, translated by J. O. Urmson, London & New York: Bloomsbury, 2014; *On Aristotle's Physics 4.1–5 and 10–14*, translated by J. O. Urmson, London & New York: Bloomsbury, 2014; *On Aristotle's Physics 5*, translated by J. O. Urmson, London & New York: Bloomsbury, 2014; *On Aristotle's Physics 6*, translated by David Konstan, London & New York: Bloomsbury, 2014; *On Aristotle's Physics 8.1–5*, translated by István Bodnár, Michael Chase, Michael Share, London & New York: Bloomsbury, 2014; *On Aristotle's Physics 8.6–10*, translated by Richard D. McKirahan, London & New York: Bloomsbury, 2014.
Joannes Stobaeus, *Sermones* [or *Anthology*], in *Ioannis Stobaei Anthologium*, three volumes, edited by Curtius Wachsmuth & Otto Hence, Berlin: Weidmannsche Buchhandlung, 1894–1912; no English translation found.
Joannes Stobaeus, *Eclogues* [*Physical and Moral Extracts*], edition annotated by Arnold Hermann Ludwig Heeren, *Ioannis Stobaei Eclogarum physicarum et ethicarum libri duo. Ad codd. mss. fidem suppleti et castigati annotatione et versione latina instructi ab Arn. Herm. Ludov. Heeren*, Göttingen: Vandenhoek & Ruprecht, 1792; *Ioannis Stobaei Anthologium*, three volumes, edited by Curtius Wachsmuth & Otto Hence, Berlin: Weidmannsche Buchhandlung, 1894–1912; no English translation found.
Tertullian [Quintus Septimius Florens Tertullianus], *De anima* [*Treatise on the Soul*], edited and translated by J. H. Waszink, Leiden & Boston: Brill, 2010.
Virgil [Publius Vergilius Maro], *Aeneid*, translated by Frederick Ahl, Oxford: Oxford University Press, 2008.

Other references cited by Guyau

Alighieri, Dante, *The Divine Comedy*, translated by Charles H. Sisson, Oxford: Oxford University Press, 2008.
Bain, Alexander, *The Emotions and the Will*, London: John Parker & Son, 1859.
Barni, Jules, *Les moralistes français au dix-huitième siècle*, Paris : Germer Baillière, 1873.
Bayle, Pierre, *Dictionnaire historique et critique*, Rotterdam: Reinier Leers, 1697.
Bentham, Jeremy, *An Introduction to the Principles of Morals and Legislation. New Edition Corrected by the Author*, London: W. Pickering, 1823.
Bentham, Jeremy, *Deontology or the Science of Morality*, manuscript edited by John Bowring, volume 1, London: Longman, Rees, Orme, Browne, Green & Longman, 1834.
Bentham, Jeremy, *The Influence of Natural Religion on the Temporal Happiness of Mankind*, Amherst: Prometheus Books, 2003; Bentham originally published this book under the pseudonym of Philippe Beauchamp (London: R. Carlile, 1822).
Bentham, *Deontology, Together with A Table of the Springs of Action and the Article on Utilitarianism*, edited by Amnon Goldworth, Oxford: Oxford University Press, 1983.
Cardano, Girolamo, *De Subtilitate rerum*, Johann Petreius, Nuremberg, 1550; English edition: *The De subtilitate of Girolamo Cardano*, translated by John M. Forrester, Tempe, Arizona: Arizona Center for Medieval and Renaissance Studies, 2013.
Cardano, Girolamo, *De Vita propria* [1576], Paris: Iacobus Villery, 1653; English edition: *The Book of my Life*, translated by Jean Stoner, New York: New York Review of Books, 2002.
Clark, Henry, *La Rochefoucauld and the language of unmasking in Seventeenth-century France*, Geneva: Droz, 1994.
Collé, Charles, *Journal historique ou Mémoires critiques et littéraires*, volume 2, Paris: Imprimerie Bibliographique, 1807.
D'Alembert, Jean Rond, *Essai sur des éléments de philosophie (1759)*, edited by Richard N. Schwab, Hildescheim : Georg Olms, 1965.
D'Holbach, Paul-Henri Thiry, *Système de la nature ou des loix du monde physique et du monde moral*, London: n/a, 1770 ; text published under the name of M. Mirabaud.
D'Holbach, Paul-Henri Thiry, *Système Social ou Principes naturels de la morale et de la Politique, avec un examen de l'influence du gouvernement sur les mœurs*, London: N/A., 1773.
Erasmus, Desiderius, *Colloquia familiaria et Encomium moriae* [1518], Lipsia: Holtze, 1892; English edition: *The Colloquies of Erasmus*, two volumes, translated by Nathan Bailey, edited by the E. Johnson, London: Reeves and Turner, 1878.
Feuerbach, Ludwig, *Thoughts on Death and Immortality*, translated by James A. Massey, Berkeley & Los Angeles: University of California Press, 1980.
Fouillée, Alfred, *La philosophie de Socrate*. Ouvrage couronnée par l'Académie de sciences morales et politiques, Paris: Librairie philosophique Ladrange, 1874.
Fouillée, Alfred, *Histoire de la philosophie (troisième édition)*, Paris: Delagrave, 1889.
Fox Bourne, Henry Richard, *The Life of John Locke*, volume 1, New York: Harper & Brothers, 1876.
Gassendi, Pierre, *Animadversiones in Librum X Diogenis Laërtii, qui est de vita, moribus, placitisque Epicuri*, Lugduni: Barbier, 1649.
Gizycki, Paul von, *Enleitende Bemerkungen zu einer Untersuchung uber den Wert der naturphilosophie des Epikur*, Berlin: Gärtners Verlag, 1884.
Grimm, Friedrich Melchior, *Correspondance littéraire, philosophique, et critique*, volume 2, Paris: Furne, 1829.

Helvétius, Calude-Adrien, *De l'esprit*, Paris: Duran, 1758 ; English edition: *De l'esprit, or Essays on the Mind and its Several Faculties, Translated from the French to which is now prefixed A Life of the Authors*, translated by n/a, London: J. M. Richardson, Sherwood, Nelly and Jones, 1809.

Helvétius, Calude-Adrien, *De l'homme, de ses facultés intellectuelles et de son éducation (œuvre posthume de M. Helvétius)*, London: Société Typographique, 1773.

Hobbes, Thomas, *Man and Citizen (De Homine and De Cive)*, translated by Charles T. Wood, Bernard Gert, Thomas S. K. Scott-Craig, Indianapolis & Cambridge: Hackett, 1991.

Hobbes, Thomas, *De Cive*, edited by Howard Warrender, Oxford University Press, 1983.

Hobbes, Thomas, *On the Citizen*, translated by Richard Tuck & Michael Silverthorne, Cambridge: Cambridge University Press, 1998.

Hobbes, Thomas, *Leviathan*, edited by Richard Tuck, Cambridge: Cambridge University Press, 1996.

Jouffroy, Théodore Simon, *Cours de droit naturel*, volume 1, Paris: Librairie de L. Hachette, 1843.

La Mettrie, Julien Offray de, *De la volupté: l'anti-Sénèque ou le souverain bien; l'École de la volupté; système d'Épicure*, edited by Ann Thomson, Paris: Desjonquères, 1996.

La Mettrie, Julien Offray de, *Machine Man and Other Writings*, edited and translated by Ann Thomson Cambridge: Cambridge University Press, 1996.

Lange, Friedrich Albert, *Histoire du matérialisme et critique de son importance à notre époque*, translated by B. Pommerol, Paris : Reinwald, 1877; originally published as *Geschichte des Materialismus und Kritik seiner Bedeutung in der Gegenwart*, 1866.

La Rochefoucauld, François de, *Collected maxims and other reflections*, translated by E. H. and A. M Blackmore and Francine Giguère, Oxford: Oxford University Press, 2007.

La Rochefoucauld, François de, *Reflections; or Sentences and Moral Maxims*, translated by J. W. Willis Bund & B. and J. Hain Friswell, London: Simpson Low, Son, and Marston, 1871.

Locke, John, *Some Familiar Letters Between Mr. Locke and Several of His Friends, The Works of John Locke*, volume 3, London: Arthur Bettesworth, John Pemberton & Edward Symon, 1727.

Locke, John, *An Essay concerning Human Understanding*, Oxford: Oxford University Press, 2008.

Lord King, Peter, *The Life of John Locke, with Extracts from his Correspondence, Journals, and Common-Place Books*, two volumes, London: Henry Colburn & Richard Bentley, 1830.

Martha, Constant, *Le poème de Lucrèce: morale, religion et science*, Paris: Librairie Hachette, 1869.

Mill, John Stuart, *A System of Logic, Ratiocinative and Inductive, being a connected view of the principles of evidence and the methods of scientific investigation*, London: John W. Parker, 1843.

Montaigne, Michel de, *The Complete Essays*, translated by Michael A. Screech, London & New York: Penguin, 1993.

Montesquieu, *The Spirit of the Laws*, edited and translated by Anne M. Cohler, Basia C. Miller & Harold S. Stone, Cambridge: Cambridge University Press, 1989.

Ozanam, Frédéric, *Dante et la philosophie catholique au XIIIème siècle*, Paris: V. Lecoffre, 1845.

Pascal, Blaise, *Pensées and Other Writings*, translated by Honor Levi, Oxford: Oxford University Press, 1995.

Ravaisson, Félix, *Essai sur la Métaphysique d'Aristote*, volume 2, Paris: Librairie de Joubert, 1845.
Renouvier, Charles, 'Les labyrinthes de la métaphysique. VIII – Le libre arbitre selon les épicuriens et le commentaire de M. Guyau', *La critique philosophique*, n° VIII, 25 mars 1880, dans *La critique philosophique, politique, scientifique, littéraire. Neuvième année*, Paris, Bureau de la Critique philosophique, 1880, 113–23.
Ribot, Théodule, *La psychologie anglaise contemporaine : L'école expérimentale*, Paris: Librairie philosophique de Ladrange, 1870.
Ritter, Heinrich, *Histoire de la philosophie*, translated by Clément-Joseph Tissot, Paris: Librairie philosophique de Ladrange, 1835–6.
Rousseau, Jean-Jacques, *Lettres de Deux Amans, Habitants d'une petite Ville au pied des Alpes*, Amsterdam: Marc-Michel Rey, 1761.
Rousseau, Jean-Jacques, *Julie, or The New Héloïse. Letters of Two Lovers Who Live in a Small Town at the Foot of the Alps*, translated by Philip Stewart and Jean Vaché (The Collected Writings of Rousseau, volume 6), Lebanon NH: Dartmouth College Press & University Press of New England, 1997.
Salisbury, John of, *Policraticus, sive de nugis curialium et de vestigiis philosophorum*, Leiden [Lugduni Batavorum]: ex officina Ioannis Maire, 1639; English edition: *Policraticus: Of the frivolities of courtiers and the footprints of philosophers*, translated by Cary J. Nederman, Cambridge: Cambridge University Press, 1990.
Spencer, Herbert, *Principles of Psychology*, London: Longman, Brown, Green and Longmans, 1855.
Spinoza, Benedict de, *Ethics*, London & New York: Penguin, 1996.
Spinoza, Benedict de, *Complete Works*, translated by Samuel Shirley, edited by Michael L. Morgan, Indianapolis & Cambridge: Hackett, 2002.
Strauss, David Friedrich, *The Old Faith and the New: A Confession*, translated by Mathilde Blind, second edition, London: Asher & Co., 1873.
Volney, Constantin-François, *Les ruines. La loi naturelle*, Paris: Librairie de la Bibliothèque nationale, 1879; *La loi naturelle* was originally published in 1793 with the subtitle *Catéchisme du Citoyen français*.
Zeller, Eduard, *Die Philosophie der Griechen*, Leipzig: Verlag R. Reisland, 1882 [Tübingen: Fuess Verlag 1862].

General bibliography

Ansell-Pearson, Keith, 'True to the Earth: Nietzsche's Epicurean Care of Self and World', in Horst Hutter and Eli Friedland (eds.), *Nietzsche's Therapeutic Teaching for Individuals and Culture*, London & New York: Bloomsbury, 2013.
Ansell-Pearson, Keith, 'Heroic-Idyllic Philosophizing: Nietzsche and the Epicurean Tradition', *Royal Institute of Philosophy Supplements*, 74, 2014, 237–63.
Bachofen, Johann Jakob, *Myth, Religion, and Mother Right: Selected Writings of J. J. Bachofen*, translated by Ralph Manheim, Princeton: Princeton University Press, 1967.
Boase, Alan Martin, *The Fortunes of Montaigne. A History of the Essays in France, 1580–1669*, London: Methuen and Co., 1935; New York, Octagon, 1970.
De Champs, Emmanuelle, *Enlightenment and Utility: Bentham in French, Bentham in France*, Cambridge: Cambridge University Press, 2015.
Deleuze, Gilles, 'Lucretius and Naturalism', translated by Jared C. Bly, in Abraham Jacob Greenstine & Ryan J. Johnson (eds.), *Contemporary Encounters with Ancient Metaphysics*, Edinburgh: Edinburgh University Press, 2017, 245–54.

Foucault, Michel, *Ethics, Subjectivity and Truth. The Essential Works of Michel Foucault (1954–1984)*, volume 1, edited by Paul Rabinow, translated by Robert Hurley and others, London & New York: Penguin, 1994.

Fustel de Coulanges, Numa Denis, *La Cité antique, étude sur le culte, le droit, les institutions de la Grèce et de Rome*, Paris: Durand, 1864; English edition: *The Ancient City: A Study on the Religion, Laws and Institutions of Greece and Rome*, translated by Willard Small, Boston: Lee & Shepard, 1877.

Gombaud de Plassac, Josias; Nicole, Pierre & Huet, Pierre-Daniel, 'Trois extraits autour de Montaigne', *Cahiers philosophiques*, 114, 2008, 88–96.

Grimal, Pierre, *A Concise Dictionary of Classical Mythology*, edited by Stephen Kershaw, translated by A. R. Maxwell-Hyslop, Oxford & Cambridge: Basil Blackswell, 1990.

Hadot, Pierre, *Qu'est-ce que la philosophie antique?* Paris: Gallimard, 1995.

Hadot, Pierre, *Philosophy as a Way of Life*, edited by Arnold I. Davidson, translated by Michael Chase, Malden & Oxford: Blackwell, 1995.

Hadot, Pierre, *The Selected Writings of Pierre Hadot: Philosophy as Practice*, edited and translated by Matthew Sharpe and Federico Testa, London & New York: Bloomsbury, 2020.

Irwin, Terence, *The Development of Ethics*, volume 1, Oxford: Oxford University Press, 2007.

James, William, *The Will to Believe*, New York, Dover, 1956.

Kant, Immanuel, *Ethical Philosophy*, translated by James W. Ellington, Indianapolis: Hackett, 1983.

Kant, Immanuel, *Lectures on Ethics*, translated by Peter Heath, Cambridge: Cambridge University Press, 1997.

Mitsis, Phillip, *Epicurus' Ethical Theory: The Pleasures of Invulnerability*, Cornell: Cornell University Press, 1988.

Montinari, Mazzino, 'Nietzsche e la décadence', *Studia Nieztscheana*, 2014.

Moore, G. E., *Principia Ethica*, Cambridge: Cambridge University Press, 1993.

Nietzsche, Friedrich, *The Birth of Tragedy & The Case of Wagner*, translated by Walter Kaufmann, New York: Vintage Books/Random House, 1967.

Nietzsche, Friedrich, *The Will to Power*, translated by Walter Kaufmann & R. J. Hollingdale, New York: Random House, 1967.

Nietzsche, Friedrich, *The Gay Science,* translated by Walter Kaufmann, New York: Random House, 1974.

Nietzsche, Friedrich, *Nachgelassene Fragmente 1884–5, Kritische Studienausgabe*, edited by Giorgio Colli & Mazzino Montinari, Berlin: Walter de Gruyter, 1988.

Nietzsche, Friedrich, *Dawn. Thoughts on the Presumptions of Morality*, translated by Brittain Smith, Stanford: Stanford University Press, 2011.

Nietzsche, Friedrich, *The Wanderer and His Shadow*, translated by Gary Handwerk, Stanford: Stanford University Press, 2013.

Porter, James I., 'Epicurean Attachments: Life, Pleasure, Beauty, Friendship, and Piety', *Cronache Ercolanesi*, 33, 2003, 205–27.

Rosen, Frederick, *Classical Utilitarianism from Hume to Mill*, London: Routledge, 2003.

Royce, Josiah, *Studies of Good and Evil: A Series of Essays upon problems of Philosophy and of Life*, New York: Appleton & Co., 1899.

Tarde, Gabriel, *Penal Philosophy*, translated by P. Berne, New Brunswick/London: Transaction Publishers, 2001.

Thomson, Ann, *Bodies of Thought. Science, Religion and the Soul in the Early Enlightenment*, Oxford: Oxford University Press, 2008.

Tolstoy, Leo, *What is Art?* translated by A. Maude, Introduction by V. Tomas, Indianapolis: Hackett, 1996.
Volpilhac, Aude, 'Du bon et du mauvais usage des Essais au XVIIe siècle', *Cahiers philosophiques*, 114, 2008, 85–7.

Texts by Jean-Marie Guyau

Books

La morale d'Épicure et ses rapports avec les doctrines contemporaines, Paris: Germer Baillière, 1878; seventh edition, Paris Félix Alcan, 1927; new French edition by Gilbert Romeyer Dherbey and Jean-Baptiste Gourinat, Paris: Encre Marine, 2002.
La morale anglaise contemporaine. Morale de l'utilité et de l'évolution, Paris: Germer Baillière, 1879; second edition, Paris: Félix Alcan, 1885.
Vers d'un philosophe, Paris: Félix Alcan, 1881.
Les problèmes d'esthétique contemporaine, Paris: Félix Alcan, 1884.
Esquisse d'une morale sans obligation ni sanction, Paris: Félix Alcan, 1885; second edition established by Alfred Fouillée, Paris: Félix Alcan, 1890; English edition: *A Sketch of Morality Independent of Obligation or Sanction*, translated by Gertrude Kapteyn, London: Watts & Co., 1898.
L'irreligion de l'avenir. Étude sociologique, Paris: Félix Alcan, 1887; English edition: *The Non-Religion of the Future*, translated by n/a, London: William Heinemann, 1897.
L'art au point de vue sociologique, edited by Alfred Fouillée, Paris: Félix Alcan, 1889.
Éducation et hérédité. Étude sociologique, edited by Alfred Fouillée, Paris: Félix Alcan, 1889; English edition: *Education and Heredity: A Sociological Study*, translated from the second edition by W. J. Greenstreet, introduction by G. F. Stout, London: Walter Scott, 1891.
La genèse de l'idée de temps, edited by Alfred Fouillée, Paris: Félix Alcan, 1890; English translation in J. A. Michon, V. Pouthas, & J. L. Jackson (eds.), *Guyau and the Idea of Time*, Amsterdam: North Holland Publishing Co., 1988.
La première année de lecture courante, Paris: Colin, 1875.
La littérature chrétienne du IIe au VIe siècle. Extraits des Pères de l'Eglise latine, suivi d'extraits des poètes chrétiens, Paris: Delagrave, 1876.
L'Année enfantine de lecture, Paris: Colin, 1883.
L'Année préparatoire de lecture courante, Paris: Colin, 1884.
La méthode Guyau. Lecture par l'écriture, Paris: Colin, 1893.

Articles

'La contingence dans la nature et la liberté selon Épicure', in *Revue Philosophique*, t. IV, 1877, 47–71.
'La théorie d'Épicure sur la mort et ses rapports avec les théories contemporaines', in *Revue des séances et travaux de l'Académie des Sciences morales et politiques*, t. CXI, 1879, 350–77.
'L'hérédité morale et Herbert Spencer', in *Revue philosophique*, t. VII, 1879, 308–15.
'L'origine des religions', in *Revue philosophique*, t. VIII, 1879, 561–84.
'La morale de Darwin', in *Revue bleue*, t. XVI, 1879, 860–5.

'Les plaisirs du beau et les plaisirs du jeu, d'après l'école de évolution', in *Revue des deux Mondes*, t. XLVI, 1881, 750–78.
'Un problème d'esthétique. L'antagonisme de l'art et de la science', in *Revue des deux Mondes*, t. CX, 1883, 356–87.
'Critique de l'idée de sanction', in *Revue philosophique*, t. XV, 1883, 243–81.
'L'évolution de l'idée de temps dans la conscience', in *Revue philosophique*, t. XIX, 1885, 353–8.
'Les hypothèses sur l'immortalité de l'âme dans la philosophie de l'évolution', in *Revue des deux Mondes*, t. L XXVII, 1886, 176–201.
'La religion et l'irreligion de l'avenir', in *Revue bleue*, t. XII, 1886, 240–6.
'Le pessimisme comme religion de l'avenir', in *Revue bleue*, t. XII, 1886, 308–13.

Books edited & translated

Epictetus, *Manuel, précédée d'un Étude sur la philosophie d'Épictète* par Jean-Marie Guyau, suivi d'extraits des *Entretiens d'Épictète et des Pensées de Marc-Auréle*, Paris: Delagrave, 1875.
Pascal, Blaise, *Entretien avec M. de Saci sur Épictète et Montaigne*, précédé d'une Notice par Jean-Marie Guyau et suivi d'extraits de Montaigne; *De l'autorité et du progrès en philosophie*, suivi d'extraits et d'éclaircissements relatifs à l'histoire de l'idée du progrès, Paris: Delagrave, 1875.
Epictetus, *Manuel*, Greek text, Paris: Delagrave, 1876.
Cicero, *Des suprêmes biens et des suprêmes maux (livres I et II, exposition et critique de la philosophie épicurienne)*, traduit par Desmarais, suivie d'extraits et d'éclaircissements relatifs à l'histoire de l'épicurisme, Paris: Delagrave, 1875.
Cicero, *De finibus bonorum et malorum (livres I et II)*, Latin text, Paris: Delagrave, 1876.
Étude sur la Philosophie d'Épictète et traduction du Manuel d'Épictète, Paris : Delagrave, 1875.
La littérature chrétienne du IIe au VIe siècle, Extraits des Pères de l'Église latine, suivi d'extraits de poètes chrétiens, Paris: Delagrave, 1876.

Texts on Jean-Marie Guyau[1]

Andolfi, Ferruccio, 'Nietzsche et Guyau. Consentements, dissonances, silences', *Corpus*, 46, 2004, 109–24.
Ansell-Pearson, Keith, 'Free spirits and free thinkers: Nietzsche and Guyau on the Future of Morality', in Jeffrey A. Metzger (ed.), *Nietzsche, Nihilism, and the Philosophy of the Future*, New York: Continuum, 2009, 102–24.
Ansell-Pearson, Keith, 'Beyond Obligation? Jean-Marie Guyau on Life and Ethics', *Royal Institute of Philosophy Supplement*, 77, 2015, 207–25.
Ansell-Pearson, Keith & Testa, Federico, 'Jean-Marie Guyau on Life and Morality', in Mark Sinclair & Daniel Whistler (eds.), *Oxford Handbook of Modern French Philosophy*, Oxford: Oxford University Press, forthcoming.
Archambault, Paul, *Guyau*, Paris: Librairie Blond & Cie., 1911.
Aslan, Gabriel, *La morale selon Guyau et ses rapports avec les conceptions actuelles de la morale scientifique (Thèse pour le doctorat d'université présentée à la Faculté de Lettres de Paris)*, Paris: Félix Alcan, 1906.

Behrent, Michael, 'Le débat Guyau-Durkheim sur la théorie sociologique de la religion. Une nouvelle querelle des universaux?' *Archives de sciences sociales des religions*, 53ᵉ année, no. 142, 2008, 9–26.

Bergmann, Ernst, *Die Philosophie Guyaus*, Leipzig: Kinkhardt, 1912.

Bergson, Henri, 'Compte rendu de *La genèse de l'idée de temps* de Guyau', *Revue philosophique de la France et de l'étranger*, 21, 1891, 185–90.

Carrel, Frank, 'The Morals of Guyau', *International Journal of Ethics*, 15, 4, 1905, 457–69.

Contini, Annamaria, *Jean-Marie Guyau: Una filosofia della vita e l'estetica*, Bologna: CLUEB, 1995.

Contini, Annamaria, 'Plus que la vie. L'esthétique sociologique de Guyau', *Corpus*, 46, 2004, 67–92.

Dauriac, Lionel, 'Philosophes contemporains: J.-M. Guyau', in *L'Année philosophique. Premier année – 1890*, Paris : Félix Alcan, 1891, 191–225.

Durkheim, Émile, 'De L'irréligion de l'avenir', in *Revue Philosophique*, 23, 1887.

Durkheim, Émile, 'The Conception of Religion', in *Emile Durkheim: Selected Writings*, edited and translated by Anthony Giddens, Cambridge: Cambridge University Press, 1972, 219–22.

Dwelshauvers, Georges, 'De l'idée de vie chez Guyau' (Séance du 28 décembre 1905), discussion with R. Berthelot, L. Dauriac, edited by A. Colin, *Bulletin de la Société Française de Philosophie*, 6, 43, 1906.

Fedi, Laurent, 'Guyau et Darwin: la lecture de la vie', *Corpus*, 46, 2004, 25–46.

Fidler, Geoffrey C., 'On Jean-Marie Guyau, *Immoraliste*', *Journal of the History of Ideas*, 55, 1994, 75–98.

Fouillée, Alfred, *La morale, l'art et la religion d'après Guyau*, Paris: Félix Alcan, 1889; 'Note Biographique', Paris: Félix Alcan, 1913.

Fouillée, Alfred, 'The Ethics of Guyau and Nietzsche', *International Journal of Ethics*, 13, 1, 1902.

Franco, Vittoria, 'Individu moderne, responsabilité, éclatement des hiérarchies sociales', *Corpus*, 46, 2004, 153–72.

Hablitzel, Hans, 'Jean-Marie Guyau: penseur interdisciplinaire et sociologue', *Corpus*, 46, 2004, 17–24.

Harding, Frank Williams, *Jean-Marie Guyau (1854–1888). Aesthetician and Sociologist*, Geneva: Droz, 1973.

Høffding, Harald, *A Brief History of Modern Philosophy*, translated by Charles. F. Sanders, New York: Macmillan, 1912 [1894].

Jankélévitch, Vladimir, 'Deux philosophes de la vie: Bergson et Guyau', *Revue philosophique*, t. XCVII, 1924, 402–49.

Jordan, D., *Guyau: the Man, the Thinker, the Writer*, New York: Macmillan, 1903.

Kropotkin, Peter, *Ethics: Origin and Development*, translated by L. S. Friedland & J. R. Piroshnikoff, New York: Lincoln McVeagh/Dial Press, 1942.

Lampl, Hans Erich, *Zweistimmigkeit – Einstimmigkeit? Friedrich Nietzsche und Jean-Marie Guyau*, Cuxhaven: Junghans, 1990.

Llevadot, Laura, 'Spinoza et Guyau: l'étique du *conatus*', *Corpus*, 46, 2004, 47–56.

Maffesoli, Michel, *Au creux des apparences : pour une éthique de l'esthétique*, Paris: Plon, 1990.

Malblanc, Alfred, *L'irréligion de l'avenir d'après Guyau*, Geneva: Société générale d'imprimerie, 1904.

Molina, Enrique, *Dos filosofos contemporaneos: Guyau – Bergson*, Santiago de Chile: Editorial Nascimineto, 1926.
Moore, G. E., 'Book Review: A Sketch of Morality Independent of Obligation or Sanction. M. Guyau, Gertrude Kapteyn', *International Journal for Ethics* 9, 2, 1899.
Muller, Laurent, *Jean-Marie Guyau ou l'éthique sans modèle*, Villeneuve d'Ascq: Presses universitaires du Septentrion, 2018.
Pénaud, Dominique, 'Ce Brave Guyau', *Nietzsche Studien*, 25, 1996, 239–54.
Pinilla, Scheherezade, 'La littérature face au spleen. Génie et sociabilité dans la pensée de J.-M. Guyau', *Corpus*, 46, 2004, 93–108.
Orru, Marco, *Anomie. History and Meanings*, Winchester: Allen & Unwin, 1987.
Pastore, Annibale, *Giovanni Maria Guyau e la genesi dell'idea di tempo*, Lugano: Coenobium, 1907.
Pfeil, Hans, *Jean-Marie Guyau und die Philosophie des Lebens*, Augsburg: Benno Filser, 1928.
Picht, Carl, *Hypnose, Suggestion und Erziehung, im Anschluss an Jean-Marie Guyau*, Leipzig: Klinkhardt, 1913.
Ragghianti, Renzo, 'Hiérarchie ouverte et éthique de l'effort : Fouillée, Guyau, Durkheim', *Corpus*, 46, 2004, 93–108.
Riba, Jordi, *La morale anomique de Jean-Marie Guyau*, translated by Mariló Fedz Estrada, Paris: L'Harmattan, 1999.
Riba, Jordi, 'L'au-delà du devoir. Guyau précurseur de la morale de notre temps', *Corpus*, 46, 2004, 57–66.
Riba, Jordi (ed.), *L'effet Guyau: De Nietzsche aux anarchistes*, Paris: L'Harmattan, 2014.
Ricoeur, Paul, 'From Kant to Guyau', in J. A. Michon, V. Pouthas & J. L. Jackson (eds.), *Guyau and the Idea of Time*, Amsterdam: North Holland Publishing Co., 1988.
Riba, Jordi, & Hablitzel, Hans, 'Bibliographie', *Corpus*, 46, 2004, 13–16.
Saltel, Philippe, *La puissance de la vie. Essai sur L'Esquisse d'une morale sans obligation ni sanction de Jean-Marie Guyau*, Paris: Belles Lettres, 2008.
Sidgwick, Henry, 'M. Guyau, La Morale d'Épicure et ses Rapports avec les Doctrines contemporaines', *Mind* 4, 582, 1879.
Testa, Federico, 'Jean-Marie Guyau's Presence and Absence in the History of Philosophy', *Pli: The Warwick Journal of Philosophy*, Volume 30: Restoration and Resistance, 2019, 234–53.
Testa, Federico, 'Guyau's Spinoza: Between Epicureanism and Stoicism', *Parrhesia. A Journal of Critical Philosophy*, 32, 2020, 23–32.
Testa, Federico, 'Guyau and Nietzsche on the Temporality of Epicurean Pleasure', in Vinod Acharya & Ryan Johnson (eds.), *Nietzsche and Epicurus. Nature, Health and Ethics*, London & New York: Bloomsbury, 2020, 96–109.
Testa, Federico, 'Jean-Marie Guyau', *Bloomsbury Encyclopaedia of Philosophy*, London & New York: Bloomsbury, 2020. Accessed November 25, 2020. http://dx.doi.org/10.5040/9781350994997.0015.
Testa, Federico & Dennis, Matthew, 'Pleasure and Self-Cultivation in Guyau and Nietzsche', *The Agonist*, volume X, issue II, spring 2017, 94–117.
Walther-Dulk, Ilse, *Materialien zur Philosophie und Ästhetik Jean-Marie Guyau*, Hamburg: Verlag die Brigantine, 1965.
Walther-Dulk, Ilse, 'Sur Guyau et Nietzsche', *Sociétés*, 58, 1997, 13–24.
Walther-Dulk, Ilse, *De Guyau à Proust: Essai sur l'actualité d'un philosophe oublié*, Weimar: VDG, 2008.

Notes

1. For a more comprehensive bibliography (especially French, German and Italian sources), see Contini, *Jean-Marie Guyau: Una filosofia della vita e l'estetica* (1995) and Saltel, *La puissance de la vie. Essai sur* L'Esquisse d'une morale sans obligation ni sanction *de Jean-Marie Guyau* (2008), as well as Walther-Dulk, *De Guyau à Proust* (2008) and Riba & Hablitzel, 'Bibliographie', *Corpus,* 46, 2004. I have consulted their bibligraphies and added relevant studies of the anglophone scholarship on Guyau.

Index of Names

Académie des Sciences Morales et
    Politiques vii, xiii, xiv, xxviii, xxix,
    xxx, 16, 254
Ahasuerus 94
Alexander the Great 96
Alexandria (school of) 157, 164
Antisthenes 119
Aquinas, Thomas 83n
Archimedes 157
Aristippus, xx, 12, 17n, 19n, 27–31, 32n,
    37–40, 43n, 45n, 50, 96, 124n, 242
Aristotle, xix, 11–12, 14–16, 36, 39, 58n,
    134, 156, 163, 165, 168, 200
Augustine of Hippo, xiii, 2, 6n

Bacchus (god) 91
Bacon, Francis 135, 141, 156, 198, 207
Bacon, Roger 133, 135, 141
Bain, Alexander 89, 92, 103n, 111, 118, 125,
    130n, 229
Barni, Jules, 223
Bayle, Pierre 57, 69, 93, 99, 104n
Beauchamp, Philippe 105n
Bentham, Jeremy xiv, 3, 23, 89n, 96, 105n,
    111, 115, 118, 187–8, 194, 202,
    205–6, 221, 222n, 228n, 235n, 241
Bergson, Henri xi
Bossuet, Jacques-Bénigne Lignel 83n, 178
Brucker, Jakob 23, 93
Büchner, Ludwig 89, 94

Caius Julius 230
Calanus 96
Callicles 15, 125, 170, 214
Cardan (Cardano, Girolamo) 174
Carneades 61, 68–9, 82
Caro, Elme-Marie vii, xiii–xiv, xxix, xxx
Carrau, Ludovic vii
Cavalcanti, Guido 164
Cerberus (mythology) 91
Chapelle (Claude-Emmanuel Luillier) 166

Chrysippus 17n, 68, 82n
Cicero vii, xxx[n], xv, 1, 6n, 42, 44n, 53, 61,
    63, 67–8, 79, 80n, 83, 91, 111,
    116–17, 119, 148, 151, 153n, 239
Cocytus (mythology) 91
Colotes 158
Comte, Auguste 155, 157, 159n
Condorcet, Nicolas de 135
    Lycée xi

Dalembert (Jean-Baptiste le Rond
    d'Alembert) 220, 229, 231–2, 235n,
    237n, 241
Darwin, Charles 3, 66, 139, 220, 230
Deleuze, Gilles xix
Democritus xv, 23, 156, 173, 244
Des Barreaux (Jacques Vallé) 166
Descartes, René 83n, 141, 165–6
D'Holbach (Paul-Henri Thiry, Baron
    d'Holbach) 3, 171, 173, 188, 195,
    208, 217, 220, 229, 231–2, 236n,
    237n, 240–2, 244
Diderot, Denis 171, 173, 208, 237
Diocles 150, 151
Diogenes Laertius ix, 1, 39, 104n, 119, 124,
    144n, 158
Dupuy, Henri 165
Durkheim, Émile xi, xxiii

Eleusis 141
Epictetus xiii, 1, 113, 165
Epicurus vii–xxii, xxiii[n], xxiv[n], xxv[n],
    xxix–xxx, 1–5, 6n, 11–15, 16n, 17n,
    18n, 19n, 21–3, 24n, 27–31, 32n,
    35–41, 42n, 43n, 44n, 45n, 49–51,
    53–6, 57n, 58n, 59n, 61–4, 66–78,
    79n, 80n, 81n, 82n, 83n, 84n, 85n,
    86n, 87n, 89–99, 101–2, 104n,
    111–20, 120n, 122n, 124n, 125–8,
    129n, 130n, 131n, 133–6, 138–9,
    142, 144n, 147–52, 152n, 153n,

155–9, 159n, 161, 163–8, 170, 172–3, 177, 179, 184, 187, 191n, 195–6, 199–200, 209–10, 212, 216, 219, 221, 222n, 230, 232, 239–40, 242–5
Erasmus of Rotterdam 164, 230
Euhemerus (mythographer) 53

Farinata degli Uberti 164
Feuerbach, Ludwig, xvii, 57n, 59n, 89–90, 95, 105n
Fontenelle, Bernard Le Bovier de 229–30
Fouillée, Alfred, vii, xi–xiv, xxxi, 199, 204n
Fustel de Coulanges, Numa Denis 102n, 144n

Gassendi, Pierre xiv, xvii, 3, 23, 163, 165–6, 175n, 239, 244
Goldstein, Kurt, xxiv[n]
Gomperz, Theodor 85n
Gorgias 43n, 93, 125, 226
Gourinat, Jean-Baptiste ix, 152n
Grimm, Friedrich Melchior 223n

Hadot, Pierre viii, xv, xx, xxv[n]
Hegesias of Cyrene 89, 96–7
Helvétius, Claude Adrien xiv–xv, xvii, 3, 18n, 23, 171, 173, 184, 187, 188, 194n, 195, 199, 205–21, 222n, 223n, 225n, 227n, 229–33, 235n, 240, 242, 244
Heraclitus 12
Hercules 91, 96
Herodotus (Epicurus' disciple) 135
Hipparchus 157
Hobbes, Thomas xiv–xv, xvii, 3, 19n, 23, 120, 126, 128, 137–8, 144n, 158, 163, 165–73, 175n, 176n, 177–9, 182, 184, 186, 189n, 195–6, 199–201, 204n, 206–7, 209–12, 219, 222n, 223n, 229, 232–3, 236n, 239–40, 242–4
Horace xxv[n], 133, 140–1
Hume, David 151

James, William xi
Jesus 90, 163–4
Joannes Stobaeus 84n
John of Salisbury 164

Jouffroy, Simon Joseph Théodore 82n, 189n
Jupiter (god) 1, 37, 62, 77, 93–4, 112, 147, 150, 152

Kant, Immanuel xiv, xvi, xxiv[n], xxv[n], 3, 11, 13, 16, 51, 86n, 151, 200, 207, 239, 245
Kropotkin, Peter (Pyotr) xi
Kythera (island) 119

La Mettrie, Julien Offray de xv, xvii, 184, 229–31, 235n, 240, 242, 244
La Rochefoucauld, François de xvii, 3, 18n, 99, 177–88, 188n, 189n, 192n, 193n, 194n, 196, 206, 208–11, 221, 231
Lactantius 99, 148, 152n, 153n
Lamarck, Jean-Baptiste 66
Lange, Friedrich Albert 54, 136, 139, 151, 235, 239–40
Lazarus (Bible) 90
Leibniz, Gottfried Wilhelm 51, 83n, 85n, 231
Leucippus 63
Locke, John 135, 165, 171, 206, 221n, 222n, 232
Lucian of Samosata 1, 57n
Lucretius ix, 133–42, 143n, 144n, 147, 156, 158–9, 165, 243–4

Madame du Deffand (Marie Anne de Vichy-Chamrond) 228
Maine de Biran (François-Pierre-Gontier de Biran) 61, 64
Malebranche, Nicolas 86
Mandeville, Bernard de 240
Manlius Torquatus 177
Marcus Aurelius xiii, 1, 98
Martha, Constant 140
Menoeceus 15, 74, 92, 96
Metrodorus 21, 23, 55, 66, 76, 81n, 98, 113, 116, 119, 128, 168
Midas (king) 15
Mill, John Stuart vii, xxx, xxx[n], 3, 23, 25n, 55, 58n, 111, 118, 185, 222n, 229, 235n, 241
Montaigne, Michel de xiv, 2, 6n, 141, 164–5, 174n, 212, 234, 237n

Montesquieu (Charles-Louis de Secondat, baron de Montesquieu) 3, 173, 176n, 223n, 233, 237n
Moore, George Edward xi

Nietzsche, Friedrich xi, xix, xxi, xxiii[n], xxv[n], 106n, 190n, 204n

Orcus (mythology) 38, 43n
Orpheus (mythology) 134
Owen, Robert 118, 184

Pascal, Blaise 92, 100, 128, 130n, 141, 163, 165–6, 183, 234, 237n
Périer, Marguerite 166
Petronius 230
Phidias 150
Philodemus of Gadara 122n, 124n, 130n, 152, 154n, 230
Pico della Mirandola, Giovanni 141
Plato 12, 14–16, 28, 32n, 36–7, 43n, 51, 63, 104n, 125, 133, 156–7, 196, 214, 226n, 239
Pliny (the Elder) 157
Plutarch 1, 53, 61, 63, 75, 91, 116
Polyaenus 119
Porter, James xx
Posidonius 151
Protagoras 93
Ptolemy (king) 96
Pyrrho xiv, 2, 11, 125

Rabelais, François 165
Rambaldi da Imola, Benvenuto 164
Ravaisson, Félix 44n, 45n
Renan, Ernest 147, 151
Renouvier, Charles-Bernard 85–7
Ritter, Heinrich 136, 239
Rousseau, Jean-Jacques xxiv[n], 3, 120, 142, 144, 216, 233, 236n
Royce, Josiah xi

Saint-Just, Louis Antoine de 219
Saint-Lambert Jean-François de 3, 171, 229, 232, 234

Saturn (god) 93
Saturn (planet) 128, 130n
Schopenhauer, Arthur xv, 86, 89–90, 93, 96, 104n
Seneca xiii, xxi, 1, 95, 97, 103n, 116, 124n, 133, 141, 151, 158, 187, 230, 237n
Sidgwick, Henry xi
Sisyphus (mythology) 101
Socrates 12, 15–16, 16n, 17n, 19n, 21–2, 36, 38, 53, 63, 98, 102n, 133, 151, 156–7, 200
Spencer, Herbert 3, 23, 54, 66, 89, 102n, 139, 143n, 201, 204n, 222–3, 241
Spinoza, Baruch xi, xvii, 195–201, 201n, 202n, 203n, 204n, 206–7, 210, 224n, 232–3, 237n, 240
Strauss, David Friedrich 89–90, 94
Suard, Jean-Baptiste-Antoine 234

Tacitus 183
Tantalus (mythology) 91, 101
Tarde, Gabriel xi
Theodorus 53
Theseus (mythology) 116
Tolstoy, Leo xi, xviii[n]
Torquatus 57, 84, 116
Turgot Anne Robert Jacques 3, 141

Ulysses 103n

Vacherot, Étienne 147, 151
Vanini, Lucilio ('Giulio Cesare') 165
Velleius 57n, 74
Viau, Théophile 166
Virgil 42n, 133, 140
Volney, Constantin-François 171, 188, 229, 232–3, 241
Voltaire (François-Marie Arouet) 178, 188, 223n, 224

William of Orange 171

Zeller, Eduard 58n, 83n, 136, 239
Zeno of Citium 62, 165, 168, 195, 200, 232

Index of Subjects

action vii–viii, xvi–xx, xxviii, 4, 5, 12, 15, 18n, 22, 28, 30–1, 32n, 52, 67–9, 73, 78n, 86, 95, 104n, 114, 120, 126, 134, 147, 164–5, 177, 179, 181, 184–5, 187, 206–13, 215, 219, 221, 225n, 226n, 230–1, 234, 240–3
aesthetic, xxi–xxii, 21–2, 31, 33n, 95, 157
affect xvii, 55, 58n, 59n, 198–200, 203n
affection 100, 115, 117–19, 121n, 150, 157, 168, 181–4, 193n, 231, 236n
afterlife 89, 90, 92
agency 66, 74
alienation 57n, 59n, 172
altruism, xii, xvii, 241
anatomy, xv, xvi, xviii
animal, xix, xxvii, 12, 17n, 51, 72–3, 77, 85n, 136–8, 141–2, 145n, 148, 168–9, 171, 210, 229, 230, 243
anticipation (*protopatheia*) 18n, 49–50, 58n
aponia x, 38, 40–1, 43n, 44n, 50
architecture xv, 140
art viii, xi, xx, xxii, xxiii[n], 19n, 30, 33n, 44n, 73, 100, 112, 128, 137, 139, 145n, 152, 178, 187, 206, 213, 214, 231, 240
  of conduct vii, xii, xx, 15
  of divination 52, 73, 78n, 84n
  of living xi–xii, xx, 15
  work of xii, xxviii, 31, 99
artist xxii, 16, 31, 33n
artwork 31
asceticism 142, 174n, 202n
assembly 171–2, 219
ataraxia (ataraxy) xiv, xxix, 35, 40–1, 44n, 50, 52, 54, 56, 57n, 59n, 97, 112, 114, 120, 128, 242
atheism 147–8
atom, vii, 20–1, 23, 30, 38, 43n, 61, 63–72, 75, 77–8, 79n, 80n, 81n, 82n, 83n, 85n, 87n, 150, 165, 242

atomism xv, 165
austerity, xxi, 191n

beatitude 33n, 148
beauty xxi–xxii, xxiii[n], 27, 31, 37, 117, 167, 179, 182, 184, 203n, 219
behaviour viii, xii, 5, 6n, 52
being xii, xv, xix, 11–12, 14, 31, 35, 40–1, 42n, 44n, 50–1, 62–3, 65, 68, 70–2, 75, 77–8, 79n, 83n, 85n, 86, 92, 94–5, 99, 101, 103n, 113, 117–18, 126, 134–5, 138, 140, 143n, 147, 151, 163, 170, 172, 178, 195–8, 200, 202n, 206, 212, 226n, 233, 237n, 241–2
  animate 64
  human xiii, xvi–xviii, xxii, xxiii[n], 2–3, 12–15, 28–30, 32n, 35, 38, 49, 51–3, 56, 59n, 61–3, 65, 67–9, 71–2, 75, 77–8, 85n, 86–7, 89–90, 92, 101, 111, 117–20, 133, 135–42, 147–9, 158–9, 167–70, 173, 178, 186, 197–9, 202n, 209–10, 213–15, 218–20, 230–2, 242–3
  living xii, xv, xxvii, 12, 67, 71–2, 75
  sentient 39, 41, 51, 135
belief xxviii, xxx, 1–2, 4, 43n, 51, 53, 57n, 73–4, 89–90, 92, 96, 102, 103n, 125, 134, 137, 147–51, 178, 182, 193, 207, 209, 222n, 230, 234, 242, 245
benefaction 177, 205, 207–8
benevolence, 113, 115, 118, 173, 186, 205, 206, 208–9, 219, 222n, 224n, 232, 240
blessedness, xx, xxv[n], 31, 33n, 197
body xxvii, 40–1, 49–51, 64–5, 70–2, 79, 81n, 90, 98, 102n, 104n, 128, 150, 153n, 158, 171–2, 178, 184–6, 207, 213, 217, 233, 235, 237n, 242

calculation 12, 30, 68, 112, 157, 163
calculus xxv[n], 5, 163, 174n, 182, 222n, 234

canonics 54, 58n 149, 245n
Cartesian 165–6
causality 51, 64, 75, 82n
cause 40, 61–5, 67–9, 74–5, 77, 82n, 83n,
    85n, 87n, 90, 104n, 125, 129n, 142,
    147–8, 152n, 167, 170, 173, 178, 196,
    198–9, 207, 225n, 243
  final 147, 156
  first 51, 61, 70, 147–8
cell xv, xxvii
chance xxv[n], 33n, 41, 53, 62–3, 70–1,
    74–6, 84n, 85n, 86n, 112, 137, 173,
    185, 214, 217, 225n, 234, 240
chaos xxi, 62–3, 65, 134, 171
chemistry 157, 186, 193n
Christian 2, 97, 102n, 146n, 164, 180
Christianity 2, 13, 90–1, 111, 113, 141,
    163–4, 166, 222n, 245
city, xiv, 32, 70, 119, 125, 157, 159n, 163,
    167, 172–3, 176n
civilization 6n, 23, 135–7, 140, 142
clinamen vii, xxix, xxx[n], 61, 75–76, 78n,
    80n, 83n, 86
collision, xx, 61, 63–5, 75, 78
commonwealth 176n
community xvii, 115, 120, 216
conatus 202n
conduct, vii–viii, 52, 54, 97, 111, 116–17,
    126, 128, 183, 186, 193n, 219, 221,
    230, 243–4
  art of viii, xix, xx, 15
confidence 15, 21, 54–6, 112, 114, 115,
    121n, 130n, 181, 188n, 190n, 217,
    225n
consciousness 14, 90, 86n, 89, 90, 133, 135,
    186, 197, 243
consent xxvii, 125–6, 199
conspiratio amoris, xviii, 116
contingency vii, xxx, 61–3, 66–73, 83n,
    84n, 86n
cosmogony 140
cosmology 58n, 65, 147, 165
cosmos (*kosmos*) 65, 135
courage 18n, 55, 97–9, 111–12, 177,
    179–80, 212, 218, 226n, 230, 233
cultivation xviii, xx–xxii, 240
custom xv, xxx, 125, 127, 135, 159n, 166,
    195, 198, 205, 212, 214–18, 227n,
    237, 240–1, 244

Cyrenaic xxi, 17n, 30, 41, 53, 35n, 92, 96,
    168, 233

death vii, xii–xiii, xxv[n], xxx, 2, 4, 6n, 33n,
    35, 40–1, 43, 45, 52–3, 66, 76,
    89–102, 102n, 103n, 104n, 105n,
    106n, 111–13, 115, 126, 128, 131n,
    140, 164–5, 179–80, 183, 200, 212,
    217, 195
decadence xiii, 2, 134
deity 52, 147, 149, 152n
delight ix, xix, xxii, 12, 44n, 84n, 124n, 178,
    222
democracy 195, 201, 204n
Democritean 3
desire xix–xxi, 2, 14–15, 18n, 27–9, 32n,
    35–40, 42n, 64, 67, 93, 94–6, 100–1,
    104n, 117, 119, 128, 129n, 130n, 136,
    150, 163, 167–71, 174n, 180–1,
    183–5, 193n, 195–200, 202n, 205–7,
    210, 212, 215, 218, 220, 223
despotism 171–2, 201, 204n, 232
destiny 66, 69, 73–5, 78n, 93, 103n, 112
determinism 51, 61–2, 68, 70, 73–4, 78n,
    85n, 86n, 184, 243
devotion 98, 114, 117, 120, 182–3, 205, 209,
    231
dialectics 22
disinterestedness 3, 100–1, 107n, 114, 116,
    119, 151, 179, 182, 199–200, 221,
    229, 235
disposition xxii, 31, 41, 156, 158, 210, 225n
divination 52, 73–4, 84n
divinity 62, 70, 147, 149–50, 166
doctrine xii–xiii, xv, xix–xx, xxvi–xxxi,
    1–3, 5, 11, 14, 18n, 22–23, 25n,
    28–31, 35–6, 43n, 49–50, 61–3, 74,
    83n, 86n, 89–90, 92, 94, 95, 96–9,
    112–14, 116, 118–19, 122n, 127–8,
    130n, 133–5, 140, 141–2, 144n,
    146n, 147, 151–2, 153n, 156–7, 159,
    163–6, 168, 170–2, 174n, 177, 184,
    186–8, 197, 201, 205, 210–11, 216,
    218–21, 221n, 223, 226n, 229–33,
    239–42, 244–5
drive xii, xix, 5, 79
duration xiii, xx–xxi, 1, 5, 6n, 28, 30–1,
    38–40, 49, 50, 76, 89, 93–5, 105n,
    117, 128, 135, 185

duty xii, xvi, xviii, xxiv[n], 3, 5, 111, 128, 129n, 179, 209, 210, 216, 240, 243

education xi, 148, 152, 205, 214, 217–218, 220, 227n, 237n
effort vii, x, xxx, 30, 35–36, 39–40, 43n, 61, 94, 100, 114, 118, 120, 136, 141, 147, 149–151, 166, 173, 177, 180, 187, 196–198, 202, 205, 207–208, 210, 218, 235, 241
egoism xii, xvii–xix, 115, 117, 137, 159, 177–180, 183, 186–187, 198, 205, 207–209, 211, 229, 234, 240–242
élan 14, 80n, 81n, 85n, 176n
emancipation xvii, 54, 89, 235
embryogenesis xv–xvi, xxviii
emotion xxii, 31, 92, 138–9
empire xiii, 1, 102n, 163, 171–2
empiricism 17n, 23, 143n, 176, 217
emulation 195, 198–9
end xvii, xix, 11–15, 16n, 18n, 19n, 21–3, 27–31, 32n, 33n, 35–7, 39–40, 42n, 44n, 45n, 54, 65, 84n, 91, 95, 98–9, 101, 111–12, 114, 118, 120, 125–8, 137, 148, 159, 165, 167–9, 172, 176n, 177, 184, 201, 204n, 206, 209, 211–12, 215–17, 221, 229, 233, 234, 235, 240, 242–3
energy xii, xx, 15, 41, 95–6, 100, 105, 235, 242, 244
English school xv, xxix[n], 3, 18n, 118, 186, 198, 272, 241–2, 245
enjoyment ix, xii, xvi–xxii, xxiv[n], xxv[n], 3, 5, 7n, 12, 14, 15, 21–2, 27, 28–9, 31, 35, 37–8, 40, 44n, 49–50, 76, 92–94, 96–8, 101, 114, 126, 131n, 142, 167–9, 178, 202n, 222, 230, 236
Epicureanism vii–viii, xiii–xviii, xxi–xxii, xxiv[n], xxv, 1–3, 5, 11, 19n, 23, 27, 33n, 40, 42n, 44n, 51, 94, 96, 101–2, 111, 113, 116–18, 128, 133, 140, 142, 144n, 152, 155, 157–9, 163–6, 173, 174n, 177, 179, 186–7, 195, 197, 204n, 206, 222n, 227n, 229–34, 239–45
equality 114, 169, 226n, 229, 232–3, 237n
equilibrium 38–9, 130n, 167, 242
ethics vii–xii, xiv–xvi, xviii–xix, xxi–xxii, xxiv[n], xxix, 1–5, 11, 14, 16n, 18n, 23, 27, 30–1, 35, 37, 54, 75, 90, 111, 147, 151, 156, 165, 167, 172–3, 177, 195, 197, 199–201, 201n, 204n, 205–7, 210, 212–13, 215–18, 220, 221n, 222n, 227n, 229, 232–4, 236n, 239–44, 245n
ethocracy 205, 217
evil 6n, 12, 19, 27, 29–30, 32n, 35, 39, 40, 45n, 51, 76, 89, 91–4, 97, 99–101, 104n, 112–13, 115, 119, 120n, 125–8, 129n, 134, 147–50, 167–8, 179, 183, 195–6, 206–7, 209, 213, 234
evolution xiv–xvi, xxiv, xxvi–xxix, 66, 78, 101, 111, 134–6, 139, 141, 146n, 157, 201, 231–2, 241–2, 244
evolutionism xiv, 204n
existence xii, xxi, xxii, xxiii, xviii, 13, 17n, 23, 33n, 45n, 65–6, 69, 72, 77, 90–1, 93, 95, 97–101, 104, 104n, 125, 133, 135, 137–8, 140, 142, 147–9, 151–2, 154n, 163, 170, 172, 196, 198, 220
expenditure xii, 37
experience ix, xvi, xx–xxi, 4, 12–13, 30, 36, 49, 63–5, 76, 91, 94, 98, 100, 104n, 107n, 119, 123n, 128, 136, 140, 143n, 147–8, 178, 180, 197, 199, 215, 236n.

faith 2, 4, 55, 74, 87n, 91–2, 98, 102n, 159, 165–6, 174n, 178, 182, 231
fatalism 61–2, 163, 167, 207, 242
fate xiv, 51, 62–3, 67, 70, 72–7, 78n, 80n, 89, 103n, 164, 185, 225n, 239
fear xii, xiv, xvii, xxv[n], 6n, 11, 14, 40, 52–5, 57n, 66, 69, 74, 76, 89–96, 98–101, 103n, 104n, 106n, 112–13, 122n, 126, 128, 137, 141, 145n, 150, 164, 167, 169–70, 172, 176n, 179–80, 182–4, 195, 199, 213–17, 230, 234, 244
fecundity xii, xxxi[n], 140, 240–1
feeling ix, xxiii, 4, 18, 21–3, 64, 76, 90, 92, 95, 102n, 103n, 115, 117, 122n, 138–9, 141, 145n, 150, 164, 168, 177–8, 181–2, 184, 190n, 193n, 208, 235n
flesh xx, 6n, 9, 13, 16, 18n, 21, 37, 41, 42n, 49–50, 166–7

force xii, 23, 27, 35, 38–9, 54, 59n, 61–6, 68–9, 76, 78, 81n, 91, 95–6, 104–5, 115, 119, 125–8, 138, 142, 158, 163, 167–73, 175n, 176n, 178, 199, 200–1, 205, 208–10, 212–16, 233, 236n, 240, 244
fortune 31, 33n, 41, 57n, 62, 75–6, 85n, 114, 119, 179–80, 182–3, 185, 192n, 193n
frankness 122n, 239
fraternity 229, 232
free will 14, 63, 68, 73, 77, 85n, 86n, 87n, 242–3
freedom vii, 163–4, 167, 169, 171–2, 182, 193n, 195, 197–9, 201, 204, 207, 214, 232, 234, 236, 269n, 242–4
friendship vii, xvii–xviii, xxx, 98, 111, 113–20, 121n, 122n, 128, 144, 177, 182–3, 191n, 231, 240, 243
future xx–xxi, xxv[n], 2–5, 15, 27–9, 31, 33n, 38, 40, 49–50, 52, 58n, 61, 73–4, 76–7, 91–4, 98, 100–1, 103n, 124n, 126, 127–8, 133–4, 138, 141, 152, 172, 185, 192n, 221, 225

garden xiii, xxiv[n], 2, 157, 159[n]
genius xiv, 3, 93, 140, 152, 158, 172, 205, 214
geometry, 195, 207
  of custom(s) 195, 198, 205, 240
glory 129, 183–4, 210, 213, 218, 223n
God xxvi, 2–3, 33n, 62, 66, 73–5, 77, 83n, 96, 113, 134, 146, 148–9, 152, 153n, 154n, 158, 164, 172, 195, 197–8, 200, 214, 216, 222n, 244
gods xiv, xxiii[n], xxv[n], xxix, 31, 49, 51–3, 55, 56, 59n, 62–3, 65, 71–4, 78n, 89, 91, 102, 134, 147–52, 153n, 154n, 158, 216, 219, 230
good xix, xxiv[n], 3, 5, 6n, 11–15, 17n, 18n, 19n, 21–3, 24n, 27–31, 32n, 33n, 35, 37, 40–1, 44n, 45n, 50–1, 54–5, 59n, 75–7, 89, 92–4, 96–7, 100, 103n, 104n, 112–13, 115, 118–19, 120n, 121n, 127, 134–7, 142, 143n, 144n, 150, 158, 163, 165, 167–8, 170, 177, 179–86, 191n, 195–8, 200–1, 205–9, 211, 213–14, 216–18, 220, 222n, 226n, 228n, 230, 232–3, 235n, 236n, 237
  sovereign 13–14, 22, 27–8, 35, 40, 44n, 50, 94, 118, 168, 200
goodness 13–14, 177, 182
gratitude xxv[n], 15, 182, 191n, 209, 224n, 230
gravitation upon oneself 231

habit xviii, 5, 67, 111, 117–18, 123, 125, 210–12, 217, 219, 220, 232, 242, 244
happiness xvii–xviii, xx, xxi–xxii, xxix, 14–15, 17n, 27–8, 31, 33n, 35–41, 42n, 44n, 45n, 50–4, 56, 62, 74, 76–7, 89–92, 94, 96–8, 102, 111–17, 119, 128–9, 150, 157–9, 167–8, 180, 186, 195, 197, 198, 208, 212–15, 217–20, 222, 222n, 229–31, 235, 236n, 237n, 242–3
harmony xvii, xviii, xxi, xxix, 27–8, 30, 35, 39–42, 44, 56, 65, 99, 116, 120, 127, 130n, 138, 158, 169, 172, 205, 213, 217, 240–2
health xxix, 15, 19n, 35, 38, 40–1, 44, 50, 180, 222n
heaven xiii, xxii, 2–4, 6n, 31, 55, 62, 91, 208
hedonism xii, xx, xxii, 17n
heredity 71, 242
history vii, xii–xiii, xiv–xvii, xix, xxiv[n], xxvii–xxx, 3–5, 11, 29, 51, 135–7, 139–42, 155, 163, 165–6, 171, 186, 227n, 229, 239, 240, 242–4
  of philosophy vii, xi, xv, xxviii, xxx, 239
honour xxix, 1, 36, 78n, 94, 111, 119, 120, 169, 179, 180–1, 191n
humility 51, 177, 180–1, 183

ignorance 14, 49, 51–5, 57n, 188, 193, 213, 215, 225n, 226n, 244
illness 27, 39, 166
illusion 55, 113, 134, 196, 199, 209, 232, 241–2
image xx, 13, 16, 18n, 20n, 32n, 43n, 50, 58n, 67, 80n, 90, 95, 98, 134, 137, 149–51, 153n, 158, 166, 174n, 179, 187, 198, 213–14, 228
imagination 16, 50, 55–6, 89–93, 101, 103n, 134, 148–9, 187, 243

immortality xiii, 89–90, 93–5, 98, 101–2, 104n, 148, 158, 223n
imperturbability 40–1, 77
impetus 29, 63–4, 67, 77, 79, 104, 173, 234
impression 58n, 135, 140, 207, 214
independence vii, xvii, 36, 41, 52, 54–5, 75, 98, 167, 243
industry 133, 139, 142, 179, 228
infinity 37, 50, 65, 93–4, 152, 184, 216
instant xx–xxi, 28, 31, 38–9, 50, 52, 76, 92, 95, 101, 135
intellect xix, 15, 19n, 137, 187, 196–7
intelligence xix, 12–16, 17n, 27–8, 30, 54, 65–6, 99, 101, 135, 139–41, 149, 195–7, 208, 218, 230, 243
intelligible 14, 239
interest xvi–xviii, xxix, 1, 3, 5, 6n, 23, 37, 50, 100–12, 114, 116–18, 120, 125–8, 138, 163, 168–9, 172–3, 174n, 177–84, 186–7, 188n, 190n, 195, 197, 199–201, 205–16, 218–22, 225n, 226n, 229, 231–4, 237n, 240–4, 237n, 240–1, 243
  ethics of 1, 37, 199
instinct 5, 12, 30, 94, 164, 230
intemperance 27, 127
intuition 135, 197

joy 41, 44n, 101n, 98, 114, 195, 196–8
justice xvii, xxx, 3, 56n, 102, 117, 120, 125–9, 129n, 130n, 137–8, 141, 145n, 163, 169, 170, 177, 182, 205, 210–16, 219–20, 225n, 229, 230–1, 234, 237, 244

key idea (*idée maîtresse*) xv–xvi, xxvii, 85
knowledge, vii–viii, 4, 19n, 23, 32, 54–5, 56n, 57n, 93, 112, 135, 139, 142, 143n, 150, 153n, 176, 181, 188, 195, 197–8, 200–1, 210, 214–15, 221–2

labour 35–6, 139, 142, 149
language viii, 1, 15, 42n, 52, 56n, 68, 95, 99, 133, 135–6, 138, 139, 141, 144n, 145n, 154, 156, 165, 227n
law 3, 51, 62, 63, 69–70, 72–4, 77–9, 83n, 87, 101, 114, 119, 125–8, 129n, 130n, 134, 136–8, 140–2, 142n, 145n, 148–9, 169–70, 172, 174n, 195–200, 205–7, 209–10, 212–21, 223n, 230, 232–3, 235n, 236n, 237n, 242
  natural xvii, 17, 101, 125, 127, 149, 163, 170, 174n, 209, 233
legislation 205–6, 212, 214–20, 237n, 244
liberalism 195, 234, 244
liberation 45, 53, 55, 89, 185
liberator 1, 6n, 49, 53, 57n, 158
life xxvii–xxix, xxx[n], 2, 4–5, 6n, 11–15, 17n, 19n, 22–4, 28–31, 32n, 33n, 36, 37–40, 43n, 49–52, 64–7, 73–4, 76, 90–102, 103n, 104n, 105n, 106n, 112–17, 119–20, 122, 126–8, 131n, 134, 137–8, 140, 143n, 146n, 151, 157–8, 164–5, 168–70, 174n, 178–9, 182, 186, 187, 191n, 202n, 204n, 212, 217, 221, 222n, 223n, 225n, 233, 241–3
  blissful xx, 15, 91
  expansion of xii, 204n
  philosophy of xii
  way of viii, xii, xix, xxi, 40, 143n
  whole of (*ho holos bios*), xx–xxi, 29–31, 32n, 33n, 36, 40, 49, 114–15, 168
lifetime xi, xx, 31, 33n, 94
logic viii, xvii, 49, 53–5, 58n, 59n, 99, 115, 127, 147, 153n, 157–8, 167, 171–3, 196, 200, 211, 217, 222, 229, 239
love, xx, 1, 3, 93, 97, 104n, 111, 113–14, 116–19, 122n, 123n, 166, 169, 177, 180–3, 186, 188, 193n, 195, 197–200, 205, 207, 208–12, 216, 218, 220, 224n, 231–3, 235, 236n
  of oneself (*amour de soi*) 177, 188, 188n, 193n, 197, 224n, 227n, 236n

magnanimity 116, 179
mastery xii, xxiv[n]
materialism xv, 56n, 151, 236n
mathematics 157, 223n, 227n
matter xxvi, 2, 21, 23, 64, 70, 72, 77, 83n, 85n, 87n, 94, 112, 128, 148, 222n
meditation xiv, xxv[n], 1–2
memory, 18n, 49–50, 56n, 58n, 62, 76, 84n, 98, 100, 134, 140, 158

merit xviii, 5, 16, 18n, 54, 75, 86, 91, 165, 180–1, 185, 187, 205, 207, 211, 221, 231–2
metaphysics 11–12, 16n, 44n, 135, 155, 201, 231, 243
method ix, xv, xxvi–xxviii, xxxi[n], 133, 156, 178, 184, 198, 205, 217, 223n
Middle Ages 13, 133, 141–2, 159, 163–4
milieu xxvi–xxviii, 85n, 211, 214
mind xviii, xxi, xxvii, xxxi[n], 2–5, 6n, 11, 13, 18, 23, 30–1, 49–51, 53, 55–6, 64, 67, 72, 79, 86, 90, 98, 127, 130, 135, 137, 140, 142, 148–9, 152, 155–8, 166, 178, 180, 185–7, 192n, 196, 199, 203n, 212–13, 215, 218, 229, 233–4, 243–4
miracle, xiv, 49, 61, 70–3, 83n, 87, 135, 139, 164, 184, 244
miraculous 2, 6, 70–1, 143n, 146n, 245
misanthropy 158, 177, 187
moderation 117, 180, 203
modesty 180–1
moment xx–xxi, xxv[n], 1, 12, 23, 25n, 28–30, 32n, 33n, 39, 42, 49, 52–3, 67, 93, 95, 105n, 119, 157, 168, 184, 206, 214, 225n, 233
morality, vii–viii, xvii, xxii, xxiv[n], xxix[n], 4–5, 14, 27, 36, 107n, 118, 127, 163, 174n, 184, 195–6, 204n, 207, 209–12, 217, 219, 230, 233, 236, 239–41
movement xii, xv, xxvi–xxviii, 4, 6n, 14, 21, 28, 30, 35, 37–41, 50, 61, 63–5, 67–73, 75, 77, 79n, 82n, 83n, 84n, 86n, 98, 111, 113, 133, 136, 166, 168, 171, 183, 185–6, 192, 198, 200, 207, 209, 211, 229, 235, 240, 244

natural selection 136, 138, 230
naturalism xix, xxiv, 3, 195, 234
naturalist xvii, 11–12, 21–2, 78n, 133, 135, 141, 170, 173, 230
nature xii, xvii–xix, xxv, xxvii, 6n, 11–14, 17n, 23, 24n, 25n, 31, 32n, 36–8, 41, 42, 50–1, 54–5, 57n, 59n, 61–3, 66–73, 75–8, 83n, 84n, 85n, 87n, 93–4, 97–103, 112, 117, 119, 125–7, 130n, 133, 135–7, 141–2, 145n, 148–50, 156, 157–8, 167–71, 185, 187–8, 195–201, 202n, 203n, 205, 209–10, 213–14, 218–19, 220, 225n, 230, 232–5, 236n, 237n, 242–4
necessity xiv, xxiii[n], xxx, 12, 21–2, 24, 38, 51, 56, 61–74, 76–7, 78n, 79n, 80n, 82n, 84n, 85n, 86n, 89, 93, 97, 99, 130n, 136, 158, 167, 185, 195–201, 205, 207, 213–15, 242
nothingness 64, 66, 70–1, 75, 77, 93, 95, 97

obligation xvi, 126, 222n, 230–1
opinion xii, xiii, xxx[n], 36–7, 42n, 53–4, 57n, 58n, 59n, 68, 78n, 93–4, 120n, 121n, 147, 151, 165, 183, 193, 205, 214–16, 220, 237n, 239–40
order xxii, xxvi–xxviii, 22, 126, 128, 144n, 147, 156, 183, 185, 189n, 196, 199, 204n, 205–6, 212–13, 218, 244
organism xv–xvi, xxiv, xxvii–xxviii, 38, 70–1, 128, 140, 230

pagan xiii–xiv, xviii, 2, 49, 53, 62, 71, 103, 245
paganism, 2, 53, 62, 158
pain x, xix–xxii, xxix, xxx, 11–14, 17n, 18n, 27–31, 32n, 33n, 35–42, 43n, 44n, 45n, 49–50, 55, 62, 76, 77, 92–3, 96–100, 104, 106n, 107n, 112, 114, 118–19, 168, 174n, 183, 202n, 207, 213, 222n, 233, 240
passion xx, 177–9, 181–2, 184–6, 188n, 190, 192n, 193n, 194n, 195, 198–200, 201n, 203n, 207–8, 211–13, 217–19, 224n, 235n
peace 53, 92, 103n, 126–8, 163, 166–7, 169–73, 176n, 183, 200, 236n, 242–3
piety vii, xxx, 53, 118, 147, 150–2, 179, 207
pity 177, 182, 198, 208, 224n
phantom 51, 91–2, 148–9, 153n, 178, 181, 190n
pleasure ix–x, xii, xvi–xix, xx–xxii, xxiv, xxv[n], xxix[n], 6n, 7n, 9, 11–16, 17n, 18n, 21–3, 24n, 27–31, 32n, 33n, 35–42, 42n, 43n, 44n, 45n, 47–52, 56n, 62, 74–5, 89, 92–7, 99–101, 103n, 111–15, 117–19, 122n, 123n, 129–31, 142, 158, 165, 168, 169, 174n, 178, 182–4, 186,

189n, 195, 203n, 206–9, 222n, 229, 232–4, 240–3, 245n
   constitutive (*katastēmatikē*) 35, 39, 41, 44n
   of movement (*kinētikē*) 35, 39, 41, 42n, 101
philanthropy 118, 173, 205, 218, 220, 231–2, 244
philosophy, viii, xi–xx, xxii[n], xxiv, xxvi, xxviii, xxx, 1, 4, 11, 13, 15, 16n, 21, 23, 27, 29–30, 56n, 57n, 58n, 63, 73–4, 85n, 89, 93, 96, 98–9, 112–13, 123, 136, 142, 148, 151, 157, 163, 165, 179, 204n, 210, 223n, 230, 232, 234, 239–40, 244
   moral vii, xvi, xxiii, 29, 210
physics viii, xix, 11–12, 43n, 54–5, 58n, 144n, 196, 207, 212, 218, 227n, 239, 245n
   of custom(s), 198, 205, 207, 212, 218, 232, 240–1
physiology 49, 54, 236n
   of custom 240–1
politics xvii, 172–3, 195, 200–1, 204n, 205, 229–30, 232, 236n, 244
positivism xiv, 155, 157, 204n
power xxix[n], 4, 14, 36, 51, 54–5, 56n, 57n, 59n, 61–5, 67–7, 78n, 82n, 83n, 84n, 86n, 87n, 89, 92, 98, 101, 105n, 117, 119, 124n, 134, 157, 163, 166–9, 171–3, 178, 185, 195–7, 199–202, 204n, 206, 210, 213–18, 220, 225n, 226n, 237n
preconceptions 18n, 58n
prejudice 133, 215, 228n, 236n, 245
present (temporality) xx–xxi, xxiv[n], xxv[n], 4, 27–30, 32, 36, 40, 49–52, 58n, 62, 71, 73, 91, 98, 100–1, 133–4, 136, 138, 172, 179, 185, 217
pride (*fierté*) 177, 181
pride (*orgueil*) 177, 180–1, 183, 186–7
probity 177, 188n, 205, 210–13, 215, 219, 220, 227n
progress xiv, xvii, xxx, 5, 6n, 22, 29, 67, 71, 101, 116–18, 127, 133–42, 143n, 145n, 146n, 152, 155, 168, 170, 185, 193n, 201, 205–6, 218, 221, 233, 240, 242, 244
providence 62, 66, 74, 153n, 164

prudence 15, 21, 179
psychology xvii, xix, xxvii, 18n, 65, 135, 172, 177, 187, 198–9, 223n, 241
public safety (or 'public welfare'; *salut publique*) 205, 216, 219, 221n, 227
punishment x, 74, 91, 126–7, 129n, 206, 213, 215
Pyrrhonian (Pyrrhonism) xiv, 2, 125–6, 174n

reason viii, ix, xvi, xix–xx, xxiv[n], 2, 5, 11–13, 15, 17n, 22–3, 31, 36, 44, 54–6, 68, 71, 76, 86n, 90, 93–4, 101–2, 112, 117, 129n, 136, 140–1, 167, 169–70, 175n, 182, 192n, 195, 197, 199, 200–1, 202n, 204n, 208–9, 220, 229–30, 235n, 243
reciprocity 126, 233
religion xiii–xiv, xxiii, 1–3, 43, 49, 51–5, 57n, 59n, 71, 90–2, 95, 98, 101, 103n, 113, 133–4, 142, 143n, 146, 148, 157, 164, 205, 216, 218, 231, 234, 237n, 239, 243–5
religious enthusiasm xvi, xviii, 3–4
remorse 177, 216, 229–30, 232
Renaissance 133, 163–4
resistance 2, 61, 76, 142, 206, 223, 239
responsibility 61, 74
rest 14, 35, 38–40, 42, 43n, 57n, 64, 92, 97, 103n, 155, 168, 183, 186, 207, 215, 219, 235, 242
revolution 4, 91–2, 139, 157, 163, 166, 201, 204n, 219, 221n, 232–3
right ix, xvii–xviii, 3–4, 12, 102, 126, 128, 129n, 130n, 137, 145n, 145n, 163, 169–70, 172, 174n, 196, 201, 209, 216–17, 219, 223n, 233, 237n, 244
   natural xvii, 125–6, 163, 169, 204n, 211–12
rule xvi, xvii, xx, 14–15, 21, 27, 54, 113, 127, 130n, 137–8, 157, 168, 171, 197, 206, 209–12, 217, 219, 233–4, 243

sage xiii–xiv, xxi–xxii, xxv, xxix, 2, 27, 29, 31, 33n, 36–7, 41, 54, 56, 57, 62, 75–7, 85n, 89, 94–5, 97–9, 111–17, 119, 120n, 122n, 124n, 126–9, 158, 202n, 230, 244

sanction x–xi, 17, 126, 129n, 158, 169–70, 205, 213–15, 217–18, 220, 227n, 230–1
sceptic xiv, xviii, 2, 11, 55, 57n, 59n, 125–7, 212
scepticism xiv, 2
scholastics 133, 156, 165
science viii, xv, xix–xx, xxvi–xxviii, xxix[n], 11, 15–16, 19n, 21, 23–4, 49, 52, 54–6, 57n, 58n, 61, 71, 73, 78, 78n, 85n, 90, 98, 136, 139–41, 146n, 149, 152, 156–7, 170, 173, 197, 204n, 205–7, 210, 216–18, 229–30, 233–4, 243–5
seed xiv, 22, 61–2, 64–6, 67, 70–1, 83n, 192n, 244
self xii, xviii, xxiv[n], 11, 74, 77, 114–15, 117, 120, 168, 181, 193, 241
   affirmation of xviii
   mutilation of xviii
self-cultivation xviii, xxi
self-love (*amour propre*) xvii, 177, 180–2, 186–8, 191, 193, 196, 198–9, 207–8, 213, 215
sensation xix, xxiii[n], 13–14, 16–18, 23, 30, 37–9, 41–2, 49–50, 54–5, 58n, 59n, 76, 99, 135, 138, 143n, 148–9, 152, 153n, 168, 186, 207, 233
senses 12–14, 16–18, 23, 39, 49, 54–6, 72, 95, 97, 143n, 149, 153n, 176n, 182, 222
sensualism 17n, 19n, 135, 143n, 173, 186
sentiment xx, 4, 18n, 27, 30, 53, 55, 61–2, 75–6, 103n, 114, 130n, 150, 163, 168, 177–8, 180–1, 184, 188, 198, 207, 213, 215–16, 219, 231–2, 241–2, 244
serenity xix, 40, 49, 111, 150, 157, 167
servitude xiii, 2, 28, 37, 53, 158, 185, 193n
shock xx, 68, 79n, 80n, 207
slavery 52, 77
social contract xvii–xviii, xxx[n], 120, 125, 127–8, 138, 191n, 200
social pact xvii, 126, 133, 144n, 199
society xvii–xviii, 4, 111–13, 117, 123n, 125–7, 128, 129n, 130n, 131n, 135, 137–8, 156, 166, 168–70, 177, 183–4, 197–200, 207–9, 211, 215, 224n, 228n, 299n, 233, 237n, 242–3

sociology 133, 136, 156, 243
solidarity 61, 77–8, 85n, 116, 164
sophists 125
soul xxiv[n], xxvii, xxix[n], 2–3, 6n, 15–16, 18, 21, 29–30, 32, 33n, 40–1, 47, 49–51, 53, 55, 57n, 58n, 65, 67–9, 74, 76–77, 83n, 95, 97, 102n, 104n, 105n, 112–13, 116, 126, 128, 130, 137, 148, 151, 158–9, 165–8, 177–81, 186, 189n, 197–8, 213, 215–16, 218, 234, 242–4
sovereign 40–1, 44n, 150, 167–8, 171–2, 193n, 199, 201, 206, 210, 233, 236n
space xx, 30, 33n, 36, 38–9, 63, 65–6, 70–2, 79n, 80n, 81n, 102n, 116, 150, 164, 168, 172, 186, 234–5
species xxvii, 66, 196, 241
speculation xix, 11–12, 15, 155–7 221, 234
spirit xvi, xxvi, 2, 11, 15, 43–4, 54, 56n, 62, 100, 117, 130n, 134, 155–6, 164–6, 183–4, 214, 218, 223n, 229, 231, 242, 245
spontaneity 61, 66–7, 70–3, 75–8, 85n, 86n, 137, 158, 242–3
state x, xv, xx, 33n, 38–9, 40, 41, 43n, 44n, 45n, 53, 55, 59n, 79, 93, 97, 99, 100, 104, 124n, 128, 133, 134, 137, 156, 166–7, 169–73, 185–6, 192, 199, 205–6, 209–12, 214–16, 218–20, 227n, 233, 242
Stoic xiii, xvi–xvii, xix, xxi, 1, 3, 14, 17n, 35, 51, 58n, 61–2, 68, 73–4, 76, 85, 98, 112–14, 119, 133, 141, 164–5, 197, 198, 201, 229, 232, 237n, 239
Stoicism xiv, xvi, 3, 111, 142, 163, 166, 195, 197, 232, 239, 245
stomach (*ventre*) xxix[n], 21–3, 24n, 25n, 27, 37, 111
structure viii, ix, xv–xvi, xxiv[n], 71, 245n
struggle xiii, xvi, 1–3, 41, 49, 51, 54–5, 62, 100, 114, 137, 142, 147, 149, 151, 153, 167, 169–70, 172, 205
style viii, xxi, 113, 175n
subject xxi–xxii, 23, 35, 41, 42n, 51, 53, 120n, 155, 183, 206, 236n, 237n
   sentient 35, 41
substance 80n, 104n, 200
supernatural xiv, 2, 6n, 31, 53, 55, 65, 67, 71, 83n, 143n, 146n

superstition xiv, 49, 51–3, 54, 55n, 59n, 91, 98, 113, 146n, 164, 174, 215, 227
swerve vii, 31, 61, 63, 65, 67–72, 75, 77, 78n, 80n, 82n, 83n, 85n, 87n
sympathy xvii, 17, 115, 120, 182, 186, 195, 198, 231–3
system viii, xiv–xvi, xix, xxvi–xxviii, xxx[n], xxxi[n], 1, 3, 5, 6n, 11–12, 16, 18n, 19n, 25n, 27, 28–30, 32, 37, 49, 54, 62, 70, 74, 91, 93, 96–7, 111–12, 115, 128, 129n, 133, 135, 141–2, 147–8, 150–2, 153n, 157–8, 163–7, 171–3, 177–8, 183–4, 187, 189n, 195–7, 199, 201, 205–8, 210–12, 217–21, 226n, 227n, 229, 231–4, 237n, 239n, 240, 242–4, 245n

Talmud 164
temperance 111–12, 120n, 177, 180, 233
temporality xxi, xxv[n], 105n
time x–xvi, xviii, xx–xxii, xxiv[n], xxvii–xxviii, xxix, 1–5, 6n, 12–13, 15–16, 22, 27–9, 31, 33n, 36–7, 40–1, 42n, 49–52, 54–5, 58n, 62–7, 70–2, 75–7, 78n, 79n, 89, 91–8, 103n, 104n, 105n, 113–16, 125, 127–8, 131n, 133–7, 139–42, 151–2, 152n, 155–66, 169, 171, 173, 185, 187, 189n, 194n, 195–6, 199–201, 202n, 206, 217, 219–20, 223n, 225n, 234–5, 237n, 240–1, 244
theology 147, 151
theory xvi, xxix–xxx, 2–3, 12, 19n, 38, 55, 63, 67, 75, 83n, 85n, 89–90, 92, 94, 99, 111–20, 123n, 126, 128, 133–5, 143n, 149–50, 153n, 170, 176n, 177, 209, 214, 217, 219, 232–3, 243
theurgy 164
thought ix, xi, xiv–xxi, xxii[n], xxiv[n], xxvi–xxviii, xxx[n], xxxi[n], 1–4, 11–14, 16, 22–3, 27, 29–31, 33n, 39, 45n, 50–2, 55, 58n, 62–3, 70, 76, 81n, 86–7, 89, 92, 97–8, 100–2, 103n, 106n, 115–18, 122n, 123n, 126, 133, 139, 143, 145n, 150–2, 155–7, 166, 170, 174n, 177–80, 187, 189n, 192n, 194n, 196–8, 201, 204n, 205–8, 211, 219, 221n, 227n, 232–5, 239–41, 244–5

tranquillity xiv, 40, 52, 59n, 89, 93, 97, 99, 158, 176n, 242
trouble x, xvii, 11, 17n, 31, 35–41, 43n, 44n, 45n, 49–51, 54, 56, 57n, 59n, 76, 91, 93, 97–8, 104, 112, 115, 119, 126–8, 130n, 142, 147, 150–1, 153n, 186–7
truth xiii, xvi, xviii, 1–2, 4–5, 11–14, 49, 54–5, 58n, 62, 73–4, 84n, 86, 90, 95, 98, 130n, 135n, 141, 158, 171–2, 181, 200, 215, 218–19, 220, 234, 239–40, 242–3

underworld 42n, 43n, 89, 91–2, 101, 103n
unity xxi, xxvii–xxviii, 6n, 21–2, 28–9, 67, 85, 127, 171–2, 177, 186, 199, 201, 201n, 234
universe viii, 3, 64–5, 68–73, 77–8, 85, 90, 150, 205, 207, 211–12, 218–19, 232
useful xix, xxvi, 11, 15, 16n, 22, 30, 97, 101, 112, 115, 119, 124n, 127–8, 152, 155, 163, 168, 173, 179, 182, 184, 195–7, 200, 207, 209–11, 213, 215–16, 218–19, 225n, 226n, 227n, 228n, 231, 233, 236, 240
utilitarianism, vii, xiii–xvi, xxii, xxv, xxix, 3, 119, 157–8, 184–7, 194n, 195, 204, 222n, 226n, 229, 241, 245n
utility xv–xviii, xxi, 6n, 11–12, 15, 16n, 27, 29, 50, 54–5, 74, 111–12, 114, 126–7, 141–2, 144, 157, 167, 169–70, 177, 184, 197–201, 206, 210–12, 216–17, 219–21, 225n, 228n, 229, 233–5

value x, xiii, xxi–xxii, 2, 11, 15–16, 21–2, 39, 54, 59n, 74–5, 94, 98, 103n, 115, 127, 130n, 133, 142, 171, 178, 199, 206, 223n 229, 239, 243
vanity 101, 178–81, 183–4, 186, 188, 189n
virtue iv, xviii–xix, xxii, xxix, 5, 11–12, 14–15, 19n, 21, 27–9, 65, 68, 77, 86, 98–9, 109, 111–12, 115–18, 128–9, 130n, 131n, 147, 151, 165, 169, 177–82, 184–6, 188, 195–7, 199–200, 202n, 205, 208–11, 213–17, 221n, 222n, 224n, 227n, 229–34, 235n, 237n, 241

private 109, 111–12, 181
public 109, 111
vitalist (vitalistic) viii, xv, 6n, 79n
void 35, 38–39, 41, 43n, 63, 65–6, 69, 72, 79n, 81n, 83n, 87n, 150, 178
voluptas x, 19n, 24n, 42, 45n
voluptuousness ix–x, xxix, 21, 29, 35–7, 41, 42n, 92, 94

war 133, 137, 141, 145, 163, 167, 169–72, 208, 212, 215, 219
weight (of atoms) 30, 61, 63–5, 65, 69, 75, 79n, 82n, 83n
well-being ix, xii, xvii, 97, 123, 167, 173, 182–3, 186, 210, 235n
will 14, 28–9, 35, 50–2, 56, 61, 64, 66–7, 73, 76, 85n, 89, 100, 117–18, 170–2, 174n, 176n, 185, 193n, 195, 208, 212, 214, 222n, 236n, 243–4
wisdom xix–xx, xxiv–xxv, 15, 19n, 22–3, 30–1, 32n, 33, 36, 44n, 53–5, 77, 106n, 112–13, 119, 124n, 129, 129n, 158, 185, 213
world xii, xvi, xxiv[n], xxvii, xxx, 1–3, 6n, 12, 17n, 49, 51, 55–6, 59n, 61–3, 65–71, 74, 76–7, 80n, 81n, 84n, 85n, 86n, 91–2, 100–1, 104n, 113, 117, 134–5, 138, 140–1, 145n, 147–50, 152, 152n, 153n, 156, 164–5, 178, 187, 194n, 198, 207, 209–10, 212–13, 215–20, 222n

www.ingramcontent.com/pod-product-compliance
Lightning Source LLC
Chambersburg PA
CBHW070751020526
44115CB00032B/1644